CASHFLOW, CREDIT AND COLLECTION

Over 100 Proven Techniques for Protecting and Strengthening Your Balance Sheet

Revised Edition

BASIL P. MAVROVITIS

PROBUS PUBLISHING COMPANY
Chicago, Illinois
Cambridge, England

ISBN 1-55738-522-X

Printed in the United States of America

IPC

1 2 3 4 5 6 7 8 9 0

RR/BJS

This book is dedicated to my loving wife, Barbara.
Thanks for your support.

Table of Contents

Preface

Cash Flow, Credit and Collection is a "how to" oriented guide to managing, reporting, and enhancing credit and cash flow. It promotes proactive management of the credit function as a means of maximizing company cash flow.

I have presented new and innovative credit and cash flow methodologies, perpectives, and insights, as well as traditional approaches, for a broad spectrum of executive readers. The book is written to benefit credit practitioners, treasurers, controllers, CFOs, CEOs, and corporate presidents.

Credit and cash flow have become a focal point of corporate America over the past few years. The credit function in many companies has been turned into a profit center. Collections, days sales outstanding (DSO), past due, and risk have been closely linked to cash flow and to corporate cash and loan positions. Monthly changes in DSO are now directly correlated to changes in cash and loan positions. In many ways the credit function and cash flow are synonymous. Their strategic goals are common: to provide the required financial support of the company, to control the company's assets of cash and accounts receivable, and to provide timely and accurate information.

Cash flow is being recognized as a corporate asset that can be accelerated and enhanced through sound credit strategy.

Today, in order to be viable and competitive forces in the marketplace, companies need to emphasize a proactive approach to credit and cash flow management. Formalized approaches to enhance or maximize cash flow and credit operations must be a part of management's overall strategy.

Reactive or passive credit and cash flow management is just not good enough! Financial managers must aggressively explore, digest, implement, and manage cash flow options and alternatives.

I wrote this book in short abstracts, more than 100 of them. Each one provides a concise overview of a credit concept or strategy. In many cases, these abstracts offer action plans, including step-by-step instructions for implementing a concept or strategy. The abstracts are further clarified by a number of flow charts, schematic diagrams, checklists, and legal exhibits.

Each abstract in Chapters 1–10 is followed by a summary section that highlights five key points in the abstract.

I have made a sincere effort to share as many cost-saving and cash flow enhancing concepts as possible.

The guide focuses on four central themes relating to credit and cash flow strategy. Briefly, here is what you can expect:

Credit and Cash Flow Information Sources

The first three chapters of the book cover the complete cycle for credit and cash flow data gathering and analysis. Specifically, these sections cover collections, credit and financial analysis, and credit systems.

The abstracts in these chapters instruct, advise, and counsel the reader on how to derive, extract, and analyze credit information. Forty detailed abstracts have been dedicated to asset management for these credit and cash flow disciplines.

Cash Flow Management

The next four chapters review and discuss credit and cash flow from operational, reporting, forecasting, and strategic standpoints. The topics include lockbox, DSO, cash management techniques, and forecasting. Thirty-five detailed and probing abstracts cover advanced cash management approaches and analytical techniques for generating and/or monitoring cash flow.

One of the underlying themes I've tried to hammer home in this section is that companies must operate on less than cash flow.

Asset Control and Preservation

Chapters 8–10 offer a detailed approach to controlling and preserving credit and cash flow as an asset. These chapters cover legal issues, credit and cash flow strategies, and credit perspectives. Forty-nine detailed abstracts have been dedicated to controlling and preserving credit and cash flow. Flow charts, checklists, diagrams, and legal exhibits are reviewed and discussed in detail.

These sections serve as a legal and strategic overview that reinforces another one of the book's underlying themes: you can never possess enough credit knowledge.

You Make the Credit Call

The final two chapters comprise a truly unique interactive format: the "You make the credit call" case studies and follow-up responses to the case studies.

The 12 case studies challenge the reader to make executive decisions based on hypothetical situations. The cases are condensed presentations based on actual customer scenarios.

At the end of each case study, the reader is prompted to detail in writing his or her objectives, action items, and options for handling the situation that is described. The follow-up section lets readers compare their answers to a detailed set of possible responses.

Near the end of the guide there is also a glossary of 150 credit and cash flow terms, as well as a detailed index that highlights specific credit and cash flow concepts, approaches, and terms.

This book represents a concise presentation of my 15+ years of credit and cash flow memories and experiences with the Amerada Hess Corporation, United States Steel Corporation (now USX Corporation), Cyro Industries, a joint venture of American Cyanamid and Roehm GmbH, and Bertelsmann, Inc. During those years I always looked to enhance the performance and scope of the credit function beyond the traditional boundaries of credit extension and collections.

This book provides both the traditional and nontraditional cash flow oriented approaches, strategies, perspectives, and insights that I have seen or developed during my years as a credit professional. I think they can help you achieve many of your credit and cash flow management goals.

Good luck with your firm's credit and cash flow strategy!

Acknowledgments

There are many people I would like to thank for providing me with the inspiration to write this book. First, there is my dear family. Especially my parents Peter and Dorothea Mavrovitis. Without their tender loving care and wisdom, I could not have written the book. I would like to thank my grandmother Mary Karavida for her love and concern for me. Also, I want to thank my brother and sister, Leo Mavrovitis and Rea Hunter, who set an example for me to follow academically.

Most important of all I would like to thank my wife, Barbara, and my sons, Peter, Alex, and Evan, for their guidance, patience, and understanding. Many an hour of family time was sacrificed as I worked in my basement on this book. I would also like to thank my in-laws, Gerald and Janet Spiro, who have been a source of encouragement for my professional endeavors. I would like to thank Rutgers University and its faculty for providing me with higher education and positive life experiences at the undergraduate and graduate school levels.

Professionally, I would like to thank Vince DiPaolo, the noted financial publishing executive, who encouraged me to tackle this project and gave me my first opportunity to be published. I also want to thank Ed Salzmann, copy editor of this book, who added logic and precision to my narrative. Knowing in advance that Ed was going to be the professional editing this book enabled me to write with a strong degree of confidence.

I would like to thank former coworkers Joe Hanley and Bill Albert, who took the time to be my mentors during our working relationships. These men shared with me the financial knowledge, insights, and skills that took them many years of professional experience to develop.

Finally, I would like to thank Dr. Juergen Kraemer for giving me the opportunity to become a part of Bertelsmann, Inc. I would also like to thank Peter Blobel, my current boss, for his interest in my professional career.

1

COLLECTIONS

COLLECTION POLICIES AND PROCEDURES

Formal, written collection policies and procedures are essential to achieving the credit function's goals of generating cash flow and protecting the company's accounts receivable assets. A credit department without written policies and procedures is likely to have an undisciplined approach toward collections; such an approach can negatively impact cash flow, accounts receivable and past due levels, DSO, and possibly the level of bad-debt write-offs sustained.

A decentralized credit function, especially, will have problems without written policies and procedures. Lacking written guidelines, credit personnel located throughout the country will fail to approach the collection task in a uniform manner.

Here are some key elements of a typical corporate collection policy:

- Collection of open accounts receivable balances are the sole responsibility of the credit department.
- The scope of collections includes the timely collection of open invoices, unauthorized claims and deductions, debit memos, unearned discounts, and finance charges.
- The goal of collections is to maximize the conversion of trade accounts receivable into cash flow and minimize bad-debt write-offs whenever possible.
- Credit personnel should attempt to identify and reduce customer exposures that could lead to lengthy payouts that strain cash flow.
- Past due balances and slippage are to be minimized through effective collections.
- Collection responsibility and accountability is predicated on job classification.
- Collections are to be made in a professional and courteous manner; abusive language is prohibited, no matter what the circumstances.
- Collections are to be made in compliance with the Fair Debt Collection Practice Act.

Specific collection procedures should be in writing; they should indicate:

- How to properly document collection call conversations;
- Procedures for executing standard, bad debt, and overseas collection calls;
- Time frames for when to notify management regarding a customer's failure to pay;

- Policies regarding the cleaning up of old past-due items, and procedures for deriving individual daily collection call budgets and objectives.

All collection procedures should be written in a clear, "how-to" style. The goal is to create documentation that will not only serve to make policies and procedures uniform, but which also will be understandable and serve as a guide and a set of corporate expectations for new employees.

Clearly, a credit department must have internal rules and regulations regarding collections to ensure that cash flow is maximized and credit laws are not broken.

ABSTRACT SUMMARY

- Formal, written collection policies and procedures are essential to generating cash flow and protecting the company's accounts receivable assets.
- Without written policies and procedures, there is likely to be an undisciplined and intuitive approach toward collections.
- Having no policies and procedures can negatively impact cash flow and possibly the level of bad-debt write-offs sustained.
- Written policies and procedures are particularly important in a decentralized credit function.
- Procedures should be stated clearly, in writing and in a "how-to" manner.

CUSTOMER CONTACT CARDS

The credit function should use written customer contact cards to record and update collection calls made to customers. It's a simple way to keep facts in order. Each customer should have a customer contact card that lists the following information:

Customer Name _____ Account Number_____
Street Address _____ Telephone Number_____
City, State_____ Customer Contact_____

The cards should also contain columns for the 1) Date, 2) Balance, 3) Past Due, and 4) Comments.

The cards can be filed in alphabetical order, by account number, or using any other type of alphanumeric combination, such as alpha order by product line or by sales region. During and/or after each collection call, entries should be made summarizing the discussion with the customer; a follow-up date should be noted at the end of the entry.

A typical entry could read: "Spoke with Pete Dukey re: invoices 50511, 50823, and 50899, totaling $25,000. The check was mailed on 6/17. Follow up on 6/24 if check is not received." Note that the entry is clear, short, and to the point.

The customer contact card leaves a clean audit trail for management to review and to take action upon in the event of a credit employee's vacation, illness, or termination from the company. Recording the essence of the collection call—during or right after the call—minimizes any dependence upon memory and will eliminate unnecessary follow-up calls.

By using customer contact cards, credit staffers can also note if the customer has broken promises. Later, these broken promises can be brought to the customer's attention, accompanied by specific dates, invoices, and dollar amounts related to the unfulfilled pact.

Customer contact cards enable a corporate credit person to note when warnings, requests, or agreements were made with the customer. For example, on a certain date a credit staffer may have advised the customer that he must be current within 90 days or else provide a letter of credit or a UCC1 filing. All too often, a credit staffer will verbally warn the customer in this way, but will make no record of the discussion.

When a company files suit against a customer, the customer contact card can be invaluable in reconstructing the events leading to the suit. When the creditor makes its case, it will be able to document dates and events with specific detail, rather than providing a hazy reconstruction of events.

Once a card has been fully utilized, the credit staffer should file it away in the customer's credit file and begin a new card. Corporate credit policy will determine how long cards are retained in the file.

Some accounts receivable systems currently available allow comments or text to be recorded. Such systems now are the exception rather than the norm, but credit managers can expect that the AR systems of the 1990s will generally all have the capability to record and maintain unlimited customer contact information. Storage on the computer of customer collection call information represents the first step toward establishing electronic credit files.

In the meantime, although they may appear a bit primitive, customer contact cards remain an effective way to record collection and other customer information — information too important to merely commit to memory.

ABSTRACT SUMMARY

- Using customer contact cards for collections ensures that customer payment information is recorded accurately and maintained.
- Customer contact cards leave an audit trail for management to review and act upon.
- Recording collection call information minimizes dependence upon human memory and eliminates unneccessary follow-up calls.
- Customer contact cards can be used to document warnings, requests, and agreements discussed with the customer.
- Contact cards can be helpful in reconstructing events when a company files suit against a customer.

MONITORING THE QUALITY OF
DAILY COLLECTION CALLS

Collection calls are at the heart of corporate cash flow generated by credit departments throughout the nation. One way to improve the overall output of collection calls is to use daily collection sheets for each credit representative.

Collection sheets are not the same as customer contact cards, which summarize collection calls with individual customers. Collection sheets summarize each caller's daily collection activity for management review purposes.

Collection sheets should contain the following information in a columnar format:

1) Date
2) Customer Name
3) Number of Calls Made Re: Open Items
4) Balance
5) Past Due
6) Comments

This format enables a credit manager to review the output of the collection staff on a daily basis. By reviewing the balance and past due information, the manager can monitor the quality and quantity of collection calls made by the credit department and the resulting impact on cash flow. The last thing a credit manager for a middle-market company wants to see is collection representatives making 10 calls a day chasing past due balances under $1,000 when they could be making calls to customers with high past-due amounts and converting those accounts receivable into cash flow.

Once this monitoring program has begun, it won't be long before the credit manager can make correlations between the number of calls made each day and the ensuing level of trade receipts (see Correlation, in this chapter). The manager should be able to determine the number of days lag time there is between a quality collection call and when the actual receipt is recorded at the company's lockbox.

The manager can learn a number of things from this process. For instance, he or she might find that it takes more calls at the end of the month to generate receipts than it does at the beginning or the middle of the month. The manager might also be able to determine the optimum number of collection calls required in order to collect a desired level of trade receipts.

One tactic a credit manager can use is to formalize a call-volume goal with each representative (see Daily Collection Call Budgets, in this chapter). If the representative is expected to make a certain number of calls per day, the credit manager can monitor performance on a monthly or quarterly basis. Remember, duplicate calls to the same customer for the same items should be counted as one collection call only.

Credit managers have responsibility and accountability for the level of incoming trade receipts and past due. Thus, doesn't it make sense that these managers should formalize the delegated collection responsibility? At a minimum, the use of daily collection sheets will provide more direction to the efforts of credit representatives.

ABSTRACT SUMMARY

- Collection calls generate the bulk of corporate cash flow.
- Collection call sheets enable managers to evaluate the quality of collection call output.
- Daily collection call sheets should contain the date, customer name, number of calls made, balance, past due, and comments.
- Monitoring collection calls lets a credit manager make correlations between total calls made and the ensuing cash receipts generated.
- Duplicate calls to the same customer for the same items should be counted as one collection call only.

DAILY COLLECTION CALL BUDGETS

There is a definite relationship between the number of credit calls a company makes and its absolute level of past-due accounts receivable dollars outstanding. With this in mind, there is little question concerning the value of instituting formal, daily collection call budgets within the credit department. Each credit staffer should be required to make a certain number of credit calls each day.

The reason this strategy works is that chronic slow-paying customers generally will "sit" on cash for as long as possible. They won't budge unless they receive some pressure to do so. In fact, even current receivables don't always get paid without a little telephone contact from the credit department.

Budgeting calls is a way to ensure that this necessary contact with customers is initiated. By formalizing this process, the credit department has a better chance of meeting its past due, days sales outstanding (DSO), and cash flow goals.

The credit manager should assign daily collection call budgets to each credit staffer according to his or her collection proficiency and overall credit experience. A manager might determine that experienced staffers should generate 15 collection calls a day, while entry-level staffers will be assigned a budget of 10 collection calls per day. By allocating individual budgets, the credit manager assigns specific accountability to each credit staffer, and this accountability becomes part of the credit employee's formal performance evaluation.

Setting budgets is an effective way to communicate with credit personnel. The budgets let staffers know what is expected of them, as well as what management believes it will take to meet corporate past-due, DSO, and cash flow goals.

A budget gives a staffer direction for generating constructive collection activity. Without call budgets, collection results tend to lack consistency; they may even be volatile.

Budgets are also useful tools in evaluating credit employees. Are they meeting their budget goals in terms of calls made? Keep in mind that what a manager looks for in credit staffers is a consistent level of daily collection calls. A manager should not penalize a staffer for missing budget goals on a few occasions. However, the best staffers will generally exceed their budgets more often than they fall below them.

ABSTRACT SUMMARY

- There is a quantifiable relationship between the total number of collection calls made in a month and the level of month-end past due.
- Collection call budgets for individual staffers and for the department as a whole maximize the collection effort.

- Each staffer should be assigned daily collection call budgets based on his or her collection proficiency and overall credit experience.
- Assigning collection call budgets places specific accountability on individual credit staffers.
- Collection call budgets provide direction for staffers and a basis for formal performance evaluations.

A CORRELATION BETWEEN COLLECTION CALLS AND THE MOVING LEVEL OF PAST DUE

By monitoring and charting the level of collection calls made by each credit staffer on a daily basis, the credit manager can gain valuable insight into the relationship between call volume, on the one hand, and the company's moving monthly past due and its incoming level of cash receipts, on the other.

When charting this information, the credit manager should only count quality collection calls — not calls in which the credit staffer is chasing small dollars that will have no impact on receipts and the level of past due. Also, don't double-count duplicate follow-up calls to the same customer within a five-working-day period.

Collection call information can be integrated into a daily log that includes other accounts receivable information in the following format:

Date	Total AR	Total Past Due	Past Due	Collection Calls	Receipts
12/5	$33,000,000	$2,750,000	8.3%	26	$395,000
12/6	$32,795,000	$2,900,000	8.8%	55	$275,000
12/7	$33,500,000	$2,875,000	8.6%	34	$554,000
12/8	$33,275,000	$2,550,000	7.7%	49	$770,000
12/9	$32,990,000	$2,275,000	6.9%	58	$225,000
12/12	$33,100,000	$1,990,000	6.0%	47	$990,000
12/13	$33,675,000	$2,500,000	7.4%	36	$195,000

There will be a few days lag time between when the collection calls are placed to customers and when the corresponding past due and receipt levels surface. After a period of three to six months of daily charting, a clear relationship should develop between the number of calls made and the levels of past due and receipts.

The credit manager should be able to determine the approximate lag time in days for collection calls made and the ensuing level of incoming receipts. For instance, the data might indicate that every four working days after a high or low level of collection calls is made, there should be a corresponding high or low dollar level for incoming receipts and moving total past-due amount.

The daily log in the exhibit illustrates this lag effect. Note that the relatively large volume of calls made on Dec. 6 (55) is followed four days later by a high level of receipts ($990,000). On the other hand, when only 26 calls were made on Dec. 5, four days later there was a corresponding low level of receipts ($225,000).

The charting methodology can be an extremely helpful tool for reviewing and revising cash receipts projections based on what is known about collection call output. After a certain period of time, the credit manager might be able to determine the minimum and optimum number of collection calls per staffer per day required to achieve the credit department's past due and receipts goals.

11

ABSTRACT SUMMARY

- There is a quantifiable relationship between collection call volume and the moving level of past due.
- When monitoring the relationship between collection call volume and the moving level of past due, take into account only quality collection calls.
- There is a lag time between when collection calls are made and when the corresponding past due and receipts levels surface.
- Charting collection call output and moving past due enables a credit manager to review and revise receipts forecasts.
- Charting can enable the credit manager to determine the optimum number of collection calls required to meet past due and receipts goals.

COLLECTION LETTERS:
THE INVISIBLE COLLECTORS

Collection letters provide the credit department with a subtle way of reminding customers when their accounts are in arrears and the situation needing to be resolved. If used correctly, these letters can lend strong support to the collection effort, enhancing collections and cash flow.

Collection letters can be sent in response to a number of situations. Outstanding past-due items are a popular reason. But these letters can also be sent in the event of partial payments or unearned discounts that are taken. The letters can be either preprogrammed — that is, they can be system-driven based on a set of balance default criteria — or they can be generated manually on a selective basis.

Such letters can be especially helpful in collecting from customers with small, open past-due balances. After all, collection personnel tend to concentrate on large past-due customers when making telephone collection calls. These calls are time-consuming, and it only makes sense to concentrate efforts on the customers who owe the most money. Collection letters serve as a cost-effective means for communicating with small past-due customers that might not otherwise be contacted.

Customers will frequently write comments on the letters that elaborate about short shipments, damaged shipments, or returned material. In this way, collection letters are also a tool for enhancing the flow of information between the customer and the credit department. As a result of input received through collection letters, credit personnel are often able to identify a problem and begin solving it without ever making a time-consuming telephone collection call.

The timing and frequency of past-due collection letters is an important issue. The first letter might be sent when the account is past due six days. A second, different letter could be generated if the account is past due 21 days, and a third distinct letter could be generated if the account goes to 36 days past due. A fourth and final letter, again with a differently worded message, could be sent if the account goes to 50 or more days past due.

Each successive past-due collection letter should take on a more serious, no-nonsense tone. For instance, the *first letter* might use wording such as: "If your check for the account listed below is in the mail, please accept our thanks. Otherwise, please send your remittance now, or let us know if there are any reasons for the delay."

The *second letter*, sent when the account is 21 days past due, should contain a sterner message, such as: "This is a reminder that your account continues to be past due for payment. Unless your check is in the mail, kindly make payment at this time, or advise us if you are not able to make payment at the present time."

The *third letter*, generated when the account is 36 days past due, should refer to the previous letters and might state: "Please contact us immediately if there are any questions about the past-due account balance described in our previous letters. A response from your firm will receive our immediate and prompt attention."

The *fourth and final letter* of the cycle should convey a sense of immediacy and could read: "We had expected payment prior to this time covering the past-due items listed below. We know you appreciate the urgency of keeping your account up to date and current. Thus, please send your check today for $719.52. If your check is in the mail, please contact us to advise such."

All four letters should list the invoice date, invoice number, invoice amount and due date for the outstanding items. In addition, each letter should list the credit department contact and the number to call. Under no circumstances should any of the letters make any threats based on failure to make payments. The letters should be used simply to remind customers that they need to pay the items or communicate with the credit department regarding outstanding past-due obligations.

A *partial payment letter* could read: "Your check number 62042 recently received in partial payment in the amount of $2,500.00 is greatly appreciated. However, there is still an amount due on the invoice(s) listed below. Kindly forward an additional check to fully pay the invoice(s) listed below. If you have forwarded your payment, kindly disregard this notice." The letter should list the invoice date, invoice number, original invoice amount, and amount now partially outstanding. The letter should also list the credit department contact and the contact's phone number.

The *unearned discount letter* should be sent each time the customer generates an unearned discount. The letter might state: "Your check number 112644 in the amount of $920.82 generated an unearned discount(s) for the following invoice(s) listed below. Kindly review your records and remit a check to resolve the unearned discount." The letter should list invoice date, invoice number, discount date, postmark date, invoice amount, check number, and unearned discount amount. And, as with the other letters, it should also list the credit department contact and a number to call.

A second unearned discount letter also could be utilized when a series of unearned discounts remain unresolved after a period of time. For example, the letter could state: "Detailed below are a series of unearned discounts generated by your firm that still remain open and unpaid. Please review the items outstanding and remit a check for $617.82 upon your earliest convenience." The letter should list each unearned discount outstanding in the same form as the single unearned discount letter.

Some customers, especially proud, prompt-paying customers, may take great offense at receiving a computerized dunning or collection letter. When these situations arise, the credit department should contact the customer's management directly to advise them that the letter is a computer-generated letter and that there was no intention by the credit department to offend or imply that they don't pay their bills. The credit department may even want to suppress system-driven letters for prompt-paying customers who complain or threaten to buy elsewhere if the letters persist.

Often, collection letters will prompt the customer to make a payment that otherwise would not have been made. At other times, the letters will prompt the customer to contact the credit department about a situation preempting customer payment — a situation of which credit personnel were not aware. Some customers may resent the letters, but overall these letters are effective and cost justifiable.

ABSTRACT SUMMARY

- Collection letters can either be preprogrammed, that is, system-driven by a set of balance default criteria, or they can be manually driven or initiated.
- Collection letters are generally sent because of partial payments made, past-due items outstanding, or unearned discounts generated by the customer.
- Collection letters send a subtle reminder to customers that their accounts are in arrears and that the situation must be resolved.
- Collection letters can be especially helpful when dealing with customers with small, open past-due balances; credit personnel may not have the time to contact these customers via telephone collection calls.
- Given that a collection phone call is not viable, collection letters will often prompt the customer to make a payment that would not have been made otherwise.

BE PREPARED:
INFORMATION NEEDED FOR COLLECTION CALLS

It takes preparation to make a successful collection call. Before a credit representative calls a past due customer, he needs to review in detail the customer's statement of account. The collector needs to identify exactly which invoices he wants to collect payment for, and how many dollars he wants to collect against those invoices.

A credit representative or collection correspondent should probably spend more time preparing for the call than he does in making it.

If the credit person is working with an on-line accounts receivable system, he should access the customer's account via CRT and review the customer's payment history (if available on the system). Such a review can point out any new or emerging payment trends.

When making a collection call, credit personnel should have details of the customer's account in front of them—either on a computer screen or on a computer printout. This allows them to review with the customer recent past-due items, as well as old items that have not been resolved. Furthermore, having this information on hand prevents the need to call the customer back later with additional details. Eliminating call-backs will obviously increase productivity.

A complete review of the account prior to making the collection call will enable the credit staffer to prevent past-due slippage of old items, as well as recently past-due items. The collection call provides an opportunity to perform maintenance and cleanup work, and look beyond the 1–30 days and 31–60 days past-due aging columns.

If the credit department maintains customer collection call cards, the credit professional should review them prior to the next call. These call sheets will indicate whether the customer has failed to fulfill any outstanding commitments. A review of the call sheets might also indicate a pattern of broken promises; if so, this pattern needs to be discussed with the customer.

After making a collection call, the credit person should summarize the conversation in writing on the collection call card and log in the follow-up date that was agreed upon during the call.

Calls to certain customers—especially Fortune 500 firms—may require a bit more preparation. For instance, some companies might have accounts payable systems that are organized by purchase order rather than by vendor invoice number. This could require the credit representative to prepare for collection calls by identifying each invoice by the customer's original purchase order. (Depending on the level of accounts receivable system sophistication, individual customer accounts receivable screens should capture and detail customer purchase order information along with other invoicing detail.)

It's important to anticipate these exceptional cases. The credit staffer who doesn't will waste time on unnecessary follow-up phone calls. What good does it do to make the collection call only to be told again that the customer cannot convey any payment information without a reference to his purchase order number?

Collectors shouldn't get themselves in positions where they can be caught by surprise. To maximize collection results, collectors should be prepared for a number of scenarios that may arise during the call.

A review and planning step prior to a collection call can point out a number of issues the credit person might want to bring up with the customer. For instance, the review might indicate a need for acquiring from the customer an updated financial statement or revised bank information. If this is the case, the credit representative can make the call even more productive by using it as an opportunity to ask for this information.

A collection call that shows a lack of preparation reflects poorly on the credit person, his/her company, and ultimately has a negative impact on corporate cash flow. At a minimum, preparation will help the credit professional use the collection call to meet collection objectives.

ABSTRACT SUMMARY

- Prior to making a collection call, review the customer's statement of account in detail.

- Prior to making the call, also review the customer's payment performance in order to identify emerging payment trends.

- A complete review of the customer's accounts receivable balances prevents past-due slippage of old and recent past-due invoices.

- Before making collection calls, review the customer's collection card call sheet for commitments or broken promises.

- Collection calls can accomplish objectives other than securing payment commitments; for instance, they might be used to request updated financial information about the customer.

LENGTH OF COLLECTION CALLS

With few exceptions, collection telephone calls to customers should be short and to the point, and they should always be conducted in a professional manner.

The credit staff can only make a certain number of collection calls each day. Additional credit responsibilities are time-consuming and limit the number of collection calls that credit personnel can place. In order to maximize cash flow and accounts receivable performance, the key, then, is to make the most effective use of time spent on the telephone.

An effective call, one that has been prepared for and elicits necessary payment information from the customer, should last between one and three minutes. Once the credit person acquires the necessary payment information, he should move on to the next call. It is important to remember that the customer values his time, too.

The credit person should prepare for each collection call to avoid wasting anyone's time. Before placing the call, he should know which invoices he will seek payment information on. With certain customers, the credit person might need to have purchase order information in hand before making the call. In all cases, before making the call, the corporate credit staffer should review the customer's account using a CRT or by getting a hard-copy printout of account information. Failure to do so indicates a sloppy approach to collections.

All negotiating and collection strategy should be plotted before the collection call is made. In that way, the credit person will be in a better position to make a quick decision or commitment if necessary. Ultimately, pre-call preparation should reduce and minimize the actual time spent on each call.

So be prepared and be concise, and the desired cash flow results should follow.

ABSTRACT SUMMARY

- Collection calls should be professional and concise.
- Before calling the customer, plan a negotiating and collection strategy.
- An effective collection call should last one to three minutes.
- When necessary, obtain purchase order information in advance of collection calls to minimize the need for a second collection call.
- Never make a collection call without accessing the customer's account on the company's CRT or via hard-copy printout.

ALWAYS SECURE A COMMITMENT

One of the cardinal rules of collections is that the credit manager—or other credit department staffer—must always secure some type of payment commitment before completing a collection call. Because collections are a driving force behind corporate cash flow, the goal is to make every call to a customer productive.

Secure a commitment. If the customer says he currently is unable to send the past-due amount, find out when he can make that payment. Can he mail it five days from now? Eight, nine, or 10 days from now? If the customer indicates he is not sure if he can make the payment within five to 10 days, the credit manager should ask if he can call again in a specified number of days to discuss the status of past-due items.

Be persistent in a professional and courteous manner, but don't let the customer end the conversation unless he has at least committed to further discussion of the past due amount on a particular date. Otherwise, the call will have been a waste of time for both parties.

A key to securing a commitment from the customer is planning. Prior to each call, a credit manager should review the customer's balance and past-due amounts. Additionally, the manager should determine—within a range—what size of payment commitment he will seek. That range will, of course, have a floor—the minimum dollar commitment that the credit manager will attempt to extract from the customer. Let's say a customer is $25,000 past due by anywhere from one to 30 days. Based on the customer's total exposure and credit limit, the credit manager might determine that his minimum collection objective should be $10,000.

Don't get sidetracked if a customer says he can't mail a check for the entire balance. Ask for a partial payment, keeping in mind the predetermined minimum goal. Certain circumstances might even warrant a request for a postdated check (see Postdated Checks, in Chapter 8).

A credit person can make only so many collection calls in a day. He or she must make each call an effective one. This kind of performance can only be achieved by securing from the customer some kind of commitment to pay. Failure to secure such commitments will have a clear and negative impact on the corporation's cash flow.

ABSTRACT SUMMARY

- Make every collection call productive.
- If the customer is unable to give a payment commitment, obtain a follow-up date to contact the customer.
- Plan out collection calls in advance.

- Determine a "satisfactory payment" range. How much must the customer commit to pay in order to make the call a success?
- Partial payments, or even postdated checks in some circumstances, are better than no customer payments at all.

DEALING WITH REPEATED PROMISE BREAKERS

Unfortunately, not all customers tell the truth all the time. A small minority of customers will make payment commitments pegged to specific dates, knowing that they won't be able to meet them. A customer might make such a commitment in order to procure additional goods while on credit hold; or it simply might be the customer's management style, one that allows it to buy time with the vendor's credit department.

Either way, these customers must be reminded of a very critical point concerning the vendor/customer relationship: Credit is a privilege and not a right! Repeated broken commitments in the future could jeopardize the customer's credit limit or credit terms.

In a subtle and professional way, the credit practitioner must convey to the customer that payment commitments — in effect, the customer's "word" — must be kept in every situation unless there are overriding, explainable circumstances. The credit department can formalize this position by sending the customer a letter that reinforces it.

If the customer does not take this approach seriously and continues to break promises, then the credit department must consider holding all shipment of product until the customer remits all past-due funds. Another option is to restrict the amount of the customer's credit limit. For instance, if the customer's credit limit is $25,000, the vendor could cut it back to $10,000. The scaled-back credit limit could be put in force until the customer proves that it intends to honor payment commitments. A more drastic option would be to revoke the customer's open-account credit terms and require COD (cash on delivery) or CIA (cash in advance) terms.

Invoking COD or CIA terms, of course, might spell the end of the customer relationship. Once this action is taken, and it doesn't appear to be a short-term measure, the customer is likely to seek a new source of supply from another vendor that may be willing to tolerate the poor payment performance and broken promises. For this reason, before revoking terms, credit practitioners must determine the profit on sales to the customer in question. They should also investigate whether or not the customer's purchases have any impact on the operating profitability or capacity of a particular plant or product line. In some cases, the credit department will discover that revoking credit terms for a single customer could have a greater negative impact on the company than just losing the customer's business.

Revoking terms, therefore, is more than just a matter of the firm's corporate and credit philosophy regarding doing business with repeated promise breakers.

When the credit department allows a promise breaker to keep its open-account credit terms — for whatever reason — it's critical that department personnel keep a close watch on the customer's payment behavior. This will mean making telephone calls to monitor the customer's promises. If the customer promises to mail a check on Tuesday, the credit department needs to call the customer on Tuesday to confirm that the check, in the agreed-upon amount, is being mailed. The confirming calls should be made for a period of at least three to six months; this will enable the customer to establish a new track record of meeting payment commitments. The message will be subtle but clear: This vendor means business.

Credit personnel should also make it clear to the customer that when it is unable to make a commitment, it needs to advise the credit department. This will give the credit department an opportunity to secure a new commitment regarding the payment.

Credit personnel should stress that the vendor/customer relationship is a two-way street in which both parties must be equally cooperative and forthcoming if the relationship is to be mutually beneficial.

ABSTRACT SUMMARY

- There are a small minority of customers who will knowingly make payment commitments for particular dates that they will not be able to meet.

- Promise breakers must be reminded that credit is a privilege and not a right!

- When repeated promise breakers don't heed warnings, the credit department should consider holding new shipments of product until past-due funds are received.

- A customer's credit line may sometimes by reduced if it continues to break payment commitments.

- Enforcing COD or CIA terms is a drastic option that could lead to losing the customer's business.

ACCELERATING COLLECTIONS

When collection performance is not meeting expectations, or when the company requires additional cash flow, the credit department can accelerate collections in two basic ways. It can take internal measures generally not apparent to the customer, or it can try to accelerate collections using external measures that involve direct interface with customers. In either case, it's important to be proactive rather than reactive.

Internally, a credit manager could review lockbox efficiency, perform a ship date/invoice date audit (see Ship Date/Invoice Date Audit, in Chapter 6), review collection efficiency and the adequacy of current credit staffing, or consider changing existing credit policy and philosophy with respect to acceptable risk.

The review of lockbox efficiency should focus on major customers, since generally 80%–90% of all cash receipts are derived from 10%–15% of the company's total customer base. During the review, the credit manager should compare internal customer masterfile system information for "bill to" and "remit to" addresses to the major customer's actual postmark and envelope.

A lockbox study will enable the manager to discover internal coding errors and redirect remittances from customers who have either consolidated or relocated their payables function. Such a study can be extremely valuable in this age of mergers, acquisitions, and hostile takeovers.

A lockbox review also will enable a company to determine which of its customers are remote mailing or remote disbursing to the firm's lockbox. Ultimately, the review should verify the geographic configuration of the company's current lockbox network, while accelerating collections and cash flow.

The ship date/invoice date billing audit should cover the same major customers who are the focus of the lockbox review. A predetermined number of invoices per customer could be audited for a given month's billing activity. Or, the credit professional could decide to audit all billings for all customers for specified days of the month in question. For instance, one could audit all customer invoices generated on 6/3, 6/6, 6/13, 6/17, 6/20, and 6/25.

When conducting the audit, the credit person should compare shipment dates to invoice dates in order to determine whether his company is assigning free payment days to customers. For example, a July 19 shipment might not be invoiced until July 31. In this case, if standard terms of sale are 30 days, the seller actually extends 42 days of credit to the customer.

Considering that most companies' payment terms are based on the invoice date (except on letter of credit transactions), billing lags of this sort can be quite costly to the creditor. Not only might the seller be losing cash flow in the form of earlier collections, but there could also be an impact on the firm's balance sheet.

For instance, in the example above, the July 31 invoice probably will not be paid by the end of August. If that is the case, the company's balance sheet will reflect a higher receivables level, which must be offset by a lower cash level or an increased loan position.

When performing the audit, the credit person should note any relation between particular products and delays in billing. In a company with a decentralized billing function, certain billing groups might not be doing their jobs properly. The billing audit could make this clear.

If the credit person notes such a problem, he should gather his facts and confer with the appropriate billing personnel. The situation needs to be corrected. Be sure to explain to the billing personnel the cash flow ramifications of allowing the invoice date to lag beyond the actual shipping date.

With respect to collection efficiency, make sure that the credit department is making quality collection calls, rather than just a large quantity of calls. Credit staffers should not be chasing after past-due amounts of $250 when they could be calling customers who are past due $25,000 or more.

If the company isn't meeting DSO, past due, and total cash collection goals, a credit manager should consider whether the department has enough qualified personnel. The firm simply might not have enough collectors to meet cash flow needs. Adding members to the collection staff could be the best way to accelerate collections and cash flow.

Even in times when the need for increased cash flow is not critical, it's a good idea to periodically review the adequacy of the credit and collections staff.

As a final internal option, the credit department could implement changes in credit policy and philosophy. The firm could decide to weed out slow-paying customers or be more selective in extending credit to new customers.

These kinds of dramatic changes carry with them certain dangers, however. The main danger would be a disruption of business. A unilateral change in credit policy and philosophy might increase cash flow in the short term but, in the long term, create more harm than good. Therefore, before taking such measures, a credit manager should confer with senior financial and marketing personnel.

Now let's turn to external options.

The credit manager could offer a cash discount or increase the current cash discount as a way of accelerating collections. Other options would be to promote cash on delivery or cash in advance terms for non-prime or slow-moving inventory, increase the daily frequency of collection call output, or, under certain market conditions, restrict credit to slow-paying customers.

Before increasing discount terms or implementing discount terms for the first time, a credit manager should study the economics of such a move. How much additional cash flow will be generated by the proposed change in terms? Will unearned discounts offset the cash flow savings generated? What percent of prompt-paying customers will take advantage of increased or new discount terms?

A credit manager who increases the cash discount should be prepared to enforce the new discount terms strictly. If he or she doesn't, customers are likely to abuse the new terms by taking unearned discounts.

Cash on delivery (COD) or cash in advance (CIA) sales of non-prime and slow-moving inventory should accelerate collections by default. In most cases, the company is already offering the customer a distressed price to purchase the non-prime or slow-moving inventory. So why not maximize cash flow on the distressed pricing? The customer isn't likely to forgo the deal because of the COD or CIA terms.

A customer balking at these terms should be reminded that the deal involves a nonstandard trade sale at a distressed price. The only customers who are likely to complain about the payment terms are slow-payers with cash flow problems.

Increasing the frequency of daily collection call output by credit personnel should accelerate cash flow. However, there are diminishing returns associated with increasing collection call frequency. A credit manager needs to be careful when increasing the frequency of daily collection calls; it's important not to antagonize customers, and more frequent telephone calls might do that.

Before initiating increased collection call activity, the credit manager should hold a staff meeting. At the meeting, the manager can discuss how to increase collection calls without incurring negative customer feedback. Specifically identify the customers and aged-out items that will be impacted by increased collection call frequency.

A final external alternative for accelerating collections would be to restrict trade credit for slow-paying customers. This option has less downside risk than making a formal change in credit policy. In essence, this option implies stronger enforcement of a credit hold when customers are past due. However, this alternative is only available when competitive market conditions are opportune. Such a policy change should not necessarily be announced to the customers who are affected. Over time, the marginal exposures identified should gradually become accustomed to their orders being held if they cannot meet their payment obligations.

A company could restrict its credit with slow-paying customers—without having to initiate a formal change in credit policy—if its products are sold out, its plant is operating at full capacity, or the competitive supply for goods is tight. Yet, even under such conditions, the move could be dangerous. The company runs the risk of incurring potentially severe long-term injury if the marketplace turns around or the company's capacity becomes slack.

Customers have good memories. A vendor cannot turn the supply spigot off and on and expect the customer not to notice. A customer whose flow of credit is restricted today might be the customer a company needs in the future. If the customer believes it has been treated improperly, it might take the opportunity at a later date to look elsewhere for its goods.

Even so, under the right conditions, restricting credit on selected slow-paying customers can be a way to accelerate collections and cash flow. But, once again, before taking such action, a credit manager should confer with senior financial and marketing management to obtain their feedback on the plan. If top management gives the green light to this strategy, the credit manager needs to hold a staff meeting to discuss specific past-due criteria for restricting credit.

Ideally, this kind of credit tightening will dramatically accelerate payments from the targeted slow-payers. Such customers are likely to fear an interruption in their supply of materials, and they will often act accordingly by improving their payment habits.

The credit department can prepare a checklist (see Exhibit 1.1) of internal and external sources for accelerating collections that can be referred to in the future by credit department management.

There are many approaches to priming the collection pump. Some will work better than others. But, in all cases, it is the credit manager who must initiate the strategies and provide direction to the collections staff.

Exhibit 1.1
Checklist of Internal and External Sources
for Accelerating Collections

Internal Sources
_____ Lockbox Efficiency Study
_____ Ship Date/Invoice Date Audit
_____ Review Collection Efficiency and Staffing Adequacy
_____ Formal Change in Credit Policy Regarding Risk

External Sources
_____ Offer or Increase Cash Discount
_____ Promote COD Terms for Slow-Moving Inventory
_____ Increase Daily Collection Call Output
_____ Restrict Credit (Credit Hold) with Slow-Paying Customers

ABSTRACT SUMMARY

- Cash flow can be accelerated using either internal or external measures.
- Internal methods of accelerating collections include analyzing lockbox efficiency, performing a ship date/invoice date audit, reviewing collection efficiency and adequacy of credit staffing, and initiating a change in credit policy or philosophy.
- External methods include offering a cash discount, increasing the current cash discount, promoting cash on delivery (COD) or cash in advance (CIA) terms for non-prime or slow-moving inventory, increasing the fre-

quency of collection calls, and restricting credit with slow-paying customers.

- The credit manager must provide direction to efforts aimed at accelerating collections.
- Accelerating collections to enhance cash flow can be either proactive or reactive in nature.

ANALYZING COLLECTION PERFORMANCE

Collection performance directly impacts a company's balance sheet, as well as its cash flow, level of past due, and DSO (days sales outstanding). Simply put, without collections, there is no cash flow — unless the firm operates a pure cash business. Nevertheless, corporate America has failed to emphasize and recognize the obvious importance of this function, and there is a great need for companies to develop formalized programs for monitoring and analyzing short- and long-term collection performance. Without formalized programs, companies will not be able to identify when, how, and where the collection effort has gone astray.

There are a variety of ways to analyze collections. Some include DSO, Best DSO and Past-Due DSO analysis, past-due analysis, high-risk collection analysis, bad-debt analysis, collection call analysis, and monthly trend analysis for DSO and past due.

When analyzing collection performance, it's important to review both short- and long-term collection performance. Short-term performance implies the current year's performance analyzed on a monthly basis (including trend analysis) — i.e., actual performance against budget, and month-to-month changes in DSO, past due, and high-risk exposures. Analysis of long-term performance would involve comparing either the current year's performance to the prior year's, or analyzing a trend line of two to five years' performance.

Before moving on, let's analyze a few terms:

- Days sales outstanding (DSO): A calculation of total accounts receivable that measures month-end accounts receivable dollars to sales for the current and prior months (if necessary), and then allocates sales days to the outstanding receivables.

- Best DSO: A DSO measurement that only takes into account current month-end accounts receivable dollars. It is the "best" the DSO could have performed if there were no past-due dollars outstanding at month end.

- Past-Due DSO: A DSO measurement of outstanding month-end past-due accounts receivable. Past-Due DSO can be calculated or derived by subtracting Best DSO from Total DSO.

- DSO calibration: The concept of aging out Total DSO days for current and past-due accounts receivable dollars. For example, if there were 12 total Past-due DSO days, one would assign DSO days to 1–30 days past due, 31–60 days past due, 61–90 days past due, 91–120 days past due, and 120+ days past due, based on the past-due AR balances.

- High-risk exposures: Refers to those customers that carry a significant degree of risk with respect to extending them credit. The risk relates to payment or viability risk based on either industry, financial, derogatory, or payment information.

- Daily collection call sheets: A management tool to monitor the quality and output of collection calls per staffer. The call sheets made by each staffer list the following information for each day: customer name, number of calls made regarding the open item, balance, past due, and comments.

Before being able to perform DSO analysis, the credit manager should set monthly calendarized standards for DSO, Best DSO, and Past-Due DSO days. For instance, let's say a company's DSO historically ranges from 40 to 50 days, carrying eight to 12 Past-Due DSO days. The credit manager could set a goal limiting Past-Due DSO days to no more than 10 DSO days—the equivalent of roughly 20 –25 percent of total accounts receivable. By reviewing DSO history, monthly budgets would be set for DSO, and by subtracting the 10 Past-Due DSO day budget from each monthly DSO target, the credit manager would derive the Best DSO objective for each respective month.

In addition, the credit manager should set DSO calibration objectives (see DSO Calibration, in Chapter 5) for the Past-Due DSO days budgeted. The monthly objective of 10 past-due DSO days should now be calibrated and allocated to the past-due aging categories of 1–30 days past due, 31–60 days past due, 61–90 days past due, 91–120 days past due, and 120+ days past due. Collections can then be focused on all the past-due aging categories to minimize past-due slippage and ultimately bad-debt write-offs. Remember, all bad-debt write-offs don't result from a bankruptcy. A bad-debt write-off simply means that the receivable is uncollectable.

Once monthly DSO budgets have been set for DSO, Best DSO, Past-Due DSO, and the calibration of Past-Due DSO days, the credit manager should begin analyzing short-term collection performance by comparing actual performance to the specific objectives for each respective month.

Monthly collections are a direct function of DSO. For example, let's say month-end July accounts receivable is $20 million, July DSO is 50 days, and collections were $12.5 million. Given this scenario, we could say that if July month-end DSO was 47 days, collections would have been $600,000 higher (given that one DSO day equals $200,000). Or if July ending DSO was 3 days higher at 53 days, we could say that collections would have been $600,000 lower.

In addition to comparing actual DSO to projected DSO for a given month, credit managers should analyze the month-to-month changes in DSO, Best DSO, and Past-Due DSO. They need to dissect the components of DSO for the month to determine from where the increase or decrease from the prior month came. Can the three-day increase in the month's DSO be attributed to a rise in Past-Due DSO days or to a rise in Best DSO days? If the rise was in Past-Due DSO days, which aging categories increased?

A credit manager should determine exactly why there was a negative or positive variance from the budgeted objectives and ensuing collections. Was overall collection call output low, was there a lack of quality collection calls made, or did a few major customers negatively impact cash flow? There should be a direct correlation between the change in Past-Due DSO days and the change in past-due dollars as a percent of total AR.

Positive and negative month-to-month changes in DSO are a direct function of the level of collections. If month-to-month DSO and actual-to-budget monthly performance is consistently negative, the credit manager might have to take a closer look at the components of the budgeted DSO objectives, the quality of the AR portfolio, collection procedures, and staffing adequacy. A common problem is that DSO objectives are not realistic. They may be set too high or too low.

Analysis of long-term collection performance utilizing DSO requires the comparison and analysis of the prior year's monthly DSO, Best DSO, and Past-Due DSO performance to the current year's monthly DSO performance. For example, current year month-to-month changes could show declines, yet monthly performance represents DSO erosion when compared to the prior year's performance levels.

Again, credit managers need to determine if overall collection call output has been low, if there has been a change in market or competitive conditions, if there has been a lack of quality collection calls made compared to the prior year, or if a few major customers have been negatively impacting cash flow as compared to the prior year. They need to know whether the DSO swings and trends can be attributed to changes in the Best DSO and/or the Past-Due DSO days.

Past due analysis can be helpful if performed properly. Unfortunately, in many instances past due is misguidedly analyzed with an eye toward total past-due dollars only. Using this methodology, total past due for a month could increase in whole dollars yet be much proportionately lower as a percent of total accounts receivable — or past-due dollars could increase for a month while Past-Due DSO days decreased for the month. For example, July 1989 month-end past due could be up $500,000 as compared to the prior month of June, but reflect a much lower percentage of outstanding accounts receivable dollars. Meanwhile, Past-Due DSO days could also be lower. Thus, the analysis should be confined to analyzing past-due dollars as a percent of total accounts receivable dollars. Credit managers should analyze month-to-month changes and review historical changes for the particular month analyzed. They should also look for timing differences where a large amount of cash may have been received in the first few days of the new month.

As with DSO analysis, credit managers should set monthly budgets for past-due dollars as a percent of total AR dollars. Budgets should not be set based on absolute past-due dollar levels only. For budgeting monthly past due as a percent of AR, managers should review three to five years of AR data and past-due history and then set the monthly budgets accordingly, factoring in any monthly seasonality relating to past due. Clearly, the past-due percentage budget should have a direct correlation to the budgeted objective for Past-Due DSO days.

When measuring monthly past-due levels for short-term collection performance, the credit executive should compare the current to the prior month's past-due dollars as a percent of total accounts receivable dollars. This approach will minimize overreacting to past-due dollar increases that don't reflect an increase in the outstanding percent past due. A cross correlation for monthly collection performance would be to compare the month's actual past due percent to the budgeted past due percent for the month. In addition, one should compare Past-Due DSO days of the current month to the prior month's performance.

For longer-term analysis, credit managers can compare the current year's July percent past due to the prior year's July percent past due. They might also compare the current year's July Past-Due DSO days to the prior year's July Past-Due DSO days. Or, they can graphically compare the current year's monthly percent past due to the prior year's monthly past-due percentages to denote any longer-term collection trends. A three- to five-year comparison should be sufficient to surface any deviating trends.

Past-due analysis in dollar terms should also be evaluated by product line or business entity to analyze collection performance on the macro level for credit assignments. Collections could be strong with the exception of one product line or subsidiary that is negatively offsetting the collective efforts. This way, management will have a clear focus on where the additional collection measures must be taken in the near term.

Ultimately, past-due analysis should provide a clear indication of the efficiency of the department's collection performance.

The next task when analyzing collection performance is to correlate bad-debt performance to collection performance. This takes on macro and micro implications. On the macro level, the credit manager can measure total bad-debt dollars as a percent of total annual sales, in order to gauge overall collection performance. On sales of $100 million, bad-debt write-offs of $100,000 represent a bad-debt rate of .1 of 1 percent of total sales. This rate should be compared to established industry standards. On the micro level, when customers are classified as bad-debt write-offs, credit managers need to review the collection call card (see Customer Contact Cards, in this chapter) to determine if satisfactory collection calls and follow-up efforts were made. Bad-debt levels not only yield insights into collections, they also say something about the quality of credit extension documentation for new and existing customers. Clearly if bad-debt performance exceeds industry standards, then credit policy and procedure must be closely examined for credit analysis and extension, and for collections.

High-risk collections analysis can measure month-to-month changes in high-risk customer DSO days, Past-Due DSO days, and past-due high-risk dollars outstanding. All these measurements are ultimately a function and reflection of the collection effort. High-risk collections analysis should also shed light on the overall quality of the accounts receivable portfolio.

Credit managers should review the collection call cards for high-risk customers to ensure that high-risk collection procedures are being adhered to. They should maintain a weekly or monthly cumulative report for high-risk customers that charts their weekly or monthly total balances and past-due dollar levels. For example, the chart below lists for each month the customer's total balance/past-due balance.

1989 Monthly Moving High-Risk Exposures

Customer	Jan.	Feb.	Mar.	A	M	Jn	Jl	A	S	O	N	D
PLM Co.	90/12	115/34	65/6									
DPM Co.	43/23	88/31	99/44									
BJM Co.	89/21	92/28	96/19									
PJM Co.	44/23	34/31	46/38									
BPM Co.	65/12	77/17	90/23									
LPM Co.	106/15	94/24	86/41									

Charting moving 12-month levels for Total DSO, Past-Due DSO days, past-due accounts receivable dollars, and respective percentage calculations will enable the company to detect negative trends and potential deviations in the collection effort and in the administration of credit policy and procedure. Charting these variables with a 12-month trend line provides credit personnel with a graphic display of their collection performance.

Collection call analysis is an extremely effective measurement of collections. On a monthly basis, credit managers should review staffers' daily collection call sheets for the department as a whole and by individual credit personnel, checking the number of quality collection calls made for the month. Budgets should be set for each staffer regarding the number of quality collection calls to be made daily.

Are the credit collectors making quality or quantity collection calls? Quantity is only effective when it goes hand in hand with quality. Collection contact with small-dollar exposures has little or no impact on cash flow and past due. Thus, it should be instilled into credit personnel that high-dollar, quality collection calls must be made first in order to reduce DSO and past due, and to enhance cash flow.

Credit managers need to define "quality collection call" in writing as part of collection policy and procedure. They also need to find out the relationship between the moving total number of collection calls made to the moving level of outstanding past-due accounts receivable. This will enable them to gauge if quality collection call output is meeting cash flow needs. If a negative collection trend continues, the credit manager may have to redirect the collection effort, either by pressing for more quality collection calls, or by shuffling credit assignments among staffers.

The collection effort has a direct correlation to the level of cash flow. Budgets and measurements must be applied to collection performance as a safeguard for cash flow. These measurements will enable credit managers to redirect their short- and long-term collection policy and strategy if necessary.

ABSTRACT SUMMARY

- Collections directly impact the balance sheet, cash flow, past due, and DSO (days sales outstanding).
- Methods for reviewing collection performance include DSO and Best DSO analysis, past-due analysis, bad-debt analysis, high-risk collection analysis, monthly trend analysis for DSO and past due, and collection call analysis.
- When analyzing collections, credit managers should review short- and long-term collection performance. Short-term performance implies performance analyzed on a monthly basis, whereas long-term performance refers to comparing current year's performance to previous years' trends.
- Correlating bad-debt performance to collection performance takes on macro and micro implications.
- Collection measurements will enable credit managers to redirect their short- and long-term collection policy and strategy when necessary.

2

CREDIT
& FINANCIAL ANALYSIS

CREDIT APPLICATIONS

To be competitive in almost any marketplace, a business needs a steady stream of new customers. It is the credit department's responsibility to investigate, review, and evaluate new customer requests for open account credit terms.

Central to any effective and proper credit investigation is the credit application (see Exhibit 2.1). The credit application should provide the credit department with enough information to enter into new customer relationships and establish credit limits.

The application should request demographic information such as the firm's registered, legal namestyle; city; state; telephone number; type of business; and principal products or scope of business. It should also ask what type of legal entity the applicant is—e.g., corporation, partnership, or proprietorship. Also, if applicable, the applicant should be asked to identify its parent company, subsidiaries, affiliates, and principals. The corporate affiliation information may be especially helpful when negotiating for any corporate or personal guarantees, either up front or at a later date.

A standard credit application should request that the applicant provide at least three trade references, including their names, addresses, telephone numbers, and contact persons.

The credit manager should emphasize with sales personnel that references should come from within their company's own industry. Additionally, the dollar amounts for the high credits attained on the references should be similar or close to the amount of credit for which the prospective customer is applying.

The credit application should request at least one bank reference that includes the institution's name, address, telephone number, and contact person. Obtaining complete bank and trade reference information on the application gives the credit department the option of pursuing additional credit reference information through a written inquiry or via a verbal inquiry. Which option is selected will probably hinge on time constraints and/or the dollar level of credit being requested.

An ideal application would include written confirmation from the applicant as to the dollar amount of credit being requested. In this way, the credit department knows the amount is not simply a lowball estimate provided by the marketing department to ensure that the account is established.

If the amount of credit being requested is high enough, the supplier may want to ask the customer to submit a financial statement. When requesting such information, get the name of the person at the applicant's firm who can answer any questions or clear up any ambiguities related to the financial statement. This individual may be a key contact to develop in case payment problems arise down the road.

The credit application itself could include a request for a financial statement in the form of a checklist with a place for the applicant to mark: "Most recent year-end financial statement enclosed" or "Statement is forthcoming." Don't include on the application a notation such as "Statement declined." The application should

Exhibit 2.1

PJM Co. CREDIT APPLICATION

PJM Co., 719 Broad Street, Newark, NJ 10005

CREDIT INFORMATION

Please Complete this Form and Return in the Attached Envelope.

Name of Company _____ Date _____

Address _____

City and State _____

Phone Number _____

Products Manufactured, Distributed, or Services Performed _____

_____

Business Entity (Check One}: Corporation ____ Sub. Chap. S ____

Partnership ____ Proprietorship ____

<u>Name of Company Principals</u>   <u>Title</u>

_____

_____

_____

<u>Trade References:</u>

<u>Name</u>	<u>Address</u>	<u>Telephone</u>	<u>Contact</u>
1.			
2.			
3.			

<u>Bank Reference:</u>

Name _____

Address _____

Telephone No. and Name of Bank Contact _____

FINANCIAL INFORMATION

____ Latest Audited Report and Interim Statement Attached.

____ Customer Will Forward Directly to Corporate Credit Department.

<u>Order Data:</u>

Please indicate the type of product you wish to purchase:

____ Sheet ____ Rod ____ Tube ____ Flat Rolled ____ Carbon Plate

<u>Amount of Credit Requested</u>   <u>Name of Person Requesting Credit</u>

$ _____   _____

leave the applicant with the impression that financial disclosure is required before credit extension can be considered.

At the bottom of their applications, some companies list their terms of sale and note that the applicant must pay a finance charge on payments received beyond terms. The application might also contain a statement to the effect that the customer agrees to pay the vendor's legal fees in the event of litigation due to nonpayment. In some cases, the applicant is asked to sign a statement agreeing to the outlined terms and conditions. A vendor might have difficulty in successfully enforcing the collection of finance charges for late payments, but signing such an agreement will make customers think twice before paying late.

Credit investigations take time. Thus, it is best to avoid same-day investigations aimed at approving credit and pushing ahead with a rush order. After all, the credit investigation, if done properly, might indicate the necessity for pursuing additional financial information, or some form of guarantee or collateral. Thus, make sure that marketing is aware that plenty of lead time is required between the time the completed application is received and the date the first order is to be shipped.

Also, make sure that each member of the sales force has an ample supply of credit applications to provide potential customers. Sit down with marketing personnel and explain the logic of the credit application. Their support will be vital in getting the applications filled out properly with sufficient first-order shipment lead time.

The credit application should be a part of the vendor's written credit policy and procedure.

ABSTRACT SUMMARY

- A good credit application form will provide the credit department with enough information for it to make decisions about extending credit and setting credit limits.

- Some of the demographic information an application should ask for includes: legal namestyle, city, state, telephone number, type of business, and principal products.

- A standard credit application should also request that the applicant provide at least three trade references, at least one bank reference, and written confirmation from the applicant as to the amount of credit being requested.

- If the amount of credit being requested is high enough, the supplier might want to ask the applicant for a financial statement — or the supplier could simply include a request for a financial statement in all applications.

■ Make sure that the marketing department is aware of the necessary lead time between when the application is received and when a first shipment might be made (assuming a credit investigation is favorable).

CREDIT LIMITS

Credit limits are assigned to new customers after a credit investigation has been performed and the credit department is satisfied that the customer is creditworthy and deserves the privilege of open-account credit terms. These limits are reviewed on an ongoing basis for existing customers that are deemed creditworthy. They are generally reviewed for approval on an annual basis, unless the credit department perceives a credit problem. In that case, a thorough credit analysis should be performed immediately, including an assessment of the current credit limit.

At a given point in time, a credit limit represents the upper dollar limit of credit exposure and risk that the firm wants to take on with a particular customer. Such limits are generally used as control mechanisms, but they are not necessarily ironclad. In certain cases, credit limits do not represent the maximum or final level of credit that the firm is willing to extend to its customers.

Credit limits often are set for new and existing customers based on the customer's estimated level of monthly purchases. The limits are set based on the assumption that the customer will be paying obligations (invoices) within the firm's terms of sale. For example, if a new customer indicates that monthly purchases are estimated to be $50,000 per month with net 30-day terms, then a credit limit of $50,000 would probably be assigned. If the terms were net 60 days, with the same level of estimated purchases, the credit limit would be set at $100,000. Depending on corporate and credit department philosophy, the new customer's credit limit may take into account perceived slow payments based on the initial credit investigation.

When the new customer's monthly purchase requirements increase, a new and higher limit may be assigned based on its payment performance and a credit department assessment of the customer's financial wherewithal and viability. The newly assigned limit represents the revised "upper-end" dollar exposure that the creditor wants to assign to the new customer.

With existing customers, credit limits are generally set according to the customer's estimated monthly exposure, factoring in existing slow payment performance, if applicable and tolerable. The reason the credit department can do this is that the existing customer has developed a track record of viability. The proven track record enables the credit department to adjust the limit, and in cases of acceptable slow payers, factor slow payments into new credit limits.

Credit limits cannot be adjusted upward just because limits are exceeded. Credit analysis must first be performed. When limits are exceeded for new and existing customers, there must be justification and documentation for increasing the customer's credit limit, even if there isn't a perceived credit problem. If this weren't the case, the credit limit would lose its value as a control mechanism. In fact, when a customer begins to exceed its credit limits, this might be a sign that the customer is having difficulty managing or repaying its exposure. Limits should definitely not be adjusted upward in cases where there is a documented or perceived credit risk, overexposure, or intolerable payment performance.

The control function of the credit limit is particularly important when limits are applied to "high-risk" or "marginal" customers. The limits set for these customers should more closely represent absolute thresholds because of the great potential for bad-debt write-offs. However, even with these customers, credit limits can be adjusted upward provided there is sound company and/or credit department rationale.

When a high-risk customer is continually over its credit limit and not able to reduce its balance, the account can be characterized as being overexposed or "evergreen." Such accounts should be referred to senior financial management for review.

Credit limits for all customers should be assigned and approved using prudence. Credit personnel should always ask themselves: Can I document and justify the required limit?

ABSTRACT SUMMARY

- Credit limits are assigned for new customers after a credit investigation has been performed and the credit department is satisfied that the customer is creditworthy.
- Credit limits for existing customers should be reviewed on an ongoing basis and generally reviewed for approval on an annual basis.
- Credit limits represent the upper dollar limit of credit exposure and risk that the firm wants to take on with a particular customer.
- Credit limits should not be adjusted upward based solely on the fact that they have been exceeded. Credit department analysis of the account must first be performed.
- The role of the credit limit as a control mechanism is most important as these limits are applied to "high-risk" or "marginal" customers, those accounts where there is a question about the customer's ongoing viability and solvency.

THE OTHER THREE "C"s OF CREDIT

The traditional "three 'C's of credit"—character, capital, and capacity—are well known. However, in today's environment, there are three more "C"s of credit and risk analysis that cannot be overlooked: competition, costs, and cash flow.

In fact, these days, it might be even more important to know and understand the customer from competitive, cost, and cash flow standpoints than it is to assess character and capacity. With respect to character, the customer doesn't really have to be a nice guy to pay promptly and be a good credit risk. And, as for capacity, it can be a drain on cash flow if it is not fully and properly utilized.

Without the right products in the right marketplace, the customer may not be able to survive the competitive rigors of the near term. Today, competition has such broad implications. It is based on price, payment terms, timing, service, quality, and, in some cases, technology. A supplier needs to understand the nature and level of competition faced by each of its major customers.

Credit practitioners should make it their jobs to know who and what make the customer's market tick. Competition sometimes can put a customer out of business—especially if the customer is a small, privately held firm competing against Fortune 500 companies. So, if a price war breaks out in a customer's industry, credit personnel need to be aware of it. Furthermore, they need to be aware of the customer's game plan to mitigate these competitive factors.

Cutting costs has become a prime focus of corporate America in the mid to late 1980s. The new corporate slogan is "doing more with less." Thus, in relation to customers, it makes sense to ask: Have their costs been reduced or are they increasing their costs? What types of quality-control measures are in place to minimize costs? How well-contained are their cost of goods sold, selling, general, and administrative expenses?

Cash flow is the third new "C" of credit. Cash flow is a pure measure of a firm's wherewithal and viability. Cash flow sources of net income, depreciation, and deferred income taxes must be able to support capital spending, dividends, and changes in working capital. Otherwise, cash will be depleted and debt must be taken on.

The quality of a firm's earnings can be measured against the costs of the earnings. A firm may earn $1 million, but those earnings could, for instance, come at the expense of increasing the loan balance by $2 million. Why? The problem could be poor working capital management in the form of increased accounts receivable and inventory. If the customer is unable to secure bank borrowings, its capital appropriations will be reduced and will most probably affect its competitive ability. Thus, growth can be blunted by the lack of cash flow. And without growth, survival could be challenged.

The other "C"s of credit are meant to be a reminder.

Credit personnel need to get to know their customers up close. They need to know the terms and conditions relating to their customers' competition. They need to determine if the company is well-run and efficient, and whether it contains costs or creates them needlessly.

Credit personnel should prepare a checklist of internal prompts regarding the other "C"s in order to formalize this awareness and serve as a reminder (see Exhibit 2.2).

Credit practitioners should understand a customer's cash flow situation while deciphering the hidden costs. They should understand all the components of the customer's profit and loss statement, and be aware of accounting "gymnastics" that have no impact on cash flow but can be misleading with regard to earnings quality.

Thorough attention to the "other three 'C's" will maximize cash flow while reducing risk.

Exhibit 2.2
3 "C"s Checklist Of Internal Prompts

Competitive Prompts
_____ Are They Competitive with Respect to Price?
_____ What Are the Competition's Terms?
_____ Is Service a Factor?
_____ How Important Is Quality in the Marketplace?
_____ Does Technology Come into Play?
_____ Nature of Competition?
_____ Can They Survive a Major Price War?

Cost Prompts
_____ Are They Doing More with Less?
_____ Have Costs Been Reduced or Increased?
_____ Any Cost Reduction Programs in Place?
_____ Any Quality Control Measurements Utilized?
_____ How Well Contained Are Costs?

Cashflow Prompts
_____ Can Cash Flow Sources Support the Business?
_____ What Is the Quality of Earnings?
_____ How Strong Is Borrowing Wherewithal?
_____ Are There Any Hidden Costs Associated with Cash Flow?
_____ What Are the Industry Standards for Earnings and Cash Flow?

ABSTRACT SUMMARY

■ The traditional "three 'C's of credit" are character, capital, and capacity.

■ Three additional "C"s that can't be overlooked are competition, costs, and cash flow.

■ A supplier needs to understand the nature and level of competition faced by each of its major customers, because competition can sometimes put a customer out of business.

■ Costs are important because a company that does not minimize costs through quality-control measures will be weakened and ultimately may not survive.

■ Cash flow is a pure measure of a firm's wherewithal and viability; without a strong cash flow, a company's growth can be blunted, and without growth, the company could die.

TRADING ASSETS: THEY PAY THE BILLS

A supplier can learn a lot about a customer through a careful and thorough analysis of the firm's trading assets. Comprised of inventory and accounts receivable, a company's trading assets are its primary corporate assets, generating 90 percent or more of its required ongoing cash flow.

For the most part, viable cash flow is not generated through the sale of fixed assets or other current assets. Cash flow that results from such sales is "one time"; it isn't considered ordinary cash flow, because it will not be repeated.

On the other hand, trading assets are the mainstays of the corporate liquidity cycle, which works as follows: Inventory is sold to a customer, an invoice and receivable are generated, the receivable is collected and is converted to cash. The cycle is repeated over and over again (see Exhibit 2.3).

The quality of a customer's liquidity cycle is a leading indicator of its payment performance. The quality of that cycle can be measured by the turnover in days for accounts receivable and inventory, as well as by the ratios of accounts receivable and inventory to accounts payable. These measurements are indicative of the firm's natural cash flow independent of bank borrowings.

Comparing the turnovers for accounts receivable and inventory to the turnover for accounts payable may reveal that a customer is living on borrowed time and customer funds. There should be a close correlation between the customer's turnovers and its trade-payment performance.

A corporate credit department should analyze a customer's turnovers and ratios and compare them to industry standards. Ultimately, the analysis could lead the supplier to refuse credit or to closely monitor an account exposure.

By carefully analyzing a new customer's trading assets, the supplier may be able to avoid taking on a future bad-debt write-off candidate or potential payout account. Or, if the supplier's marketing department decides to commercially support the exposure, at least the credit department can point out what the company is getting into from cash flow and risk standpoints.

From a credit perspective, the quality of a customer's receivables and inventory cannot be emphasized enough. The ratio of accounts receivable and/or cash to accounts payable should be indicative of the degree of trade support (slow-payment tolerance) provided to the customer by vendors either voluntarily or involuntarily.

An investigation of a customer's trading assets can enhance the supplier's credit analysis, providing key additional qualitative information to assist in the credit decision.

Exhibit 2.3
Corporate Liquidity Trading Cycle

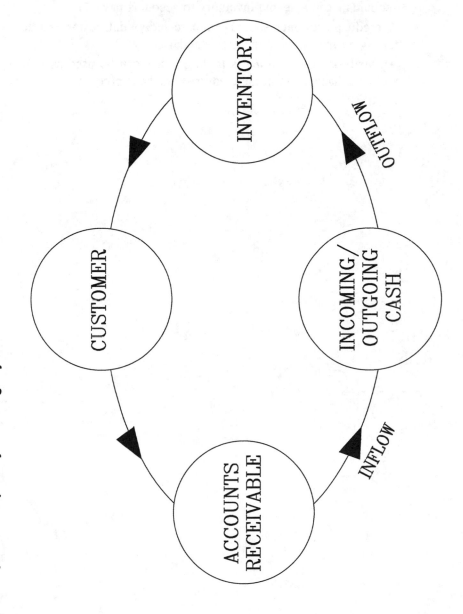

ABSTRACT SUMMARY

- Accounts receivable and inventory are commonly referred to as a company's "trading assets."
- Trading assets are the mainstays of the corporate liquidity cycle; they account for 90 percent or more of a company's cash flow.
- Liquidity and quality of trading assets can be measured by the turnover in days for accounts receivable and inventory, as well as by the ratios of accounts receivable and inventory to accounts payable.
- A credit practitioner should compare individual customer trading asset turnovers and ratios to industry standards.
- An analysis of a customer's trading assets can be used as a meaningful tool or enhancement in the credit/risk analysis process.

LIMITATIONS OF BALANCE SHEETS IN CREDIT ANALYSIS

While a customer's balance sheet is a useful tool in credit analysis, credit professionals need to remember that it is only a snapshot of a customer's financial health at a particular time. For example, while a balance sheet dated December 31, 1992, may accurately report a company's financial health until that day, that balance sheet may be far from accurate when measuring the firm's creditworthiness six months later. This is especially true when analyzing high-risk and LBO customers.

Many factors can render balance sheet data outmoded. For example, the customer may be scheduled to make a dividend or interest payment shortly after the date of the balance sheet report. Either event could negatively impact cash on hand or substantially increase or exhaust borrowings.

Between the report date and when you make your analysis the company's accounts receivable or inventory may have ballooned, again reducing cash or requiring increased borrowings. Or, the customer may have sustained heavy losses since the statement date, dramatically impacting liquidity, leverage, and the firm's long-term viability. Any of these scenarios could dramatically impact a customer's liquidity, leverage, and profitability ratios.

Since any of these scenarios could render a prior financial statement outmoded, credit professionals need to be careful to not rely solely on such statements, especially those that are six or more months old.

Dated disclosure isn't totally useless, however. Information in the statement may raise a red flag for you to consider if there could have been any major changes in the customer's financial health since the statement date. You may want to request a more recent interim balance sheet and income statement, even if the statements are unaudited or generated for management review only. The interim statements should narrow the window during which a dramatic change could take place in a firm's financial condition without you knowing it. Or, you can ask the customer for estimates of current receivables, inventory, payables, bank debt, and profitability to supplement the data in the most recent statement. You can obtain this information over the phone or during a face-to-face customer visit. Even with supplemental information, the financial statements you are using should be no more than three or four months old.

When working with a dated statement, you should factor current payment performance into your analysis. Also ask for updated trade and bank references. Whatever you do, you need to look to information beyond the dated financial statement in completing your credit analysis.

ABSTRACT SUMMARY

- A balance sheet is merely a snapshot of a customer's financial condition on a specific date.

- Events can occur between the statement date and when you are conducting your analysis that could dramatically change the customer's financial condition.

- When reviewing dated financial information about high-risk customers, ask yourself the likelihood of there having been a major change in the customer's financial condition since the statement date.

- Request interim financial statements from high-risk customers. If they aren't available, then ask for current financial data on receivables, payables, inventory, bank debt, and profitability to supplement dated financial reports.

- Make sure financial statements you work with are no more than three or four months old at the time of your analysis.

KEY LIQUIDITY RATIOS

When the information is available, financial statement analysis is one of the most critical aspects of sound credit analysis. The objective is to determine the customer's overall liquidity, profitability, and leverage/viability. This can be achieved through an analysis of key ratios and turnovers that are derived from the customer's balance sheet and income statement.

The first step in statement analysis should be to review and analyze the customer's liquidity ratios in detail. This process goes beyond simply reviewing the traditional current and quick ratios.

A thorough analysis of the customer's liquidity and payment wherewithal should encompass the following liquidity ratios and turnover levels:

1. *Current Ratio.* The traditional current ratio is calculated by dividing total current assets by total current liabilities. Let's say the current ratio is 1.55. That means there is $1.55 of current assets for every $1 of current liabilities. How liquid the 1.55 current ratio is will depend on the quality of the quick and turnover ratios.

2. *Quick Ratio.* Calculation: Divide the sum of cash, cash equivalents, and accounts receivable by total current liabilities.

    The quick ratio is a much better liquidity measure than the current ratio because it measures the ratio of cash and equivalents and receivables readily convertible into cash, on the one hand, to total current liabilities, on the other. However, a liquidity analysis must go into even greater detail. A quick ratio of .58 would mean that there is 58 cents in cash and equivalents and receivables to offset every $1 of current liabilities. Now the current ratio of 1.55 does not look as liquid as it initially appeared. For every 58 cents of quick assets there is 97 cents of inventory and other current assets.

    A further review of inventory and accounts receivable turnovers will indicate the liquidity of the current and quick ratios, as a quick ratio of 1:1 may be offset by slow moving accounts receivable.

3. *Cash/Current Liabilities.* Calculation: Divide cash and equivalents by total current liabilities. The result of this calculation indicates how much cash there is to offset every $1 of current liabilities.

4. *Cash/Total Liabilities.* This ratio also reveals liquidity more than leverage. Calculation: Divide cash and equivalents by total liabilities. Usually the quality of the quick ratio will correspond to the liquidity of the cash and equivalent ratios.

5. *Inventory/Current Liabilities.* Calculation: Divide inventory by total current liabilities. The ratio should verify the quality and liquidity of the current ratio. What good is it to have a 1.55 current ratio when 97 cents of every $1.55 of current assets is inventory?

51

6. *Fixed Assets/Total Assets.* Calculation: Divide net fixed assets after depreciation by total assets. If the ratio is .61, that means there is 61 cents in fixed assets for every $1 of total assets. This ratio should yield insights into how capitally dependent the customer is upon fixed assets for the operation of its business.

7. *Accounts Receivable Turnover.* Calculation: Divide net trade accounts receivable by net sales and multiply that ratio by 360 (days). Accounts receivable turnover calculated by this method should not be confused with days sales outstanding (DSO). The receivables turnover should reveal the degree to which the firm's quick ratio is liquid. A quick ratio of 1:1 carrying a 78–day turnover for accounts receivable may not be as quick as first presumed.

    Note, for interim statements, the days multiplier times the ratio of AR/Net sales would be 30 days times the number of months ended for the statement. Thus, for a six months ended interim statement, the multiplier would be 180 days times the ratio of AR/Net sales to derive AR turnover.

8. *Inventory Turnover.* Calculation: Divide total inventory by the cost of sales derived from the income statement, and multiply the resulting ratio by 360 (days). Inventory turnover indicates whether the subject's inventory is slow moving, or whether it is a liquid trading asset that can help generate cash flow.

9. *Accounts Payable Turnover.* Calculation: Divide accounts payable and accrued liabilities by the cost of sales derived from the income statement, and multiply the resulting ratio by 360 days. Accrued liabilities are factored into the calculation because they represent future liabilities that will have to be paid. The credit practitioner should compare the customer's accounts payable ratio calculation to payment experience. This will allow him to determine whether slow trade payments are justified from a balance sheet standpoint.

By analyzing the nine liquidity ratios and turnovers, a credit practitioner can get a clearer picture of the customer's true liquidity and ability to retire invoices within terms. When coupled with the leverage/viability ratios and profitability ratios, liquidity analysis should render a complete snapshot of overall customer risk.

Keep in mind that customer liquidity ratios can be compared to established industry standards and norms.

ABSTRACT SUMMARY

■ The liquidity ratio is one of three types of ratios the credit professional needs to calculate based on numbers provided in a customer's financial statement. The other key ratios fall into the categories of leverage/viability and profitability/operating.

■ Liquidity ratios include current ratio, quick ratio, cash/current liabilities, cash/total liabilities, inventory/current liabilities, and fixed assets/total assets.

■ The liquidity analysis also includes the calculation of three turnover ratios: accounts receivable turnover, inventory turnover, and accounts payable turnover.

■ The quick ratio is a much better liquidity measure than the current ratio.

■ Inventory turnover indicates whether the subject's inventory is slow moving, or whether it is a liquid trading asset that can help generate cash flow.

KEY LEVERAGE/VIABILITY RATIOS

Analyzing a customer's leverage/viability ratios allows a credit professional to assess the risk involved in extending open account credit. Leverage/liability ratios provide a different perspective than liquidity ratios, which enable a vendor to determine the customer's ability to meet obligations within terms.

A combination of leverage/viability, liquidity, and profitability/operating ratios should provide a good overall picture with respect to customer cash flow payments and the potential for insolvency. The liquidity and profitability/operating ratios can be cross-referenced to determine or confirm the soundness of the leverage/viability ratios.

Ultimately, the credit person should assess the probability of a customer insolvency through analysis of the leverage/viability ratios. The leverage/viability analysis should encompass the following six ratios:

1. *Total Debt/Tangible Net Worth.* Total debt to tangible net worth is calculated by dividing total liabilities by tangible net worth and factoring out of net worth intangible assets such as goodwill, patents, or trademarks. If the ratio is 3.15, which is somewhat leveraged, that means there is $3.15 of total liabilities for every $1 of tangible net worth. A total debt-to-worth ratio in excess of the 3.0-4.0 range is generally thought to reflect a leveraged and unbalanced financial condition.

2. *Total Funded Debt/Tangible Net Worth.* Calculation: Divide total funded debt of bank debt, bonds, debentures, and other similar debt instruments by tangible net worth.

    The ratio will reveal how dependent the firm is upon bank and other funded debt markets to operate the business. The ratio should provide an idea of what level of bank borrowings the customer could resort to if necessary.

3. *Fixed Assets/Tangible Net Worth.* Calculation: Divide net fixed assets, after accumulated depreciation, by tangible net worth. This measurement reveals the degree to which owners' equity (tangible net worth) has been invested in the fixed assets required to operate the business. (Note: Beware of off-balance-sheet leasehold arrangements, which tend to understate this ratio.)

4. *Accounts Receivable/Accounts Payable.* Calculation: Divide net accounts receivable by total accounts payable, including accrued liabilities. The ratio indicates the degree to which accounts receivable trading assets are leveraged. A 39-day turnover for receivables may not be that liquid if the AR-to-AP ratio is .79, meaning there is 79 cents of accounts receivable to offset every $1 of accounts payable.

5. *Funded Debt/Cash Flow.* Calculation: Divide total funded debt of bank debt, bonds, debentures, and similar debt instruments by the cash flow of the company (defined as net income less dividends paid plus depreciation).

   This ratio will reveal the degree to which the earnings capability of the firm is leveraged. The key question here is: Are the earnings strong enough to support the level of funded debt?

6. *Credit Limit/Tangible Net Worth.* Calculation: Divide the customer's required credit limit by its tangible net worth. The ratio will reveal the degree to which the credit exposure is leveraged in relation to the tangible net worth. The ratio should indicate whether a company is selling in an overexposed scenario where caution should be heeded.

An old yardstick for this final measurement was that the credit limit should not exceed 10 percent of the customer's tangible net worth. But this yardstick is outdated. In today's competitive environment, a company may need to extend credit limits where the ratio exceeds 100 percent. Of course, in such cases, the credit department needs to perform a complete customer analysis of bank, trade, and mercantile information to support such credit extension.

The leverage/viability ratios reviewed above should provide a clear indication of the customer's ongoing viability. These ratios reveal financial wherewithal and potential vulnerability to adverse business conditions.

For further insights into customer leverage, one can compare the ratio output to established industry norms and standards.

ABSTRACT SUMMARY

- Leverage/liability is one of three sets of ratios that credit professionals need to calculate and analyze in order to gauge the credit risk of extending open account credit to a customer. The other two ratio groupings are liquidity ratios and profitability/operating ratios.

- The leverage/viability analysis should include an investigation of six key ratios: total debt/worth, total funded debt/worth, fixed assets/tangible net worth, accounts receivable/accounts payable, funded debt/cash flow, and credit limit/tangible net worth.

- A total debt-to-worth ratio in excess of the 3.0-4.0 range is generally thought to reflect a leveraged and unbalanced condition.

- Beware of off-balance-sheet leasehold arrangements, which tend to understate the fixed assets/tangible net worth ratio.

- In today's competitive environment, a company may need to extend credit limits where the customer's credit limit/tangible net worth ratio exceeds 100%.

KEY PROFITABILITY/OPERATING RATIOS

When analyzing a customer's financial statement, the third type of ratio to calculate — in addition to liquidity and leverage/viability ratios — is the profitability/operating ratio.

By reviewing profitability ratios, a credit practitioner can analyze the customer's current ability to generate true cash flow in the form of earnings. He knows that if earnings can't generate sufficient true cash flow to sustain working capital and fixed asset requirements, then bank borrowings will be required. Further analysis may reveal that the customer does not have sufficient overall financial wherewithal to justify the required bank borrowings.

An analysis of various ratios will indicate how effectively management deploys capital. It can also help a credit person gauge management's overall operational and administrative capabilities.

A review of a three- to five-year trend line for the profitability ratios will provide information upon which to base judgments about the future or near-term earnings wherewithal of the firm. Listed below are eight key profitability/operating ratios that can be derived for analysis from the customer's balance sheet and income statement:

1. *Addition to Retained Earnings/Tangible Net Worth.* Calculation: Divide the current year's addition to retained earnings from net income by the year's ending tangible net worth.

    When calculating this ratio, don't use accumulated retained earnings or the beginning net worth. As a cross-check for this ratio, one could analyze the earnings before taxes/tangible net worth ratio. However, for credit review purposes, the "addition" ratio measures the amount of the annual return on equity that is reinvested in the business — as opposed to the total annual return on equity. (Earnings before taxes can be significantly reduced by taxes and dividends.)

    Note: The lower the customer's tangible net worth, the more likely it is that the ratio may be misleadingly high.

    The credit analyst needs to remember that he is not a stockholder assessing earnings potential for capital appreciation and dividend income, which net income/tangible net worth and net earnings before taxes/tangible net worth ratios both assess. When performing the three forms of ratio analysis, credit practitioners are assessing liquidity and credit risk with respect to cash flow and insolvency.

2. *Addition to Retained Earnings/Total Assets.* Calculation: Divide the current year's addition to retained earnings by the ending total assets. Again, this ratio will help determine the net amount of the return on assets that has

been reinvested in the business to sustain operations and support future growth.

3.   *Addition to Retained Earnings/Net Sales.* Calculation: Divide the current year's addition to retained earnings by the total net sales. Here the ratio enables one to measure the net amount of return on every dollar of sales that is reinvested in the firm.

4.   *Addition to Retained Earnings/Addition to Debt.* Calculation: Divide the current year's addition to retained earnings by the current year's addition to debt. Note: One needs at least two years of financial statements to determine the debt addition, unless a source and application of funds analysis is part of the complete financial statement that has been provided.

This ratio enables one to determine the hidden cost of earnings for the current year. For example, there might be two companies with similar sales and net earnings, but one company may have reduced debt while generating the earnings, while the other firm may have incurred additional debt to generate the earnings.

Overall, the "addition" ratios highlight the quality of the net amount of earnings that have been retained for reinvestment when measured against the yardsticks for the sales, equity, asset, and debt variables.

5.   *Net Sales/Net Fixed Assets.* Calculation: Divide net sales by ending total fixed assets. This ratio is especially useful in determining the productivity of the the fixed assets that the company is deploying.

6.   *Net Sales/Total Assets.* Calculation: Divide net sales by ending total assets. This ratio presents a much broader picture of asset deployment but can be a valuable ratio when compared to industry standards.

7.   *Gross Profit/Net Sales.* Calculation: Divide the subject's gross profit by net sales. Here one can gauge the efficiency of the firm's manufacturing operations. The key question to answer: Are the margins sufficient to sustain selling, general, administrative, and interest expenses?

8.   *Selling, General, and Administrative Expense/Net Sales.* Calculation: Using the income statement, add together the selling, general, and administrative expense. Divide the sum by net sales.

This ratio provides an indication of the efficiency of management and staff in operating the business. If the ratio is excessively high, it might indicate that significant cost-cutting will be required for the firm to operate at profitability levels necessary for generating cash flow.

As with the ratios previously discussed, it can be beneficial to compare a customer's profitability ratio outputs with those of other companies within the firm's industry.

Once profitability ratios are calculated, the credit person can cross-check the results against liquidity and leverage/viability ratios.

ABSTRACT SUMMARY

- The profitability/operating ratio is one of three types of ratios the credit professional needs to calculate based on numbers provided in a customer's financial statement.
- Profitability ratios can help a customer analyze a customer's ability to generate true cash flow in the form of earnings.
- When performing profitability/operating ratio analysis, the credit practitioner needs to remember that he is assessing liquidity and credit risk. He should not act as a stockholder would—assessing earnings potential for capital appreciation and dividend income.
- The "addition" ratios highlight the quality of the net amount of earnings that have been retained for reinvestment when measured against the yardsticks for the sales, equity, asset, and debt variables.
- Profitability ratios can be cross-checked against the results of liquidity and leverage/viability analysis.

INDUSTRY STANDARDS FOR
FINANCIAL STATEMENT ANALYSIS:
A COMPANY CAN DEVELOP ITS OWN

When analyzing customer financial statements, it's prudent to compare them to industry standards such as the norms published by Dun & Bradstreet or Robert Morris Associates. The credit department can compare the customer's financial condition and operating performance to the standards set by other companies in the customer's industry. Simply comparing one company's ratios to another company's—when the two firms are from different industries—generally provides no meaningful information. In fact, it could be misleading.

Credit practitioners can take financial statement analysis a step further by developing their own industry standards. These standards could be developed based on financial disclosure from the vendor's own customer base. In many cases a vendor sells to enough companies in a particular industry or industries to develop such standards.

For example, if a company is a steel manufacturer, its credit department might have sufficient financial disclosure from diverse end-users—such as fabricators, distributors, and contractors—that will enable it to develop individual industry standards for each of the respective end-user groups. An over-the-counter pharmaceutical company might be able to establish distinct standards for wholesalers, drug stores, hospitals, and discount chains.

A vendor must have a minimum universe of seven to 10 customers within an end-user group to develop standards for that group. The more customers the vendor has within each sector, the more valid the standards will be. Once the customer universe for each sector has been established, credit personnel can create data bases within each sector that identify the upper, median, and lower quartiles for each ratio analyzed.

If the firm had 40–50 customers within each industry sector, then it could develop substandards within each industry group according to the level of sales or total assets for each subgroup. For example, if the steel manufacturer had a base of 45 distributors, individual standards could be set for distributors with sales of $100,000–$4.99 million, $5 million to $24.99 million, $25 million to $49.99 million, etc.

Not only will this give the company standards for each sector for comparative purposes, but the assessment of each individual industry sector should shed light on the overall quality and liquidity of the company's accounts receivable portfolio. Standards can be applied both to the analysis of existing customer financial disclosure and the analysis of new customer investigations. With standards and substandards in place, red flags should arise when new or existing customers fall well below established norms for the specific ratios analyzed.

Ultimately, credit personnel can compare their internally developed standards to the published standards of D&B and/or Robert Morris Associates. They might find out that their customer base as a whole exceeds or falls short of the published standards. Again, this would shed light on the overall liquidity and quality of the company's accounts receivable portfolio.

The development of standards can be especially helpful if the company is selling to several leveraged buyout companies. The LBO phenomenon is still relatively new, and it might be helpful to consider these companies, because of their similar leverage and financial characteristics, as a distinct industry sector.

No matter what industry sector is being analyzed, the credit department can establish "negative" standards for that sector based on prior bad-debt write-offs that have occurred within the sector. Negative standards can be used as another means of useful comparison when analyzing existing accounts. Does an existing account exhibit some of the same negative standards of previous bad-debt write-off accounts? Existing customers that fit the profile of the established norms for the bad-debt accounts could be on the road to insolvency as well.

As time passes and the data base grows, internal standards will become an invaluable tool for credit analysis and extension. The analyst will be in a better position to take proactive rather than reactive measures when negative comparisons have been identified to the established sector standards or to the bad-debt write-off norms. Thus, if the company has the financial disclosure data base, its credit personnel shouldn't just analyze individual customers on the micro level. They should also analyze and merge financial information from companies in the same industry sectors to establish standards on a macro level as well.

ABSTRACT SUMMARY

- A company with sufficient customer financial disclosure for a particular industry can develop its own internal industry standards that can be compared to published standards.

- The more customers a company has within each sector, the more valid will be the internal industry standards that it develops. A company needs a minimum of seven customers within an industry sector to develop internal standards for that sector.

- Within each sector, credit personnel can establish upper, median, and lower quartiles for each financial ratio analyzed.

- Standards can be applied not only to the analysis of existing customer financial disclosure, but also to the analysis of new customer investigations.

- When a credit department has in place standards and substandards based on industry sectors, red flags will arise when new or existing customers fall well below the established norms for the specific ratios analyzed.

SOURCE AND APPLICATION OF FUNDS: THE REAL MEASURE OF CASH FLOW

Performing a "source and application of funds" analysis from one quarter ending to the next provides a clear measurement of a customer's cash flow. Such an analysis can also pinpoint the source of the cash being generated.

If such an analysis indicates that depreciation (a noncash item) or debt is generating the lion's share of cash sources, the credit person will want to question the customer's viability. Another possible red flag can go up if the analysis shows that the customer's main source of cash is the issuing of stock. Equity cannot be issued perpetually to fund operations.

On the application side, it's a good idea to investigate where are all of the customer's cash sources are going. One can tell a lot about a company's management by reviewing how it allocates its cash. Key application components include capital spending, dividends, changes in working capital, and changes in any other asset and/or liability accounts.

A source and application of funds analysis should be used to assess the impact of the sources and applications and how they tie into their respective asset and liability account entries.

All the sources and applications either increase or reduce cash. Increases to asset accounts, aside from cash, are offset by reductions to cash, while decreases to asset accounts are offset by increasing cash. Correspondingly, increases to liability and equity accounts are offset by increasing cash, while decreases to liability and equity accounts are offset by reducing cash.

Here's a type of a source and application of funds analysis:

SOURCES	12/31/XX (full year)
Net Income	100,000
Depreciation	32,000
Deferred Income Tax	17,000
Short & L.Term Debt	220,000
Stock Issue	200,000
TOTAL SOURCES	569,000

APPLICATIONS	
Capital Spending	121,000
Dividends	298,000
AR Increase	127,000
Inv. Increase	24,000
AP Decrease	25,000
TOTAL APPLICATIONS	595,000

CASH FLOW	(26,000)
OPENING CASH (1/1/XX)	109,000
CHANGE	(26,000)
ENDING CASH (12/31/XX)	83,000
OPENING LOAN (1/1/XX)	175,000
CHANGE	220,000
ENDING LOAN (12/31/XX)	395,000

The source and application of funds analysis will indicate if capital spending is either neglected or excessive. Additionally, the impact of dividends on the customer's cash and loan positions will be evident. For instance, a company might be borrowing through the debt markets to support its dividend payout.

Changes in working capital, and especially increases in working capital net of cash increases, have always been misunderstood by the credit community. Increases in accounts receivable and inventory are not always positive. They may be positive for a growth company, but they still come at the expense of cash and often require increased borrowings to generate the required level of cash.

Accounts payable figures can also be misinterpreted. Just remember: An increase in accounts payable has a favorable impact on cash while a reduction of payables comes at the expense of cash.

When performing a source and application of funds analysis, be careful to include all items that have impacted cash. The analysis is only a true measure of cash flow if the net result of sources offset by applications equals the actual change in the cash position for the period.

ABSTRACT SUMMARY

- Performing a source and application of funds analysis highlights the true sources of cash.
- Key applications components include capital spending, dividends, changes in working capital, and changes in any other asset and/or liability account.
- From one quarter to the next, changes for an asset or liability account must be offset by an entry to cash, which either reduces or increases cash.
- Increases to asset accounts, aside from cash, are offset by reductions to cash; decreases to asset accounts increase cash.
- Increases to liability and equity accounts increase cash; decreases to liability and equity accounts reduce cash.

RESORTING TO SUMMARY FIGURES

Consider the following scenario: A customer's credit exposure is on the rise and the credit department of the supplier firm has none of the customer's financial information on file. The credit manager calls the customer, but his request to have a financial statement mailed to him is denied. The credit manager then asks the customer if he can make a visit to review the numbers in person. Again, the answer comes back: "No."

The supplier needs some type of financial disclosure in order to continue shipping product, but so far the customer isn't budging. Is there a way to avoid a stalemate here?

Possibly. The credit person might consider settling for limited summary figures, conveyed over the phone by the customer.

These figures could include total current assets, total assets, current liabilities, total liabilities, and stockholders' equity (see Exhibit 2.4). The credit manager could also ask the customer for dollar levels of accounts receivable, inventory, accounts payable, and bank debt, as well as turnover levels in days for accounts receivable, inventory, and accounts payable.

By obtaining summary totals for current assets through stockholders' equity, the supplier can reconstruct a skeletal balance sheet that will yield insights into the customer's liquidity and leverage. The dollar levels for accounts receivable through bank debt will make a fuzzy picture a little bit clearer. True turnover levels in days should confirm prior assumptions about liquidity and leverage. With these summary figures, the credit manager could calculate current ratio, working capital, total debt to worth, bank debt to worth, and other ratios (see Exhibit 2.5).

In the scenario above, the credit manager should verbally advise the customer that he is relying on the summary numbers as the means for extending credit. He should also send to the customer a confidential certified letter restating the numbers and the fact that those numbers are the basis for the extension of credit.

If the customer provided honest numbers, he is not likely to balk at the letter. However, if the customer has fraudulently misled the supplier, the certified letter at least lays the legal groundwork for a potential lawsuit if payment problems ensue.

Although limited in detail, summary figures—along with other credit data in the customer's file—can provide enough information upon which to base a credit decision. A decision based on summary figures and other credit data is better than a decision based on no financial information whatsoever.

Nevertheless, using summary figures in this fashion is best avoided except as a final option under under special conditions and circumstances.

Exhibit 2.4
Summary Figures Checklist

____ (Determine as of Date for Summary Figures)
____ Total Current Assets
____ Total Assets
____ Total Current Liabilities
____ Total Liabilities
____ Total Bank Debt
____ Stockholders' Equity
____ AR Dollars
____ Inventory Dollars
____ Accounts Payable Dollars
____ AR Turnover
____ Inventory Turnover
____ Accounts Payable Turnover
____ Sales
____ Net Income

Exhibit 2.5
Summary Figure Analysis Checklist

____ Current Ratio
____ Quick Ratio
____ Working Capital
____ Tangible Net Worth
____ Bank Debt/Tangible Worth
____ Total Debt/Tangible Worth
____ Credit Limit/Tangible Worth
____ Return on Sales
____ Return on Equity

ABSTRACT SUMMARY

- Summary figures are a form of limited financial disclosure.
- Summary figures are an alternative to reviewing hard-copy financial information.
- With summary totals for total current assets, total assets, current liabilities, and total liabilities, a credit professional can determine net worth and reconstruct a skeletal balance sheet.
- With the above summary figures, one can derive the customer's current ratio, working capital, and total debt to worth.
- Confirm with the customer—both verbally and in writing—the company's intention to use the summary figures as the means for extending credit.

UNDERSTANDING THE CUSTOMER'S BORROWING/FUNDING ARRANGEMENTS

When performing credit and financial analyses, the credit department analyst needs to understand the mechanics, rules, and regulations that govern the customer's borrowing/funding arrangements. The last thing a vendor wants to do is base a credit decision on an incorrect assumption regarding these arrangements.

Middle-market companies—firms with between, say, $5 million and $500 million in annual sales—generally have four avenues for borrowing cash. They are bank credit lines, bank revolving credit agreements, long-term fixed-rate agreements, and factoring. (Commercial paper, private placements, bonds, and debentures are borrowing/funding alternatives that are primarily used by larger corporations.)

These four financing vehicles generally are used to finance capital expenditure requirements, ongoing working capital needs, and peak period or seasonal financing requirements.

Bank credit lines usually run for a period of one year, at which time they are reviewed. The bank credit line can be canceled at any time by the bank without the creditor being in violation of the credit line. The bank credit line usually is not supported by a detailed document—such as is the case with a revolving credit agreement—although there usually is legal wording relating to conditions of default.

Bank credit lines are a form of short-term debt and are classified as current liabilities on the balance sheet.

The credit line can be referred to as being on an "offering basis." This implies that there is no formal commitment on the bank's behalf to provide the funds. Credit lines can be extended on a secured or unsecured basis. Typical security would be accounts receivable, inventory, fixed assets, or a blanket lien on all the company's assets.

A vendor should find out if its customer's credit line is on a secured or unsecured basis. This information may be important to know later if the vendor is contemplating a suit or is negotiating collateral from the customer.

In the case of negotiating collateral, the vendor's credit practitioner will want to know if there are sufficient assets to cover his firm's secured position after the bank. Some credit lines require a "cleanup period," which means that the borrower must be debt-free of the bank for a predetermined period of 30 to 60 days each year. Failure to achieve debt-free status during the cleanup period would put the company in violation of the credit line, in which case the entire borrowing could be immediately declared due and payable. The bank, at its option, could do so by invoking what is known as an "acceleration clause." Litigation could follow if the company does not immediately retire the debt.

The reason for the cleanup period is that the bank doesn't want to get into an evergreen loan situation where the credit line is being renewed annually by the customer without any evidence of loan reduction wherewithal.

The credit practitioner should know whether a customer's credit line requires a cleanup period. If it does, the credit person needs to be aware of the timing on the cleanup period. It could coincide with a major credit decision, such as dramatically increasing the customer's credit limit.

Credit-line-related short-term borrowings are usually based on either the prime rate, or rates on certificates of deposit, banker's acceptances, or possibly Eurodollars. Borrowings are usually fixed for 30, 60, 90, 120, or 180 days, and there is usually a provision for overnight borrowings at prime.

The bank will usually put a margin on all borrowings with the possible exception being prime-based borrowings. This means that the company might be able, for instance, to borrow at the banker's acceptance rate plus 50 basis points. The margin charged is usually indicative of the bank's perception of the quality of the credit. The bank may charge the borrower an annual fee ranging from 1/8 to 3/4 percent for the credit line.

Revolving credit agreements are committed credit facilities in which there is a lengthy loan agreement that spells out the terms and conditions of the revolving credit agreement. Unless the borrower is in violation of the agreement or in default, the bank cannot refuse to lend the borrower money. Here the borrower has the best of both worlds. The borrower can utilize short-term borrowing instruments that are classified as long-term debt on its balance sheet. The only exception occurs in the last year of the revolver when the indebtedness would have to be classified as a current liability due within one year.

The text of the revolving credit agreement will cover definitions, loans, conditions to borrowing, representations and warranties, covenants, defaults and remedies, change in circumstances, opinion of counsel, and a promissory note.

The credit analyst must be aware of covenants and events of default. Covenants are either agreements to conditions or performance clauses required of the borrower. Operating covenants could cover working capital, cash flow, debt to worth, and restriction of dividends. A conditional covenant could require, for instance, that the borrower provide quarterly financial statements within 60 days of the end of a quarter. If the customer violates the covenants, it violates the revolving credit agreement, thus giving the bank the option of declaring the loan in default and invoking the acceleration clause, which would make all loans outstanding due and payable immediately regardless of the scheduled maturities.

Obviously, violating these covenants could be devastating to a company. A vendor to a company with such covenants would be wise to make sure that the firm is currently complying with them.

Revolving credit agreements generally run three to five years. "Revolvers" can be all revolving, or revolving and part term with a possible commitment reduction required. For example, a revolver can be three years revolving and two years term, whereby at the end of the third year the loan is converted to a term loan—or, depending on the subject's financial condition, the borrower could ask the bank to extend the revolving period.

Commitment reductions are sometimes incorporated into straight revolvers and revolvers with term periods. The commitment reduction implies that the borrower must reduce its outstanding borrowings over time to coincide with predetermined reductions of the total lending commitment. For example, one may have a five-year revolver in which the commitment will be reduced by 1/8 over the last eight quarters of the agreement, beginning with the first quarter of the fourth year. Thus, as the commitment gets reduced, the borrowings must be reduced commensurately.

A vendor needs to be aware of the commitment reduction and the timing for the reductions. If not, the vendor could be extending credit based on the assumption that the customer has ample availability, when in fact the bank's commitment to lend funds is being reduced.

Revolvers can be structured on a secured and unsecured basis. Borrowing options are generally the same as mentioned under the credit line scenario, although the borrower probably will be offered a greater selection under the revolving facility. There is usually a quarterly commitment fee of 1/8 to 3/4 of a percent, however the fee is usually assessed on the unused portion of the borrowings for the period in question.

In many ways, long-term fixed-rate agreements have the same makeup as revolving credit agreements. The language of the loan agreement and restrictions and covenants are all similar. The key difference, of course, is that these long-term agreements have a fixed borrowing rate. Thus, there isn't a variety of borrowing instruments to utilize. The borrower here most likely has ongoing or permanent borrowing needs whereby it wants to hedge its income statement against interest rate fluctuations by fixing the rate of interest it will be paying over the life of the long-term borrowing period. As with a revolver or credit line, if the borrower is in violation of the agreement, the lender can invoke the acceleration clause. Thus, covenant compliance is critical.

Long-term fixed-rate borrowing arrangements usually run from three to 10 years.

Factoring is a nonbank source of funding that is available to companies that need cash. Factoring does not necessarily imply that the borrower is a poor credit risk. Yet, for certain firms, factoring may be the only alternative because of their inability to negotiate bank financing.

In essence, the factor credit-checks and approves orders referred by the parties factoring their receivables, purchases the ensuing receivables, and provides funds in return for the receivables purchased. The factoring relationship is on a secured basis. The factor will most likely possess a lien on accounts receivable and inventory. Factors often will also advance funds against inventory based on an agreed-to formula. Payments from the factor can be on an "advance basis" or "at maturity." On an advance basis, once the party factoring the receivables submits an invoice, the factor advances funds less a fee, and a percentage of the receivables is withheld for returns and allowances. On an "at maturity" basis, the factor remits funds monthly based on the average due date of the receivables purchased.

The factoring arrangement can be with or without recourse. "With recourse" indicates that the party factoring its receivables is financially responsible for any bad-debt losses sustained by the factor. Under "without recourse" terms, the party factoring its receivables bears no financial responsibility for losses sustained by the factor.

Clearly, with factoring there are greater restrictions and less borrowing options than with credit lines and revolving credit agreements.

These are some basics regarding the borrowing/funding arrangements of many middle-market companies. A credit practitioner needs to be fully aware of the nature and structure of any such arrangements involving his customers. Sound credit decisions depend on this knowledge.

ABSTRACT SUMMARY

- The four avenues that middle-market firms use for borrowing cash are bank credit lines, bank revolving credit agreements, factoring, and long-term fixed-rate agreements.

- Bank credit lines, which are generally up for review on an annual basis, are a form of short-term debt and are classified as current liabilities on the balance sheet.

- Revolving credit agreements generally run three to five years. They can be all revolving, or revolving and part term with a possible commitment reduction required.

- Long-term fixed-rate agreements are similar in most ways to revolving credit agreements except that they have a fixed borrowing rate and they run from three to 10 years.

- Factoring is generally a nonbank source of funding available to companies that need cash. The factor credit-checks and approves orders, purchases the ensuing receivables, and provides funds.

OBTAINING BANK UPDATES OVER THE PHONE

There are basically three ways to obtain information about a customer from its bank. A credit practitioner can make the request in writing, over the telephone, or through a third party such as his company's bank.

The most productive method is having credit department personnel obtain the information over the phone from someone at the customer's bank—preferably the customer's lending officer. This method should be used for problem accounts and for new and existing customers that have significant exposures.

Written bank inquiries usually provide the least amount of information for assessing the customer's overall creditworthiness. With a written inquiry, the credit person usually is only able to obtain "account since," average balances, and minimal loan information. Additionally, written inquiries do not allow a credit person to ask follow-up questions.

Third-party inquiries are usually more informative than written inquiries, but usually less informative than a concise direct call placed to the bank by a credit department staffer. With third-party calls, one loses the opportunity to steer or control the scope of the conversation.

A direct inquiry over the phone enables a credit person to really probe the existing banking relationship. Again, the ideal person to question is the customer's lending officer rather than a clerical person in the bank's credit department. The corporate credit person should have a planned set of questions, but based on the banker's responses, he or she can ask for additional information.

In addition to asking for basic information—i.e., "account since" date, average balance information, and borrowing information—also consider asking some of the following, more detailed questions:

- Does the customer have any history of NSF (non-sufficient funds) checks?

- Has the bank extended the customer a formal line of credit? If so, then ask:

- Is the credit line on a revolving or an offering basis?

- Is the line secured (and with what collateral?) or is it unsecured?

- Is the line personally guaranteed by the owners?

- Any corporate guarantees?

- How much is currently outstanding? What is the customer's current availability?

- If the credit line is revolving, when does it expire?

- If it is revolving, are there revolving and term portions to the line?

- If offering, is there a cleanup period? For 30 days?

- If offering, when is the line reviewed? In what month?
- How often is the line utilized? For what purposes?
- Has the customer ever been in violation of the covenants?
- Would you (the bank) increase the line of credit if the company requested?
- Can you tell me if operations were profitable? How and why?

Some subjective questions a credit person might consider asking include:

- Which of the following types of companies would you (banker) describe the customer as? A growth company? A mature company? An emerging company? A leveraged firm? An unbalanced one?
- Would you recommend the customer for the amount of credit my company is extending?

If the banker's responses do not reflect well on the company, or even if they cast some doubt about the firm, a credit person might want to ask: "Has the company ever had any history of bankruptcy, suits, judgments, or liens?"

If the customer is a public company and undergoing loss operations, one might want to ask: "On what basis is the bank extending credit and why?"

The caller might not get to ask all of these questions during the update. Nevertheless, in order to ensure a thorough update, it's wise to have an extensive checklist of key questions at hand.

Don't be surprised if the banker believes that the questioning is too probing. The banker might even balk at responding to certain questions. In that case, the credit professional needs to explain that he is simply trying to gather as much information as possible in order to make a sound credit decision on behalf of the customer.

The banker's answers to certain questions might even influence how the corporate credit person pursues negotiations with a customer. For instance, knowledge of maturity and/or expiration dates of loans and loan agreements can be extremely helpful in structuring the time frame of a commitment. Knowledge of maturities will enable the credit person to know when there will be a drain on the customer's liquidity.

Learning about a customer's current availability and levels of debt outstanding enables the credit person to make direct correlations to how his company is being paid by the customer. Additionally, once the credit professional knows the customer's levels of bank support and availability, there might be an opportunity to press the customer to borrow funds in order to reduce its balance. If the customer has no availability, that's good information for the creditor to have as well.

Direct bank inquiries via telephone are time consuming. Thus, be selective about which inquiries are made by phone and which ones are made either by mail or through a third party. The same philosophy that applies to collection calls can be applied to bank inquiries: devote the most phone time to matters relating to large-dollar exposure accounts. Don't make verbal inquiries regarding minimal-dollar exposure accounts, or discount or prompt-paying customers.

ABSTRACT SUMMARY

- Banking information about a customer can be obtained in three ways— in writing, via telephone, or through a third party such as the creditor's bank.

- Written inquiries usually provide the least amount of banking information.

- Verbal bank updates should be utilized for problem accounts and for significant new and existing exposures.

- Knowledge about maturities and/or expiration dates of loans and loan agreements can yield insights about potential strains on liquidity.

- Knowledge about current customer availability and outstanding borrowings can provide insight into a customer's current payment habits.

VERBAL TRADE REFERENCES

Trade references can be an invaluable tool in supplementing credit analysis for new and existing customers. For existing customers, the objective in obtaining trade references is to compare the customer's current payment performance to how the customer is paying other vendors. If the trade reference is sought for a potential rather than an existing customer, the objective is to learn enough from other vendors to make some projections about how a customer will pay if granted credit.

Trade reference information can be compared to liquidity ratios derived from the customer's financial statement in order to gain a better perspective on potential payment performance.

Trade references can provide information on whether other vendors are tolerating delinquency or possibly extending credit terms. Additionally, trade information can reveal if the customer's payments to other vendors meet the company's payment criteria for new customers.

A credit practitioner has two options for obtaining trade information. The first option is the written inquiry. The credit professional can make a written request for trade information using a standardized trade inquiry form (see Exhibit 2.6). There is nothing wrong with this method, but most credit experts will agree that greater insight into the customer's payment habits can be achieved through the second option, the verbal inquiry.

Verbal inquiries are more time-consuming. Thus, they should be limited to high-risk or high-exposure accounts.

Here are some suggested questions for the verbal inquiry:

- How long has the customer been an account?
- What are your terms of sale?
- What is the recent high credit in dollars?
- What dollar amount is currently outstanding?
- Is there any past due, and if so, how is it aged out beyond terms (i.e., 1–30 days past due, 31–60 days past due, 61–90 days past due, 91–120 days past due, and 120+ days past due)?
- If the customer is beyond terms, ask: Is the customer presently on credit hold?
- Does your firm assess a late charge for slow payments?
- Have you had any NSF (non-sufficient funds) check experience with the customer?
- Has the customer broken promises relating to payment commitments?
- Do you have any guarantees or any other form of collateral?

Exhibit 2.6
Standardized Trade Inquiry Form

/PLM/

PLM Company
1967 W. Granville
Teaneck, NJ 07871

To: ⌐   ⌐

Date _____ 19 _____

L   ⌐

Gentlemen:

In order to complete our credit files, we will appreciate your answering the following concerning the account listed below. All information will be treated confidentially and is received without responsibility attaching to the Company or individuals furnishing same.

Re: ⌐   ⌐

L   ⌐

REASON FOR INQUIRY
We have first order for $
We are revising our credit file
Customer refers us to you

CREDIT EXPERIENCE	Our Experience	Your Experience	MANNER OF PAYMENTS	Ours	Yours
Sold Since			Discounts		
Date of last sale			Prompt & Satisfactory		
Terms of sale			No. days beyond invoice terms		
Highest credit last 12 months	$	$	CASH - our request		
Total owing including notes	$	$	CASH - Customer's request		
Amount beyond terms incl. notes	$	$	Placed for collection		

COMMENTS *(Account in dispute - unjust claims - takes unearned discount - pays on account - account secured - account guaranteed - have financial statements, etc.)*

_____

_____

_____

_____

_____

_____

FURNISHED BY —   _____
                          (Signed)

A stamped, self-addressed envelope is enclosed for your convenience. Your prompt attention to our request will be appreciated.

Cordially,

ORIGINAL - Return to Us
DUPLICATE - Retain for File

- Have you ever visited the customer's facilities? If so, what do you think of their operation?

- Do you have financial disclosure on hand?

- Are you aware of any other derogatory information relating to the customer?

The references contacted may not choose to answer all of these or other questions. Questions relating to finance charges, guarantees, visits, financial disclosure, or derogatory information might not be received well. But ask anyway. If a credit person is persistent, he or she will be surprised at the level of insight these inquiries can provide.

Even if the trade contact shies away from some questions, the verbal inquiry should yield more and better information than the written inquiry. In addition to standard trade information, a verbal inquiry can exceed the written inquiry by yielding information about the aging of past due, whether the customer is on credit hold, NSF check experience, and broken promise experience.

Written inquiries generally only yield standard trade information such as: sold to since, high credit, and maybe the balance currently outstanding. In addition, the written reference will usually never have any written embellishment attached.

Verbal trade-reference updates can be invaluable when customers are experiencing payment and financial problems. When payment problems arise, the credit person can speak with other vendors and find out if they are restricting credit or working with the customer. This information can affect future credit decisions with respect to the customer.

Trade references can also be used as cross-checks against financial information provided by the customer. For instance, compare the trade reference information to the turnovers for accounts receivable and accounts payable drawn from financial statements. The credit practitioner might find that a customer with a 33-day accounts receivable turnover and a 39-day accounts payable turnover, with a positive AR/AP ratio, is paying the firm's invoices in excess of 30 days. In this scenario, it appears the customer is investing or deploying the funds for purposes other than paying off its trade obligations on a timely basis. For instance, the customer might be slow-paying its trade obligations so it can pay off bank debt.

Another use for the information provided by trade references is to compare it with the existing customer's payment performance. If the two differ — for instance, if the customer is paying other vendors more promptly — the corporate credit person will want to ask the customer why.

One note of caution: Always try to obtain references from vendors that are in the same or a similar industry. It is highly unlikely that the customer uses only one firm as a supplier of a particular type of product, so seek out the other suppliers and use them as trade references, especially when it comes to new customers.

ABSTRACT SUMMARY

- Trade references supplement credit analysis for new and existing customers.
- A credit practitioner has two options for obtaining trade information — the written inquiry or the more time-consuming verbal inquiry.
- Written inquiries generally only yield standard trade information such as: sold to since, high credit, and maybe the balance currently outstanding.
- Verbal inquiries generally yield more and better information; they can exceed the written inquiry by providing information about the aging of past due, whether the customer is on credit hold, NSF check experience, and broken promise experience.
- Not all questions in the verbal inquiry will be received well, especially those related to finance charges, guarantees, visits, financial disclosure and derogatory information. But ask anyway.

CUSTOMER VISITS

Customer visits provide an opportunity for the credit practitioner to review financial information, discuss credit requirements, negotiate collateral and improved payments, assess customer character and culture, and promote goodwill.

If the visits are well planned, they can yield insights that are not available through the traditional vendor/customer telephone relationship. In effect, they put the credit person in a better position to make a sound credit decision.

A properly executed customer visit can make financial information "come to life," as fixed assets and inventory leap off the balance sheet and take a physical form.

Customer visits can provide a wealth of information about accounts receivable. During the visit, the credit person should ask the customer for the current dollar level of accounts receivable and turnover in days (DSO), and compare that information to the most recent available financial statement for the firm.

The key is to look for deviations or unfavorable trends. If the customer's payments are slow, the credit person needs to try to understand why. But at the same time he needs to remember the vendor's proper role. A vendor should not allow itself to be cast in the role of a banker. Because, in fact, by making slow payments, the customer substitutes trade credit and support for bank borrowings.

What there is no substitute for is the customer visit. It's the only way to get a true picture of the customer's level of inventory and the only way to gauge the efficiency and strength of the customer's work force.

A plant tour might also provide some additional credit references. Labels on the inventory packaging will generally reveal the names of other suppliers to the customer. These references should be able to provide a good picture of how accounts payable is managed at the company.

Make the visit count. When it's over, the credit person should come away with necessary information for making sound credit decisions, and the customer should feel he has met with a problem solver, someone who wants to continue a mutually beneficial relationship.

ABSTRACT SUMMARY

- Visits can be utilized to review financial information, discuss credit requirements, negotiate collateral and improved payments, assess customer character and culture, and promote goodwill.
- Customer visits can yield insights that are not available through the traditional vendor/customer telephone relationship.
- A well-planned and executed customer visit can make financial information "come to life."

- If customer payments are slow, the credit person needs to understand why; the customer visit is a good place to find some answers.
- During a plant tour, note the names of other suppliers on inventory packaging; they are potential credit references.

QUESTIONS TO ASK ON CUSTOMER VISITS

The cardinal rule when making customer visits is to always be prepared. Study the customer's credit file in advance of the visit. Review financial and credit agency information, and update bank and trade references to get a current picture of the customer's financial state.

The most important task in preparing for a customer visit is to draw up a list of questions to ask during the visit. The credit person should select questions whose answers will yield a better understanding of the company's relationship with the customer and where that relationship is going.

Questions should be clear, concise and well timed. Plan out the flow of questions. It's best to begin with "soft" or general questions. Save the most difficult questions for when the customer is relaxed and comfortable.

The following is a list of general questions that should apply for most customer visits:

- How are your products sold and marketed?
- How would you characterize the scope of your market penetration?
- Who is your primary competition? On what basis are they competitive? Price/quality/delivery?
- Do you have any foreign competition? What is their impact on the market?
- Who are the end-users of your product or service? Is their any seasonality in their businesses?
- Do you have other suppliers who provide the same product as we do? Who are they?
- What are your payment arrangements with these other suppliers? Do they tolerate delinquency?
- Do any of your suppliers have guarantees, UCC1 financing agreements, or letters of credit?
- Do you import material from overseas?
- What were your sales and income for the current period?
- What is your projection for sales and income for the full year?
- What is your outlook for next year?
- Any plans for internal expansion or acquisitions?
- What is the dollar and day level of your backlog?
- How many days per week and how many shifts are you operating?

- What is the current dollar level and turnover in days for accounts receivable and inventory?
- What are your current credit-line arrangements with your bank?
- Are accommodations secured? Revolving? Is there a cleanup period?
- How much is currently outstanding and what is your present availability? Any plans to increase your credit line?
- For what purposes do you usually borrow?

Consider asking the following questions when the customer has experienced severe payment difficulties:

- When and how will your payments to our company improve?
- What factors have contributed to your slow trade payments?
- Are any of your competitors experiencing the same problems?
- Has any major business been lost recently and why?
- Can we formalize a weekly payment program in order to reduce the present exposure?
- What are your recommendations for resolving your payments problem so we can best service your account?
- Have you considered filing for bankruptcy?
- Do you have any plans for making personal loans to the business or for generating a capital infusion via some other means?
- Are you prepared to provide us with collateral in order to continue our relationship?
- What cost-saving measures have you taken in order to turn things around?

Not every question on this list needs to be asked during the visit. Select questions that are necessary to create a clearer understanding of the customer's business; also ask the questions—the sometimes tougher questions—that need to be answered before the relationship can continue.

Don't be afraid to ask tough questions, but do consider how those questions are timed. The difficult questions need to be asked at the right time, preferably when the credit person has clearly established a rapport with the customer.

Like any speech or presentation, a customer visit demands planning and preparation. Only by planning out a line of questioning can the credit person hope to satisfy the credit department's information needs.

A well-planned and executed customer visit generally will be informative, paying dividends to both the supplier and the customer.

ABSTRACT SUMMARY

- Prepare for customer visits by reviewing the credit file for financial, credit agency, bank, and trade information.

- Before making the visit, draw up a list of questions for discussion with the customer.

- Develop a separate list of questions for customers that are exhibiting severe payment difficulties.

- Begin the visit with "soft" and general questions. Save the most difficult questions for when the customer is relaxed and comfortable.

- Don't be afraid to ask the customer difficult questions, but ask such questions at the appropriate time.

PLANT TOURS

Customer visits are invaluable. They can help a credit person perform a credit analysis, assess the customer's credibility, resolve old items, negotiate collateral or guarantees, and engender goodwill. However, too often credit professionals fail to take advantage of a key opportunity that a customer visit provides: the plant tour.

The plant tour can be a great complement to a customer visit. Touring a customer's operations can bring the customer's financial information to life. A tour provides an opportunity to further confirm balance sheet and profit-and-loss disclosures provided by the customer.

A tour of the customer's facility can deepen the credit person's understanding of the customer's business and provide other valuable information. For instance, a tour provides an opportunity to view the customer's raw materials and finished goods inventory. By eyeballing the inventory, one can get a feel for whether the levels indicated in the customer's statement are accurate. Claims about levels of obsolete inventory can also be investigated.

Viewing a customer's inventory also provides an opportunity to learn the identity of the customer's other suppliers of raw materials. Packaging labels from most suppliers are in large, bright print and are easy to read.

A plant tour also offers a chance to evaluate the customer's manufacturing and shipping configuration. Are there enough loading bays and dedicated areas for manufacturing, or will there be a need for further expansion that may require borrowings and further leverage the customer's financial condition? Or, conversely, does the customer have too much space and not enough company to utilize all the space effectively? Too large a facility can be a monthly drain on overhead, thereby potentially impacting cash for raw material suppliers.

A tour can also answer questions about possible excess capacity. Are all the customer's machines at work, or are some idle? The credit person needs to recognize that idle capacity utilization can place a major strain on profits, cash, and trade payments to raw material suppliers. A credit professional can use the plant tour to get a better understanding of the customer's manufacturing process, which in turn might provide clues about the customer's payment performance. For instance, one might learn that the turnaround time it takes for the customer to receive raw materials, convert them into finished product, ship, invoice, and collect from its customers is longer than 30 days. This could explain why the customer has been having difficulty meeting the vendor's 30-day payment terms.

Enough can't be said about the value of plant tours. A credit person who plans to visit a customer to discuss the account relationship would be wise to request a tour in advance, and thereby gain a more complete perspective of the customer's overall financial strength.

ABSTRACT SUMMARY

- Plant tours provide an opportunity for the customer's financial information to come to life.

- During a plant tour, one can verify inventory levels indicated on the customer's financial statement and acquire insights about potential levels of obsolete inventory.

- Plant tours can reveal the identities of additional raw materials suppliers, who can be used for future trade references.

- Plant tours provide insights into the efficiency of the customer's manufacturing and shipping configuration.

- Plant tours reveal insights into the customer's manufacturing process.

BAD-DEBT WARNING SIGNALS

Bad-debt warning signals come in a variety of forms. Signs of trouble can range from a dramatic change in the customer's payment performance—a customer might go from being a prompt payer to paying slow by 15-30 days—to a sudden flight of key employees from the company.

These signs and others should trigger a complete credit analysis of the customer in question.

A credit practitioner must develop a sixth sense for picking up on warning signals. A credit person can't just wait for a series of adverse events to occur before taking preventive action. He or she must be proactive in responding to perceived bad-debt warning signals.

Other examples of potential bad-debt warning signals include a customer faced with:

- An IRS tax lien for nonpayment of taxes
- Fixed-asset revaluations
- Qualified financial statements from auditors
- Marked changes in the customer's financial statements with respect to liquidity and viability
- Suits or judgments
- Layoffs or the shutdown of entire shifts
- COD payment terms from most of its vendors
- A major write-off of one of its receivables
- Operations that have lost money continuously for more than a year
- The loss of one of its customers that makes up 10 percent or more of its annual sales volume
- If the business is family-owned, the retirement of an elder family leader, leaving other unqualified family members to run the business
- Principals who bow out of the day-to-day decision-making when the going gets tough

Also watch out if customers exhibit the following behavior:

- Excessively and repeatedly delay generating financial statements
- Break promises with respect to payment remittances
- Delay payments due to "bogus" disputes or claims
- Violate bank lending agreement covenants

84

- Have a sudden rash of NSF (non-sufficient funds) checks
- Offer to pay the account with post-dated checks
- Delay paying employee payrolls or NSF payroll checks
- Maintain excessively low inventory levels
- Repeatedly promise a capital injection or loan without results

Prepare a checklist of bad-debt warning signals that can be used as a quick reference guide. Having such a guide minimizes the chances of an oversight. All high-risk customers should be reviewed against the checklist on an annual basis. A review of the checklist can be incorporated into the credit department's annual procedure for approving high-risk customers' credit limits.

Usually, bad-debt customers will manifest more than one of the warning signals listed above, and in some cases the company will manifest many of the warning signals before it becomes insolvent. Again, the supplier's objective is to take preventive action at the first sign of potential problems.

When warning signals are manifested, initiate a complete and thorough credit evaluation of the customer. Such a review might entail another round of calls on the customer's existing trade references, obtaining updated bank information, requesting interim or monthly financial information, and even visiting the customer in order to obtain a better perspective on its financial health.

The key is to recognize the signals and take action in a timely manner so as to reduce the company's exposure.

ABSTRACT SUMMARY

- Bad-debt warning signals should trigger a complete credit investigation.
- Credit practitioners need to develop a sixth sense in identifying bad-debt warning signals.
- Potential bad-debt customers usually manifest more than one bad-debt warning signal.
- A credit professional doesn't wait for adverse circumstances before taking preventive and proactive measures.
- Customer visits will help confirm any suspicions the credit person has about a customer giving off bad-debt warning signals.

ANNUAL CREDIT FILE REVIEW AND CREDIT LINE APPROVAL FOR EXISTING ACCOUNTS

All customer credit files should undergo an annual review that coincides with the annual review of the customer's credit limit. Credit limits should be reviewed and approved in accordance with the vendor's written policy covering credit-limit approval authority.

For the credit file and credit limit reviews, make every effort to obtain financial disclosure. With financial information at hand, the credit professional is in a better position to evaluate risk when making credit decisions. If the customer has balked at providing disclosure in the past, current credit-limit requirements or payment performance may make it necessary for the vendor to readdress the financial disclosure issue with the customer.

Some customers will still refuse to provide financial disclosure. If such is the case, the credit person should ask if he or she can confidentially review the figures during a customer visit. Another strategy would be to ask if it would be possible to contact the customer's accountant to review the financial information.

For these annual reviews, the vendor should request an updated financial statement, even if the customer's purchases have declined. Some customers will go so far as to claim they do not generate financial statements. Such claims need to be challenged. After all, Internal Revenue Service guidelines require the preparation of a balance sheet and income statement in order to file a corporate or sole proprietor tax return.

For customers providing financial disclosure, the credit file and credit line reviews should be scheduled for between 90 and 120 days after the customer's year-end statement date. For example, a customer with a December 31 year-end should be scheduled for a file and credit-limit review the following March or April. By that time, the customer's statements should be completed and ready for distribution.

For customers that don't provide financial disclosure, set the review date one year from the date that the business relationship began. Then update the file accordingly on an annual basis.

If a customer's payment performance declines or if the company suffers a financial setback, don't wait for the annual review period to perform a complete credit analysis. Under these circumstances, a vendor can request interim financial disclosure from the customer. A credit department representative might also be sent to visit the customer to review and discuss its problems. Trade and bank references should also be updated at that time.

A vendor should have specific financial and payment criteria for identifying the "high-risk classification" customers within its accounts receivable portfolio. The credit files of these customers will demand special attention during the annual review. Their files should be updated to contain the latest information available from

86

Dun & Bradstreet (provider of the industry standard in credit reports), as well as bank and trade references.

D&B information will provide a broad insight into the customer's trade payments. In addition, D&B provides public information on customers such as prior bankruptcy filings, UCC1 filings, suits and judgments, and IRS tax liens.

The process of updating trade references could yield valuable information. For instance, one might learn that other suppliers to the high-risk customer — suppliers in the same industry — are beginning to restrict credit to the customer. This could call for an adjustment in the vendor's credit strategy.

Updated bank information on the customer will help complete the picture, as will old customer visit reports, which should be kept in the credit file for at least three years. The picture — in terms of corporate liquidity and financing wherewithal — is not always a pretty one, however. In fact, the updated picture of the customer's overall financial condition may make it necessary for a credit person to make another visit to the customer in order to finalize a credit decision.

The procedure for reviewing customer credit files and limits should be in writing as part of a company's credit policy and procedure. The company should also put in writing the requirements for file documentation according to customer classification.

The process of keeping updated credit files can be even more critical in a company with a geographically decentralized credit function. However, the process can be standardized and kept under better control through the use of a credit file review form (see Exhibit 2.7).

The form provides an audit trail relating to the credit analysis and approval of the credit limit. Communication and company information is detailed in the first part of the form. From there, an audit trail is constructed that tracks when particular types of credit information — e.g., D&B reports or bank references — were updated. Within this section is the "authorized by" signature and date for approval of the credit limit.

Annual payment history is recorded on the form, along with capsulized financial information. Part of the form can be dedicated to additional bank reference comments.

The vendor should house all negotiated collateral, guarantees, letters of credit, notes, and other legal instruments in its corporate safe. Copies can be kept in the credit files, along with all original joint authorizations and high-risk evaluation forms.

The vendor's credit department should keep the data base for updating individual customer credit limits on its accounts receivable software system. Review-date information should be a part of customer credit screens. This way, the credit representative is always aware of when the next annual credit limit review is scheduled.

A company's data processing department can create and run a monthly report that indicates which customer credit limits are up for review. At the same time, the

Exhibit 2.7
Credit File Review Form

Account Name

Subsidiary of

Division of

Address   (street)

Related companies/Divisions sold

City   State   Zip

Account No.

Phone   Contact

DATE REQUESTED			D&B	Credit	Credit Limit	Risk	
D&B	Bank	Stmt.	Rating	Line	Authorized By	Code	Date

PAYMENT HISTORY ($000)

Year	Sales	High Credit	Payments

FINANCIAL HISTORY ($000)

Stmt. Date	Curr. Assets	Curr. Liab.	Total Assets	Total Liab.	Tangible Net Worth	Net Sales	Net Income

report should list customers whose accounts receivable balances during the past month exceeded their credit limit, and these customers' files should be reviewed.

Remember, as part of credit policy and procedure, credit-limit reviews should be performed at a minimum of once per year for every customer. However, a complete review might be warranted at any time if there are signs that the customer is encountering financial difficulties.

ABSTRACT SUMMARY

- All customer credit files should undergo an annual review that coincides with the annual review of the customer's credit limit.
- If a customer's payment performance declines or it suffers a financial setback, don't wait for the annual review period to perform a complete credit analysis.
- A review of high-risk customer classifications and exposures should contain updated financial, bank, and trade reference information, as well as the latest Dun & Bradstreet credit bureau report.
- When performed in conjunction with a review and analysis, updated bank information paints a picture of corporate liquidity and financing wherewithal.
- The procedure for reviewing customer credit files and limits should be part of a credit department's written policies and procedures.

WEEDING AND PURGING CREDIT FILES

Credit professionals love to hoard customer information in their files. And, while making sound credit decisions does require reviewing file information, the value of that data diminishes as it ages. The challenge is to keep in a file only that information that is useful and to purge the rest.

Every customer file should contain Dun & Bradstreet and mercantile reports, trade references, financial statements, risk assessments, and customer correspondence. It also should contain internal memos such as reports on customer visits and correspondence with your marketing department.

You ought to maintain a formalized policy regarding what information to keep in a customer file and for how long. You should retain for at least two years routine customer correspondence, customer collection call sheets, and copies of customer payments. Retain for three years financial statements, trade references, bank information, significant customer correspondence relating to delinquencies, payouts, or guarantees, and bank correspondence. Also keep for three years customer visit reports, credit references, year-end sales payment records, D&B and other mercantile agency reports, and published articles about the customer.

You should keep on file for at least three years risk assessments, credit limit approvals, negotiated collateral such as UCC1s, and corporate or personal guarantees. Also keep on file indefinitely in-force and expired letters of credit, bankruptcy notices, NSF checks, and other negative information. Maintain permanently information about bad-debt write-offs.

Except for information marked permanent or indefinite, you should review and purge active credit files at least once a year. You can weed and purge when you make your annual review of the customer's credit limit.

When weeding and purging files, you focus on the quality of the information in the credit file. Frequently purged files are more streamlined with information easier to access.

ABSTRACT SUMMARY

- Weed and purge credit files on an ongoing basis as information becomes dated.
- Maintain routine customer correspondence and customer collection call sheets for two years.
- Keep financial statements, customer correspondence, customer visit reports, credit references, and year-end payment records for three years. Also retain for three years D&B and other mercantile agency reports, and published articles about the customer.

- Retain indefinitely risk assessments, negotiated collateral such as UCC1s, corporate or personal guarantees, in-force and expired letters of credit, and bankruptcy notices.
- It makes sense to weed and purge your files the same time you make your annual customer credit review.

3

CREDIT SYSTEMS

SELECTING AN ACCOUNTS RECEIVABLE SOFTWARE SYSTEM

The first step in selecting accounts receivable software is to outline required system characteristics and attributes. They should be prioritized in the form of a "needs and wants" list, which can be used as a qualifying hurdle for software vendors. The "needs and wants" list for an accounts receivable system could elaborate on the following system functions:

- Credit screen formats
- Cash application formats
- Credit menus
- Cash application menus
- Credit reports (daily, weekly, monthly)
- Cash application and accounting reports
- Audit trails for all daily activity, cash receipts, cash application, and write-offs
- Control mechanisms for cash application and write-offs
- Automatic cash application capability
- MICR (magnetic ink character recognition) encoding
- System-generated chargeback invoices
- Computer-driven dunning letters
- Capability to charge interest for late payments
- Interface to billing system
- Interface to order entry system
- Customer payment history calculation capability

The "needs and wants" list will help establish priorities. For instance, one might determine that automatic cash application is a high priority "need," while system-generated chargeback invoice capability is a mid-level "want." Keep in mind that whatever needs a software vendor's basic package does not provide will have to be paid for as enhancements to the basic system. (Extensive enhancements can sometimes exceed the cost of the basic package.)

Within the listing of functional needs and wants, the credit person should outline in greater detail the specific attributes or characteristics desired in the software. If, for instance, credit reports are either a want or a need, list the specific daily credit reports that are desired—e.g., monthly past due report, daily cash activity report, customer masterfile change report, or daily accounts receivable totals and aging report. For each report listed, describe the report's format, its purpose, and why it would be desirable to have. Indicate what the consequence would be of not having such a report as a system feature.

The process of generating a "needs and wants" list can be quite beneficial. It forces the credit person to consider the many potential features of accounts receivable software and provides some framework for making the purchase decision.

When the list is complete, distribute it to vendors. Ask them to review the list and indicate the number of "man-hours" that will be required to program desired system features that are not offered as part of the basic software package. Some packages can be eliminated from consideration at this point because of the cost of excessive programming requirements.

The winning software vendor will probably provide a reasonable number of the credit person's needs in its basic package. Some enhancements will probably be required, but the outlay for this work will be minimized as a result of the "needs and wants" analysis process.

ABSTRACT SUMMARY

- The first step in purchasing (or internally programming) accounts receivable software is to generate a list of required system attributes and characteristics.
- System characteristics and attributes should be prioritized in the form of a "needs and wants" list, which can be used as a qualifying hurdle for software vendors.
- Whatever needs a software vendor's basic package does not provide will have to be paid for as enhancements to the basic system.
- If extensive, enhancements can sometimes cost more than the basic software package.
- Within the functional "needs and wants" list, one should outline in greater detail the specific attributes or characteristics desired in the software package.

INTERFACING ORDER ENTRY WITH ACCOUNTS RECEIVABLE

Sometimes it seems that people at the same company are working against each other. A classic example involves order entry and credit personnel. The order entry staffer is intent on seeing that when a customer asks for product, the customer gets it in a timely fashion. The credit staffer would like to see this happen, too, but not at the expense of a potential bad debt or overexposed account.

Because their primary goals are different, at times order entry and credit personnel may seem to be working at odds. Fortunately, today's automated systems can be configured in ways that will enable both departments to meet their objectives and allow the company to be the ultimate winner.

Under many traditionally configured systems, however, it seldom happens that both departments get what they want. A brief description of two common systems makes it clear why:

1. At some companies, every customer order must be referred to and approved by the credit department. Period. Customer service cannot ship any goods unless the credit department gives the order a "thumbs up" sign.

   Under this system, the credit department can be assured of a great degree of control over the quality of the accounts receivable portfolio. But, at the same time, the system has problems. For one thing, checking out every customer order can be extremely time-consuming. The constant checking of information can turn credit staffers into CRT operators — keeping them from other cash-flow generating duties.

   It's pretty obvious that this system runs counter to the goals of order entry personnel. Such a system can also bring the manufacturing, warehousing, and shipping departments to a grinding halt. In a word, it's slow.

2. A second way of configuring the system relieves the credit department of the burden of reviewing all customer orders and can speed the order review and approval process. It involves designating dollar limits for orders.

   For example, the supplier can designate that ABC Company has a $2,500 order limit. Shipping can occur almost immediately on all orders falling below the $2,500 order limit. Only orders exceeding the limit automatically go to the credit department for review. Under this scenario, order limits would be entered for each customer within the order entry system but not the accounts receivable system. When the customer order is entered into the order entry system, there is a check of the pending order amount against the designated order limit.

   Although less cumbersome, this type of system presents some major problems for the credit department. Under this scenario, customer orders can be approved without anyone checking to see if the customer is over its designated credit limit—or anyone checking to determine how the order will affect the customer's total exposure with the customer, factoring in the unshipped order backlog. Additionally, such a system has no mechanism for checking to see how past due the customer might be.

From a credit perspective, the system could be disastrous. A customer with a $2,500 order limit could potentially get approval for 50 separate orders of $2,499 each. Order entry personnel, keeping their primary goal in mind, might get creative and split a $10,000 order into five separate $2,000 orders just to avoid having to refer the order to credit for approval.

The solution can be to institute an order entry/billing system interface with accounts receivable (see Exhibit 3.1). Under this configuration, the order entry system interfaces with accounts receivable and checks to see if, for instance, the existing order plus the balance exceeds the designated credit limit. If it does, the order is rejected and referred to credit for approval to ship.

Other interface hurdles can be introduced as well. For example, order entry could be required to check with accounts receivable to determine if 33 percent or more of the assigned credit limit is past due. Or, a company might develop an exposure hurdle whereby order entry searches its records for the customer's unshipped backlog and adds that to the accounts receivable balance to compare the total exposure to a designated total exposure limit or credit limit.

Creating an automated interface between order entry and credit calls for a long-term commitment and the cooperation of the data processing department. Without such a system, the company may have to resign itself to the fact that in most situations, either the efficiency-oriented goals of the order entry department or the control-oriented goals of the credit department will have to be sacrificed to some extent. As a result, the quality and service levels for the credit, customer service, manufacturing, warehousing, and shipping functions will suffer.

ABSTRACT SUMMARY

- By interfacing its order entry/billing system with accounts receivable, a company can perform automated credit checks.
- Interfacing order entry and accounts receivable expedites orders while providing an internal control.
- Order entry hurdles alone do not provide the controls that an interface can provide.

Exhibit 3.1
Flow Chart of Order Entry Interface with Accounts Receivable

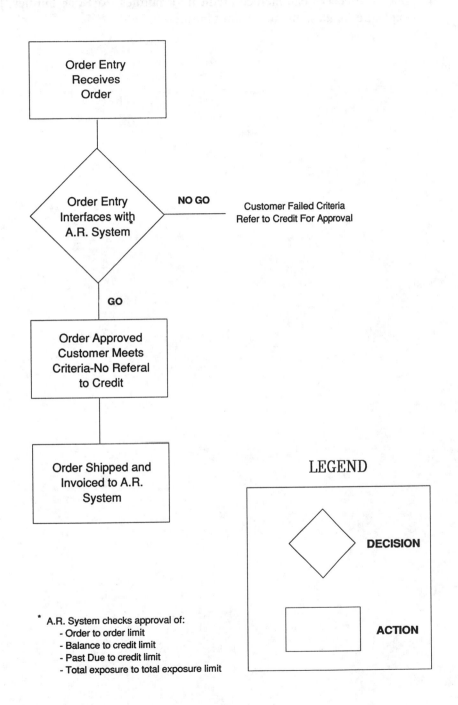

LEGEND

DECISION

ACTION

* A.R. System checks approval of:
  - Order to order limit
  - Balance to credit limit
  - Past Due to credit limit
  - Total exposure to total exposure limit

- Without an interface or order entry hurdles, all orders must be referred to the credit department, possibly delaying customer shipments.
- Interface checks can include credit limit hurdles, past due hurdles, total exposure hurdles, and order limit hurdles.

CREDIT SYSTEMS: AUTOMATIC CASH INPUT USING MICR NUMBERS

Companies using a bank lockbox service can substantially add to the value of that service by having the bank encode on a tape the MICR numbers for each check deposited.

MICR stands for "magnetic ink character recognition." MICR numbers are the numbers that appear in the lower left-hand field of the check (see Exhibit 3.2). For only pennies per item, a company can have its lockbox bank encode the MICR numbers on a tape and thus perform a critical phase of the accounts receivable update cycle.

A lockbox service generally processes daily cash deposits for presentment, photocopies checks, batches check deposits, microfilms checks, transmits checks, and reports lockbox deposits. But a company can also request the encoding of MICR numbers on remittance checks.

Once the MICR numbers are on a tape, the numbers from each check can be matched against a customer's internal accounts receivable customer number through an interface with the supplier's accounts receivable system. This interface can be achieved in one of two ways:

1. If it has the capability, the lockbox bank can transmit the MICR numbers directly to the supplier's computer system, or
2. The lockbox bank can transmit the MICR numbers to an intermediary data reporting service, which can then interface with the supplier's accounts receivable system.

Either way, the interface can be accomplished overnight — after the day's cash is processed but before the next working day begins. The result is that remittance checks received at the lockbox are automatically input onto the customer's accounts receivable screen on a next-day basis.

In a manual environment, the process is much slower. The supplier cannot input the customer remittance until paper backup from the lockbox is received in the mail. But in an automated environment, thousands of items each month can be input through the recapture and transmission of MICR encoding.

The benefits of this process go beyond time saved in inputting customer cash, however. By having the cash posted to the customer's account on a next-day basis, the credit department ensures that it will make fewer unneccessary collection calls to customers whose cash has actually been received but not yet properly recorded. Even more important, the process can help the credit department more accurately assess whether it should hold off shipping product to a marginal customer; if that customer's remittance check — or cash in advance payment — has arrived, the credit

Exhibit 3.2
Location of MICR Numbers on Checks

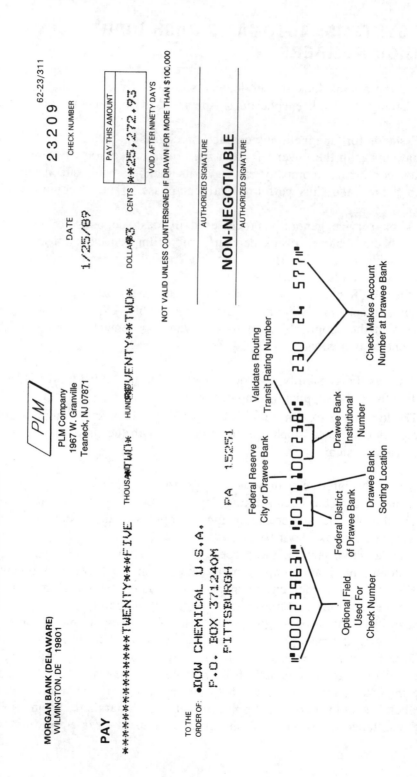

department will know it sooner than if an accounts receivable clerk were manually inputting each item.

Another benefit of MICR input via the lockbox is that in many cases it can reduce the need for accounts receivable clerical help—or at least allow AR clerks to work on other projects such as resolving deductions and old invoice items. But more significant is the fact that it enhances the quality and integrity of a company's individual customer accounts receivable information. With better information, credit managers can be assured that their people will have the opportunity to channel their energies into more positive efforts.

ABSTRACT SUMMARY

- Lockbox MICR encoding yields automatic cash input, which has significant benefits as compared to manual inputting.

- MICR numbers are the numbers that appear in the lower left-hand field of the check.

- Automatic cash input is achieved when the MICR numbers from each check encoded by the lockbox bank are matched against the customer's internal accounts receivable customer number via an interface with accounts receivable.

- One way a company benefits from an MICR interface is that its credit department will not make unneccessary collection calls to customers whose cash has actually been received but not properly recorded.

- MICR encoding and interface free up accounts receivable and credit personnel time for more productive activities.

OVERCOMING "COMPUTERITIS"

Financial analysts and accounting and treasury personnel across the nation are using the personal computer as a decision-making and reporting tool. Despite the numerous potential benefits and applications, however, the corporate credit function has been slow to accept the PC as a management tool.

Like most people, credit personnel are averse to change. And so most of them still struggle in a pencil-and-paper environment that limits their decision-making capabilities. This is unfortunate because credit PC utilization opens up new horizons for decision-making and credit reporting. The following are some of the benefits derived from PC utilization:

- Greater timing, speed, and accuracy in generating reports and making decisions;
- Enhanced credit modeling capabilities beyond the limits of a mainframe or manual environment;
- Online access to credit data;
- Data processing department independence with respect to the printer queue and programming requests;
- Paperless records storage with all records on disk; and
- More time available for pursuing other credit tasks that will generate cash flow.

The credit person has two options with respect to software programs: buy one or create one using spreadsheet software such as Lotus 1-2-3 or Framework II. For a number of reasons, the do-it-yourself approach often works best. For one thing, there are few available PC-based credit software packages. And if one of these packages is selected, it's quite likely that the required enhancements will be costly. Once again, remember that the cost of enhancements can sometimes exceed the cost of the basic package.

With self-designed and created software, the credit person controls his own destiny.

Creating credit software sounds more difficult than it is. The first step is to take all of the company's manually driven credit reports and automate them on the PC. Because the PC will now be performing the calculations, the credit person might even want to add fields or columns of information to these reports. The reports will not only be generated faster, but they will have more information.

Most credit people are under the impression that they must use sophisticated mathematical formulas to do modeling. But that is not the case at all. Most models—including financial statement analysis and cash forecasting models—can be programmed using formulas based on simple addition, subtraction, multiplication, and division.

PC utilization offers a whole new array of credit reports while providing decision-making models that enhance and protect cash flow. The time has come for credit personnel to take advantage of PC technology. A small investment in time — for, say learning Lotus 1-2-3 or Framework II — can pay off big in terms of career enhancement.

ABSTRACT SUMMARY

- The credit function has been slow to accept the personal computer despite its many potential benefits and applications.

- Credit PC utilization provides significant benefits when compared to a pencil-and-paper environment.

- Benefits of using a PC include: better report-generating capability, enhanced credit modeling, online access to credit data, independence from the DP area, paperless records storage, and more time to perform other cash-flow generating credit activities.

- Program options are twofold: buy software from a vendor or create it internally.

- Programming internally with spreadsheet software appears to be the best option based on the lack of available PC-based credit software and the cost of enhancing off-the-shelf packages.

GENERATING PC-BASED CREDIT REPORTS

With the aid of a personal computer, a corporate credit department can develop a wide variety of credit reports both for internal credit analysis and for review by senior managers. These reports, which analyze and expound upon cash flow and credit risk, can be generated without using the company's mainframe computer. However, credit staffers can use these reports in conjunction with mainframe-generated reports to expand decision-making and analytical capabilities. Thus, by using the PC, a credit person can enhance internal and management reporting capabilities.

Some of the reports that a PC can produce for internal credit department use include: collateral listing reports, individual high-risk customer DSO reports (see Exhibit 3.3), customer credit hold reports, and credit file review reports. On the other hand, the PC can also generate reports for senior management covering customer-extended credit terms, month-end customer high-risk and DSO analysis (see Exhibit 3.4), customer bad debt, product DSO, and accounts receivable delinquency by product line.

Very few, if any, mainframe accounts receivable systems generate these types of specialized credit reports, which are so effective in helping to identify potential cash flow shortcomings and opportunities.

Credit staffers can use the personal computer to generate reports that are subjective — reports that could not be produced simply by retrieving data from a mainframe's data base. For example, the company's mainframe can't determine which of the company's customers are high-risk accounts. That is a subjective determination that might change from one month to the next, based on shifting performance and criteria. Only by using a PC can a credit person alter the criteria from month to month in order to generate such subjective reports.

In fact, today most reports of this nature are being generated in time-consuming, error-prone, pencil-and-paper environments. Generally, an accounts receivable computer system that generates collateral reports or individual customer DSO reports does not provide customer-risk reporting capabilities as part of its basic reporting package. However, the credit person can custom-design PC software to write such reports.

Generating internal reports and reports for senior management review via the PC is the first level of enhanced decision-making and analytical capabilities that the PC offers to credit users. At the next level, credit staffers can use a PC to create credit models.

Exhibit 3.3
High-Risk Customer DSO by Product Line as of 04/30/XX

Name	Product	Balance	Past-Due	Current	Actual DSO
ABC	BOARD	$ 19,622	$ 5,640	$ 13,982	120
DEF	BOARD	2,374	2,374	0	100
HIJ	BOARD	182,761	33,814	148,947	76
KLM	BOARD	151,875	79,284	72,591	62
NOP	BOARD	78,342	11,250	67,092	79
QRS	BOARD	75,548	75,548	0	105
TUV	BOARD	53,460	0	53,460	30
WXY	BOARD	249,190	0	249,190	61
	BOARD TOTAL	813,172	207,910	605,262	73
AA CO.	LINER	$ 26,071	$26,071	$ 0	120
BB CO.	LINER	37,057	1,417	35,640	56
CC CO.	LINER	64,276	14,913	49,363	62
DD CO.	LINER	46,769	0	46,769	57
	LINER TOTAL	174,173	42,401	131,772	65
EE CO.	CARTON	$778,580	$295,152	$483,428	73
FF CO.	CARTON	57,339	17,235	40,104	83
GG CO.	CARTON	39,590	0	39,590	60
	CARTON TOTAL	875,509	312,387	563,122	73
HH CO.	CONTAINER	$229,500	$19,162	$210,338	107
II CO.	CONTAINER	114,445	69,304	45,141	120
JJ CO.	CONTAINER	9,451	0	9,451	30
	CONT. TOTAL	353,396	88,466	264,930	114
KK CO.	SCRAP	$22,586	$6,445	$16,141	84
	SCRAP TOTAL	22,586	6,445	16,141	84
	CO. TOTALS	$2,238,836	$657,609	$1,581,227	78

Exhibit 3.4
Month-End Customer High-Risk and DSO Analysis as of 11/30/XX

Customer Name	Terms	Product	Risk Code	Security	Cr. Line	Balance	Past Due	Backlog	$ Exposure*	Ex/CLine	Curr.Pymts.	Yr. Ago Pymts.
AAA Industries	n30	Board	P.B.	none	10,000,000	139,000	77,500	33,900	172,900	1.73%	sl 30-60	sl 15-30
Acme Paper	n30	Container	LEV.	P.G.	75,000	33,000	1,000	7,000	40,000	53.33	Ppt	Ppt-sl 6
Ainex Paper Dist.	1%30n60	Carton	S.P./H.R.	none	66,000	49,000	45,000	16,000	65,000	98.48	sl 60+	sl 15-45
Appleton Press	n30	Container	H.R.	P.G.	150,000	81,500	26,500	11,500	93,000	62.00	sl 31-45	sl 31-60
Astrapape Inc.	n30	Liner	LEV.	none	100,000	121,000	2,500	12,500	133,500	133.50	sl 6-30	sl 6-15
Canterberry United	n30	Board	M.R.	none	500,000	331,900	0	125,000	456,900	91.38	Ppt	Disct-Ppt
Conners Co. Inc.	n30	Liner	S.P.	none	50,000	65,000	22,000	9,000	74,000	148.00	sl 30-45	sl 15-30
Davidson Enterprises	n30	Board	M.R.	none	275,000	211,000	0	33,000	244,000	88.73	sl 6-10	sl 6-30
Dennis Co.	n30	Liner	LEV.	none	100,000	89,000	12,000	20,000	109,000	109.00	Ppt-sl 6-10	sl 6-15
Donaldson Paper	n30	Container	H.R.	none	90,000	66,000	25,000	3,500	69,500	77.22	sl 15-30	sl 30
Fort Monterey Paper	n30	Container	M.R.	1/c200k	200,000	455,000	171,000	47,600	502,600	251.30	sl 6-15	sl 6-15
Fortune Paper	n30	Carton	PAY./P.B.	none	75,000	123,500	119,500	0	123,500	164.67	sl 75+	sl 15-45
Gordon Paper	n30	Liner	PAY./P.B.	P.G.	100,000	211,000	211,000	0	211,000	211.00	sl 60+	sl 60+
Hardy Thompson Inc.	n30	Liner	LEV.	none	100,000	64,000	0	12,500	76,500	76.50	Ppt-sl 6-10	sl 6-15
Home Magazine Inc.	n30	Carton	PAY./P.B.	P.G.	75,000	70,000	69,000	0	70,000	93.33	sl 120+	sl 60+
Jillson Inc.	n30	Liner	LEV.	none	100,000	71,000	24,000	9,100	80,100	80.10	Ppt-sl 6-10	Ppt
Johnson Jones Inc.	n30	Board	S.P.	none	300,000	266,000	88,000	75,000	341,000	113.67	sl 30	sl 30
Johnson Paper Co.	n30	Liner	LEV.	none	30,000	55,000	21,500	12,500	67,500	225.00	Ppt-sl 15-30	Disct-Ppt
Lincoln News	n30	Carton	S.P	none	75,000	49,000	31,000	15,500	64,500	86.00	sl 6-30	sl 15
Louisville Industries	n30	Carton	S.P.	none	100,000	22,000	5,500	10,000	32,000	32.00	sl 31-45	sl 31-60
Paper Man, Co. Inc.	n30	Carton	S.P.	none	100,000	50,000	6,000	6,000	56,000	56.00	sl 30	sl 15-30
Sampson & Howard	n30	Container	H.R.	P.G.	775,000	445,750	65,000	28,700	474,450	61.22	sl 31-60	sl 15
Spring News Inc.	n30	Board	M.R.	none	425,000	245,700	0	65,000	310,700	73.11	Ppt-sl 6-10	Ppt
Stevens Publishing	n30	Carton	PAY./P.B.	2nd UCC1	75,000	35,000	35,000	0	35,000	46.67	sl 90+	sl 31-60
Tulley Publishing	n30	Board	M.R.	none	1,000,000	576,000	22,500	154,000	730,000	73.00	Ppt	Ppt
TOTALS						3,925,350	1,080,500	707,300	4,632,650			

* Exposure = balance + backlog

Exhibit 3.4 (continued)
Month-End Customer High-Risk and DSO Analysis as of 11/30/XX

High-Risk DSO Analysis

TOTAL DSO (days)	59
Total Accounts Receivable	21,355,000
Total High Risk Accounts Receivable	3,925,350
Total High-Risk Past Due	1,080,500
High-Risk Accounts Receivable/Total Accounts Receivable	18.38%
High-Risk Past-Due/Total Accounts Receivable	5.06%
Total High-Risk DSO	10.85
High-Risk Past-Due DSO	2.99
One DSO Day	361,949

Terms Legend

CIA = Cash in advance
COD = Cash on delivery
NCRI = Net Cash upon receopt of Invoice
n30 = Net 30 days
1%10n30 = 1% 10 days net 30 days
n45 = Net 45 days
n60 = Net 60 days
1%30n60 = 1% 30 days net 60 days
Other = Terms are greater than 60 days

Security Legend

Bond = Bond from Bonding Company
C. Gty = Corporate Guaranty
C.C. Gty = Cross Corporate Guaranty
C.L. = Comfort Letter
DEP. = Deposit
LC = Letter of Credit
P.G. = Personal Guaranty
UCC1 = Uniform Commercial Code Lien

Risk Code Legend

H.R. = High Risk
LEV. = Leveraged
M.R. = Moderate Risk
PAY. = Payout
P.B. = Potential Bankruptcy
S.P. = Slow Paying

Payments Legend

Disct = Discount
Disct-Ppt = Discount to Prompt
Ppt = Prompt
Ppt-sl = Prompt to slow
sl = slow

ABSTRACT SUMMARY

- Using the personal computer, the credit department can generate customized credit reports independent of the company's mainframe computer system.
- PC utilization enhances internal and management reporting capabilities.
- For internal analysis, the PC can generate collateral listing reports, individual customer DSO reports, customer credit hold reports, and credit file review reports.
- For senior management review, the personal computer can produce reports on customer high risk, customer bad debt, product DSO, and accounts receivable delinquency reports by product line.
- PC-driven internal reports and reports for senior management review represent the first generation of credit PC utilization.

PC-BASED DECISION-MAKING MODELS

After the credit department has customized and automated its credit reports, the next step is to develop PC decision-making models.

The process of programming new credit reports and revising existing reports gives credit personnel the ability to present groups of credit data in customized formats. Once this initial phase of automation is completed, true modeling of credit data can take place, thereby further enhancing decision-making capabilities.

Credit personnel can design and program a variety of PC decision-making models using spreadsheet software such as Lotus 1-2-3 or Framework II. Daily cash forecasting, monthly DSO forecasting, individual customer DSO analysis, customer profitability models, and customer financial statement analysis models (see Exhibit 3.5) are just some of the decision-making options that are readily programmable without the assistance of data processing personnel. By entering balance sheet and P&L data, the model automatically calculates the ratios based on predetermined formulas, as well as the variance to the industry standards. For the specific exhibit rendered, the data entry phase should last no more than five to ten minutes.

Using these decision-making models will add to the credit person's control over:

- Customer exposures
- Days sales outstanding
- Cash flow
- Delinquency
- Extended terms
- Bad-debt write-offs

Credit personnel should also be able to achieve greater timing, speed, and accuracy in credit decision making. Building these models provides expanded capabilities and approaches to analyzing existing credit data—compared to the previously limited, pencil-driven environment.

Customized models enable a credit person to make correlations, adjustments, modifications, and decisions relating to credit data. Once these models are designed, the credit department can begin to make effective use of the wealth of available cash flow and profitability data that is probably underutilized or going untapped. The decision-making model's output data can be integrated with individual customer, product line, or subsidiary/division accounts receivable data to produce previously unavailable credit decision-making data.

To begin the process of designing PC decision-making models, first outline the objectives for each model. Most modeling can be executed with formulas that utilize addition, subtraction, multiplication, and division to some degree. Remem-

Exhibit 3.5
Automated Customer Financial Statement Analysis Model

Enter Below:
Current Date: 07/19/XX
Company Analyzed: DPM Co.
Year End: 12/31/88
Prepared By: B. P. Mavrovitis

Enter Below Balance Sheet Items:

Assets		Liabilities & Equity:		P&L Performance:	
Current Assets:		Current Liabilities:		Sales	66,022
Cash	46,884	A/P	4,435	COGS	27,415
A/R	17,508	Accruals	7,115	Op. Profit	7,331
Inventory	19,456	S.T. Bank Debt	0	Int. Exp.	-3,082
Other	876	L.T. Bank Due	300	Int. Inc.	4,604
Total Current	84,724	Other	0	NBT	8,853
Fixed Assets		Total Current	11,850	Tax	-3,187
PPE	31,049	Long-Term Liabilities:		NAT	5,666
Less. Dep.	7,929	L.T. Bank	39,329		
Net PPE	23,120	Def. Inc. Tax	5,008		
Other	2,800	Other	0		
Total Assets	110,644	Total Liabilities	56,187		
		Equity:		Equity Reconcilliation:	
		Common Stock	84	Opening Equity	49,311
		Cap in Excess	42,465	NAT	5,666
		Retained Earn.	14,902	Dividends	0
		Less Trea. Stk.	-506	Less Adj.	520
		Less Misc.	-2,488	Ending Equity	54,457
		Total Equity	54,457		
		Tot. Lia./Eq.	110,644		

Exhibit 3.5 (continued)
Automated Customer Financial Statement Analysis Model

	Calculated Ratios Output	Industry Standard	(+ fav/- unfav) Variance
Current	7.15	1.55	361.27%
Quick	5.43	.85	539.29%
Debt/Worth	1.03	.80	-28.97%
Bank/Worth	.73	.35	-107.92%
ROE	11.49%	15.00%	-23.40%
ROS	8.58%	5.00%	71.64%
A/R Curr. Assets	.21	.60	-65.56%
A/R-A/P	3.95	1.20	228.97%
Net PPE/Tot. Assets	.21	.35	-40.30%
A/R Turnover	95.47	45	-112.15%
Inv. Turnover	255.49	60	-325.81%
A/P Turnover	58.24	38	-53.26%
Interest/Sales	4.67%	5.00%	6.64%
Cash/Curr. Liab.	3.96	.18	2,160.83%

ber, the layout of the models must conform to the format and logic of the spreadsheet software being used. Thus, where necessary, model using rows and columns logic — the standard layout and spreadsheet architecture for Lotus 1-2-3 and Framework II.

The data entry phase can take anywhere from two minutes to more than an hour, depending on the modeling. For instance, cash forecasting data entry will be more time-consuming than entering data for a customer profitability model. But don't let the data entry phase be a constraint against full use of credit PC decision-making models. The more time-consuming data entry work can be delegated to the clerical level.

Ultimately, credit department PC-based decision-making enhances credit and corporate objectives. A natural byproduct of this type of modeling is that credit personnel increase their cash flow orientation, and this conciousness is reflected in their everyday credit analysis.

Decision-making models can be fine-tuned to the micro level for customer cash flow and risk analysis or they can encompass the broader cash flow picture on the macro level, assessing the overall cash flow capabilities and risks of the accounts receivable portfolio.

ABSTRACT SUMMARY

- PC decision-making models represent the second step in credit PC utilization.
- Benefits include greater timing, speed, and accuracy in credit decision making.
- PC decision-making models provide greater control of customer exposures, customer profitability, DSO, cash flow, delinquency, extended terms, and bad-debt write-offs.
- By utilizing PC decision-making models, credit can make effective use of cash flow and profitability data that is available yet usually underutilized or untapped.
- PC decision-making applications can include: daily cash forecasting, monthly DSO forecasting, individual customer DSO analysis, customer profitability models, and customer financial statement analysis models.

PC PROGRAMMING USING
SPREADSHEET SOFTWARE

Working with spreadsheet software such as Lotus 1-2-3 or Framework II is not as difficult as many nonusers believe. All it takes is the ability to add, subtract, multiply, and divide — and an interest in improving reporting, decision-making, and modeling capabilities.

The goal of spreadsheet software is to emulate an actual paper spreadsheet — just as if it were layed out in front of someone. The spreadsheet on the screen is comprised of columns and rows. The columns are usually in alpha form beginning with column "A" in the extreme left-hand corner of the screen, followed by columns "B," "C," and so forth as one moves to the right. Most spreadsheets have more than 24 columns, thus when one gets to the 25th column it is usually labeled "AA."

Rows start at the top of the spreadsheet and are usually labeled on the left-hand side of the spreadsheet in ascending order. Thus, row one is at the top of the spreadsheet while the highest numbered row is at the bottom of the spreadsheet. The idea is to place data and formulas in the individual cells whose locations are identified by the column and row number. Let's take a look at a typical spreadsheet:

	A	B	C	D	E	F	G	H
1								
2	Customer		Balance		Past Due		Past Due	
3	ABC Co.		25,000		5,000		25.00%	
4	DEF Co.		100,000		41,000		41.00%	
5	GHI Co.		30,000		10,000		33.33%	
6	JKL Co.		10,000		1,000		10.00%	
7								
8								
9								
10	Totals		165,000		57,000		34.55%	

In cells A2, A3, A4, A5, A6, A10, C2, E2, and G2 are entered text or labels to help identify the variables being programmed.

In cells C3, C4, C5, C6, E3, E4, E5, and E6 are entered individual customer data that will be manipulated by designated formulas.

Formulas to carry out calculations have been entered in cells C10, E10, G3, G4, G5, G6, and G10. The formula cell reads the formula command and then executes the calculation in the same cell in which the formula has been placed. Note that the formula in cell C10 would be C3 + C4 + C5 + C6; the formula for cell E10 would be E3 + E4 + E5 + E6; and the formula for cell G3 would be C3 divided by E3, or in formula terms, C3 / E3. Cell G4's formula would be C4 / E4.

It's not really that complex or difficult to understand! A credit manager or staffer can create very sophisticated and high-powered programs using formulas based solely on addition, subtraction, multiplication, and division. There is no need for complex formulas involving calculus or statistics.

Using spreadsheet software can extend reporting, decision-making, and modeling cababilities. Calculations that would take hours can be executed in seconds once the appropriate formulas are in place. The PC enables the credit person to program models to analyze balance sheets, calculate DSOs, and analyze month-end accounts receivable data. And the work can be achieved in a manner that is more timely and accurate than it would be in a pencil-and-paper environment.

Individual text and formulas within spreadsheets, as well as entire spreadsheets, can be easily copied using the program's system commands. Monthly accounts receivable formats and reports can be copied in a matter of seconds, eliminating the need to recreate the formulas and formats for the next month's report. Only the new month's data must be input into the copied report. Calculations and updated detail will automatically follow by generally depressing the "enter" and "recalc" (recalculation) keys.

One final, important point on the use of spreadsheet software by credit professionals: It allows one to work independent of the company's mainframe computer, and thus independent of the data processing department.

ABSTRACT SUMMARY

- Using spreadsheet software such as Lotus 1-2-3 or Framework II is not as difficult as some nonusers believe.
- Spreadsheet software is based on the same concepts as the paper spreadsheet, which is composed of columns and rows.
- The idea is to enter data and formulas in the individual cells whose locations are identified by the column and row number.
- One can create very sophisticated and high-powered programs by simply using formulas based on addition, subtraction, multiplication, and division.
- Calculations that would otherwise take hours can be executed in seconds once the appropriate formulas are in place.

CREDIT'S ROLE IN ELECTRONIC
DATA INTERCHANGE

Electronic data interchange, or EDI, is becoming a popular buzz word among corporate credit professionals. EDI is the electronic transaction of routine business data using formats that are standardized and machine readable. Among other things, it is looked upon as an electronic tool that will enhance the credit department's ability to accelerate cash flow, monitor and report credit data, and perform cash forecasting.

EDI will create a number of changes affecting how credit departments conduct their business. Some of these include:

- Electronic invoicing of customers (as opposed to a paper-generated invoice);

- Electronic receipt of payments from customers via the automated clearinghouse, or ACH, (as opposed to receiving paper checks or wire transfers via a wire transfer payment network), thereby reducing credit's reliance on a geographic network of lockboxes;

- Electronic interchange of credit experience (as opposed to the verbal or written interchange of credit experience); and

- Electronic access to customers' accounts payable systems, which enables the credit practitioner to make an "electronic collection call" to determine whether payment is forthcoming.

It is clear that a company utilizing EDI will be able to generate dollar savings through enhanced cash flow and reduced costs. So how can a company get started?

The first step will be to get the treasury and data processing departments committed to EDI. The treasury department, which is often responsible for the credit function, should be an easy sell. After all, the treasury area depends on cash flow to provide financial support for the company. The DP department could be tougher; DP will have to support the various EDI applications the credit department will want to implement.

The credit department will want to focus initially on the two applications within the cash flow timeline that will have the greatest impact—electronic invoicing of customers and electronic receipt of payments.

Electronic invoicing provides an immediate benefit by cutting down on the assignment of free payment days that results from paper invoicing. These free payment days are created when the invoice date lags behind the actual shipment date. But they are generally eliminated by electronic invoicing, which ensures that the shipment date and invoice date are the same.

To invoice a customer electronically, tapes must be sent to the company's bank or through a third-party network in ANSI X12 formats. ANSI X12 refers to a committee chartered by the American National Standards Institute for the purpose of developing EDI standards.

To receive payments electronically, a company's bank must be capable of receiving from the customer's bank the payment information on tape in the ANSI X12 format. If the company's bank can't receive ACH payment information, the company can still receive electronic payments. However, it would have to have the customer's electronic payment directed to a correspondent bank that would, in turn, advise the company's bank when funds were received.

Why EDI? An immediate reason involves some of the nation's largest firms— Fortune 100 companies. These megacompanies, with their enormous economic clout, are beginning to force their vendors to invoice them electronically rather than via paper. Some of these same firms are requiring their vendors to electronically accept and confirm purchase orders, which impacts the order entry/credit release cycle.

Many companies that do business with the federal government realize that they can benefit by taking advantage of the government's program for paying vendors electronically. Rather than receiving a check, which is subject to mail and presentation float, vendors to the government are receiving payment electronically through a program called Vendor Express.

With the backing of major companies like General Motors Corp., as well as the U.S. government, it appears that EDI is here to stay. Sooner or later most companies will be forced to start doing business the EDI way. So why not start now? It could result in significant cash flow dividends.

ABSTRACT SUMMARY

- EDI can enhance the credit department's ability to accelerate cash flow, monitor and report credit data, and perform cash forecasting.
- EDI can be applied to the following credit applications: electronic invoicing of customers, electronic receipt of payments from customers via the ACH, and electronic interchange of credit experience.
- EDI can generate dollar savings through enhanced cash flow and reduced costs.
- EDI implementation will require a commitment from the treasury and data processing departments.
- Any company doing business with the U.S. government can take advantage of EDI now through the government's Vendor Express program in which vendors are paid electronically.

4

LOCKBOX

THE BENEFITS OF OPENING A LOCKBOX

Opening a single lockbox or a multi-lockbox network can help a company achieve quicker access to funds from customer remittances while freeing up credit personnel to pursue other cash-flow generating activities.

A lockbox offers several advantages over the alternative — receiving checks at the company's office location. By opening a lockbox, a company can:

- Enhance customer collections;
- Accelerate the availability of funds by reducing customer mail float and check presentation float;
- Obtain earlier notification that customer payments have been received;
- Reduce human error; and
- Free up accounts receivable staff for other tasks.

When remittance checks are sent to an office location, they must be coded and deposited in the bank for check processing and presentment for cash availability. That's a time-consuming process that subjects the company to many potential delays.

One of the biggest problems a lockbox can help the company overcome is mail float, the time (in days) it takes from the date of postmark for the customer's check to be received at its designated "remit to" destination.

A lockbox network with an optimal geographic configuration can reduce and even eliminate unnecessary mail float. As an example, consider a firm located in Philadelphia with a customer in Indianapolis. It will certainly take a check mailed from Indianapolis to Philadelphia much longer to arrive at its destination than it would if the Philadelphia firm had its customer mail the check to a lockbox in, say, Chicago or Cleveland (see Exhibits 4.1 and 4.2).

In other words, having the Indianapolis customer send its check to a Midwestern lockbox location would cut down on mail float.

Geographic stratification is not the only reason for using a lockbox. There are mail float delays to be expected any time a company has checks remitted to its office. Thus, even a company located in Chicago would be able to cut down on mail float using a Chicago lockbox site.

Most lockbox banks pick up remittance mail 15 or more times a day, while companies without lockboxes collect checks once or twice via their daily mail pickups from the local post office. A unique zip code enables the post office to process mail destined for a lockbox on a more timely basis.

Lockboxes operate as much as 24 hours a day, picking up, updating, and processing customer remittances in a regimented and organized manner. A company

Exhibit 4.1

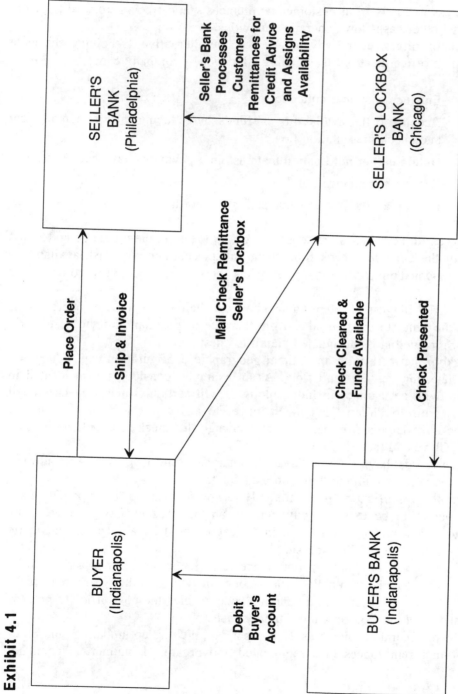

Exhibit 4.2

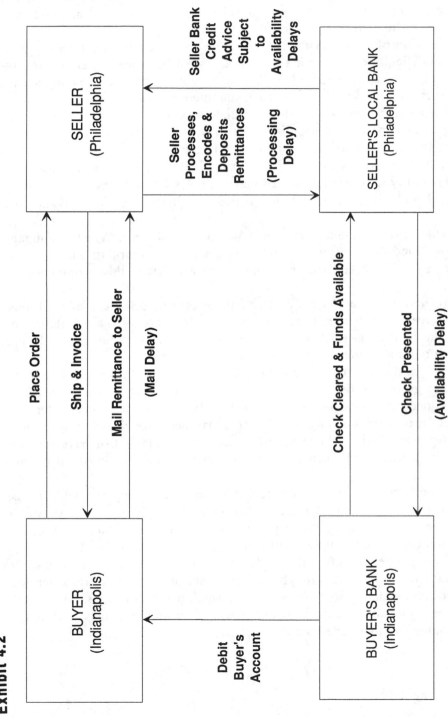

having its checks remitted to the office will process remittances in a much less disciplined fashion.

Credit managers at companies that don't use a lockbox or lockbox network should ask themselves: How many times have customer remittances been received at the office on the last day of the month but not reflected as paid at month-end because I wasn't able to make the deposit?

This situation illustrates that failure to use a lockbox not only raises month-end DSO and delinquency levels; it also affects the balance sheet. Accounts receivable will likely be higher at month end, which either hurts the company's cash position or increases the firm's loan balance and interest expense.

In the example above, availability of funds would be enhanced dramatically by clearing a customer's Indianapolis check at a lockbox in Chicago or Cleveland—rather than presenting the item to a Philadelphia bank for processing and ultimate availability. Even if a company is located in the same city as its designated lockbox, availability for checks presented may not be as favorable as for a company with a formal lockbox arrangement that includes a preset negotiated availability schedule.

As noted above, lockboxes also cut down on human error. When a company has checks remitted to its office, a check may come in the morning but staff may fail to deposit the check until the next day. With a lockbox, this simply doesn't happen.

Additionally, when checks are received at the office, each piece of mail must be handled three times before it reaches the bank. A piece of mail will first be handled by the mail room staff, then by accounts receivable personnel, and once again by mail room staff transporting the checks to the bank.

This reliance on internal staff can backfire. For instance, internal staffers have been known to go on vacation or get sick. What happens when they are out of the office and no one remembers to take care of their duties? In a worst-case scenario, checks could be floating around in the wrong departments for days before eventually being deposited. This problem is more acute at companies that have too few qualified, trained staffers who can fill these positions during vacations and periods of illness.

With a lockbox, the credit department may also notice improvements in the payment performance of marginal customers—based simply on the company's greater efficiency in collecting and reporting on incoming remittances. And, the company will receive much timelier notification of NSF checks.

One of the greatest benefits of a lockbox is that it frees up employees to do more important work than sift through mail. A bank, through its lockbox service, can do the sorting, coding, and processing for a small per-item charge. For a small additional fee, a lockbox bank will also telecopy customer names and dollar amounts for same-day remittances on a daily basis.

Another service the bank can perform is MICR encoding. This process enables individual remittances to be automatically input to their respective accounts in the company's accounts receivable system.

MICR encoding eliminates the need to have accounts receivable personnel manually input each customer's remittance to its account in the AR system. The process saves time and reduces human error—once again for just a few cents per item. And, once again, the fees will buy additional staff time that can be spent on more important work.

ABSTRACT SUMMARY

- With a lockbox, a company can: enhance customer collections, accelerate availability by reducing mail float and presentation float, obtain earlier payment notification, reduce human error, and free up staff for more productive tasks.

- Companies that receive and process customer checks for deposit at their offices are subject to several possible delays and a greater risk of human error.

- A lockbox can narrow the notification time for NSF customer checks by improving mail time and handling, and by reducing presentment float.

- For a small per-item charge, a lockbox bank will assume the task of sorting, coding, and processing customer remittances, allowing staff to do other work.

- A bank can also provide a company with MICR encoding, the first step in a process that allows the company to have remittances automatically input to its accounts receivable system.

REVIEWING THE ECONOMICS OF
OPENING A LOCKBOX

Opening a lockbox would appear to offer a company a number of benefits. But there's no sense in signing up to use a bank's lockbox services if the move cannot be justified on an economic basis.

A company considering the lockbox option should take the time to project out the savings that using a lockbox will generate, and then contrast those savings with the cost of operating the lockbox. Lockbox savings can be quantified in the form of reduced mail and check presentation float, as well as man hours that will be saved by freeing up credit personnel from mail sorting and processing duties.

Let's start by quantifying mail float savings. The first step is to perform a mail survey of the company's major customer data base (see The Major Customer Study, in Chapter 6). These customers will likely represent 85–90 percent of the company's total cash receipts.

For each of these customers, gather two or three recent check remittances along with their envelopes. Then plot the number of days from the postmark date that it took before each in-house item was deposited at the company's bank.

Next, obtain Phoenix-Hecht mail-time surveys from lockbox banks under consideration. Phoenix-Hecht is a Research Triangle Park, NC, cash management research firm that plots and constantly updates mail float times from check origin points to various potential collection cities, based on their zip codes. The firm's lead bank or candidate banks should be able to provide independent surveys showing the average mail float times for checks originating at certain locations and sent to their lockbox site.

As an example, let's say a company is based in Rochester, NY, and it is considering a single lockbox location in Chicago. If one of the company's major customers is located in Los Angeles, the credit practitioner needs to determine from Phoenix-Hecht data the average mail time for a check sent from Los Angeles to the proposed lockbox location in Chicago. This same process should be repeated for all of the company's major customers.

The next step is to compare, by customer, the availability the company will get on funds remitted to the lockbox, and then compare that to the availability the company received on those checks when they were remitted to the office.

Once this information is gathered, it should be charted in columnar fashion, as shown in Exhibit 4.3.

On the chart, note that in-house mail time represents the average of the two to three check remittances that were plotted.

In order to derive the lockbox savings for ABC Co., the credit practitioner would multiply the annual sales to the company ($500,000) by the company's cost of funds (8.5%) and divide the answer by 360 days to arrive at the daily cost of

Exhibit 4.3
Lockbox Economics/Chicago Lockbox vs. In-House Processing

Customer City/State	Phoenix-Hecht Mail Time	In-House Mail Time	Mail Time Differential	Lock Box Availability	In-House Availability	Availability Differential	Total Mail/Avail. Differential	Annual Sales	Cost of Funds	Annual Savings
ABC Co. Carson, CA	2	5	3	1	3	2	5	$ 500,000	8.5%	$ 590.28
DEF Co. L.A., CA	2	6	4	1	3	2	6	$1,500,000	8.5%	$2,125.00

funds ($118.06). That figure is then multiplied by the total mail/availability differ-ential of five days to arrive at the gross annual lockbox savings ($590.28).

The gross annual lockbox savings represents the money the company will save by using a lockbox instead of having checks sent to the office. (It does not factor in the cost of operating the lockbox, however.)

At the end of the study, determine what percent of total annual sales the study group comprised. Based on that percentage, the credit practitioner can estimate what the company's total annual savings would be if it began using a bank's lock-box services.

The manpower savings of using a lockbox can also be quantified. Start by determining the total number of employee hours that are required on a monthly basis to process checks received in-house. Then calculate the number of hours that will be freed up for other tasks if the company uses a lockbox, and annualize the savings.

After determining lockbox savings based on reduced mail time and freed-up man-hours, the credit practitioner must determine the annual costs of operating a bank lockbox. To determine these costs, credit practitioners should review the past 12 months of in-house receipts to calculate the average number of items that are deposited monthly. Next, they need to obtain quotes from two or three lockbox banks at the preferred location. They will need quotes on both per-item and fixed-fee charges.

Typical bank charges include: monthly account maintenance, annual box rent-al, per-item charges for photocopying and processing, a data transmission charge, and a postal charge. Based on the company's average monthly number of items and these quotes, credit practitioners can estimate how much the banks would charge them per month and per year.

Before comparing the savings to the costs, credit practitioners should net out costs that the local bank was charging for check handling and processing. They then can subtract the net costs from the gross savings to determine whether using a lockbox is justifiable.

ABSTRACT SUMMARY

- Savings from the use of a lockbox can be quantified based on reductions in mail and check presentation float and freed-up manpower.

- To quantify the mail float savings, the company needs to perform a mail survey of its major customer data base.

- In the process of calculating mail float savings, the credit practitioner can use data supplied by Phoenix-Hecht, a Research Triangle Park, NC, cash management consulting company. Phoenix-Hecht plots and constantly updates mail float times from check origin points to various potential collection cities by zip code.

- The manpower savings associated with using a lockbox or a lockbox network can be derived by calculating the number of hours that will be freed up for other tasks—and then annualizing the cost of those man-hours.

- Before comparing lockbox savings to lockbox operating costs, a credit practitioner should net out local bank charges for check handling and processing.

SELECTING A LOCKBOX LOCATION

A company should select the site of its lockbox (or lockboxes) based primarily on the geographic distribution of its major customers—the top 10 percent or 15 percent of its customer base. In most cases, these customers will account for three-quarters or more of the company's total collected cash receipts.

The process should begin with the credit practitioner charting out information in the major customer data base. In this case, the chart should include the customer's name, the location from which it remits checks, the product it buys, the amount of product it buys in dollars (annual sales), and the region where it is located (see Exhibit 4.4).

Through this process, the company can determine from where the majority of its remittances are being sent. By including product data, the practitioner can determine where the majority of cash flow is derived by product line or product group.

The "Region" column should make it clear from which regions the company is generating the highest volumes of remittances.

Based on the "Remit from City/State" column, the credit practitioner can further pinpoint possible lockbox sites, keeping in mind that the site or sites selected should be near one of the 12 Federal Reserve district headquarter cities. The availability schedules in outlying areas aren't as favorable as those provided to lockboxes in or near one of these cities.

The Fed's district headquarters are located in: Boston; New York; Philadelphia; Cleveland; Richmond, VA; Atlanta; Chicago; St. Louis; Minneapolis; Kansas City, MO; Dallas; and San Francisco.

Once credit practitioners have determined which cities appear to be the top candidates for a lockbox based on geographic proximity to customers, they should consider mail time to these locations. That's where data provided by Phoenix-Hecht can come in handy again.

If, for instance, Philadelphia, and Newark, NJ, both appear to be potential sites for locating an Eastern lockbox, then having some hard data about mail time will help in selecting between the two sites. The credit person will want to investigate the mail times from the sites of major customers—let's say Rochester, NY, and Cranston, RI—to both Philadelphia and Newark. The process should be repeated for all major customers.

The mail times to Philadelphia and Newark could turn out to be quite comparable. When potential lockbox sites are closely matched on this basis, the determining criteria will probably be the availability schedules at the candidate sites.

Companies that already have lockboxes in place might want to go through this exercise just to reaffirm that their lockboxes are in the best locations.

Exhibit 4.4
Major Customer Study by Geographic Dispersion

Customer Name	Remit From City/State	Product	Annual Sales	Region
ABC Co. Inc.	Rochester, N.J.	Compound	$525,000	East
DEF Co. Inc.	Cranston, R.I.	Mixer	$329,000	East
GHI Co. Inc.	Rockville, M.D.	Compound	$710,000	East

ABSTRACT SUMMARY

- The selection of lockbox locations is primarily a function of the geographic distribution of major customers.

- Performing a study of major customers and their geographic locations will help a company decide where some potential lockbox sites might be.

- In the major-customer study, a credit practitioner can chart out geographic and sales volume information about the company's major customers — the customers who are generating three-quarters or more of all the company's cash receipts.

- Based on the charted information, the company should be able to identify several potential lockbox sites; the next step is to investigate independent survey information about mail times to those cities.

- If two lockbox sites both look good from geographic and mail-time standpoints, the deciding factor will probably be the availability schedules that the company will get at each location.

SELECTING A LOCKBOX BANK

Once a company determines the optimal location for its lockbox, it can proceed to the next step in the process: selecting a lockbox bank. In order to get a competitive deal, the company will need to do a certain amount of comparison shopping. Close scrutiny of at least two to three candidate banks is recommended.

When reviewing potential banks, the credit practitioner should devise a bank selection grid (see Exhibit 4.5) based on the following criteria:

- *Pricing of lockbox services.* Pricing may be the most critical criteria. When shopping for a lockbox bank, there are a number of items that should be compared on each competitive bid. These include: monthly account maintenance charges, per-item processing charges, per-item photocopying charges, per-item micro encoding charges, per-batch charges, and daily data transmission charges.

When reviewing pricing, credit practitioners should make sure that one bank is not charging for a service that the other banks are not. For example, maybe only one of the three or four candidate banks has a special processing cutoff charge.

Once all the charges are unbundled and compared, the company can assign rankings to each bank for their pricing. The rankings can be reflected in the grid.

- *Availability schedule for checks presented.* Obviously, availability is important. It means the difference between cash flow for the company and delayed cash flow.

Surprisingly, availability can vary dramatically at banks located in the same city. Banks in the same city may have different availability schedules and required cutoff times for deposit availability.

Credit practitioners will want to obtain a copy of each bank's proposed availability schedule. Then they can compare the availability that each bank will grant for major-customer out-of-town checks. Once the comparisons are completed, they can again assign each candidate bank a ranking and note it in the selection grid.

- *Service.* Service could be a very critical factor in selecting a lockbox bank. To begin the comparison process, credit practitioners should request a tour of bank facilities to gauge efficiency. They should ask to meet with lockbox processing personnel as well as the lockbox manager—all the while looking to get a feel for the quality of responses they might get to inquiries.

Exhibit 4.5
Lockbox Selection Grid

Bank Criteria	Score Bank 1	Score Bank 2	Score Bank 3	Comments
Pricing	5	5	3	
Availability Schedule	4	3	3	
Service	5	5	4	
Operating Hours	5	4	4	
Mail pickups	5	5	4	
Equipment or Technology	5	5	3	
Processing Method	4	5	3	
References	5	4	4	
Total Score	38	35	28	

During the facilities visit, a credit person should try to make some judgments about how well-trained lockbox personnel are in processing customer remittances. What type of customer service department does the bank offer?

A company can't afford spending time reconciling its lockbox statements. So service must be timely and accurate.

- *Operating hours.* Potential lockbox banks should be asked: Is the lockbox open 24 hours a day, seven days a week, or is it open five days a week for eight hours a day? On what holidays does the bank process remittances for next-day presentment? Is there a Saturday or Sunday deposit made?

If the operating hours are thin, the company might lose availability on cash that has been received at the box but not processed due to the operating hours. In effect, such items become next-day rather than same-day items.

Each bank should be ranked based on the extent of their operating hours.

- *Mail pickups.* The frequency of mail pickups is critical with respect to the bank's ability to maximize its processing capabilities on any given day. The more mail pickups, the greater the amount of incoming remittances that can be processed. Some lockbox banks pick up incoming remittance mail as many as 15 times per day, whereas other banks may only have three to five daily mail pickups.

A company also needs to learn the times that these mail pickups are made during the day. It's especially important to learn at what time the bank makes the final pickup for which it can process remittances for same-day availability and ledger credit.

Again, the credit practitioner should rank each prospective lockbox bank based on the number of its mail pickups.

- *Systems equipment and technology.* What type of systems equipment and technology do each of the banks utilize? Are they using state-of-the-art processing equipment to accelerate processing and check presentments? Or are they utilizing outdated and antiquated technology that unnecessarily delays or duplicates tasks? And how committed is the bank to upgrading future lockbox technology?

A tour of each bank's lockbox processing center will give an indication of the quality of its processing technology. After comparing technology, assign a rating to each of the banks.

- *Processing method.* The work can be done using an assembly line approach where several people are involved in the processing of cash, or it can be done using a batch method where one person is responsible for all the tasks relating to an account.

Once again, a lockbox tour of each bank should reveal the efficiencies of each of the respective bank's processing methods. After comparing individual processing methods, assign a score to each bank.

- *References.* The company should ask each bank for two to three active lockbox references. Before they are contacted, the credit practitioner should develop a questionnaire for use in interviewing people at these companies. Typical questions will include: How would you rate the bank's error levels? How timely is their service on inquiries? Do you feel that pricing is competitive? How often has the bank missed making a deposit? Have you encountered any major problems with your lockbox? Are you notified of NSF checks on a timely basis? How intelligible is the bank's account analysis (monthly or quarterly charge) format? What are the major criticisms you have of the lockbox? Is the lockbox following your processing instructions? On a scale of one to 10, how would you rate the lockbox?

After reviewing responses to these questions, assign a score to each candidate bank.

After assigning scores to each bank on the basis of these eight criteria, the credit practitioner should be able to select a lockbox bank—or at least narrow down the candidates.

If, however, when the process is completed the banks' scores are relatively close, the credit person might want to review the criteria again. If the ratings remain close, the decision may ultimately come down to selecting the bank that offers the most in terms of potential cash management benefits beyond the scope of lockbox services.

ABSTRACT SUMMARY

- Once a company justifies the economics of having a lockbox, and selects an optimal city for the lockbox, it must then select a lockbox bank.
- When selecting a bank, consider at least two or three that are located in the city that has been selected as the optimal lockbox site.
- Criteria for bank lockbox selection should include: pricing, availability schedule, service, operating hours, mail pickups, systems equipment and technology, processing method, and references.
- Select a lockbox bank or narrow down the candidates after assigning scores to each of the banks for the eight criteria.
- If the competing banks are rated fairly equal, the decision may come down to selecting the bank that offers the most in terms of potential cash management benefits beyond the scope of lockbox services.

LOCKBOX INSTRUCTIONS

Once a company has justified the economics of using a lockbox, and has selected a lockbox site and a lockbox bank, it must complete the cycle by preparing instructions indicating how the bank should handle the company's lockbox account, including the specifics of how to handle certain contingent events. The instructions will be primarily geared toward meeting the needs of accounts receivable personnel and the accounting department.

By providing instructions tailored to the company's needs — as opposed to the bank's standard instructions — the company will ensure that accounts receivable personnel are able to operate in a more efficient manner when executing AR system updates and maintenance. Putting the instructions in writing will eliminate any potential misunderstandings related to lockbox processing.

The instructions should incorporate control mechanisms for the tracking and handling of cash. Lockbox reconciliation time will be minimized by having controls in place. Credit will benefit from the special instructions for the handling of unusual and returned items.

Detailed below are representative lockbox instructions geared toward the needs of accounts receivable and accounting personnel:

1) Acceptable payee namestyles are as follows:
   (a) ABC Co.
   (b) ABC
   (c) ABC Industries
   (d) Alexander Division
   (e) DPM Division
2) Maintain a microfilm record of each check processed.
3) Do not process checks drawn on non-U.S. banks. Call accounts receivable at (201) 837-4451 to advise of receipt and return checks to:

   ABC Co. Inc.
   P.O. Box 1206
   Megion Drive
   Emerson, New Jersey 07630
   Attn: Accounts Receivable Dept.
4) Prepare photocopy of each check processed (both sides).
5) Clip together check photocopy and any material received with the check in the following order:
   (a) Check photocopy
   (b) Remittance advice

    (c)   Envelope

    (d)   Other material received

6)   Group the checks into batches of no more than 50 checks.

7)   For each check batch:

    (a)   Prepare adding machine tape on amounts of each check in sequential order. Write the batch number at the top of the tape.

    (b)   Date the batch slip according to the deposit date.

    (c)   Number each day's batches consecutively, beginning with the number one each day.

    (d)   Prepare a credit advice in duplicate for the aggregate amount of the total deposit processed including the total number of items.

8)   Mail all material first class to the address for instruction #3. On the last two workdays of each month, all remittance information is to be sent via next-day delivery.

9)   The scenarios outlined below should be handled in the following manner:

    (a)   Unsigned checks: Deposit with notation requesting check-maker's bank to obtain signature.

    (b)   Undated checks: Affix remittance envelope date.

    (c)   Postdated checks: Hold and process if dated within a three-day period. If dated beyond three days, forward checks to address for instruction #3.

    (d)   Checks marked "Payment in Full": Do not deposit. Forward checks to address for instruction #3.

    (e)   Variance in figure and written amount: Guarantee amount if an enclosure indicates correct amount. Otherwise, forward to address for instruction #3.

    (f)   Returned checks: Once the check has been returned the first time, contact Ms. R. Hunter or Mr. G. Spiro at ABC Co. and advise them of customer name, check number, dollar amount, and payor bank. Immediately redeposit check. If a check is returned a second time, contact ABC Co. and redeposit the check unless noted "Do not redeposit."

    (g)   Unacceptable payee: Contact Ms. R. Hunter or Mr. G. Spiro at ABC Co. and advise them of customer name, check number, dollar amount, and incorrect payee name. If still unacceptable, return checks to address for instruction #3.

Lockbox instructions should become a part of written credit department policy and procedure. To enhance the quality of the instructions that are submitted, credit practitioners can create a checklist to help insure against any omissions (see Exhibit 4.6).

All of these instructions should be reviewed by the company's accounts receivable, accounting, and treasury personnel to ensure that each group's needs are served. The lockbox bank should be sent a letter that outlines these instructions and asks the bank to sign a duplicate set, noting its acceptance of the instructions.

Periodically, the company might want to send a credit representative to visit the lockbox site to observe the firm's account being processed and confirm that instructions are being followed.

Exhibit 4.6
Instructions Checklist

_____ Acceptable Payee Namestyles
_____ Microfilm
_____ Non-U.S.-Bank Check Handling
_____ Photocopy: Front/Back
_____ Deposit Handling
_____ Check Handling
_____ Mailing Instructions
_____ Unsigned Check Procedure
_____ Undated Check Procedure
_____ Postdated Check Procedure
_____ Payment-in-full Handling
_____ Variance in Body & Figure (check)
_____ Return Check Handling & Notification
_____ Unacceptable Payee Handling & Notification

Deviations should be reviewed and discussed with the company's account officer at the bank or the lockbox supervisor.

Lockbox instructions should be reviewed periodically to spot any need for additions or deletions.

ABSTRACT SUMMARY

- Lockbox instructions will be primarily geared toward meeting the needs of the company's accounts receivable and accounting personnel.

- Specific instructions tailored to the company's needs should enable the accounts receivable department to operate in a more efficient manner when executing accounts receivable system updates and maintenance.

- The company should incorporate into the instructions control mechanisms for the tracking and handling of cash.

- Lockbox instructions should be reviewed with accounts receivable, accounting, and treasury personnel to ensure that each group's needs are served.

- Periodically the company would be wise to send a credit representative to the lockbox bank to confirm that instructions are being followed.

LOCKBOX ISSUES

After selecting a lockbox location and a lockbox bank, a company must make some decisions about three issues before beginning to use its new lockbox service: bank compensation for the lockbox services rendered, the disposition or movement of funds generated from daily lockbox receipts, and the communications flow for the daily lockbox receipts.

With respect to bank compensation, the company needs to decide if it will pay the bank on the basis of fees or on the basis of balances. Compensation via balances means that the firm will be required to have a predetermined amount of average daily balances left with the lockbox in order to receive the lockbox services. With a fee-basis pricing structure, there are no balance requirements and the lockbox will be compensated by fees only according to account activity.

With a fee-basis pricing structure, the company will probably be charged fees monthly or quarterly based on the activity in the account during the period in question. Typical fees are for lockbox rental, account maintenance, per-item photocopying, per-item processing, MICR encoding, data transmission, batch processing, and postage.

In the opinion of this credit professional, bank compensation based on fees is more desirable than compensation based on balances. In fact, fees are generally better when paying banks for any type of cash management service.

Companies that pay with balances sometimes end up borrowing from the bank when average balances fall below the required level. Many cash management practitioners disapprove of this practice, however, believing that borrowing to meet a balance requirement violates the cash management cardinal rule of only borrowing to fund a net cash flow shortage. A company should only borrow when it is short of funds and in need of cash, they would say.

Another problem with paying via balances is that the company runs the risk of overfunding the balance requirement without receiving compensation for the excess balances generated.

Most companies that have gone the balance route have done so because they feel that they are getting the services for free. After all, they reason, no charges are reflected in their budgets. In reality, of course, the company is not getting these services for free. Paying with balances has an implicit opportunity cost—the cost of what the company might have done with that cash if it weren't sitting idle in the bank.

When paying with balances, a company is also more subject to swings in interest rates. If rates decline, the company's balance requirements will increase. Fees, on the other hand, do not fluctuate with interest rates.

The recent trend among corporations has been to have bank compensation based on fees as opposed to balances.

The next issue concerns the disposition or movement of funds generated from the lockbox receipts. Even if the company pays for its lockbox on a balance basis, what will it have done with the daily funds that are in excess of the daily balance requirement? The most clear and logical choice is to transfer funds on a daily basis and concentrate them at the company's main bank, which is referred to as the firm's concentration bank.

In other words, the company would operate its lockbox on a quasi zero-balance basis. Everyday, all lockbox receipts would be transferred from the firm's lockbox account to its main or concentration bank. This could be done even with balances as the basis for pricing; the company could leave balances in a separate account from the lockbox receipts, which would be transferred daily to the firm's main bank.

The mode of transfer can be an electronic depository transfer check (EDTC) or a paper depository transfer check (DTC). Only wire transfer of funds will shift the availability of funds immediately from the lockbox to the concentration bank. The two other modes, EDTC and DTC, will have at least a one-day availability lag. The choice between the three concentration options becomes a function of the economics relating to the per-item concentration costs versus the opportunity savings derived due to accelerated availability.

The final issue is that of communications regarding the reporting of daily lockbox receipts. Should the company ask for a phone call at the end of the day advising it of the total receipts received? Or, should the company request a telecopy of the customer name and dollar amount for each item received for a particular day?

Another option would have the firm electronically retrieving the information via a microcomputer or a dumb terminal at the end of the business day.

The first two options will probably incur an additional small monthly fee. However, self-initiated electronic retrieval would probably not incur an additional fee. The company might determine that receiving lockbox receipt detail on a next-day basis will be satisfactory.

ABSTRACT SUMMARY

- After a company has selected a lockbox bank, it still must deal with how it will compensate the bank, how funds generated from daily lockbox receipts will be handled, and what sort of communications it will require from the bank regarding the day's lockbox activity.

- With respect to compensation, the main decision is whether the company wants to pay the bank with fees or on a balance basis.

- More and more companies are paying with fees, because they realize the implicit opportunity cost of keeping idle funds in the bank and they prefer to avoid borrowing funds just to meet a minimum balance requirement.

- Another negative of paying via balances is that when interest rates go down, minimum balance requirements go up. Fees, on the other hand, are not affected by interest rate swings.
- Many companies concentrate and transfer their lockbox receipts daily to the company's main bank, also known as the company's "concentration bank."

5
DSO

DAYS SALES OUTSTANDING:
MEASURING CREDIT DEPARTMENT PERFORMANCE

The calculation known as DSO — days sales outstanding — is one of the most valuable yardsticks for measuring credit department performance. The calculation, specifically referred to as the Last-In First-Out (LIFO) DSO method, measures total accounts receivable dollars at month-end against sales days outstanding for the current and prior months.

(All references to DSO in this text refer to the LIFO DSO method, as opposed to the Average DSO calculation or any other recognized method. The LIFO method assigns sales days outstanding in 30-day increments to period-ending AR by subtracting current and prior months' sales in successive 30-day layers until the AR balance is netted to zero. The author favors DSO analysis via the LIFO method, which employs actual sales and AR data to calculate an actual DSO as opposed to using average sales and AR data to compute Average DSO. Average DSO can be used for comparative rather than primary DSO analysis.)

Another measure that can be used to evaluate credit department personnel — a variation on DSO — is Best DSO. It measures current dollars against current month sales and prior month sales.

An analysis that combines DSO and Best DSO can provide insight into the factors that are influencing accounts receivable performance. For example, let's say the company's selling terms are net 30 days, Best DSO is 45 days, and DSO is 51 days. This tells us that six days of the DSO are attributable to delinquency (51 days minus 45 days). We can also note that extended terms have a 15-day impact on the DSO (45 days minus 30 days standard terms).

What do these figures say about collection performance? In this case, with only six DSO days attributed to delinquency, the credit department's collection efforts shouldn't be the main source of concern. The major influencing factor on AR and DSO performance appears to be the 15 DSO days attributed to extended terms.

Comparing DSO and Best DSO when reviewing the current month's performance against the prior month's is especially helpful in spotting trends with respect to delinquency and extended terms. For example, let's say the firm's current month's DSO is 51 days with a Best DSO of 45, when in the previous month DSO was 48 days and Best DSO was 41 days. What does that say about collection performance?

It says that the current month's collection performance was not really that bad. Despite the three-day increase in the DSO figure (51 days), the spread between Best and Actual DSO narrowed to six Past-Due DSO days, as opposed to seven in the previous month. The negative swing in DSO was due primarily to extended terms, which show up in a comparison of Best DSO for the two months. The swing from a Best DSO of 41 days to a Best DSO of 45 days reflects a four-day increase in extended terms — not poor collection performance.

If sales terms had remained constant (if Best DSO had remained at 41 days), then the company would have actually showed a one-day improvement in DSO in the second month (47 days).

Monitoring DSO and Best DSO, and comparing the two figures from month to month, will provide credit professionals with a clear understanding of how accounts receivable are performing. In particular, when making forecasts, they will know the limitations of their receivables. For instance, if they know that extended terms will add 15 days a month to the company's standard 30-day terms, they will never mistakenly budget DSO performance in the 35-39 day range. Unless management changes its policy toward extending credit terms, achieving that range simply will not be possible.

Knowing the levels of DSO and Best DSO will enable credit professionals to set performance goals. For instance, goals can be set for Past-Due DSO days and Extended Terms DSO days. A credit manager might ask personnel to stay within eight days for Past-Due DSO days and five days for Extended Terms DSO days.

Setting clearly defined target levels makes credit department personnel cash-flow oriented. It keeps them conscious of how DSO can be impacted by delinquency and extended terms.

By monitoring DSO and Best DSO on a monthly basis—and comparing the figures on a month-to-month basis—the credit professional is in a position to identify changes in credit or marketing philosophy that may be in conflict with cash flow and overall corporate goals.

ABSTRACT SUMMARY

- Days sales outstanding (DSO) is one of the most useful measures of cost flow and credit department performance.
- DSO measures total accounts receivable dollars at month end against sales for the current and prior months, and converts the relationship into Accounts Receivable DSO days outstanding.
- Best DSO measures only current dollars against recent sales.
- DSO – Best DSO = Past-Due DSO days.
- Best DSO – Standard Terms of Sale = Extended Credit Terms DSO days.

CALCULATING DSO

Calculating DSO for accounts receivable is a fairly straightforward exercise. It consists of quantifying outstanding accounts receivable dollars in terms of days of outstanding sales.

The only variables required to perform the Total DSO calculation are period-ending accounts receivable in dollars and recent sales. The number of sales months required for the calculation will depend on existing delinquency and extended terms.

The Last-In First-Out DSO calculation method assigns sales days outstanding in 30-day increments to period-ending AR by subtracting current and prior months' sales in successive 30-day layers until the AR balance is netted to zero.

For each sales month fully applied against AR, 30 days sales outstanding are assigned. If, in the final monthly layer, the AR balance is less than or equal to that month's sales, the remaining AR is divided by that month's sales, and the ensuing ratio is multiplied by 30 days to determine the number of sales days outstanding for the final monthly layer. To determine the final DSO calculation, each month's sales that are fully applied against AR are individually allocated 30 days sales outstanding and are added along with the final partial layer quantified in days sales outstanding to derive the LIFO DSO.

Let's now compute a DSO that is under 30 days:

Variables
July-ending AR $ 29,000
July sales 35,000

Step 1: Subtract July sales from July accounts receivable to determine if DSO is greater or less than 30 days ($29,000 – $35,000 = –$6,000)]. The answer, –$6,000, tells us that $6,000 of current month sales have been collected and DSO is less than 30 days. Had July AR been greater than July sales, then DSO would be greater than 30 days. If July AR was in excess of both June and July sales, then DSO would be greater than 60 days.

Step 2: Determine the percent of July sales represented by the $6,000 (–$6,000/$35,000 = –17.14%). This calculation tells us that 17.14% of July sales were collected, or 82.86% of July sales are still open and outstanding as July accounts receivable.

Step 3: Since we know that the DSO will be under 30 days, we want to determine how many DSO days the $6,000 collected represents of July sales (–17.14285% × 30 days = –5.14 days).

Step 4:   Add the days of July sales collected, −5.14, to the 30 days for July sales to determine the DSO (−5.14 + 30 = 24.86 days sales outstanding). In rounded terms, we arrive at a DSO of 25 days.

Now let's calculate a DSO in excess of 30 days sales:

Variables
July-ending AR $ 105,000
July sales   35,000
June sales   39,000
May sales   33,000

By quickly reviewing the variables, we can determine if the company's accounts receivable balance is greater than 30, 60, or even 90 days of sales. In this case, AR is greater than 60 days of sales but less than 90; July-ending AR, $105,000, is greater than the sum of June and July sales, $74,000, but less than the sum of May, June, and July sales, $107,000. Thus, we know that DSO is greater than 60 days but less than 90 days. Let's now perform the complete computation for July DSO in step form:

Step 1:   Subtract current month July sales (30 days) from July AR ($105,000 − $35,000 = $70,000).

From this calculation, we know that DSO is greater than 30 days, specifically that $70,000 of AR is older than 30 days and is uncollected. We now go to the next prior month's sales layer (June sales) to perform Step 2.

Step 2:   Subtract the next prior month's (June) sales from the $70,000 of receivables greater than 30 days outstanding ($70,000 − $39,000 = $31,000).

Step 2 reveals that DSO is greater than 60 days by $31,000. Note that the $31,000 of remaining AR uncollected is less than the next month's layer of sales; May sales were $33,000. Thus, we can determine that DSO is greater than 60 days but less than 90 days.

For Step 3, we want to determine what percent the $31,000 of open AR represents of May's 30 days of sales.

Step 3:   Divide the remaining open AR greater than 60 days sales by May sales ($31,000 / $33,000 = 93.9%).

In this case, 93.9% of the third month's sales are open and uncollected receivables. Based on this percentage, we can now determine in Step 4 how many May DSO days are outstanding for May sales.

Step 4:   Multiply 93.9% times the number of days representing May sales. (93.9% × 30 days = 28.18 DSO days.) The answer, 28.18 DSO days, represents DSO days that are in excess of 60 days.

Step 5:   Add the DSO days in excess of 60 days to the 60 days sales outstanding that were fully allocated in Steps 1 and 2. (28.18 May sales + 30 days July sales + 30 days June sales = 88.18 DSO days.) The DSO for this example is 88.18 or, rounded off, 88 DSO days.

Hopefully the firm's terms of sale are net 60 days or greater.

To recap: The LIFO DSO calculation assigns days sales outstanding in 30-day increments to period-ending AR by subtracting current and prior months' sales in successive layers until the AR balance is netted to zero.

DSO calculations and theory can be applied to any level for accounts receivable. A credit practitioner can derive DSO in total, or by product line, subsidiary, risk group, or individual customer.

Increases or decreases to DSO directly impact cash and accounts receivable balance sheet positions. Thus, DSO is one of the best tools for gauging the strength of cash flow. Monitoring and controlling the various DSO calculations discussed in this chapter should be a key component of any company's credit and cash flow strategy.

ABSTRACT SUMMARY

- DSO is merely a way of quantifying outstanding accounts receivable dollars in terms of outstanding sales. The Total DSO calculation allocates sales days to the total outstanding accounts receivable dollars open.

- Variables required to calculate DSO are period-ending accounts receivable and current and prior months' sales.

- The number of sales months required for the calculation is a function of existing delinquency and extended terms.

- DSO calculations and theory can be applied to any level of accounts receivable. Days sales outstanding can be derived in total, or by product line, subsidiary, risk group, or individual customer.

- DSO is one of the best measures of cash flow. Increases or decreases in DSO directly impact cash and accounts receivable balance sheet positions.

CALCULATING BEST DSO

Best DSO is a days sales outstanding calculation that takes into account current accounts receivable dollars only. Monitoring Best DSO and Total DSO, and comparing the two, will yield insights about extended terms and Past-Due DSO days.

A brief example will help explain how. Let's say the company's Total DSO is 47 days and its Best DSO is 38 days. What does this tell a credit or treasury professional? First, for a customer with standard net 30-day terms, it says that eight of its Best DSO days can be attributed to extended credit terms (38 Best DSO – 30 days standard terms = 8 DSO days). Second, by subtracting the Best DSO from the Total DSO, a credit/treasury professional can determine past due or delinquent DSO days. In this case, 47 (Total DSO) minus 38 (Best DSO) equals 9 (Past-Due DSO days).

Calculating Best DSO is virtually the same as calculating Total DSO. Again, the only difference is that Best DSO is calculated based on current accounts receivable dollars, while Total DSO is calculated on total accounts receivable dollars (which includes current and past-due accounts receivable dollars).

The variables needed to calculate Best DSO are current accounts receivable dollars and recent sales. The Best DSO calculation allocates sales days to the current accounts receivable dollars outstanding and not past due. In essence, the Best DSO allocates sales days outstanding to current and non-past-due receivables using the same LIFO method employed to calculate Total DSO.

Let's calculate Best DSO for the month of July with the following hypothetical variables:

July-ending AR	$ 105,000
July-ending current AR	60,000
July sales	35,000
June sales	39,000
July Total DSO	88 Days
Standard terms	30 Days

First, we check to see if July-ending current AR is less than or equal to July sales. In this case, July-ending current AR of $60,000 is greater than July sales of $35,000.

(If July-ending current AR was less than or equal to July sales, we would then multiply the ratio of July current AR to July sales by 30 days to derive the Best DSO.)

Let's now begin the Best DSO calculation.

Step 1: Subtract July sales from July-ending current AR ($60,000 - $35,000 = $25,000).

Answer: The difference is $25,000 of July-ending current AR
that is greater than 30 days outstanding.

Next, compare the remaining uncollected current AR over 30 days old ($25,000) to the next prior month's sales for June ($39,000) to determine if there will be carryover or residual uncollected current AR that would be allocated to May sales. Since uncollected current AR over 30 days old of $25,000 is less than June sales of $39,000, we now want to determine the ratio of remaining uncollected current AR to June sales.

Step 2:   Divide $25,000 uncollected current AR over 30 days outstanding
by $39,000 June sales.

Answer: 64.1% of June sales are current and in the form of uncollected
accounts receivable.

We now want to determine how many June DSO days are represented by the 64.1% of June sales.

Step 3:   Multiply 64.1% times 30 DSO days representing June sales.

Answer: 19.23 DSO days of June sales are outstanding.

Next, we want to add the DSO days accounted for and allocated in Steps 1 and 3 to derive Best DSO.

Step 4:   Add 19.23 DSO days (June sales) to 30 DSO days derived
from July sales.

Answer: Best DSO is 49.23 or, rounded off, 49 days.

What does this tell us? To begin with, if the Best DSO is 49.23 days on standard terms of net 30 days, then 19.23 days of Best DSO can be attributed to extended credit terms. Additionally, we learn that 39 DSO days can be attributed to Past-Due DSO days (88 Total DSO – 49 Best DSO = 39).

A credit/treasury professional can gather some revealing insights into accounts receivable using Best DSO analysis. Not only can Best DSO be calculated based on Total DSO, but it can also be calculated by product lines, group, subsidiary, risk group, or individual customer.

Extended credit terms have an implicit opportunity cost. Thus, Best DSO is one of the best measures of lost cash flow. Increases or decreases to Best DSO and Past-Due DSO days directly impact cash and accounts receivable balance sheet positions.

Monitoring and controlling the Best DSO and Past-Due DSO should be a key component of a company's credit and cash flow strategy.

ABSTRACT SUMMARY

- Monitoring Best DSO along with Total DSO will yield insights about extended terms and Past-Due DSO days.

- By subtracting Best DSO from the company's standard terms of sale, one can determine the number of DSO days that can be attributed to extended credit terms.

- The difference between Best DSO and Total DSO is Past-Due DSO days.

- Calculating Best DSO is virtually the same as calculating Total DSO. The only variance is that Best DSO is calculated using current accounts receivable dollars instead of total accounts receivable dollars.

- In addition to being calculated based on the company's Total DSO, Best DSO can also be calculated for specific product lines, as well as for groups or subsidiaries within the company. It can also be calculated by risk group or for an individual customer.

DSO CALIBRATION

When reporting days sales outstanding to senior management on a monthly basis, why not report the DSO aged out in days?

For example, let's say month-end total accounts receivable is $22.55 million, current dollars is $20.1 million, past due is $2.45 million, and Total DSO is 46 days on net 30-day terms. One DSO day would equal $490,000 ($22.55 million / 46), past due would be equivalent to five DSO days ($2.45 million / $490,000), and current dollars of $20.1 million would equate to a Best DSO of 41 days ($20.1 million / $490,000). Also, let's say that past-due dollars are aged out as follows:

1-30 days past due	$ 1,470,000
31-60 days past due	323,000
61-90 days past due	167,000
91-120 days past due	88,000
120+ days past due	402,000
Total past due	$ 2.45 million

The credit manager could report DSO and past-due information in the following format:

	Dollars ($ Millions)	DSO Days
Total AR	$ 22.550	46
Current AR	20.100	41
Past-Due AR	2.450	5
1-30 Past Due	1.470	3
31-60 Past Due	.323	1
61-90 Past Due	.167	0
91-120 Past Due	.088	0
120 + Past Due	.402	1

By calibrating the DSO and aging the Past-Due DSO days as well as the past-due dollars, a credit/treasury manager can get a good feel for past-due slippage from one aging category to the next.

Calibration should enable the credit practitioner to more readily explain both positive and negative changes in monthly past-due DSO days outstanding.

By aging out the Past-Due DSO days, a manager can gauge if there are significant aged-out items that may be deemed uncollectable and which can impact the company's profit and loss statement (P&L). When past-due data is quantified and aged out in DSO terms, it enables managers to take preventive action.

ABSTRACT SUMMARY

- DSO calibration ages out Past-Due DSO days.
- DSO calibration can be part of a credit or treasury manager's DSO reporting format.
- DSO calibration allows one to monitor AR for past-due slippage.
- Preventive measures can be taken when past-due data is quantified and aged out in DSO terms.
- DSO calibration can be used as a tool to prevent significantly aged-out items from impacting the firm's profit and loss statement (P&L).

FINE-TUNING DSO: CALCULATING DSO IN TENTHS

Credit professionals looking for more precision in their DSO analyses should calculate DSO days in tenths rather than rounding them off to the nearest whole number. Calculating days sales outstanding in tenths provides a much more accurate measure of DSO and cash flow.

When DSO calculations are rounded off to the nearest whole number, there is the possibility of overstating or understating DSO performance. In fact, by rounding off, credit practitioners run the risk of miscalculating DSO by nearly an entire DSO day. Such miscalculation can occur when breaking down monthly DSO into Total DSO, Best DSO, and Past-Due DSO, as well as when comparing all of these DSO measurements to the prior month's or prior year's performance.

Let's take a look at two examples of how "rounded DSO" can paint a misleading picture. In the first example, we will compare a month's rounded components of Total DSO, Best DSO, and Past-Due DSO days to the same components being calculated in tenths. Let's begin by establishing that the actual Total DSO calculation is 47.4 days and Best DSO is 39.5 days. If we round off during the calculation, we will arrive at a Past-Due DSO of 7 days (47 − 40 = 7). However, a more precise calculation shows that Past-Due DSO days equal 7.9 (47.4 − 39.5 = 7.9). Clearly, rounding off here understates true Past-Due DSO days by almost a full day. Rounding off can overstate DSO performance in the same fashion.

In the second example, we will compare the current month's DSO to the prior month's DSO. Ultimately, we want to measure the month-to-month increase or decrease in total DSO days. Let's say that the current month's DSO is 45.5 days and the prior month's DSO is 43.4 days. If those figures are rounded off, the comparison would be between 46 days for the current month and 43 days for the prior month. That comparison shows a three-day increase in Total DSO over the prior month. But, of course, this overstates the true DSO increase — which is actually 2.1 days.

As these examples illustrate, calculating the various DSO measures to tenths and making comparisons in tenths will yield a precise accounting for DSO. The more precise the calculation is, the truer will be the picture of the credit department's contribution to cash flow.

ABSTRACT SUMMARY

- Days sales outstanding calculations will be more precise if figures are calculated to the nearest tenth rather than the nearest whole number.
- Rounding off DSO measurements can throw off Past-Due DSO figures by almost a full DSO day.

■ Rounding off DSO measurements can also skew month-to-month comparisons by up to one full DSO day. For instance, when DSO has actually only increased by 2.1 days from one month to the next, a rounded off calculation could indicate an increase in DSO of three full days.

■ DSO calculations can be both under and overstated when numbers are rounded off.

■ Calculating DSO in tenths will provide a more accurate and precise picture of DSO performance and the credit department's contributions to cash flow.

TRACKING CUSTOMER DSO

The credit department should track DSO on an individual-customer basis for all the company's high-risk accounts. The customer DSO is a valuable yardstick for assessing existing customer risk.

DSO is a measurement of outstanding accounts receivable quantified in sales days. By monitoring a high-risk customer's six- to 12- month DSO trend line, a credit professional can learn a lot about the company's anticipated cash flow and credit risk.

DSO for high-risk customers is the type of data that the credit department will want to share with marketing and senior financial management in the course of making key credit decisions. For instance, a customer on 30-day terms but with a rising DSO that has hit 100 days will certainly merit serious discussion. Excessive customer DSO levels should be red-flagged by credit practitioners.

There are some companies that rely on their accounts receivable payment systems to provide them with information on payment performance — and thus anticipated cash flow and credit risk. However, the truth is that most AR payment systems don't reflect current delinquency when calculating payment performance. On such systems, delinquent invoices aren't always reflected until they are paid. For example, early in the year the AR payment system might show that a certain company has a 100% prompt payment performance. However, the case might be that the customer had a zero balance at the previous year end, paid off its first purchase of the year, but has yet to pay off another bill since that time. The customer could conceivably have a past-due balance of $150,000 on total year-to-date sales of $175,000, but the AR system still shows the company as a 100% prompt payer.

Furthermore, some accounts receivable software calculates payment performance on the total number of invoices paid but doesn't take into account the dollar value of invoices paid. Under this scenario, a company might have a customer that makes 25 payments over the year. The customer promptly pays off 20 invoices totaling $20,000 but slow pays five invoices totaling $250,000. What might the AR system report about such a customer? That's right — 80% prompt!

Calculating a high-risk customer's individual DSO requires the same information as calculating Total DSO. The credit practitioner will need the customer's month-end accounts receivable balance and its sales over the past few months. The number of months sales needed will depend on the total delinquent and extended-term AR dollars outstanding.

To take the exercise a step further, credit practitioners can calculate individual high-risk customers' Best DSO. This way they can can determine the number of Total DSO that are current and those that are past due.

To determine an individual customer's Delinquency DSO days, credit practitioners need to subtract the customer's Best DSO from its Total DSO. The number of days that can be attributed to extended credit terms can be calculated by sub-

160

tracting Best DSO from the firm's standard terms of sale. For example, let's say the customer's Total DSO is 74 days, its Best DSO is 45 days, and standard terms of sale are net 30 days. Twenty-nine of those days are Delinquency DSO days (74 total minus 45 best), and 15 DSO days can be attributed to extended credit terms (45 best minus 30 standard terms). The 29 Past-Due DSO days reveal the customer is not meeting the agreed-upon 45-day extended terms arrangement.

The high-risk customer DSO reporting format for internal and management purposes might be configured as follows:

Name	Balance	Past Due	DSO	Best DSO	Delinquent DSO Days	Extended Terms DSO
ABC	$ 75,000	$ 50,000	90	30	60	0
DEF	$100,000	$100,000	60	0	60	0

Once this information is charted, a credit practitioner can calculate Total DSO, Best DSO, and Delinquency DSO days for the entire high-risk group in the aggregate. For example, the sum of all customer balances may equate to an 89-day DSO when calculated on total high-risk sales.

An additional strategy is to compare high-risk accounts receivable balances in Total DSO days, Best DSO days, and Delinquent DSO days against the total company DSO. For example, total company accounts receivable might be $1 million with a 50-day DSO. High-risk balances are $200,000, of which $100,000 is past due. The total high-risk balances represent 10 DSO days ($200,000 / $1 million = 20%; 20% × 50 DSO days = 10 days) and high-risk past-due balances are five DSO days of the 50-day total company DSO.

DSO should not be looked upon only as a macro tool for analyzing total company accounts receivable. It can also be used on the micro level to analyze individual customer risk. By using DSO on the individual customer level and in the aggregate for high risks, a company can determine the quality of its accounts receivable portfolio.

Programming this discipline on spreadsheet software such as Lotus 1-2-3 takes no more than one to two hours.

The automated spreadsheet can save much time while generating accurate customer calculations in rapid fire.

ABSTRACT SUMMARY

- The credit department should track DSO on an individual basis for all high-risk customers in the company's accounts receivable portfolio.
- The customer DSO is an important yardstick for assessing existing customer risk.

- To calculate monthly DSO for high-risk customers, a credit professional will need the customer's month-end accounts receivable balance and its sales over the past few months.

- DSO is not a macro tool alone. Calculating DSO on individual customers and in the aggregate for high risks can provide credit practitioners with valuable information about the quality of their accounts receivable portfolios.

- These DSO calculations can be performed on a personal computer; it only takes a few hours to program the spreadsheet software.

MONITORING AND TRACKING PROJECTED
DSO BEFORE MONTH END

Credit managers make monthly DSO projections. Once those projections are made, however, they don't have to wait until month-end reports are prepared to see how accurate they were. DSO projections can be monitored on an ongoing basis.

Monitoring DSO performance for a particular month — during that month — enables managers to revise DSO forecasts. This is important because DSO also impacts the projected dollar level of receipts for the month.

The process of monitoring DSO is relatively simple. Let's say that for the month of June a credit manager has projected a DSO of 41 days. Using the build-up and roll-forward methods for projecting month-end accounts receivable and monthly cash receipts respectively (see Build-Up, in Chapter 7, p. 227), he can contrast the moving level of actual receipts during the month to the required level of receipts from the roll-forward calculation to attain the 41-day DSO (see Roll-Forward, in Chapter 7, p. 229).

To calculate the required projected receipts, using projected sales he will first quantify what a 41-day DSO amounts to in terms of month-end accounts receivable dollars. Next, he will take the month's actual opening accounts receivable, add projected sales, and subtract the projected month-end accounts receivable level to derive the required projected cash receipts to generate a 41-day DSO.

Let's say that the calculations indicate that $10 million in receipts is required in order to meet the 41-day DSO projection. As a final step, he will allocate over the workdays in the month the projected $10 million cash receipts using either the cycle value approach from history (see Time Series, in Chapter 7, p. 231) or by using a totally subjective process.

Mondays are usually the strongest cash receipts days for the month while Tuesdays are usually the weakest. What the credit manager wants to do is compare actual cumulative receipts to the required cumulative projected receipts required to attain the 41-day DSO. He should chart daily receipts information in columnar form (see Exhibit 5.1).

If there is a shortfall of cumulative actual to cumulative projected receipts, a credit manager will know that DSO is off target, and he will be able to quantify the remaining actual receipts required in order to make up the current shortfall. In the exhibit, actual receipts are lagging the required projected level by $1.72 million.

By dividing the $10 million by 30 days, the credit manager can determine that one DSO day equals $333,333. Since actual receipts are lagging by about $1.72 million, then it is clear that he is faced with a more than five-day DSO deviation from the projected 41 days ($1.72 million / $333,333 = 5.16 DSO days).

The credit manager can now assess the likelihood of making up the $1.72 million shortfall over the remaining June cash days. If necessary, he can adjust the DSO projection upward and lower the receipts projection. This information will be

Exhibit 5.1
Tracking Projected DSO vs. Cash Receipts Required

Date	Day of Week	Days Actual Receipts	Cumulative Actual Receipts	Moving Level Required	Cumulative Actual vs. Forecast (+Fav./–Unfav.)
June 17	Tuesday	$250,000	$4,050,000	$5,775,000	–$1,725,000
June 18	Wednesday	325,000	4,375,000	6,075,000	–$1,700,000
June 19	Thursday	400,000	4,775,000	6,425,000	–$1,650,000
June 20	Friday	205,000	4,980,000	6,700,000	–$1,720,000

extremely helpful to treasury personnel when they are forecasting monthly receipts and disbursements to determine month-end cash and loan positions.

Near the end of any given month, the credit manager can calculate a very accurate preliminary DSO estimate by contrasting the cumulative actual receipts to the required projected receipts. The excess or shortage can be quantified into decreases or increases to the projected DSO.

Monitoring and tracking projected DSO can be a very strong cash management tool for both credit and treasury. Through the use of relatively simple methodologies, credit managers can keep their fingers on the pulse of DSO and cash receipts performance. Once again, this process of monitoring and tracking DSO in midstream can be repeated for individual customers. Monitoring and tracking on either the micro or macro level will enhance decision making and accounts receivable reporting.

ABSTRACT SUMMARY

- A credit or treasury professional need not wait until the end of the month to gauge the accuracy of monthly DSO projections.
- By monitoring and tracking projected DSO during the month, the credit department has the option of revising DSO forecasts, and thus the projected dollar level of receipts for the month.
- By contrasting the moving level of actual receipts during the month to the required level of forecasted receipts, one can determine if a DSO projection is on target.
- If there is a shortfall of cumulative actual to cumulative projected receipts, it means that the DSO forecast is off target.
- Monitoring and tracking DSO projections on either the micro or macro level will enhance decision making and accounts receivable reporting.

6

CASH MANAGEMENT

WHAT DOES IT MEAN WHEN WORKING CAPITAL INCREASES?

Credit personnel have traditionally looked upon increases in working capital, net of cash increases, as having a favorable impact on the financial statement they are analyzing. But that isn't always the case. An increase in working capital is a positive factor only if the company's financial circumstances and growth mode warrant the increase.

Recall T account theory, which says that for every debit there must be a corresponding credit offset entry to complete the entry. This means that on a cash flow basis an increase in accounts receivable (debit) either comes at the expense of a reduced cash balance (credit), an increased loan balance (credit), or an increase in accounts payable balance (credit). An increase in accounts receivable cannot come at the expense of equity.

Companies that are in a mature stage are looking to reduce working capital in order to generate cash for investments or to reduce their loan balances. Reductions to working capital usually translate into reductions of accounts receivable and days sales outstanding. A reduction of inventory, barring a writedown, translates into newly created accounts receivable that should be readily convertible into cash within a short time period. Thus, reductions of working capital usually free up cash that is tied up in accounts receivable or inventory.

Increases to accounts receivable and inventory are actually cash detractors rather than cash generators; they come at the expense of either reducing cash, increasing the loan balance, or increasing accounts payable. Hidden within the increase in working capital may be an increase in long-term borrowings to fund the increase.

Let's look at the impact on a cash flow basis of a $300,000 month-end increase of accounts receivable on either cash, loans, or accounts payable (see Exhibit 6.1). In Case One, cash is decreased by $300,000 if loans or accounts payable are not offset. In Case Two, loans are increased by $300,000 if cash is not reduced or payables increased. In Case Three, payables must increase by $300,000 if cash is not reduced or if loans are not increased. One way or the other, accounts receivable increases from period to period will offset one of the three accounts.

In actuality, a customer's unexplained or unanticipated increase in working capital is generally a sign of its poor management of accounts receivable and inventory.

Remember, certain mature and/or growth-mode customers will require either increases in accounts receivable or inventory buildups due to their increased level of business activity.

So, a credit practitioner shouldn't jump to any conclusions before reviewing the entire financial statement.

Exhibit 6.1
T Account Illustration of Offsetting Impact
of Increase In Accounts Receivable

CASE ONE: Accounts Receivable Increase with Offset to Cash

	Accounts Receivable				Cash	
	Debit	Credit			Debit	Credit
Opening Balance	500					
				Opening Balance	1000	300 Entry
Increase	300					
				Ending Balance	700	
Ending Balance	800					

CASE TWO: Accounts Receivable Increase with Offset to Loans

	Accounts Receivable			Loans	
	Debit	Credit		Debit	Credit
Opening Balance	500			700	Opening Balance
Increase	300			300	Entry
Ending Balance	800			1000	Ending Balance

CASE THREE: Accounts Receivable Increase with Offset to Accounts Payable

	Accounts Receivable			Accounts Payable	
	Debit	Credit		Debit	Credit
Opening Balance	500			400	Opening Balance
Increase	300			300	Entry
Ending Balance	800			700	Ending Balance

Any analysis can be taken a step further by comparing the subject's working capital performance to established industry standards. One might even be advised to call the customer to discuss the increase in working capital to make sure that the increase is justified or required as a result of favorable rather than declining business conditions.

ABSTRACT SUMMARY

- Increases in working capital, net of cash increases, can have a negative impact on cash flow.
- T account theory states that increases in accounts receivable come at the expense of reducing cash or increasing loans or accounts payable.
- Working capital reductions of accounts receivable and inventory generate cash flow.
- Long-term borrowings sometimes offset increases in working capital.
- A credit professional needs to understand the nature of a working capital increase before passing judgment on the customer.

THE MAJOR CUSTOMER STUDY: INSIGHTS INTO CASH FLOW, DSO, AND RISK

A study of major customers can tell a credit practitioner a lot about the company's cash flow, DSO, and the level of risk posed by its accounts receivable portfolio. After all, a commonly accepted rule of thumb is that about 80%+ percent of a company's receipts are derived from 10 percent to 15 percent of its customers—the major customers.

But which companies exactly should be included in a major-customer study? The credit practitioner conducting such a study will need to set a threshold based on sales volume. For some companies, the list of "major customers" will include only customers with annual purchases of at least $500,000 a year. For others, the sales-volume cutoff point might be much lower, say $10,000.

In performing the study, the credit practitioner should chart out the following information on each major customer in a columnar format: customer name, city/state, product purchased, terms, balance, past due, credit limit, current year sales, prior year sales, current year payment history, prior year payment history, current year high credit, prior year high credit, most recent net worth (if available), balance/credit limit ratio and credit limit/net worth ratio.

Once this information is compiled in a columnar format, the credit practitioner can classify the company's risk by credit line distribution and corresponding payment performance, as shown in Exhibit 6.2. (In the example, note that delinquency is more tolerated with lower exposures—accounts with lines under $50,000.) To fine-tune the analysis, one could assess major customer risk by reviewing credit line distribution and payment performance by product line as well.

Knowing the payment patterns for groups of customers with selective credit limits enables the credit practitioner to understand the positive and negative impact that these customers can have on AR and DSO performance, and ultimately cash flow in the form of trade receipts.

Now, having performed a study of major customers, when credit practitioners project a decline in DSO, they can look at individual customers to see if the projection is realistic.

Additionally, once the credit department develops a list of major customers based on sales volume, it can use the same list to perform a customer remittance study, a ship date/invoice date audit, or when justifying lockbox economics.

ABSTRACT SUMMARY

- Major customer studies yield insights into cash flow, DSO, and risk.
- Generally, 80%+ percent of a middle-market company's receipts are derived from 10 percent to 15 percent of its customers.

Exhibit 6.2
Major Customer Payment Performance by Credit Line Group as of 7/31/XX (In 000's)

Major Customer Credit Line Group	AR Balance	Percent of Credit Line Group AR	Percent of Major Customer AR
Lines Under 50K Paying Prompt	1,213	69.75%	7.41%
Lines Under 50K Paying Slow 1-15	288	16.56	1.76
Lines Under 50K Paying Slow 16-30	109	6.27	.67
Lines Under 50K Paying Slow 31+	129	7.42	.79
Lines Under 50K Totals	1,739	100.00	10.63
Lines 50-99K Paying Prompt	2,299	76.33	14.05
Lines 50-99K Paying Slow 1-15	307	10.19	1.88
Lines 50-99K Paying Slow 16-30	226	7.50	1.38
Lines 50-99K Paying Slow 31+	180	5.98	1.10
Lines 50-99K Totals	3,012	100.00	18.41
Lines 100-249K Paying Prompt	5,215	83.28	31.87
Lines 100-249K Paying Slow 1-15	611	9.76	3.73
Lines 100-249K Paying Slow 16-30	238	3.80	1.45
Lines 100-249K Paying Slow 31+	198	3.16	1.21
Lines 100-249K Totals	6,262	100.00	38.26
Lines 250K & Over Paying Prompt	4,156	77.65	25.40
Lines 250K & Over Paying Slow 1-15	555	10.37	3.39
Lines 250K & Over Paying Slow 16-30	345	6.45	2.11
Lines 250K & Over Paying Slow 31+	296	5.53	1.81
Lines 250K & Over Totals	5,352	100.00%	32.70
Major Customer Totals	16,365		100.00%

- Risk should be classified according to credit limit thresholds.
- An analysis of the company's major customer credit limit/net worth ratios will reveal how leveraged the overall accounts receivable portfolio is.
- The major customer listing can be used as the data base for a customer remittance study, a ship date/invoice date audit, or when justifying lockbox economics.

PERFORMING A CUSTOMER REMITTANCE AUDIT

The credit department should perform a customer remittance audit periodically. Objectives of the audit will be to confirm the geographic configuration of the lockbox network, measure customer mail float, correct internal coding and "remit to" errors, identify remote mailing and remote disbursing customers, and adjust for changes in customers' accounts payable locations. Ultimately, the objective is to accelerate incoming cash flow and its deposit availability by redirecting misdirected customer remittances.

Companies that aren't using the lockbox services of a bank can still benefit from this type of cash flow audit.

Performing the audit will put the credit professional in a good position to redirect and accelerate cash flow. The information derived from the audit can help the company improve DSO performance through reductions in mail and check presentation float. Cash tied up in the mail will be available sooner for investments or loan paydowns.

The audit should include the high-dollar volume customers included in the major customer study.

To perform the audit, select a recent month of cash receipts activity that is reflective of recent major customer remittance patterns. Collect all check remittances for the major customers, along with the envelopes that the checks were sent in. Chart the following information based on the checks and envelopes (see Exhibit 6.3).

When this information is charted, credit practitioners can compare the "bill to" locations in the billing system to the postmark locations that are stamped on the envelopes. In this way, they can correct internal coding and billing errors. For instance, they might find that the "bill to" address has changed due to a consolidation of payables resulting from a corporate takeover.

Having the correct "bill to" address will eliminate invoices getting lost in the customer's system. Correcting the "bill to" location will also eliminate mail and check presentation float.

Additionally, the check date should be compared to the postmark date to identify customers who are generating unearned cash discounts. In some cases, those discounts are being claimed based on the check date rather than the later postmark date. The postmark date should be subtracted from the date the check was received at the lockbox to determine the number of days of mail float.

Take a look again at the information charted in Exhibit 6.3. As a result of coding this customer in the billing system for a Flint, MI, "bill to" location—instead of the correct Philadelphia location—the creditor probably added two or three days to the mail float. In addition, at least a one-day delay in availability was probably sustained.

Comparing the payor bank location to the customer's postmark location, the credit professional will also be able to determine if the customer is remote disburs-

Exhibit 6.3
Customer Remittance Audit Format

Customer	Bill To Location	Check Date	Check Amount	Postmark Date	Postmark City, State	Lockbox City, State	Date Ck. Recv'd	Days Mail Float	Payor Bank	Payor City, State	Comments
ABC Co.	Flint, MI	9/20	$39,000	9/25	Phil., PA	Chic., IL	9/29	4	Mellon	Phil., PA	Change box to Philly Reconfirm bill to

ing. This refers to the practice of remitting checks that are drawn on distant banks. An example of remote disbursement would be a Philadelphia company mailing a remittance check that is to be drawn on a Spokane, WA, bank.

The customer's goal in remote disbursing the check is to give the appearance of prompt payment while maintaining the use of funds for a longer period of time. Of course, this hurts the supplier who effectively suffers a loss of cash flow. Therefore, in most cases, the supplier identifying a remote disbursing customer should confront the customer about the practice.

Another customer practice that can slow down payments is remote mailing. An example of remote mailing would be a customer located in Baltimore that sends remittance checks to a company location in Portland, OR, where the checks are then mailed to vendors.

The customer remittance audit can also help a credit professional identify and put a stop to remote mailing.

(To verify the depth or scope of the study, add up the entire check amount column for all the major customer remittances audited, and compare this total to the total cash receipts for the month in question.)

There is no question that the information provided by one of these audits can significantly enhance the availability on incoming receipts. Adjustments in "sold to" and "remit to" locations will accelerate cash flow, and redirecting remittances to the proper lockbox will reduce mail float and thus minimize monthly past due. Performing this audit will make the credit department more cash flow conscious and aware of its impact on the treasury department.

At a minimum, the audit should verify the geographic fit of a lockbox network, alert the practitioner to any unnecessary lockbox locations, and identify any additional lockbox sites that may be required.

The customer remittance audit is just another way for the credit department to document and quantify its link to the cash flow timeline.

ABSTRACT SUMMARY

- The customer remittance audit should include the company's major customers with the highest sales volume.
- The audit's goals are to confirm the geographic configuration of a lockbox network, measure customer mail float, correct internal coding and "remit to" errors, identify remote mailing and remote disbursing customers, and adjust for changes in customer accounts payable locations.

- The audit can help a company to get quicker access to funds that have been previously tied up in the mail.

- Adjustments made in "sold to" and "remit to" locations will accelerate cash flow, and redirecting remittances to the proper lockbox will reduce mail float and check presentation delays.

- An added benefit of performing the customer remittance audit is that credit employees are reminded of their vital role in generating corporate cash flow.

SHIP DATE/INVOICE DATE AUDIT

Performing a ship date/invoice date audit is another means of internally accelerating cash flow. The objective in performing the audit is to identify any inefficiencies in the firm's order entry/billing system. More specifically, the goal is to identify where the company might be assigning free payment days to customer invoices.

The unintentional granting of free payment days occurs when there is a lag in time between the actual shipment date and the invoice date. For example, a shipment to a customer might be made on Monday the 19th, but the invoice might be dated Friday the 23rd. In this case, the customer is granted four free payment days. If the company's terms of sale are net 30 days, the customer in effect is granted 34-day terms (see Exhibit 6.4).

This may not appear to be a very critical problem. However, when customer invoices are paid one, two, or three days after month end, the unintentional assignment of free payment days and the associated opportunity costs appear more glaring.

The assignment of unintentional free payment days can potentially impact month-end past-due levels, DSO, and, most important of all, the level of month-end cash and accounts receivable for balance sheet purposes. (As was discussed earlier in this chapter, increases in accounts receivable at month-end are offset by reductions to cash or by increases to the company's loan balance. Conversely, month-end reductions of accounts receivable favorably impact and increase cash, or the cash flow can be utilized to reduce borrowings.)

In conducting the study, the credit practitioner can randomly select invoices or audit an entire month's billings covering the major customer data base. Or, one might select invoices from a billing date or a range of billing dates. Either way, the following information needs to be charted in a columnar format:

Customer Name	Invoice Number	Invoice Amount	Ship Date	Invoice Date	Days Lag
ABC Co.	61722	$215,700	6/20/89	6/24/89	4

If the company has more than one order entry/billing location, the credit practitioner might want to add an additional column labeled "order entry location." This will enable the credit practitioner to determine whether the various order entry locations are performing at different levels of efficiency. It might be that one particular billing location is assigning free payment days, while others are not.

If the credit practitioner is able to identify any problems with the timing and dating of shipments versus the invoice dates assigned and generated, the problems should be documented and discussed with the appropriate billing or order entry personnel. During the course of these discussions, make sure to highlight the impact

Exhibit 6.4

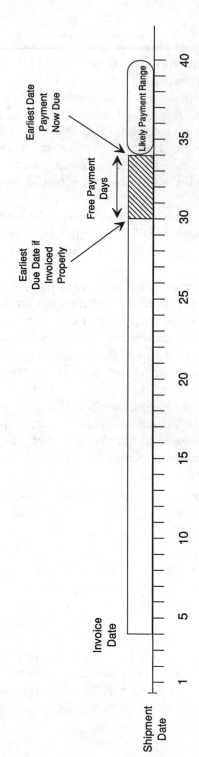

of the invoicing lag(s) in cash flow terms. That means relating the invoicing lag(s) to the opportunity costs of foregoing the month-end collections.

Exhibit 6.5 provides the formula for an opportunity cost calculation. In the example, note that the opportunity cost of generating a $215,700 invoice four days beyond the shipment date is $251.65. If a company with $200 million in annual sales averaged a four-day lag on all invoicing, its annual opportunity cost would be $233,333, based on a 10.5 percent cost of funds.

Tightening up any lag between ship date and invoice date will not only accelerate or increase cash flow, but it will also help the company promote a more efficient image to customers.

Exhibit 6.5
Opportunity Cost of Free Payment Days

Variables

A = Invoice Amount   215,700
B = Opportunity Cost Rate   10.5%
C = Days Invoice Delay   4
D = Opportunity Cost of Invoice Delay

Formula

$$[(A \times B) / 360] \times C = D$$

Answer

$$[(215,700 \times 10.5\%) / 360] \times 4 = 251.65$$

ABSTRACT SUMMARY

- Ship date/invoice date audits represent one way of accelerating corporate cash flow.

- Lags between shipment date and invoice date represent free payment days.

- Inefficiencies in the company's order entry/billing system may be assigning free payment days to customers.

- Free payment days negatively impact month-end DSO, past-due, cash, and loan positions.

- When discussing invoicing lags with the appropriate order entry/billing personnel, quantify the free payment day opportunity costs of delayed cash flow.

THE TOTAL EXPOSURE CONCEPT

When assessing customer risk and credit exposure, credit personnel tend to look only at the customer's total accounts receivable balance due—the longtime yardstick for measuring potential bad-debt losses and lost or delayed cash flow. However, to really assess risk and total credit exposure and their impact on working capital and cash flow, one must also consider two other variables: 1) pending orders produced and ready to ship, and 2) unfilled order backlog.

If goods are produced for a customer that becomes insolvent or otherwise unable to pay, it may be difficult to resell the pending orders produced and/or the order backlog at list price to other customers. At best, the company might be able to unload the goods at a distressed price. This can hurt, considering that the firm has probably already paid the supplier of raw materials for the product.

If the original customer is unable to pay for the product, the supplier could end up losing out-of-pocket expenses for raw materials as well as the anticipated cash flow on the material produced, shipped, and invoiced.

In the case of a payout arrangement with the troubled customer, the supplier may not incur a bad-debt loss, but it still has working capital tied up in the accounts receivable balance, the pending orders produced, and the backlog of orders. Clearly there is an implicit opportunity cost involving the supplier's cost of funds to borrow or the rate of lost interest on potential investments due to the delay in cash flow and out-of-pocket expense incurred.

The lesson here is that when there are extended cash flow problems with customers, make sure that the marketing department is aware of the situation. It will do the company no good to have marketing knocking on such a customer's door looking for new orders and increased market share.

Additionally, a credit practitioner should contact production and warehouse personnel and advise them to halt or delay production of the unfilled order backlog.

One way to track total customer exposure would be to perform an ongoing roll-forward analysis, as shown in Exhibits 6.6 and 6.7.

This proactive credit-risk management method enables the practitioner to chart the customer's total customer exposure at any point in time during the month and be in a position to take corrective action if necessary. The exhibits also reveal that exposure assessments can be made by reviewing the total exposure/present balance, total exposure/credit limit, and total balance/credit limit ratios.

To formalize control of marginal customer exposures, an electronic mail communications network can be established via PC. The network would link credit with production, warehousing/shipping, and customer service and marketing personnel regarding specific production, customer inventory, and shipment restrictions.

To recap: When monitoring customer exposures, it's important to closely watch the customer's total accounts receivable and past-due balances. It's also necessary to keep an eye on pending orders ready to ship and the order backlog. Taking these precautions will allow the credit practitioner to contain items that may

Exhibit 6.6
Total Exposure Formula

Months Opening Accounts Receivable Balance

plus (+)

New Orders Shipped During the Month to Date (Invoiced and Uninvoiced)

plus (+)

Orders Ready to Ship

plus (+)

Order Backlog

less (-)

Cash Received Month to Date and Credits Issued

equals (=)

Total Customer Exposure to Date (Moving Customer Exposure)

Exhibit 6.7
Total Exposure Sample Calculation

Customer Name Analyzed:	PJM Co. Inc.
Analysis Date:	September 20, 1989
Credit Limit	$100,000
Months Opening Balance	$ 96,109
plus (+)	
New Orders Shipped Month to Date (Invoiced and Uninvoiced)	10,501
plus (+)	
Orders Ready to Ship	7,500
plus (+)	
Order Backlog	21,000
less (-)	
Cash Received Month to Date & Credits Issued	12,750
equals (=)	
Total Customer Exposure to Date [a]	$122,360
Present Balance as of Analysis [b]	$ 93,860
Total Exposure/Present Balance Ratio	130.36%
Total Exposure/Credit Limit Ratio	122.36%
Total Balance/Credit Limit Ratio	93.86%

[a] Total Customer Exposure to Date $122,360 = ($96,109 + 10,501 + 7,500 + 21,000 − 12,750)

[b] Present Balance as of Analysis $93,860 = ($96,109 + 10,501 − 12,750)

impact the total company picture with respect to working capital management and cash flow.

ABSTRACT SUMMARY

- The customer's total accounts receivable balance does not represent the company's full exposure for potential bad-debt losses.
- Accounts receivable balance plus pending orders produced and unfilled order backlog are more representative of the total credit exposure and potential risk.
- Allocating inventory and future production for excessively slow-paying customers has a negative impact on working capital and cash flow.
- A credit practitioner should review orders pending and unfilled backlog for workout and marginal customers to contain the company's total exposure and working capital outlays.
- The formula for tracking moving customer exposure is shown in Exhibit 6.6.

DOLLARIZING THE CREDIT FUNCTION

Credit managers need to scc the big picture. They need to see it, their department personnel need to see it, and they need to make sure that management sees it. For that reason, calculating and reporting accounts receivable detail and days sales outstanding (DSO) figures is only the first step in the reporting process.

Credit department personnel and top management must be made to understand what those figures mean to the company in terms that have a real impact. The way to achieve this goal is to show how changes in accounts receivable and DSO are directly related to the company's month-end cash and loan balances. Specifically, this can be achieved by comparing changes in the company's month-end cash and loan balances to the current month's DSO performance vs. budget, and by comparing the cash and loan changes to current month's DSO performance vs. prior month's DSO performance — in the latter case by performing a "what-if" analysis.

On a cash flow basis, month-to-month increases in accounts receivable are offset by reductions to cash or increases in the company's loan balance. Conversely, when the credit department is able to reduce accounts receivable from one month to the next, that reduction will show up as an increase in cash or a reduction to the firm's loan balance.

In accounting lingo, one might say that an increase in AR is a debit to receivables, which is offset by either a credit to cash (reduction) or by a credit to the loan balance (increase).

Credit managers should take advantage of this relationship to give greater focus to the work of their departments and to better illustrate the impact that credit activities can have on their corporations. They can do this by making correlations between changes in their accounts receivable/DSO numbers and their cash/loan balances.

Let's try an example. Exhibit 6.8 contrasts March 1989 AR and DSO performance with budget and prior month's performance, along with March 1989 loan activity summarized. March 1989 DSO was 58 days, one day under budget but four DSO days better than February 1989 DSO performace. The ending March 1989 loan was $9.3 million, reflecting a $100,000 paydown for the month of March.

Now let's make some correlations and see how the credit department DSO performance contributed to the loan reduction. First, we want to compare actual March 1989 DSO performance to March 1989 budget in order to determine the impact on the loan balance (see Exhibit 6.9). For March, DSO was one day under the budget of 59 days DSO. We now want to quantify in AR terms what the budgeted 59-day DSO would have been in dollars. In essence, we are grossing up the 59-day budgeted DSO using March and February sales. The 59-day budget is calculated, based on March sales of $14,154 and February sales of $12,728:

Step 1:   Allocate 30 days DSO to March sales of $14,154

186

Exhibit 6.8
Accounts Receivable Totals

MARCH 1989
(000's)

Product	Balance	Past Due	DSO	Budget	Best DSO	Past-Due DSO
Flat Rolled	16,179	4,251	73	73	56	17
Carbon	6,760	918	44	49	38	6
Distribution	3,273	346	46	46	43	3
Total	26,212	5,515	58	59	47	11

FEBRUARY 1989

Product	Balance	Past Due	DSO	Budget	Best DSO	Past-Due DSO
Flat Rolled	16,061	3,933	75	74	55	20
Carbon	7,768	1,604	46	48	38	8
Distribution	3,243	364	47	48	46	2
Total	27,072	5,901	62	62	48	14

MARCH LOAN ACTIVITY
(000's)

March Opening Loan	$9,400
Loan Change (+ Unfavorable/– Favorable)	–100
March Ending Loan	$9,300

Exhibit 6.9
Cash Flow Gain or Shortfall versus Budget Comparison

	DSO Days	AR Dollars (000's)
Actual AR	58	$26,212
Budgeted AR	59	26,458
Cash Flow Gain/– Shortfall		$ 246

Since the DSO is 59 days, in Step 2 we must allocate and quantify what 29 DSO days represent of February sales.

Step 2:   Multiply $(^{29}/_{30})$ times full February sales of $12,728
$$(((^{29}/_{30}) \times \$12,728) = \$12,304)$$

Step 2 reveals that $12,304 of February sales equate to 29 DSO days for February.

For Step 3, to complete the calculation we want to sum the March and February sales allocated in Steps 1 & 2, respectively.

Step 3:   Add March sales of $14,154 representing 30 DSO days
to February sales of $12,304 representing 29 DSO days
for February sales to derive the AR balance for the 59-day
DSO budget.
($14,154 (30 days March) + $12,304 (29 days February)
= $26, 458 AR on the 59 day DSO budget.)

The difference between March actual DSO of 58 days, representing AR of $26,212, and March budget's DSO of 59 days of $26,458 is $246 (see Exhibit 6.9). The credit department can now state that performance of 58 days DSO (one day under budget) represents 246% of the actual loan paydown for the month (see Exhibit 6.11). Or we can say if DSO was at the budget level of 59 days, the company would have had to borrow $146,000 ($100,00 loan reduction minus $246,000 lost budgeted savings = -$146,000 cash shortfall).

If actual March 1989 DSO was over budget, the credit department would have negatively contributed toward increasing the firm's loan balance.

Next, let's compare March 1989 DSO performance to February 1989 performance. DSO in March was at 58 days, reflecting a four-DSO-day decline from February. We now want to compare February DSO of 62 days to March's actual of 58 days by quantifying February's 62-day DSO into accounts receivable balances with sales data used to calculate March DSO. This way the two monthly DSO figures of 58 and 62 days are computed on a like-for-like basis. The difference between actual March accounts receivable and February's 62-day DSO expressed with March's sales data represents the cash flow savings or loss that impacts the firm's cash and loan positions (see Exhibit 6.10).

The 62-day February DSO expressed with March's sales data is based on March sales of $14,154, February sales of $12,728, and January sales of $13,468:

Step 1:   Allocate 30 days DSO to March sales of $14,154.

Since February DSO is greater than 60 days, we want to fully allocate 30 days DSO to February sales in Step 2.

Exhibit 6.10
March vs. February Performance Comparison

	Actual DSO Days	AR Dollars (000's)
March Actual AR	58	$26,212
February DSO Using March Data	62	27,780
Cash Flow Gain/ – Shortfall	4	$ 1,568

Step 2:   Allocate 30 days DSO to February sales of $12,728.

Since February DSO was 62 days, in Step 3 we must allocate and quantify what two DSO days represent of January sales.

Step 3:   Multiply ($\frac{2}{30}$) times full January sales of $13,468
($(\frac{2}{30}) \times \$13,468 = \$898$)

For Step 4, to complete the calculation, we want to sum the March, February, and January sales allocated in Steps 1, 2, and 3, respectively.

Step 4:   Add March sales of $14,154 representing 30 DSO days to
February sales of $12,728 representing 30 DSO days
and January sales of $898 representing two DSO days to
derive the accounts receivable balance for the February
62-day DSO, on a like-for-like basis ($14,154 (30 days March)
+ $12,728 (30 days February) + $898 (two days January)
= $27,780 or 62 DSO days using March data).

Note that the difference between $27,780 and March's actual $26,212 (58 DSO days) is a cash savings of $1,568. In other words, March's improved DSO performance represents 1568% of the month's loan balance reduction (see Exhibit 6.11). Or we could say that if March DSO performance had been flat at 62 days the company would have had to borrow $1.468 million rather than the $100,000 loan paydown ($100,000 loan reduction minus $1,568,000 lost DSO savings = -1,468,000 cash short-fall).

Exhibit 6.11
March Loan Correlations

March Opening Loan	9,400,000
Loan Change (+ Unfavorable/– Favorable)	–100,000
March Ending Loan	9,300,000
March Actual vs. Budget (– Unfavorable/+ Favorable)	246,000
March Actual vs. Budget Contribution to Change	246.00%
March Actual vs. February (– Unfavorable/+ Favorable)	1,568,000
March Actual vs. February Contribution to Change	1568.00%

Thus, we can see how making these correlations can assist the credit department in its dealings with top management. But how can this type of process help credit personnel see the big picture, and how can it help them focus their efforts?

The answer is formalized and calendarized monthly DSO objectives. The credit manager can set performance objectives for the entire department based on these. For example, the credit department might attempt to ensure in the aggregate that DSO performance for the year will be a net offset to the loan balance. Or for a company that is in an investment mode, the target could be that DSO performance will be a net contributor to an increase in the company's cash position.

The point is that credit professionals should be thinking in terms of cash flow. By doing so, they can get into the habit of quantifying the impact that their efforts have on the cash flow timeline. The first step in making this a habit is to understand the impact that a reduction of accounts receivable and DSO can have on the company's cash and loan positions.

ABSTRACT SUMMARY

- Correlating accounts receivable balances and days sales outstanding performance to cash and loan positions enhances the reporting and analysis of cash flow.
- Month-to-month increases in accounts receivable are offset by reductions to cash or increases to the loan balance.

- Month-to-month changes in past due and DSO have a direct relationship to the month-to-month changes in cash and loan positions.
- Credit can contribute to cash flow, but it can also detract from cash flow.
- Formalized DSO objectives can be directly pegged to cash and loan needs and performance.

DOCUMENTING CONTRIBUTIONS
TO PROFITABILITY

If credit professionals only had to make credit decisions regarding customers or potential customers with clean credit histories and strong financial conditions, the job would be simple. That's why, in terms of their role as credit granters, credit practitioners must be at their best when making decisions regarding marginal customers.

Selling to marginal customers and monitoring their payment habits and financial viability is really the "bread and butter" of a credit practitioner's job. Anyone can grant credit to a General Motors or IBM. Where credit professionals really earn their pay is by making tough, informed decisions about marginal customers that can lead to increased profitability without exposing the company to excessive risk.

In effect, credit professionals have their greatest opportunity to add to corporate profits when they make sound and documented credit decisions involving marginal customers.

In order for the credit department's contributions to be fully recognized, profits generated through selling to high-risk accounts need to be quantified. The way to accomplish this is to compare the additional variable business costs incurred to the incremental profitability associated with selling marginally classified accounts. "Variable business costs" simply refers to the non-fixed costs such as raw materials and direct labor costs that the company incurs in order to operate the business. The theory is that revenues from marginal customer sales less the added variable costs equals incremental profitability to the firm—as fixed costs will be absorbed whether or not the sales are being made to the marginal customers.

The first step in this process will be to develop criteria for identifying which customers are to be considered high-risk or "marginal." These criteria will vary from company to company.

Once marginal customers have been identified, the credit professional can begin to quantify the credit department's contribution to incremental profitability by charting the information shown in Exhibit 6.12.

Let's take a look at how we can arrive at an incremental contribution to profits of $54,465.02 based on sales to ABC Company (see Exhibit 6.12). The first step is to derive the cost of slow payments (see Exhibit 6.13, Step 1). This is calculated by multiplying the $100,000 year-to-date sales figure by the percentage of slow payments, in this case 55 percent. The answer here is that $55,000 of sales are paid slow.

The $55,000 is then multiplied by the cost of funds of 8.5 percent. The answer, $4,675, is then divided by 360 days to obtain the daily cost of slow funds, $12.99. (Note: The calculation assumes a 360-day year, as short-term debt instruments are generally calculated on that basis.) The daily cost of slow funds is then

Exhibit 6.12
Documenting Credit Department Contribution to Profitability

Customer	YTD Sales	% Slow Payments	# of Days Slow	Cost of Slow Payments	# of Days Extended Terms	Cost of Extended Terms	Funds Cost	Variable Cost %	Variable Costs	Incremental Contribution
ABC Co.	$100,000	55%	14	$181.81	15	$354.17	8.5%	45%	$45,000	$54,465.02
DEF Co.	$ 50,000	0%	0	$ 0	0	$ 0	8.5%	45%	$22,500	$27,500.00

Exhibit 6.13

Step 1/Cost of Slow Payments

Variables
A = Year-to-Date Sales
B = Percentage of Slow Sales
C = Cost of Funds
D = Number of Days Slow
E = Cost of Slow Payments

Formula
$(((A \times B) \times C) / 360) \times D = E$

Answer
$(((100{,}000 \times 55\%) \times 8.5\%) / 360) \times 14 = \$181.81$

Step 2/Cost of Extended Terms

Variables
F = Year-to-Date Sales
G = Cost of Funds
H = Number of Days Extended Terms
I = Cost of Extended Terms

Formula
$((F \times G) / 360) \times H = I$

Answer
$((100{,}000 \times 8.5\%) / 360) \times 15 = 354.17$

Step 3/Incremental Contribution

Variables
J = Year-to-Date Sales
K = Variable Cost Percent on Sales
L = Cost of Slow Payments
M = Cost of Extended Terms
N = Incremental Contribution

Formula
$J - ((J \times K) + L + M) = N$

Answer
$100{,}000 - ((100{,}000 \times 45\%) + 181.81 + 354.17) = \$54{,}464.02$

multiplied by the 14 days of slow payments to equal the year-to-date cost of slow payments, $181.81.

The next step is to calculate the cost of extended terms (see Exhibit 6.13, Step 2). In this case, $100,000 is multiplied by the funds cost of 8.5 percent and the answer is divided by 360 days to derive the cost of one day's extended terms, $23.61. This figure is multiplied by the 15 days additional terms to derive a year-to-date cost of extended terms of $354.17.

The variable cost percentage of 45 percent is then multiplied by the year-to-date sales, $100,000, to arrive at $45,000, the year-to-date variable costs associated with those sales.

The three figures that have been calculated—year-to-date costs for slow payments, extended terms, and variable expenses—are then added together ($181.81 + $354.17 + $45,000). The sum, $45,535.98, is then subtracted from total sales of $100,000 to equal the incremental contribution of $54,464.02 (see Exhibit 6.13, Step 3).

Once the incremental contributions to profit are calculated for individual customers, the credit professional might consider determining incremental contributions to profits by product or division, if fixed breakouts are available by product line. The contributions will differ significantly if costs vary a lot between products or divisions.

To derive a net-net figure, the credit practitioner can subtract bad-debt write-offs for any of the marginally classified accounts against the product or division totals.

In addition to quantifying credit's contribution to profitability, this exercise might reveal that the company is operating at a loss with specific customers. In some cases, once fixed costs are factored into the equation with the marginal customers' slow payments and the cost of extended terms, the product or division will show narrow or zero net margins.

However, the main emphasis here is to illustrate how the credit department can use these calculations to show senior management how the department is contributing to profitability by selling to marginally classified customers. Reports based on the calculations above might be sent to top management on a monthly or quarterly basis.

By quantifying its contribution to profits, credit is once again documenting its important role in the cash flow timeline.

ABSTRACT SUMMARY

■ The credit professional's greatest opportunity for contributing to profits—and his greatest opportunity for exposing the company to unnecessary risk—is in his role of granting credit to marginal customers.

- In order to have their contributions fully recognized, credit professionals need to quantify incremental profits generated through selling to high-risk accounts.

- Important calculations involved in quantifying these profits include: year-to-date costs of slow payment, year-to-date costs of extended terms, and year-to-date variable costs associated with sales to marginal customers.

- Where possible, the credit professional might want to also calculate incremental profits from high-risk sales by product or division.

- Monthly or quarterly reports to senior management detailing these incremental profits will draw further attention to the link between the credit department and company profitability.

CREDIT AS A PROFIT CENTER

The credit department has not been traditionally looked upon as a corporate profit center. And that's ironic, considering that the credit department is responsible for 95 percent or more of a company's total monthly cash flow.

Clearly the credit department should be viewed as a profit center and reported on in those terms. The department can both add to cash flow and reduce cash flow. It adds to cash flow through reductions in accounts receivable. It negatively impacts or detracts from cash flow when it allows days sales outstanding to rise or when bad-debt write-offs occur. Each of these credit yardsticks, as well as others, can be quantified into revenues and costs generating a credit department profit and loss statement.

Credit managers need to look at their departments in the terms of an income statement. Revenue sources for the department include:

- Monthly DSO reductions below budget quantified at cost of funds;
- Interest income from notes or assessing finance charges for late payments;
- Incremental profitability from selling to high-risk customers (see Documenting Contributions, in Chapter 6, p.192);
- Bad-debt recoveries; and
- Credit saves. (The term "credit save" refers to a successful attempt at reducing or "zeroing out" a high-risk customer's balance prior to the customer's bankruptcy. At-risk cash flow that is collected as opposed to being lost as a bad debt.)

Credit costs that the department can incur include:

- Credit department salaries;
- Hardware and software expense;
- Bad-debt write-offs;
- Monthly DSO increases above budget;
- Mercantile and other subscription expenses; and
- Travel and living expenses incurred in visiting customers and attending seminars.

The sum of revenue less credit costs equals the credit department's net profitability or net loss (see Exhibit 6.14). In the exhibit, note that the PLM Co. credit department has operated profitably and in the black by $865,000. The credit revenue/credit cost ratio is a very favorable 5.29:1. Factoring out incremental profitabil-

Exhibit 6.14
PLM Co. Credit Department P&L Analysis
Covering Year-End 12/31/88

REVENUE SOURCES

Monthly DSO Reductions Quantified	$ 121,400
Interest Income	10,500
Incremental Profitability	851,109
Bad-Debt Recoveries	4,118
Credit Saves	79,433
Total Revenue Sources	$1,066,560

   less (–)

CREDIT COSTS

Credit Department Salaries	$ 126,500
Hardware/Software Costs	22,000
Bad-Debt Write-offs	16,603
Monthly DSO Increases Quantified	23,110
Mercantile & Other Subscription Expenses	3,500
Travel & Living Expenses	9,717
Total Credit Costs	$ 201,430

   equals (=)

Credit Department Net Profitability	$ 865,130
Credit Revenue/Cost Coverage Ratio	5.29

ity, credit revenues still exceed costs by $14,201, while coverage ratio is a positive 1.07:1.

When credit managers start thinking of their department activities in this way, then obviously their first goal will be to operate in the black. Beyond that, credit managers can set more optimistic goals relating to both the revenue and cost components of their "income statement."

Credit managers with this profit-center mentality are more likely to engage in a conscious effort to recover bad-debt write-offs. They might also set budgets for travel and living expenses by forecasting potential out-of-state trips.

In fact, the credit department will be more successful if credit managers devise formal credit and cash flow strategies to operate in the black. They should start with DSO and develop a collections plan to reduce Past-Due DSO days. Then they might focus on a whole host of questions related to cash flow:

Are receipts being directed to the correct lockbox location? Have I performed a ship date/invoice date audit recently to enhance cash flow? Are there any potential credit-save candidates that require immediate action? What measures can I take to minimize these potential bad-debt write-offs?

How else can my department maximize cash flow?

Formalize this game plan, get it approved by top management, and put it into action. The result will be a credit department functioning as a profit center that can quantify its contributions to the corporation's net profitability.

ABSTRACT SUMMARY

- Although the credit department is responsible for almost all of the company's cash flow, it has not traditionally been looked upon as a corporate profit center. But it should be.

- The credit department can contribute to cash flow and it can negatively impact cash flow.

- Credit department "revenue sources" include monthly DSO reductions, interest income from notes or finance charges, profits generated through selling to marginal customers, debt recoveries, and credit saves.

- Costs incurred by the credit department include salaries, data processing costs, bad-debt write-offs, monthly DSO increases above budget, subscription expenses, and travel and living expenses.

- The credit department is likely to be more successful—and achieve greater recognition—if credit managers devise formal credit and cash flow strategies for operating in the black.

ADVISING CUSTOMERS OF DISCOUNT BENEFITS

Customers may not be aware of the dollars they could save by taking advantage of the discount terms your firm offers for early payment. By telling clients they can save dollars and showing them how much, you can both build customer goodwill and improve your company's bottom line.

Increased customer discount activity translates into increased monthly cash flow for your firm. It also means improved accounts receivable liquidity, reduced customer exposures, and lower monthly days sales outstanding (DSO). It also reduces the loan balance of net borrowers and increases the volume of investible funds for net investors.

Some firms encourage customers to take advantage of early payment discounts when their bank financing dries up. They either can't borrow for some reason or they have exceeded their bank line of credit. Getting customers to pay faster is a way of boosting cash flow without more borrowing.

The first step to getting more customers to pay early is to educate them to the benefits of early payment. A letter from the credit department should quantify how much a customer saves by paying early and explain, in simple terms, the economics of discounting.

There are two ways to quantify the benefits of early payment. The first approach, the *discretionary method,* is fairly simple. It compares the benefits of discounting against two scenarios. In the first, you compare the benefits of discounting against having the payment amount in a 0 percent interest checking account. In the second scenario, you compare the savings generated by paying early against the interest earned by investing the payment amount.

Assumptions:

> Payment amount due = $ 100,000
> Terms = 1% 10; Net 30
> Investment Rate = 6%

Scenario 1: Early payment vs. Idle funds

$100,000 x 1% early payment discount =$1,000.00
$1,000 (early payment savings) x 6% (interest rate earned
       for remaining 20 days) = $3.29
Monthly savings for taking 10-day payment discount = $1,003.29
Annual savings (Monthly savings x 12) = $12,039.48

Scenario 2: Early payment vs. investing

$100,000 x 6% (interest earned on funds invested for 10 days) = $164.38
$100,000 x 1% (savings generated by early payment) = $1,000.00
Savings for taking 10-day payment discount = $1,164.38
x 6% investment for remaining 20 days = $3.83
Gross savings for taking 10-day payment discount = $1,168.21
− ($100,000 x 6%) for 30 days = −$500.00
Net monthly savings for taking 10-day payment discount = $668.21
Annual savings (Net monthly savings x 12) = $8,018.52

Scenario 2 quantifies for the customer the opportunity cost or effective interest rate of paying on the due date as opposed to taking a discount at 10 days.

Next, let's calculate the benefit of early payment using the *effective interest rate* approach. This method calculates the interest rate cost for paying in net 30 days as opposed to paying the invoice discounted by 1 percent in 10 days. If the customer's cost of funds to borrow is less than the effective interest rate then the customer should borrow and discount.

Assumptions:
Terms 1% 10; Net 30
Discount (D)= 1%
Discount Date Due (DD) is the 10th day
Net day due (N) is the 30th day

The formula is computed as follows:

Effective interest rate or opportunity cost = $[D/(1 - D)] \times [365/(N - DD)]$

Opportunity Interest Cost = $[.01/(1.0 - .01)] \times [365/(30 - 10)] = 18.43\%$

In this case, by paying in 30 days the customer is effectively borrowing from the vendor at a rate of 18.43 percent. If the customer can borrow at a lower cost of funds, then it makes good economic sense to do so and pay the invoice within 10 days and get the discount.

In your letter to customers, highlight the potential costs of not discounting as well as the benefits derived from discounting trade invoices. You could enclose the letter with invoices. Or, you could address the letter to the customer's CFO or controller. In either case follow up with a phone call to major customers to clarify any questions they may have relating to discounting. Ultimately, discounting is a win-win situation for both the vendor and its customers.

ABSTRACT SUMMARY

- Increased customer discount activity translates into increased monthly cash flow, improved AR liquidity, reduced customer exposures, and reduced monthly DSO ratio.
- Send a letter quantifying and detailing in simple terms the economic benefits of discounting for customers.
- Quantify the discount benefit to the customer by using the *discretionary* or *effective interest rate* approach.
- The *discretionary* approach utilizes two scenarios to document the merits of discounting. Discounting vs. having idle checking funds, and discounting vs. investing.
- The *effective interest rate*, or opportunity cost, approach derives a cost of funds rate for borrowing from the supplier to pay in 30 days 100 percent of the invoice versus paying 99 percent in 10 days. If the customer's cost of borrowing is less than the effective interest rate it makes sense for the customer to borrow and pay early to earn the discount.

REQUESTS FOR EXTENDED CREDIT TERMS

When reviewing requests for extended credit terms, credit professionals need to keep two factors in mind. One is the cost of delayed cash flow that will be incurred by granting such requests. The second factor, sometimes overlooked, is whether individual requests fall within federal price discrimination guidelines.

A credit practitioner can keep a handle on the first factor—the cost of delayed cash flow—by calculating Best DSO. This term refers to the days sales outstanding (DSO) calculation that computes DSO based on current accounts receivable dollars only. In the Best DSO calculation, past due is netted out.

The difference between the company's Best DSO and its standard credit terms are the DSO days that can be solely attributed to extended credit terms. For example, if Best DSO is 39 days and standard terms are 30 days, then nine days of the Best DSO can be attributed to extended credit terms. How else could the nine DSO days beyond the standard 30-day terms still be classified as current and not past due?

Knowing the number of DSO days that can be attributed to extended credit terms will give the credit professional a clear picture of how extended terms are affecting corporate cash flow and DSO performance.

Federal price discrimination laws may have an even greater impact on extended credit term requests, however. According to the Robinson-Patman Act, credit terms must be treated as part of price. In order for extended credit terms to be in compliance with the federal law, the request for such terms must be an unsolicited price change based on financial hardship or a request to meet a competitive situation.

Given this law, sales personnel cannot offer new and existing customers extended terms because they want to get or keep their foot in the customer's door. Robinson-Patman dictates that terms cannot be used as a marketing tool unless there is a competitive situation to be met.

Clearly, all companies should have formalized procedures for the review and disposition of customer requests for extended credit terms. The procedure should be designed to ensure legal compliance with Robinson-Patman while providing a formal mechanism for placing corporate accountability with the marketing department.

The formal procedure should have four phases: 1) The salesperson receives the request; 2) the salesperson prepares an extended credit terms form that documents the request's validity; 3) the marketing manager recommends the request; and 4) the request is approved by the director of marketing, the treasurer or controller, and the credit manager (see Exhibit 6.15).

The formalized review mechanism enables one to quantify the opportunity cost and profitability of the customer's request for extended credit terms. With a formal procedure in place, all levels of credit, treasury, marketing, and senior management are kept aware of any potential changes or deviations in credit and marketing philosophies. In addition, all levels of management are made aware of the working capital, cash flow, and risk implications of granting extended credit terms requests.

The formalized mechanism helps prevent the abuse of extended credit terms. Granting extended terms to some companies would be either unprofitable or simply too risky. But the mechanism will also enable the treasurer or controller to factor the impact of total extended terms requests into short-term cash flow forecasts and short- and long-range working capital requirements.

Granting extended credit terms without documentation or justification can lead to legal problems; the company could be engaging in price discrimination without even being aware of it. Thus, a company would be wise to have legal counsel review its formal procedure to make sure it complies with the Robinson-Patman Act.

ABSTRACT SUMMARY

- Two factors should impact requests for extended credit terms: the cost of delayed cash flow and federal price discrimination guidelines.

- Credit professionals can gauge the cost of delayed cash flow using the Best DSO calculation. Best DSO lets the credit practitioner determine exactly how many DSO days can be attributed solely to extended terms.

- The federal law known as the Robinson-Patman Act dictates that, in order to be in compliance, an extended credit terms request must be an unsolicited price change based on financial hardship or a request to meet a competitive situation.

- All companies should have a formal procedure for the review and disposition of customer requests for extended credit terms.

- The formal review mechanism will enable the company to quantify the opportunity cost and profitability of the proposed extension of credit terms; it will also ensure that the marketing department is accountable for its role in extending credit terms.

Exhibit 6.15
Flow Chart Covering Requests for Extended Credit Terms

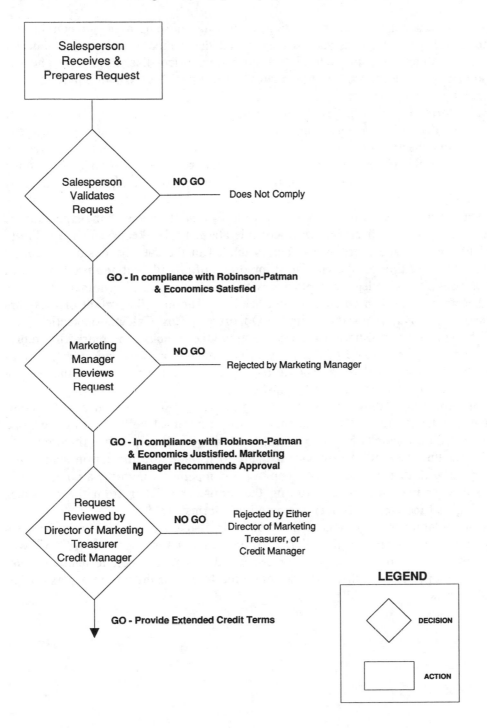

THE EXTENDED CREDIT TERMS REVIEW AND APPROVAL FORM

A formal mechanism for recommending, reviewing, and approving or denying extended credit terms requests should ensure that the company does not violate the Robinson-Patman Act, the federal law governing price discrimination. The key component of the process is the Extended Credit Terms Review and Approval form (see Exhibit 6.16).

The form should be prepared by the marketing representative for review and approval or denial by the marketing manager, the director of marketing, the credit manager, and the treasurer or controller. The marketing manager will only recommend or deny the request, whereas the credit manager, the treasurer or controller, and the director of marketing will pass final judgment and either approve or deny the request.

The form serves several purposes. It ensures that all levels of management are aware of the business decision under consideration. It also keeps management apprised of the cost and profitability factors related to the specific customer request for extended credit terms. Perhaps most important of all, diligent and prudent use of the form should ensure legal compliance with respect to price discrimination.

The form is broken down into four sections. The most important of these are the Purpose and Duration section and the Opportunity Cost Calculation section.

The Purpose and Duration section (Section One) requires the marketing representative to list the purpose of the request, documentation provided, and the duration of the request. This section should clearly elaborate the purpose of the request in order to show compliance with Robinson-Patman.

The Robinson-Patman Act states that terms are part of price. In order to comply with the law, a request for extended credit terms must be an unsolicited price change based on financial hardship or a request to meet a competitive situation.

Under Purpose and Duration, make sure to include documentation supporting compliance with this law, such as a copy of a competitor's invoice, a competitor's price list, a competitor's letter offering the terms, or a letter from the customer requesting that the company meet a competitor's terms.

Documenting the duration of the request is also important. If the customer's financial condition improves or the competitive situation no longer exists, there will be no legal reason or justification for continued extended credit terms. The customer needs to know that there is a definite time frame for the temporary extension of credit terms.

Exhibit 6.16
Extended Credit Terms Review & Approval Form

To: Marketing Manager/Region _____
     Director of Marketing
     Credit Manager
     Treasurer

Re: _____   _____
     (Customer's Complete Trade Style)   (Headquarters, City & State)

1. Purpose & Duration

    * Purpose of Request (Check off purpose)
      ___ To meet competition (attach documentation)
      ___ To accommodate customer due to exceptional financial or operating problems

    * Documentation Provided (Check off documentation)
      ___ Invoice copy
      ___ Price list
      ___ Competitor's letter offering terms
      ___ Customer's letter offering terms
      ___ Other (Explain)

    * Duration of Request
      Beginning with shipments dated _____ and ending with shipments
          dated _____

2. Product Demographics

    * Product Information
      Products involved _____ Required credit line _____
      Existing terms _____ Proposed terms _____
      Order entry shipping point _____ Plant location _____

    * Tentative Shipment Schedule
      Projected month of delivery
          (1) (2) (3) (4) (5) (6) (7) (8) (9) (10) (11) (12) Total
      Dollar value of shipments

      __ __ __ __ __ __ __ __ __ __ __ __ ____

    * Marketing Evaluation
      Current year sales to customer _____
      Current percent of business _____
      Prior year sales to customer _____
      Estimated sales volume next 12 months if terms approved $ _____
      Profit on sales for specific product _____
      General desirability, growth potential, deduction frequency and other
          marketing factors to be considered _____
      _____

(Exhibit 6.16 continues on next page)

Exhibit 6.16 (continued)

3. Opportunity Cost Calculation

    - Variables
        - (a) Estimated Sales $ _____
        - (b) Cost of Funds % _____
        - (c) Number of additional days with new terms _____

    - Calculation

    _____ (×) _____ ÷ 360 (×) _____ = $ _____
    Variable A   times   Variable B divided by 360 times   Variable C Opportunity Cost

4. Recommendation and Approval

    Recommended by _____   _____
    Marketing Manager   (Date)

    Approved by   _____   _____
    Credit Manager   (Date)

    _____   _____
    Treasurer   (Date)

    _____   _____
    Director of Marketing   (Date)

If properly executed, the Purpose and Duration section ensures legal compliance and sets a specific expiration date for the terms accommodation.

The Opportunity Cost Calculation (Section Three) determines the financial costs the company will incur by granting the extended credit terms. The calculation can be performed as follows:

1. Multiply the estimated sales during the time frame by the company's cost of funds.
2. Divide the figure derived above by 360 (days) to determine the cost of one day of extended terms.
3. Multiply the one-day cost by the total number of days by which terms are being extended to derive the final opportunity cost to the firm.

For example, say that estimated sales will be $100,000 over the extended terms time frame, the cost of funds is 8.5 percent, and the number of additional days will be 30. The calculation would be performed as follows:

1. $100,000 × 8.5% = $8,500
2. $8,500/360 = $23.61 (cost of extending terms one day)

3. $23.61 \times 30 = 708.33 (opportunity cost)

Approval or denial of the extended credit terms request will be much easier once the company knows the opportunity cost.

Other sections of the form include:

- Product Demographics (Section Two). This section requires marketing to review and justify the marketing benefits of providing the extended credit terms. Marketing must also indicate the tentative shipping schedule over the next 12 months.

Marketing is forced to commit to a shipping schedule it believes to be realistic. And, based on this information, credit can estimate how high the company's exposure will be once extended terms have been factored in. Depending on the shipment schedule and new terms, the customer's required credit line could present an exposure problem.

Under the marketing evaluation subsection, marketing must review current and prior year sales, market share (current percent of business), and profit on sales, and then indicate why the business is desirable. Based on these product demographics, the marketing representative or the marketing manager may simply choose not to pursue the business any further. The marketing manager would then simply withhold a recommendation.

- Recommendation and Approval (Section Four). The marketing manager recommends approval or denies the request. If a recommendation is offered, the form is reviewed for potential approval by the credit manager, the treasurer or controller, and the director of marketing. Cross-functional ground rules should be established for the disposition or appeal of rejected requests.

The formal review process puts the marketing department in a better position to make a solid and detailed business recommendation. It also places some of the accountability for credit terms extension with the marketing department.

Marketing will be forced to legally document and quantify the economics relating to the customer's request for extended credit terms. Furthermore, by having the director of marketing approve the request, accountability will be placed at the highest level of the marketing department.

But don't forget that: treasury and credit must also review and approve the request. So these departments will share accountability with the marketing department.

ABSTRACT SUMMARY

- The key component of a formal process for reviewing extended credit terms requests is the Extended Credit Terms Review and Approval form.
- The form should be prepared by the marketing representative for review by the marketing manager, the director of marketing, the credit manager, and the treasurer or controller.
- The two most important sections in the form are the Purpose and Duration section and the Opportunity Cost Calculation section.
- The form will ensure that all levels of management are aware of the cost and profitability factors related to the request for extended credit terms.
- The form will also ensure that the marketing department remains accountable for the business decision, along with credit and treasury.

RECOVERING LOST OR HIDDEN CASH FLOW

Many companies have significant dollars of lost or hidden cash flow that with a concerted effort can be converted to "found money" or cash flow.

In many cases, hidden cash flow can be recovered through the resolution and collection of old items that are aged out over 90 days past due. The old items could include invoices skipped, collectable customer deductions, short payments, unearned customer discounts, and interest or service charges due for late payments. All of these potential items may have aged out against the cash flow timeline. But, through a planned effort, the credit department can try to collect these outstanding items and resolve the items that are deemed uncollectable.

Taking aggressive action to recover these hidden cash flow items can pay large dividends. Not only can the credit department generate unexpected cash flow in this manner, but it can also minimize potential bad-debt write-offs if the items are aged out indefinitely.

With the Tax Reform Act of 1986, companies can no longer accrue for bad debts. Instead, when accounting for bad debts, they must use the direct write-off method. Hence, without aggressive action from the credit department, these old items could impact the company's monthly or quarterly profit and loss statement at the time of direct write-off.

The first step in the action plan to recover the lost or hidden cash flow is to identify the total dollar amount and establish a count for items that are 90 or more days past due. The next step is to identify item counts and dollar amounts by the type of aged-out item. The item and dollar distributions may reveal specific insights or flaws in the collection process. This exercise will give the credit person an idea of the potential dollars that can be recovered—as well as a good feel for the magnitude of detail work that must be performed.

Next, the credit manager should have the accounts receivable system generate a report that includes, by customer, every item that is 90 or more days past due. For each customer, the report should indicate the accounts receivable information shown in Exhibit 6.17. Any companies that are unable to run a similar mainframe report can have clerical personnel detail the information manually by reviewing the 90+ days past-due aging category.

The end of the report should list total dollars and a total item count for items 90 or more days past due. Then, for each of the item categories, dollar and item count totals should be included. When added together, these should foot to the report totals.

Once the report has been generated, the credit department can identify the customers that represent the largest exposures with respect to lost or hidden cash flow. Phase I of the recovery effort will focus on these customers.

Exhibit 6.17

report date 12/06/89
page number 54

MAVCO INC
Account number: 00617
Address: 888 Sheffield Road
Teaneck, New Jersey 07666
Phone: (201) 837-4451

Item Date	Item Number	Item Type	Due Date	Amount Due	Reference Number
5/18/88	De714	Deduction	6/17/88	$ 719.00	112645
5/21/88	114909	Invoice	6/20/88	1,205.52	PO 920
6/20/88	Di1126	Un. Disct.	7/19/88	1,000.00	092082
	Customer 90+ Past Due Total			$2,924.52	

Next, credit managers should throw down a challenge to their credit staffs. They should challenge them to collect, resolve, or write off X number of dollars and items that are 90 days or more past due—within the next 90 to 120 days. At the same time, however, credit managers need to stress that efforts must continue at minimizing new items aging out into the 90+ days past-due category. These challenges should focus on targets that are aggressive but realistic.

Each collection staffer might start by pursuing one customer per day, or possibly five items. At that rate, staffers will be spending an average of 15 to 30 minutes per day pursuing hidden cash flow, and they can do so without neglecting their other responsibilities.

A good time for staffers to pursue these items might be either right after lunch or during the 15 to 30 minutes prior to the end of the work day.

Once the recovery effort proceeds, credit managers could have each collection staffer maintain a log for the items being pursued. The log would appear as follows:

Date	Customer Name	Item #/ Type	Item Date	Amount Due	Comments	Resolution Status
12/6/88	MAVCO	De714/Ded	5/18/88	$ 719.00	Mld. Backup	Open
12/6/88	MAVCO	114909/Inv.	5/21/88	1,205.52	Needs POD	Open

As items are resolved, the "resolution status" column can be updated as either "paid" or "written off." Using this method, at any point in time the credit department can identify for management exactly how much lost or hidden cash flow has been recovered into the cash flow cycle.

Hopefully, this type of concerted effort will result in a significant recovery of dormant, aged-out dollars, and a favorable effect on the firm's Total DSO and Past-Due DSO days.

ABSTRACT SUMMARY

- Lost cash flow could include invoices skipped, collectable customer deductions, short payments, unearned customer discounts, and interest or service charges due for late payments.
- By taking aggressive action to recover hidden cash flow items, the credit department can generate unexpected cash flow and at the same time minimize potential bad-debt write-offs.
- The first step of the action plan to recover the lost or hidden cash flow is to identify the total dollar amount and item count for items that are 90+ days past due.
- As Phase I of the recovery effort, credit practitioners need to identify and focus on the customers that represent the largest exposures with respect to lost or hidden cash flow.
- Collection staffers should maintain a log of the items they are pursuing.

CREDIT PERSONNEL WITH CASH MANAGEMENT RESPONSIBILITIES

Depending on the size of your company, you may be assigned cash management as well as your ongoing credit management responsibilities. Many firms don't have a person titled treasurer but instead may have a controller supervising the treasury or cash management function. As a result, some cash management responsibilities may filter down to the credit manager.

Cash management is the management of the firm's cash inflows and outflows through the effective use of cash management services. Within any cash management responsibility one or all of the following three universal cash management objectives should apply:

- To provide financial support required by top management.
- To manage the company's cash and accounts receivable assets.
- To provide timely and accurate current data and forecasts regarding cash, accounts receivable, and loans.

Following are a number of corporate cash management responsibilities:

- Maintaining bank relationships for bank borrowings and/or cash management services.
- Daily reporting of bank account debits and credits.
- Daily funding of bank accounts.
- Lockbox relations.
- Check disbursements.
- Wire transfers.
- Bank borrowings, including negotiating loan agreements.
- Leasing.
- Investments.
- Foreign exchange strategy and purchases.
- Corporate insurance covering property damage, general liability, and workers' compensation insurance.
- Forecasting cash and loan positions.

Bank account reporting entails monitoring the daily bank reports to know your firm's daily funding requirements. You then decide to borrow if you forecast a deficit; invest if you show a surplus; or do neither if your forecast projects being at or near a zero dollar balance. Managing lockbox relations involves coordinating, reporting, and monitoring all lockbox activities. Check disbursement involves not only responsibility for disbursing checks but authorizing stop payments, etc.

Managing wire transfers involves controlling the process of paying and receiving funds electronically via a wire transfer network. Bank borrowing responsibilities include funding daily and fixed borrowing requirements, as well as negotiating bank loan agreements. Leasing activity entails maintaining leasing relationships and contacts. Investment management includes evaluating bank risk, calling for rates, placing investment, and deciding the accounting treatment for the investment.

If your company has an overseas payable or receivable, you may need to hedge your risk of exchange rate fluctuations increasing your liability or diminishing your asset between now and when the payable or receivable comes due. Corporate insurance responsibilities include procuring the required level of coverage to protect your assets and cash flows.

It is unlikely that you will become responsible for all 12 areas, but one or more could become your duties. To whatever extent your duties expand, so has your value to your firm and your value in the marketplace.

If you take on cash management responsibilities you may want to join a regional or local cash management group. Cash management groups help you grow professionally by enabling you to share with and learn from others handling the same responsibilities. You can develop from association members a network of contacts for advice and guidance.

You may also want to subscribe to cash management trade periodicals like *The Journal of Cash Management, Practical Cash Management,* or *Corporate Cashflow* magazine. Attending cash management seminars and conferences also can enhance your cash management skills.

The TMA (Treasury Management Association) offers a CCM (Certified Cash Manager) certificate that is analogous to the NACM's CCE Program. As like the CCE, attaining CCM status requires one to be very well versed in all facets of cash management.

ABSTRACT SUMMARY

- Cash management is the management of the firm's cash inflows and outflows through the effective use of cash management services.
- The three universal cash management strategy objectives are to provide financial support; control the company's assets; and to provide timely and accurate financial information.
- Cash management responsibilities range from maintaining bank relations to executing foreign exchange strategy.

- ■ Cash management groups benefit you by providing a network of contacts and information.
- ■ Attending seminars and reading cash management periodicals can enhance your cash management skills.

7

FORECASTING

AUTOMATIC CREDIT-APPROVAL MODELS

Based on specified dollar limits and guidelines, the credit department can design models to facilitate the automatic approval of credit limits and orders for new customers. Creating an automatic credit-approval structure will save the credit department precious time that can be better allocated to other credit tasks that generate cash flow. A model is shown in Exhibit 7.1.

New orders in excess of the designated ceiling for automatic order and credit limit approval will require a complete credit investigation. For example, a certain model could assign a $25,000 automatic credit limit, while the customer's order is for $30,000, thus requiring a complete credit investigation to justify the required line in excess of the ceiling.

All too often the credit department receives credit applications from marketing/sales personnel for potential customers who do not end up buying any product. With this in mind, it is difficult to justify performing time-consuming credit investigations of these applicants. It makes more sense to attempt to qualify such applicants using an "automatic" method that takes into account approval guidelines set by the department.

The automatic credit-approval approach makes the most sense when applied to customers requiring small credit limits — say, $100 to $1,000. Allocating credit department resources to thoroughly investigate these customers would be a waste of time and money.

The credit department can establish guidelines for automatic credit approval based on a variety of criteria. For example, one might establish automatic credit-approval limits based on applicants' Dun & Bradstreet credit ratings. D&B, the dominant commercial credit reporting service, assigns companies number classifications based on their credit strength. A "1" is a high credit appraisal, "2" is a good credit appraisal, "3" is fair and "4" is a limited appraisal. Within each of these numeric rankings, there are further alpha and numeric indicators of estimated net worth.

Depending on the firm's credit philosophy and policy, companies rated 5A2 or 5A3 on down to HH2 or HH3 may not be eligible for automatic credit approval. In fact, this author recommends that only applicants with a "1" composite credit appraisal be made eligible for automatic credit/order approval. Customers with composite appraisals of "2" or "3" should be subjected to standard credit investigations.

When using these ratings for automatic credit approval, the credit department still needs to set a ceiling on credit/order limits. In other words, no matter how high a credit applicant is rated by D&B, it should only be able to achieve automatic approval of a credit limit or an order with a dollar value at or below the specified ceiling figure. For example, a firm could set policy that the maximum automatic credit line or order approval amount for the highest credit appraisal would be $25,000. At the low end of the spectrum, the lowest eligible credit appraisal would be eligible for a $1,000 automatic credit line or order approval.

Exhibit 7.1
Flow of Automatic Credit Approval Process

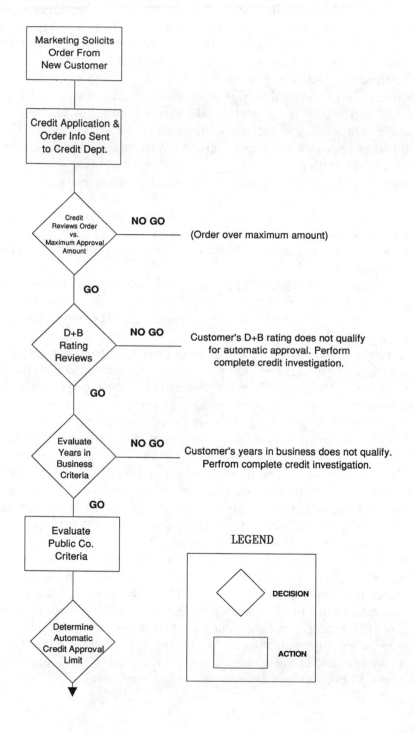

Another way to set guidelines for automatic credit approval would be to set up a "years-in-business" formula. With this method, one might say that companies in business for 20 years or more are automatically eligible for credit up to a designated dollar amount; companies in business for, say 15-19 years, would be eligible for a lesser amount; companies in business 10-14 years would be eligible for yet a lesser amount, and so on.

A firm could decide to allocate $1,000 for each year that the customer is in business. Thus, a customer in business for 15 years would qualify for a $15,000 automatic credit or order approval limit. A maximum ceiling of $20,000 could be established regardless of the number of years that the customer has been in business.

The credit department might also want to establish a minimum years-in-business cutoff for automatic credit approval. The company could restrict automatic credit approvals to companies that have been in business for at least 10 years, for instance.

If the credit department chooses to implement a years-in-business formula, its minimum cutoff point should be five years. Statistics clearly indicate that a high percentage of firms in business less than five years do not survive.

Another criteria for automatic credit approval could be whether the applicant is a public company listed on the New York, American, Chicago, or Over-the-Counter (NASDAQ) exchanges. This information is readily available from a Standard & Poor's stock guide or any of the other stock guides published and usually available free of charge from brokerage firms. If the applicant is indeed listed on one of these exchanges, the credit department might want to use one of the other criteria — D&B rating or the "years-in-business" formula — as an additional check on the applicant. For example, a $25,000 credit limit could be automatically assigned to companies listed on the New York Stock Exchange provided they have a "1" composite D&B appraisal.

When selecting the method or methods that will be used in any automatic credit-approval mechanism, it is a good idea to do a historical check using the chosen method to evaluate accounts that eventually went bad, as well as currently active COD accounts. The goal will be to see if the chosen method would have weeded out the bad accounts and not allowed the company to do business with the COD accounts. This process might point up flaws in the mechanism, allowing adjustments to be made before actual customer implementation.

Furthermore, once the automatic approval system is up and running, the credit department should review how well the customers who have received automatic credit approval are meeting the company's standards. (If a customer receiving a credit limit through the automatic mechanism becomes a payment problem, or if its credit requirements exceed the automatic approval amount assigned, the credit department should perform a complete credit investigation.) Note, the automatic credit-approval model is designed to facilitate timely shipment and establishment of new customers' initial credit requirements. Thereafter, the credit department should review the subject's balances prior to extending further credit.

Remember, initial credit approval may be automatic, but credit is a privilege and not a right that is automatic!

ABSTRACT SUMMARY

■ Creating an automatic credit-approval structure for handling relatively small requests for credit will save many man-hours that the credit department can better spend on other activities that generate cash flow.

■ Criteria for automatic credit approval could be based on D&B credit rating information, years in business, or whether the applicant is a public company listed on one of the major stock exchanges.

■ When a company uses D&B ratings as one of its criteria, it should only allocate automatic approvals to applicants with a composite rating of "1"—the highest rating.

■ A company should test its automatic credit-approval criteria against old bad-debt accounts and currently active COD (cash on delivery) accounts to see if they would have qualified for credit under the proposed guidelines.

■ If an "automatic" customer becomes a payment problem, or if its credit requirements exceed the automatic approval amount assigned, the credit department should perform a complete credit investigation.

CREDIT SCORING MODELS

Credit personnel can use credit scoring models to determine the creditworthiness of new customers and, by modifying the models, existing customers as well. A credit scoring model is a program that reviews customer information and assigns either dollar values or numerical values for each category under review. Each category can be of equal importance or the categories can be weighted.

Credit information used in the scoring model can be derived from a properly structured credit application and from the company's credit investigation. Additionally, credit personnel can use financial information provided by the customer.

New customer information reviewed and rated in the scoring model might include the applicant's number of years in business, credit rating from Dun & Bradstreet, public company information, trade reference results, bank accommodation information, and ratings on selected financial criteria from the customer's financial statement. Or the credit scoring model could be based solely on financial statement information.

Based on information provided in the customer's financial statement, credit personnel can assign scores to the following ratios or financial calculations:

- Current ratio
- Quick ratio
- Cash/current liabilities ratio
- Cash/total liabilities ratio
- Bank debt/worth ratio
- Total debt/worth ratio
- Inventory/total current assets ratio
- Accounts receivable/accounts payable ratio
- Accounts receivable turnover in days
- Accounts payable turnover in days
- Inventory turnover in days
- Return on sales
- Return on shareholders' equity
- Earnings times interest charged multiple

The financial statement credit scoring model can be designed to test certain ratios. Let's say a model scores 10 ratios (see Exhibit 7.2). For each ratio examined, the scoring model will assign a score of from 1 to 5. One way to assign these scores would be to base them on some type of published industry standards. For

Exhibit 7.2
Credit Scoring Model (based solely on customer financial information)

Ratio Category	Scoring Guide					Assigned Score
	1	2	3	4	5	
Current	2.5	2.0	1.5	1.0	Under 1.0	
Quick	1.5	1.25	1.0	.75	Under .75	
Tot. Debt/Worth	.5	.75	1.0	1.5	Over 1.5	
Credit Limit as % of Net Worth	5%	10%	15%	25%	Over 25%	
Net Profit on Sales	8.0	6.0	3.5	1.0	Under 1%	
AR Turnover	30	40	50	60	Over 60	
Inv. Turnover	30	40	50	60	Over 60	
AP Turnover	30	40	50	70	Over 60	
AR/AP Ratio	2.0	1.5	1.25	1.0	Under 1.0	
Inv./Total Current Assets Ratio	.30	.35	.4	.6	Over .6	

Total Score

Legend

10-15	Strong Account
16-25	Good Account
26-35	Watch
36-40	Control
41-50	Get Out

instance, D&B and Robert Morris Associates publish industry standards by SIC number for numerous financial ratios.

If the applicant's current ratio is one of the ratios in the model, the credit department might want to assign a score of 1 if the ratio is greater than or equal to 2.0, a 2 if the ratio is less than 2.0 but greater than 1.75, on down to a low score of 5. If 10 ratios are all rated on a scale of 1 to 5, then the best total score an applicant could receive would be 10. The worst possible total score would be 50. Depending on the total customer score, the new customer order would be either approved or held for further review before shipment.

For existing customers, the financial statement credit scoring model would not approve individual orders, but rather approve or reject the customer's required credit line based on the overall score. Thus, use of the scoring model would coincide with the existing customer's annual credit limit review. Obviously, credit investigations performed on an exception basis prior to a scheduled annual credit limit review would also utilize the model.

A very high overall score would probably indicate high risk with respect to viability and suggest the negotiation of some form of collateral.

As we all know, there are new and existing customers who absolutely refuse to provide financial disclosure when applying for credit. Thus, credit personnel might find it necessary to construct three types of scoring models—one that incorporates a rating for a customer's financial statement, a subjective model that does not, and a hybrid model that incorporates financial statement and subjective criteria into the scoring.

The most effective model will be one that incorporates a rating of the customer's financial statement, credit application information, and credit investigation results.

ABSTRACT SUMMARY

- Credit scoring models can be used to determine the creditworthiness of new and existing customers.

- Credit scoring models review new and existing customer information and assign either dollar values or numerical values to each category under review.

- For new customers, sources for credit scoring information include the customer's financial statement, the company's credit investigation, and information provided on a credit application.

- The company's scoring method for financial ratios can be based on published industry standards, such as standards for financial ratios published by Dun & Bradstreet and Robert Morris Associates.

- Some customers refuse to provide financial information. Thus, credit personnel may need to construct three models—one that incorporates financial statement information, a subjective model that does not, and a hybrid model that incorporates financial statement and subjective criteria into the scoring.

ACCOUNTS RECEIVABLE FORECASTING USING THE "BUILD-UP" METHOD

Credit personnel can use a relatively simple formula to forecast month-, quarter-, or year-ending dollar levels for accounts receivable. The accounts receivable information is extremely helpful to treasury management and senior financial management when they are projecting the impact of working capital changes on the firm's cash and loan positions.

The accuracy of the accounts receivable projection will depend on the strength of sales and DSO assumptions. In order to proceed with the accounts receivable build up calculation, we will assume that we have already arrived at accurate projections on monthly sales and monthly DSO. Monthly sales projections should be available from the controller's area or from the department of financial analysis; DSO projections are prepared by the credit department.

Let's say it's early in the month of March and our goal is to project the dollar level for month-end accounts receivable for March, which coincides with the firm's quarterly financial statements. (Note, in early March we could also project the dollar level for year end December 31st AR. Under this scenario, we would need a December DSO projection, along with projected monthly sales for the December quarterly time frame.) Assume the following variables to project the March-ending accounts receivable dollar level:

Projected March sales	$27,000
Actual February sales	30,000
Actual January sales	26,000
March-ending DSO projection	64 days

(Again, if these variables are not reasonably accurate, the accounts receivable projection will probably be inaccurate.)

With the detailed information above, we can now project the March-ending dollar level for accounts receivable. In essence, what we want to do now is back into the accounts receivable projection by allocating actual and projected sales to build up and derive the accounts receivable level that equates to the projected DSO.

If we know that the projected March DSO is 64 days, we can project accounts receivable by building up the 64-day DSO projection through using the actual and projected sales numbers. Thus, a 64-day DSO would be calculated into accounts receivable dollars as follows:

Step 1: March projected sales of $27,000 = 30 days of DSO

Step 2: February actual sales of $30,000 = 30 days of DSO

Step 3:   Determine the dollar value represented by four DSO days of
              January sales by multiplying January actual sales by the portion
              of the month represented by four days.
              ($26,000 × ($\frac{4}{30}$ days) = $3,467)

Step 4:   For the final calculation, add together the monthly sales numbers
              for January, February, and March that equal 64 days DSO.

March 30 days DSO	$ 27,000
February 30 days DSO	30,000
January 4 days DSO	3,467
Projected March AR	*60,467*

Although it is a simple calculation, the build-up calculation for accounts receivable provides very accurate accounts receivable projections. The projected accounts receivable information will be of great value to credit, treasury, and senior financial management. It also enables the credit department to project monthly cash receipts using the roll-forward method.

ABSTRACT SUMMARY

- The accounts receivable build-up calculation enables the credit department to forecast month-, quarter-, or year-ending levels for accounts receivable.
- Accounts receivable projections are extremely helpful to treasury management and senior financial management as they project the impact of working capital changes on the firm's cash and loan positions.
- The accuracy of the accounts receivable projection will depend on the strength of sales and DSO assumptions.
- Despite its simplicity, the AR build-up calculation is very accurate.
- The AR build up calculation also enables credit personnel to project monthly cash receipts using the roll-forward method.

CASH RECEIPTS FORECASTING USING THE ROLL-FORWARD METHOD

Taking the accounts receivable build-up calculation one step further will allow credit personnel to forecast monthly cash receipts. In a previous abstract, we saw how credit personnel can use sales and DSO projections and a build-up calculation to forecast month-, quarter-, or year-end accounts receivable in dollars (see "Build Up," in this chapter, p. 227). With all of this information, plus opening accounts receivable information, credit personnel can project monthly cash receipts.

Once again, a relatively simple methodology can yield very accurate cash receipt forecasting.

Remember, the quality and accuracy of the roll-forward receipts projection will be strongly impacted by the accuracy of sales and DSO projections. These should be based on a calendarized budget or a business plan—or at least on a review of some valid data base.

The calculation is fairly straightforward. It begins with a forecast of period-ending dollar levels for accounts receivable using the build-up method. Let's say a credit practitioner wants to forecast April receipts. Then he would proceed with the cash recipts roll-forward forecast as follows:

Assumptions:

Opening April AR	$ 100,000
Projected April sales	41,000
Projected ending April AR	91,000

[Quantified using the AR build-up method]

Step 1: Identify the April 1 opening accounts receivable balance, in this case $100,000 (same as March 31 AR balance).

Step 2: Add projected April sales to the April opening AR [$41,000 + $100,000 = $141,000].

Step 3: Subtract projected month-end April accounts receivable (derived using the build-up method based on projected April DSO and sales) from the sum of projected April sales and April opening accounts receivable ($141,000 − $91,000 = $50,000). The answer, $50,000, is the projected monthly cash receipts.

In essence, this forecasting formula is a variation on the following formula:

Opening AR ($100,000) + Projected Sales ($41,000)
– Projected Collections = Projected Month-Ending AR ($90,000)

The variation from which we derived our monthly cash receipts looks like this:

Opening AR ($100,000) + Projected Sales ($41,000)
– Projected Month-Ending AR ($90,000)
= Collections (Projected Cash Receipts)

The formula appears as if it's performing a reconciliation of the cash receipts forecast. Note, the roll-forward method can be used to project cash receipts for any month regardless of how far out the projections are. For example, in March one could project June's cash receipts. Under this scenario, one would need sales projections for the May time frame, and a May DSO projection to derive opening June AR, and projections for the June sales time frame, and June DSO, to derive June cash receipts.

Forecasted receipts can be measured against actual receipts to determine the month-end DSO increase or decrease. During the month, if actual receipts are lagging or are far in excess of the forecast, credit personnel might want to revise cash receipts and DSO projections.

Here again is a decision-making and forecasting tool that can benefit senior financial management as well as credit management.

To take the exercise an additional step in the "micro" direction, credit personnel can generate a daily cash receipts forecast based on the total cash receipts forecast (see Time Series, in this chapter, p. 231).

ABSTRACT SUMMARY

- An accounts receivable build-up calculation of period-ending AR can be taken a step farther to project monthly cash receipts.
- The quality and accuracy of the roll-forward receipts projection will be strongly impacted by the accuracy of sales and DSO projections.
- In order to project monthly cash receipts, credit personnel need to know the opening accounts receivable for the month, projected sales for the month, and projected month-end AR.
- The formula for projecting monthly cash receipts looks like this: Opening AR + Projected Sales – Month-Ending AR = Collections (Projected Cash Receipts)
- Forecasted receipts can be measured against actual receipts to determine the month-end DSO increase or decrease. During the month, if actual receipts appear to be off the forecast, credit personnel might want to revise cash receipts and DSO projections appropriately.

TIME SERIES OR CYCLE VALUE DAILY CASH RECEIPTS FORECASTING

Time series or cycle value cash forecasting is a relatively simple mathematical forecasting methodology that can generate accurate projections of future daily cash receipts. The credit professional's goals in using this methodology are to determine what percentage of total projected monthly cash receipts will occur on each "cash day" of the month, and, based on this projection and a forecast of monthly cash receipts, to forecast actual cash receipts for those days.

In essence, the goal is to generate a daily cash receipts forecast for a particular month or months.

To do so will require a review of historical data. When forecasting daily cash receipts, credit professionals need to evaluate and manipulate receipts data for the past six to 18 months. They need to determine what percentage of the total receipts from that period were from the first Monday of the month, the second Monday of the month, the third Monday, and the fourth and the fifth Monday, if applicable.

The same sort of analysis must be performed for each cash day of the week — Monday through Friday. The goal is to determine percentage values for every day of all the weeks of the month.

The sum of all the percentage values should equal 100 percent.

In the process, it might be revealed that the sum of all Monday percentages has, over the period analyzed, equaled 35–40 percent of total monthly cash receipts. On the other hand, the analysis might reveal that all Tuesdays in the aggregate accounted for only 7 percent of the month's total cash receipts during the period analyzed.

The analysis will also reveal differences in receipts for the same day of the week during different weeks of the month. For instance, there may be significant differences between the percentage of receipts from first Tuesdays and fourth Tuesdays.

Having arrived at percentage values for each cash day of the month, credit personnel can look next to project actual cash receipts for those days in the upcoming month. The next step will be to project the total cash receipts for the month in question.

There are several options for projecting the upcoming month's total cash receipts. One would be to use a moving monthly average of cash receipts based on the past four months of receipts. Another approach would be to construct a correlational model between receipts and current and prior months' sales and accounts receivable history. Or, in a two-step process, one could forecast month-end AR using the build-up method in order to forecast total monthly cash receipts using the roll-forward method. The final step is to apply the individual day's percentages against total projected cash receipts.

Let's say that total cash receipts for the upcoming month were projected to be $1.25 million, based on one of these methods. In order to make a forecast of actual receipts for a particular day of the upcoming month, we would need only to multiply that $1.25 million by the percentage value assigned to that specific day in the month's cycle. If we want to project what the cash receipts will be for the third Tuesday of the month, and we have assigned a percentage value of 1.3 percent to that day, we simply need to multiply $1.25 million by 1.3 percent. Our forecast for cash receipts on that day: $16,250.

The forecasting methodology described here can also be applied to the daily forecasting of check disbursements or freight payments.

ABSTRACT SUMMARY

- Time series or cycle value cash forecasting can generate accurate projections of daily cash receipts.

- This type of forecasting should be based on a six- to 18-month historical analysis of receipts data.

- Based on prior receipts history, credit personnel can assign to each day of each week of a month values that indicate the percentage of monthly cash receipts that can be expected on that day.

- The sum of all the cycle value percentages for each day of each week of the month should equal 100%.

- To forecast actual cash receipts for particular days of the upcoming month, simply multiply the assigned percentage value by the forecasted dollar figure for the month's total receipts.

FORECASTING CUSTOMER VIABILITY

Credit personnel are constantly faced with the difficult challenge of projecting whether a customer will remain viable. Usually this task is performed in a subjective manner; gut feel and intuition frequently are the only tools of analysis that credit personnel use.

When bad-debt warning signals appear, however, credit personnel can take their subjective analysis a step further by performing "if-then" modeling that features source and application of funds analysis and projecting balance sheet scenarios. "If-then" modeling might be performed annually for all customers whose credit limits exceed a certain designated dollar amount, such as $100,000 or $1 million. It might also be performed for customers with lower credit limits, if they are considered high-risk accounts. One of the better applications for "if-then" modeling would be analysis of leveraged buyout customers. Here analysts can compare their projections to the LBO's current and future debt service requirements.

"If-then" analysis can be compared to existing red flags, such as IRS tax liens, NSF checks (non-sufficient funds), violations of bank loan agreements, suits and judgments, excessive slow payments, and broken promises. The objective of the analysis is to determine whether the customer has sufficient financial wherewithal to continue as an ongoing concern based on the scenarios projected.

The "if-then" analysis will be performed in two steps. The first is the source and application of funds analysis and projection.

Let's say that the analysis will be performed covering actuals for the year ended 12/31/88, and credit personnel will project the entries for the year ending 12/31/89. From the source and application projections, they will be able to determine if projected cash flow is sufficient to sustain operations or if bank borrowings will be required to fund capital expenditures and increases to working capital accounts. In some cases, the customer being analyzed will have reached the limit of its credit agreement and thus may not be able to borrow in order to sustain operations. This exercise becomes especially critical when analyzing LBOs and firms with a deficit tangible net worth.

Credit department personnel will also want to factor into the analysis the impact of projecting loss operations on cash flow and financial wherewithal.

Based on the source and application of funds projections, credit personnel will be able to perform the second phase of the "if-then" analysis—constructing a projected balance sheet. By adding or subtracting the source and application entries to the actual 12/31/88 balance sheet items impacted, they can determine whether the projected balance sheet will be in compliance with the covenants for a specific credit agreement that may be in effect. Personnel can review covenants relating to working capital, current ratio, quick ratio, as well as the following typical bank covenant ratios: total debt/tangible net worth, bank debt/tangible net worth, and debt/cash flow.

The analyst can portray source and application of funds analysis using a variety of balance sheet scenarios. Exhibit 7.3 shows an example of the "if-then" method.

The two source and application cases portrayed reflect profitable operations (Case 1) and loss operations (Case 2). Clearly one can see the impact of a $10 million negative earnings swing on cash flow. Required borrowings to fund operations are $17.3 million higher under the loss scenario. The customer may not have availability to underwrite and support the loss operations scenario—or the loss operations could put the customer in default of the bank's performance covenants.

We can determine whether Case 2 places the subject in default by performing the second step: constructing a projected balance sheet based on the sources and applications projected.

Case 2 also implies that creditors are putting pressure on the customer; note that payables declined by $3.5 million from the 12/31/88 year-end level.

Under Case 2 projections, the customer would most likely have to scale back its capital spending and omit paying a dividend in order to prioritize the applications and ration whatever borrowings are available. The scaling down of capital spending could hurt the customer from a competitive standpoint, while the dividend omission will certainly have a negative impact on the company's public trading of its stock or debt securities.

Case 2 assumptions reflect poor working capital management; accounts receivable and inventory display a combined increase of $12 million over the 12/31/88 actual balance sheet levels. On the other hand, Case 1 reflects profitable operations and better working capital management for accounts receivable, inventory, and accounts payable. Case 1 also assumes creditors are putting less pressure on their customer to reduce their balances than does Case 2.

(Note that the analyst can portray more than two cases to reflect a greater range of how the customer will perform for the projected year.)

Now let's construct balance sheets from each of the cases to further measure viability and determine whether the customer will violate bank covenants (see Exhibit 7.4).

Once the source and application cases have been projected, analysts can construct the balance sheets. When constructing the balance sheets, they should note that each source and application entry will either increase or decrease the balance sheet item affected. Increases to asset accounts are debits that reduce cash offset by a credit to cash. Reductions to asset accounts are credits that increase cash offset by debiting cash. Likewise, increases to liability and equity accounts are credits that increase cash offset by a debit to cash. Reductions to liability and equity accounts are debits that reduce cash offset by a credit to cash.

Thus, there will be a positive or negative impact on cash. For example, if accounts receivable for the year increased by $3.5 million, accounts receivable on the projected balance sheet would be debited $3.5 million (increase) and there would also be a corresponding $3.5 million credit offset to cash (reduction). Net

Exhibit 7.3
XYZ Company Source and Application of Funds Projections

Sources	Actual 12/31/88	Case 1 Projection 12/31/89	Case 2 Projection 12/31/89
Earnings Before Extraordinary Gain	9,800	7,500	–2,500
Depreciation	2,100	2,600	2,600
Stock Issue	0	0	0
Debentures	0	0	0
Extraordinary Gain	0	0	0
Deferred Income Tax	150	150	150
Other	0	0	0
Total Sources	12,050	10,250	250
Applications			
Capital Spending	9,000	12,000	12,000
Dividends	3,000	3,000	3,000
Change in AR	1,750	3,500	7,000
Change in Inventory	1,250	3,000	5,000
Change in Other Current Assets	200	200	500
Change in Other Long-Term Assets	0	0	200
Change in AP (–Inc., + Dec.)	750	1,250	3,500
Chg. in Other Curr. Liab. (–Inc., + Dec.)	0	0	0
Chg. in Other L.T. Liab. (–Inc., + Dec.)	300	0	0
Currency Adjustment (–Inc., + Dec.)	0	200	200
Treasury Stock Repurchase	0	300	300
Other	0	0	0
Total Sources	16,250	23,450	31,700
Cash Flow	– 4,200	–13,200	–31,450
Chg. in S.T. Borrowings (+Inc., – Dec.)	3,200	3,000	12,800
Chg. in L.T. Borrowings (+Inc., – Dec.)	1,000	10,500	18,000
Net Cash Flow	0	300	– 650
Opening Cash & Marketable Securities	750	750	750
Change (–Dec., + Inc.)	0	300	– 650
Ending Cash	750	1,050	100
Opening Loan	11,300	15,500	15,500
Change	4,200	13,500	30,800
Ending Loan	15,500	29,000	46,300

Exhibit 7.4
XYZ Company Balance Sheet in (000's)

	Actual 12/31/X1	Debit (+)	Credit (−)	Case 1 Projection 12/31/X2	Debit (+)	Credit (−)	Case 2 Projection 12/31/X2
ASSETS							
Cash	750	23,750	23,450	1,050	31,050	31,700	100
Accounts Receivable	29,059	3,500		32,559	7,000		36,059
Inventory	10,677	3,000		13,677	5,000		15,677
Other Current Assets	1,221	200		1,421	500		1,721
Total Current Assets	41,707			48,707			53,557
Fixed Assets	45,332	12,000		57,332	12,000		57,332
Less: Depreciation	21,989		2,600	24,589		2,600	24,589
Net Fixed Assets	23,343			32,743			32,743
Other Assets	500			500	200		700
Total Assets	65,550			81,950			87,000
		Debit (−)	Credit (+)		Debit (−)	Credit (+)	
LIABILITIES & EQUITY							
Accounts Payable	27,424	1,250		26,174	3,500		23,924
Accrued Liabilities	2,998			2,998			2,998
Other Current Liabilities	1,300			1,300			1,300
Short-Term Bank Debt	4,200		3,000	7,200		12,800	17,000
Current Maturities	0			0			0
Total Current Liabilities	35,922			37,672			45,222

Exhibit 7.4 (continued)

	Actual 12/31/X1	Debit (−)	Credit (+)	Case 1 Projection 12/31/X2	Debit (−)	Credit (+)	Case 2 Projection 12/31/X2
LONG-TERM LIABILITIES							
Long-Term Debt	11,300		10,500	21,800		18,000	29,300
Deferred Income Tax	2,500		150	2,650		150	2,650
Other Long-Term Liabilities	0			0			0
Total Liabilities	49,722			62,122			77,172
EQUITY							
Common Stock	1,000			1,000			1,000
Additional Paid in Capital	3,000			3,000			3,000
Preferred Stock	5,000			5,000			5,000
Less: Treasury Stock	0	300		300	300		300
Retained Earnings	6,828	3,200	7,500	11,128	5,700		1,128
Equity (Net Worth)	15,828			19,828			9,828
Total Liabilities & Equity	65,550			81,950			87,000
RATIO ANALYSIS							
CURRENT RATIO	1.16			1.29			1.18
QUICK RATIO	.83			.89			.80
WORKING CAPITAL	5,785			11,035			8,335
BANK DEBT/WORTH	.98			1.46			4.71
TOTAL DEBT/WORTH	3.14			3.13			7.85
BANK DEBT/CASH FLOW	1.30			2.87			463.00

income of, say $7.5 million, will credit (increase) retained earnings by $7.5 million and have a $7.5 million favorable debit to cash. (Note: A $3-million dividend will debit (reduce) retained earnings and credit (reduce) cash by that amount. In the end, if net cash is not sufficient to withstand all the entry offsets, then borrowings must be utilized. Note, for each source and application entry there must be a debit or credit to the corresponding balance sheet account and a credit or debit offset entry to cash. In Case 1, AR increases by $3,500. The entries are debit AR $3,500, credit cash $3,500. Repeat the process for each source and application entry. Note, in Case 1 the $23,750 of debits (increases) to cash are comprised of: Earnings $7,500, Depreciation $2,600, increase in Deferred Income Tax $150, increase in Short-Term Debt $3,000, and an increase in Long-Term Debt $10,500. The $23,450 of credits (decreases) to cash are comprised of: Capital Spending $12,000, Dividends $3,000, increase in Accounts Receivable $3,500, increase in Inventory $3,000, increase in Other Current Assets $200, decrease in Accounts Payable $1,250, decrease in Currency Adjustment $200, and Treasury Stock repurchase $300. See Exhibit 7.5 for details of each cash and balance sheet entry for Case 1 only.

In Case 2 there was a negative cash flow of $31.45 million, with only $750,000 of opening cash. Thus the XYZ company had to borrow $30.8 million while drawing down cash from $750,000 to $100,000. Without this step, the company would have had a negative cash balance of $30.7 million on the balance sheet without borrowing, which is unrealistic.

If there is a negative cash position when constructing the balance sheet, then the actual amount of the borrowings reflected in the "source and app" once applied to cash should enable the balance sheet cash level to tie into the "source and app" cash level.

The constructed balance sheets will enable analysts to perform ratio analyses with the projections. They can then compare the projected ratios to industry standards or the customer's actual covenants with its banker.

The Case 2 ratios clearly reflect an unbalanced financial condition with the strong likelihood that the XYZ Company is in violation of its bank covenants. The bank debt/worth and total debt/worth ratios mushroom from 12/31/88 actual levels of .98 and 3.14 to 4.71 and 7.85, respectively.

Under the Case 2 scenario, the bank would probably restrict the customer's borrowings by requiring it to justify each request for funds. The Case 2 working-capital increase over the 12/31/88 actual level reflects poor asset management and creditor pressure as opposed to more favorable circumstances accompanying an increase in working capital, such as a new product introduction or a significant growth mode that requires building up AR and inventory levels. Clearly, Case 2 portays a path to insolvency within the near term.

The two-step "if-then" analysis should enable credit personnel to envision potential operating scenarios and their impact without having to wait for "intuition to come to fruition." A more proactive stance can be taken with high-risk customers

Exhibit 7.5
Balance Sheet Entries for Case 1 Source and Application[*]

Sources	Case 1 '89 Projection	Balance Sheet Entries
Earnings Before Extraordinary Gain	7,500	Debit cash 7,500 credit retained earnings 7,500
Depreciation	2,600	Debit cash 2,600 credit depreciation 2,600
Stock Issue	0	No entry
Debentures	0	No entry
Extraordinary Gain	0	No entry
Deferred Inc. Tax	150	Debit cash 150 credit deferred inc. tax 150
Other	0	No entry
Total Sources	10,250	

Uses		
Capital Spending	12,000	Debit fixed assets 12,000 credit cash 12,000
Dividends	3,000	Debit retained earnings 3,000 credit cash 3,000
Change in Accounts Receivable	3,500	Debit AR 3,500 credit cash 3,500
Change in Inventory	3,000	Debit inventory 3,000 credit cash 3,000
Change in Other Current Assets	200	Debit other curr. assets 200 credit cash 200
Change in Other Long-Term Assets	0	No entry
Change in AP (– Inc., + Dec.)	1,250	Debit AP 1,250 credit cash 1,250
Chg. in Other Curr. Liab. (– Inc., + Dec.)	0	No entry
Chg. in Other L.T. Liab. (– Inc., + Dec.)	0	No entry
Currency Adj. (– Inc., + Dec.)	200	Debit retained earnings 200 credit cash 200
Treasury Stock Repurchase	300	Debit treasury stock 300 credit cash 300
Other	0	No entry
Total Sources	23,450	
Cash Flow	–13,200	
Chg. in S.T. Borrowings (Increase – Dec.)	3,000	Debit cash 3,000 credit short-term borr. 3,000
Chg. in L.T. Borrowings (Increase – Dec.)	10,500	Debit cash 10,500 credit long-term debt 10,500

* (Cross reference with Exhibit 7.4)

once the range of parameters and the perceived consequences of the parameters have been identified.

ABSTRACT SUMMARY

- When bad-debt warning signals appear, "gut feel" and intuition are the tools most frequently used to analyze a customer's ongoing viability.
- Credit personnel can take subjective viability analysis a step further by performing "if-then" source and application of funds analysis and balance sheet scenarios and modeling.
- The objective of the "if-then" analysis is to determine whether the customer has sufficient financial wherewithal to continue as an ongoing concern. The process includes projecting the customer's ability to comply with loan covenants.
- The second phase of "if-then" analysis is constructing a projected balance sheet.
- The "if-then" form of analysis is particularly valuable when examining leveraged buyout (LBO) customer risk.

FORECASTING BAD-DEBT WRITE-OFFS

The Tax Reform Act of 1986 has created a clear need to accurately forecast bad-debt write-offs. Businesses are no longer able to accrue for bad debts but instead must utilize the direct write-off method of accounting. With the current tax law there is no more contingency P&L planning for a rainy day.

Forecasting bad-debt write-offs can be performed in two modes. Credit personnel can execute bad-debt forecasts based on historical bad-debt write-off data, or they can perform an intuitive bad-debt forecast based on a subjective analysis.

The historical forecast would involve reviewing bad-debt write-offs for the previous five years. The review would consist of plotting dollar totals for annual bad-debt write-offs, as well as plotting the percent of annual sales represented by those write-offs in each year.

In performing the historical analysis, credit personnel might note a clear pattern with respect to the percent of total sales represented by bad-debt write-offs from year to year. If so, they will want to project the current year's bad-debt write-offs by multiplying the projected percentage of bad-debt write-offs by the current year's projected annual sales.

For example, let's say bad-debt write-offs during the past five years were .35 percent of total sales. If sales for the upcoming year are projected at $100 million, then the projection for bad-debt write-offs for that year would be $350,000 ($100 million × .35% = $350,000).

Credit practitioners might also be able to document a mathematical progression of the historical dollar totals for write-offs as a means of making a forecast. Or, another historical methodology would be to review the ratio of total bad debt write-off dollars as a percent of year-end accounts receivable over the past five years. If there appears to be a mathematical pattern, credit personnel could perform a build-up forecast of year-end accounts receivable to forecast the current year's bad debts as a percent of the projected year-end accounts receivable.

A more intuitive approach to forecasting bad-debt write-offs would be to analyze the aged trial balance for accounts receivable. This would entail reviewing each of the customer exposures in the aged trial balance. Credit personnel would review these exposures and, based on subjective criteria, select those exposures where there is believed to be a strong likelihood that the company will be unable to collect all or portions of the customer's accounts receivable balance.

Another intuitive approach would be to review past-due aging totals for total accounts receivable, and then estimate the percent of total dollars 61-90, 91-120, and 120+ days past due that will be uncollectable and will have to be written off as bad debts. For example, credit personnel might determine that ultimately the company will only be able to collect 85 percent of dollars 61-90 days past due, 65 percent of dollars 91-120 days past due, and 40 percent of dollars 120+ days past due.

A credit practitioner will probably want to try both the analytical/historical and the intuitive approaches to forecasting bad-debt write-offs for balance sheet and P&L purposes. Forecast output for each method can be compared to get a better feel for their potential for accuracy.

If credit personnel only intend to use one of these approaches, it's probably best to use the analytical/historical approach. This approach is strong because history tends to repeat itself in clearly defined mathematical patterns.

ABSTRACT SUMMARY

- Bad-debt write-off forecasts can either be based on historical bad-debt write-off data or subjective analysis.

- A historical forecast can be generated through a review of bad-debt write-offs of the past five years. As a part of this review, credit personnel should plot the dollar totals for annual bad-debt write-offs, as well as annually what percent of total sales was represented by bad-debt write-offs.

- Another historical methodology would be to review the ratio of total bad-debt write-off dollars as a percent of year-end accounts receivable over the past five years to determine if there is a quantifiable mathematical relationship.

- One intuitive approach to forecasting bad-debt write-offs is to analyze the aged trial balance for accounts receivable, including a review of each of the customer exposures in the aged trial balance.

- Another intuitive approach would be to review past-due aging totals for total accounts receivable, and determine the percent of total dollars 61-90, 91-120, and 120+ days past due that would be uncollectable and eventually written off as bad debts.

FORECASTING DSO BY MONTH

Every year the credit department should perform a monthly DSO forecast for the coming year. Monthly DSO projections can provide the department with budgeted objectives. These projections also can be used to perform a build-up method forecast of dollar levels for accounts receivable, which treasury and senior management can use in assessing the impact of changes in working capital on cash and loan positions (see "Build-Up," in this chapter, p. 227).

Furthermore, using DSO projections, credit personnel can perform a two-step roll-forward calculation to project monthly cash receipts.

To forecast DSO by month, credit professionals need a three-to five-year data base of actual monthly DSO performance. They can chart the monthly DSO data in the following format:

DSO by Month

YEAR	JAN	FEB	MAR	APR	MAY	JUN	JULY	AUG	SPET	OCT	NOV	DEC
1988	46	49	47	43	45	44	41	42	47	49	46	48
1987	44	45	45	50	41	42	42	43	45	46	46	47
1986	41	46	44	42	42	44	50	41	43	44	45	46
1985	42	44	46	44	41	48	40	41	42	43	45	47
AVG	43	46	45	45	42	45	43	42	44	46	46	47

The four-year average for each of the months will provide a starting point for the monthly forecasts. Additionally, credit practitioners will want to look at each particular month's history and highlight any seasonality or other trends. These can sometimes be identified by charting each individual month's DSO performance on graph paper. DSO performance data that appears to be an aberration from historical trends might, in some cases, be omitted from the analysis.

When performing the forecast, credit personnel may want to attach weighted averages to more recent performance as they make adjustments to the four-year averages. For example, when projecting January DSO, they may want to attach a greater degree of value to January performance for 1988 and 1987 and assign a lower weighted average to the 1986 and 1985 January DSO performance. For example, we may determine, based on history, that a weighted score of 40 percent should be assigned to 1988, 30 percent to 1987, 20 percent to 1986, and 10 percent to 1985. Thus, the weighted average for January DSO is 44 days. The computations are as follows:

—40% weighted average × January 1988 (46 days) = 18.4 days
—30% weighted average × January 1987 (44 days) = 13.2 days
—20% wcighted average × January 1986 (41 days) = 8.2 days
—10% weighted average × January 1985 (42 days) = 4.2 days

44.0 days

Of course, the other option would be to simply adopt the pure four-year average of January DSO performance as the January forecast for the upcoming year.

The company's data processing department might be able to help design a statistical program that would mathematically smooth or massage the data.

One way to test the validity of monthly DSO projections is to project out dollar levels using the accounts receivable build-up method. This exercise will enable credit personnel to determine if the absolute dollar levels projected out are representative for the projected monthly DSOs. For example, a 37-day projected DSO for October 1989 once built up and quantified may indicate extremely low ending October 1989 AR. Credit personnel would have determined that the projected level for October AR was not representative of prior activity. At that point, they can rereview assumptions relating to projected DSO and projected sales.

If the forecast appears representative, they can then translate the projected DSOs and corresponding accounts receivable dollar levels into projected monthly cash receipts using the roll-forward method. By reviewing the projected receipts, they can determine if the projected monthly receipts levels are capable of being attained. Based on their knowledge of historical monthly cash receipts collections, credit personnel might determine that a $22 million cash month is unattainable.

No matter which method credit personnel select for projecting monthly DSO, they need to perform this or some other type of cross-check. In fact, on the first pass at the forecast, they might generate projections based on weighted averages and pure averages, and contrast the output from the two different methodologies.

One of the worst mistakes that can be made in forecasting monthly DSO is to avoid analyzing historical data in the process. Subjective forecasts that fail to take into account historical data aren't likely to be as accurate as those that do.

ABSTRACT SUMMARY

- Monthly DSO projections can serve as budgeted objectives for the credit department.
- DSO projections can also be used to perform a two-step roll-forward calculation to project monthly cash receipts.
- When forecasting DSO by month, credit personnel will need to work from a three- to five-year data base of actual monthly DSO performance.

■ When reviewing historical DSO data, look at each particular month's history and highlight any seasonality or other trends.

■ To test the validity of potential monthly DSO projections, project out dollar levels using the accounts receivable build-up method.

THE FORECASTING AUDIT

How detailed is credit department forecasting? Is the department forecasting monthly cash receipts, DSO, customer DSO, accounts receivable, and annual bad-debt write-offs? If not, why not? After all, the credit department should be the authority on these cash flow matters.

The credit department possesses a great amount of detailed and subjective information about these forecast variables. So it is important to assess whether the department is taking advantage of the opportunities afforded by cash management forecasting.

This can be accomplished if the credit department performs an annual audit of its forecasting activities. Through an audit, credit personnel can determine whether the scope of the department's forecasts and its output are meeting forecasting needs and wants.

Each forecast should be evaluated and reviewed based on financial and technical criteria. For each forecast that the credit department performs, credit personnel should chart the following information in a columnar format: name of forecast, distribution, frequency, objectives, perceived company benefit, department of benefit, hardware required, and software type. The chart should appear as shown in Exhibit 7.6.

The goal at the beginning of the audit is simply to come to grips with the scope of the forecast effort. The first question in the audit should be: Are there any other forecasts that the credit department should be performing but isn't? Credit personnel might also want to question why they have omitted another forecasting methodology for, let's say, forecasting cash receipts.

The next point of concern is whether the frequency of particular forecasts is sufficient to meet the objectives and desired benefits. In assessing this question, credit personnel might find that their DSO needs require the DSO forecast to be updated and revised periodically.

Also of interest in the audit: What is the objective of the particular forecast and how is it benefiting someone? The objective and benefit are the driving forces behind the forecast. So credit personnel will want to question whether the right benefit is being derived, and whether the appropriate department is enjoying that benefit.

Credit personnel will also want to confirm that existing computer hardware is sufficient to meet forecast requirements. The credit department could be performing a mainframe application on a microcomputer, thereby limiting performance capabilities.

Also ask: Is the source of the software satisfactory? If not, the credit department may have to look beyond the company's data processing department in order to meet its forecasting needs. Viable alternatives to consider include internal programming by the credit function using personal computers, as well as purchasing off-the-shelf software packages.

Exhibit 7.6
Forecasting Audit Grid Analysis

Name	Distribution	Frequency	Objective	Benefit	Department Benefiting	Hardware	Software
Receipts forecast	Treasury V.P. Finance	Monthly	Cash Flow planning	Quantifies Needs	Treasury	Mainframe	Internal
DSO forecast	Treasury V.P. Finance Fin. Planning	Annually/ Updated quarterly	Monitor DSO	Controls Cash Flow	Treasury Credit	Micro	Internal
AR forecast	Treasury Accounting	Annually/ Updated quarterly	Balance Sheet accuracy	Asset Management	Treasury	Micro	Internal

Once credit personnel have evaluated forecast specifications, they can make a subjective evaluation of the overall quality of the forecasts. Are forecasts reasonably accurate, and do they meet set objectives and provide the desired benefits? Or are the forecasts too often inaccurate and of no real value? In some cases, the credit department might be using the wrong methodology in deriving a forecast. If there are shortcomings along these lines, they need to be corrected.

Ultimately one needs to ask: Are the forecasts meeting the overall objectives and needs of the firm? If the answer is "no," the credit department will need to make some changes to improve the forecast output.

The results of the audit may produce far-ranging changes in the scope and methods of a credit department's forecasting. But even if this does not occur, the audit will provide credit personnel with a better picture of the department's forecasting output and capabilities. For this reason, such an audit should be performed every year or two.

ABSTRACT SUMMARY

- Every year, the credit department should annually perform an audit of its forecasting activities.

- The audit is conducted to determine whether the scope of forecasting activities is sufficient to meet the needs and wants of the firm, and also whether the output of forecasts is generally accurate and valuable.

- For each forecast, the credit department should chart the following information in a columnar format: name of the forecast, distribution, frequency, forecast objectives, perceived company benefit, department of benefit, hardware required, and software type.

- The first question in the audit should be: Are there any other forecasts that the credit department should be performing but isn't?

- After credit personnel evaluate the forecast specifications, they should make a subjective evaluation of the overall quality of the credit department's forecasts.

8

LEGAL ISSUES

WHEN IS IT TIME TO "GO LEGAL"?

One of the toughest dilemmas a credit practitioner faces is whether to refer a customer account to a collection agency or attorney. Credit practitioners would rather avoid the legal fees of outside collection efforts. However, they also must consider the possibility that all other internal avenues for collecting the debt have been exhausted.

Generally, it is best to exhaust all internal collection options before turning to outside help. Of course, the key is knowing when internal efforts are no longer likely to bear fruit.

It may be time to refer an account when a workout customer:

- Repeatedly breaks payment commitments;
- Stops paying down its account for 60–90 days or more;
- No longer returns telephone calls; or
- Is paying off other suppliers but shows no intention of paying your balance down.

In most cases the credit practitioner should try to establish a formalized weekly payment program to which the past-due customer can reasonably adhere. As long as a customer is making an effort to reduce the balance, there should be no reason to refer the account. The credit practitioner might even want to consider accepting a postdated check; despite the fact that postdated checks do not afford the same protection under bad check laws as other checks, a postdated check is still better than no check at all.

Before referring an account, consider offering to convert the receivable to an interest-bearing note that is collateralized either personally or by the customer's assets. If the customer consents to this arrangement, and then defaults on the note, the credit practitioner will be able to pursue legal avenues with personal or corporate assets that can be readily attached.

One point to consider before sending the customer a final demand letter: a credit professional should be prepared to follow through on any ultimatum. It's not wise to use a final demand as a bluff.

Typically, a demand letter will state that if the customer does not contact the creditor within 10 working days regarding the open balance due, the creditor will refer the account to an attorney or collection agency. A credit person sending such a letter must be prepared to follow through with the threatened legal action. If he doesn't, he loses all credibility with the customer. He also may be costing the company money by wasting time that could be effectively spent by an attorney or collection agency in resolving the matter.

Time, in these situations, is critical. A creditor who unnecessarily procrastinates may find that other creditors are one step ahead. They may have already beaten a path to a court and attached the debtor's assets. Thus, even if one succeeds in court, there may not be sufficient assets left to satisfy the company's outstanding balance.

The credit practitioner must always act in the best interests of the company — and not simply in the manner that might appear to be in the best interests of the credit function. So when it's time to go legal, do it. And don't look back.

ABSTRACT SUMMARY

- Before turning to a collection agency or attorney, the credit professional should exhaust all internal collections options.
- As long as a past-due customer is making a good faith effort to reduce its balance, it may not be necessary to place the account for collection.
- Some signals that it may be time to refer an account are a workout customer that repeatedly breaks payment commitments, or one that no longer returns phone calls.
- Before referring an account, consider offering to convert the receivable to an interest-bearing note that is collateralized either personally or by the customer's assets.
- A credit professional shouldn't give a customer any ultimatums unless he is prepared to follow through with the promised legal action.

COLLECTING VIA THE LEGAL CYCLE

Utilizing the legal cycle to collect accounts receivable can be a slow, drawn-out process (see Exhibit 8.1). Getting paid will involve leaping a number of hurdles. However, in some cases, legal means are the only hope a company has for recovering the money it is owed.

The first step in the process is to make sure the company has a winning case. Legal fees to file a lawsuit and attach or liquidate assets can be very high, and the company will probably have to make a significant commitment in terms of manpower in preparation for the case. There is also the possibility of a countersuit. So it's a good idea to first ask the question: "Can we win this suit?"

The creditor also needs to determine whether the debtor has any tangible assets to attach or liquidate. It does a company no good to win a case against a debtor that has no assets to attach or liquidate.

The bottom line is that a company has no business allocating corporate funds and manpower to a court fight that it cannot profit from.

Once the company determines that it wishes to pursue collections through the legal system, the first step is to select legal counsel that will prepare a lawsuit against the nonpaying customer. The jurisdiction of the suit will most likely depend upon where the debtor is domiciled.

The attorney will file a suit against the customer in the form of a complaint of nonpayment. Although laws in each state differ, each requires that the debtor respond to the suit within a reasonable time frame.

When the case comes before the court, the creditor needs to be prepared to have credit personnel testify, and to produce detailed records evidencing the debt and nonpayment. A credit department's collection call cards are generally quite valuable in a court proceeding.

If the creditor wins the case, a judgment will be entered by the court on the creditor's behalf. Remember, however, winning a judgment does not guarantee payment from the debtor. A judgment merely sets the amount of money that the debtor owes the creditor.

It is the creditor's job to successfully execute the judgment. In most states, a judgment gives the creditor lien rights to the debtor's property.

In order to satisfy a claim, the court may attach a debtor's assets or liquidate them. After the judgment, the judgment creditor must ask the court to issue a writ of execution. The court will then direct the writ to the sheriff to levy upon the debtor's property, which can be liquidated via a sheriff's sale. A writ of execution and a sheriff's sale can be stayed if the debtor files for bankruptcy, however.

Under a liquidation, the creditor is paid in accordance with the priority lien rights relating to the asset being sold. Under the attachment scenario, the debtor's assets are placed in the custody of the court until the judgment is satisfied.

Asset attachment or liquidation are the two final steps a creditor can take in the post-judgment collection rights process.

253

Exhibit 8.1
Flow Chart of Legal Cycle

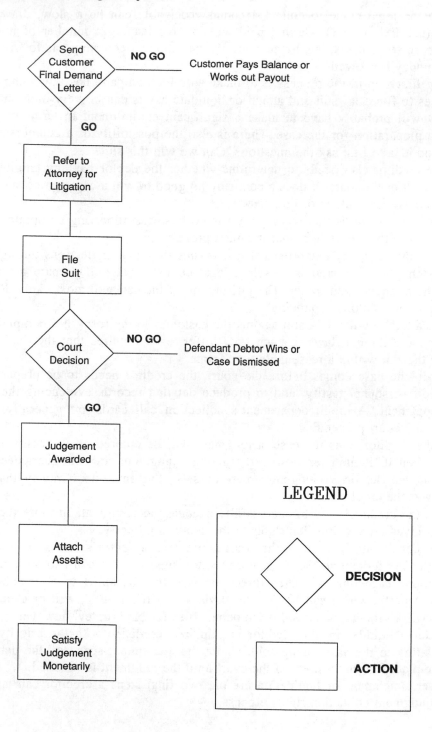

Send Customer Final Demand Letter — **NO GO** → Customer Pays Balance or Works out Payout

GO

Refer to Attorney for Litigation

File Suit

Court Decision — **NO GO** → Defendant Debtor Wins or Case Dismissed

GO

Judgement Awarded

Attach Assets

Satisfy Judgement Monetarily

LEGEND

DECISION

ACTION

ABSTRACT SUMMARY

- The first step within the legal cycle is to select legal counsel that will prepare a suit against the nonpaying customer.

- Before making a claim, be sure it is valid; litigation costs are high and an invalid claim could draw a countersuit from the defendant.

- When a creditor wins such a case, a judgment is entered with the court records on the creditor's behalf.

- Winning a judgment does not guarantee payment; a judgment merely sets the amount of money that the debtor owes the creditor.

- After a creditor is awarded a judgment, the debtor's assets may be attached or liquidated by the court to satisfy the claim.

SELECTING A COLLECTION AGENCY

Selecting a collection agency isn't a trivial matter. The agency or agencies that a company selects will, in effect, become the last hope for generating cash flow from bad-debt write-off accounts.

A good way to ensure that the process is systematic and thorough is to create a collection agency selection grid, including information about various prospective agencies (see Exhibit 8.2).

In order to complete the collection agency selection grid, the credit practitioner will have to make a number of inquiries of the agencies and their references. First, obtain from the agency the following information:

- Years in business
- Collection fee on recoveries
- Does the agency charge a non-contingency fee?
- Does the agency send a free final demand to the customer?
- Is the agency a member of the Commercial Collection Agency Section of the Commercial Law League of America?
- Does the agency have nationwide coverage?
- Is the agency bonded?
- Does the agency have a trust account where collected funds are deposited?
- Does the agency file bankruptcy proof of claim forms on behalf of clients?

With the exception of reference information, the answers to these questions will provide the credit professional with almost all the information he needs. The process of making the inquiries should also be helpful in providing a preliminary impression of the agency's overall scope, style, and professionalism.

The number of years that an agency has been in business should be a critical factor in the selection process. One of the biggest mistakes a company can make is to select an agency that eventually becomes insolvent; when that happens, the client firm often loses recovered receivables. Years in business is a helpful indicator in gauging the likelihood of insolvency. In many cases, it's best to select an established agency.

Fee structure is another critical variable, but it should not be the deciding factor. Many times, the selection will ultimately be determined by the agencies' answers with respect to bonding, a trust account, or CLLA membership.

Anyone selecting a collection agency should contact at least two and preferably three customers that are currently using the services of the collection agency in

Exhibit 8.2
Collection Agency Selection Grid

Selection Criteria	ABC Agency	XYZ Agency	Comments
Years in Business	2	25	
Collection Fee %	25%	25%	
Non-contingency Basis	No	No	
References	Good	Excellent	
Free Final Demand	No	Yes	
Nationwide Coverage	No	Yes	
Member CLLA	No	Yes	
Derogatory Information	None	None	

question. One should contact the references and ask them to answer the following questions:

- How long have you been doing business with the collection agency?
- Have you ever had disputes with the agency regarding balances due?
- Have any referred accounts ever complained about the agency's collection practices?
- Have you ever had to take away an account from the agency due to unprofessional conduct or poor handling?
- How successful is the agency in collecting on referred accounts?
- Does the agency remit collected funds on a timely basis?
- Do you know of any derogatory information regarding the agency?
- Why do you do business with the agency?
- What is the fee structure with the agency?
- Has the agency provided your firm with nationwide service? If so, were you satisfied with their results?
- How would you rate the agency's collection style?
- How would you rate the overall level of service?
- How would you rate the agency's overall performance?

These reference questions should provide a good indication of whether the credit practitioner's company should even consider doing business with a particular collection agency. References should be able to offer insight into the agency's ethics and overall conduct. If possible, ask the agency for references from firms in a similar industry with similar sales volume.

At this stage, the credit person should have all the information he or she needs to fill out the selection grid. This grid can be used to evaluate a single candidate or multiple candidates.

Having a formal procedure for selecting a collection agency is important because it will help a company make the right choice, and in so doing, ensure maximum recovery of lost cash flow within prescribed legal and ethical standards. The process for selecting a credit agency should be a part of written credit department policies and procedures.

ABSTRACT SUMMARY

- Choosing the right collection agency is important because the selected agency will represent the vendor's last hope for realizing any cash flow from a bad-debt write-off.

■ Creating a selection grid, with information about the various agencies being considered, can assist in the selection process.

■ One of the more critical factors to consider is how many years the agency has been in business.

■ In selecting an agency, fee structure is important, but it should not be the deciding factor.

■ Before selecting an agency, contact at least two or three of its customers for references.

MEASURING COLLECTION
AGENCY PERFORMANCE

A company should measure the performance of each of its collection agencies on an ongoing basis, using a variety of formal and informal yardsticks (see Exhibit 8.3). Monitoring the agencies' performance is necessary to ensure that they are charging competitive fees and meeting expected performance standards with respect to the administration and collection of bad-debt write-off referrals. In essence, the credit department will profit from keeping a collection agency report card.

One simple measure of collection performance is to track the percentage of dollars collected as a function of total dollars referred. For example, let's say that during a particular year, total referrals to a particular agency were $100,000, and the agency collected or recovered $22,000. That agency's collection rate that year would be 22%.

When measuring collection performance in this way, note that when recoveries or collections carry over into the next year, the open amount referred should be carried into the next year's total collections and referrals. For example, a company may refer a $25,000 account to an agency, which collects $5,000 in the first year, leaving an open balance of $20,000. The next year the agency recovers an additional $8,000 from the same customer. Thus, when calculating the agency's performance in the second year, be sure to add the $20,000 open balance to the agency's total referrals for the second year.

The same type of collection rate analysis can be performed on individual accounts. A credit practitioner can measure collection agency performance on a per-customer basis. An individual collection rate per customer can be established by calculating individual customer collections as a percentage of the customer's total dollars referred. Results from this analysis may reveal that the agency's collection performance is not as strong as its overall collection rate appears to indicate. The per-customer collection rates might show that the agency had success with just one or two referrals, which dramatically skewed the total collection rate in its favor.

Taking the exercise one step further, a credit professional might want to analyze the agency's collection rates for major accounts—high-dollar referrals. The agency could be having great success in collecting amounts under $25,000, but great difficulty in making any headway with major bad-debt referrals. If that's the case, the company might want to consider referring high-dollar accounts to another agency.

Another measure of collection agency return is a turnover analysis of the dollars referred to the collection agency. In essence, this involves performing a days sales outstanding (DSO) calculation of total dollars outstanding with the agency contrasted to total dollars referred to the agency. In this case, total dollars outstand-

Exhibit 8.3
Sample Existing Collection Agency Report Card

Category	Score	Comments
Overall Recovery rate	4	
Net Overall Recovery Rate	4	
Major Account Recovery Rate	4	
Current Agency Turnover Rate	4	
Average Turnaround for Initial Recoveries	4	
Prompt Remittance of Funds	4	
Fee Structure	3	
Dispute Frequency	5	
Debtor Complaints	5	
Overall Collection Style	4	
Outside Derogatory Info	5	
Overall Agency Score	45	

OVERALL AGENCY SCORE LEGEND

50-55	Strong agency scored strong in all areas
42-49	Scored well overall
34-41	Above average but can improve
28-33	Average score. Check recovery rates and fees
20-27	Scored poorly. Review all scores. Consider change
Below 20	Performance unacceptable. terminate relationship

CATEGORY SCORING GUIDE
5–Best Possible Score
4–Good But Not the Best
3–Meets Expected Requirements
2–Needs to Improve
1–Performance Unacceptable

Date: 09/20/XX
Agency Evaluated: DPM Collection Agency
Disposition: Approved For Current Year's Referrals

Reviewed By: B. P. Mavrovitis
Signature:

ing would replace total accounts receivable and total dollars referred would replace sales in the true DSO calculation.

For example, assume it's the month-end of April and the activity was as follows:

Dollars open as of month ending April and uncollected:	$ 25,000
January referrals for collection:	10,000
February referrals for collection:	9,500
March referrals for collection:	10,000
April referrals for collection:	7,500

Referrals from January through April equal $37,000. The agency has collected $12,000 of this total, leaving $25,000 uncollected and open. Based on these figures, the credit person can perform a DSO calculation on the $25,000 in open referrals (see Calculating DSO, in Chapter 5, p. 149).

Combined April and March referrals are $17,500 and equate to 60 days. Since the $25,000 in open referrals is greater than the April and March referrals, the collection agency DSO is greater than 60 days. To determine how much greater, the credit person would first subtract $17,500 from $25,000, getting $7,500, which represents open referrals that are greater than 60 days old. He would then divide the $7,500 of open referrals greater than 60 days by the third month's referrals of $9,500 to see what percent of the third month's referrals are still open and outstanding. The answer is 78.947%. He then multiplies 78.947% by 30 days for the third month, which rounds to 23.68 days, and adds the 23.68 days to the 60 days open referrals for April and March to derive a collection agency DSO performance of 83.68 days on open referred balances with the collection agency.

The credit department should also be keeping track of how long it takes for the company's various agencies to remit funds collected from referred accounts. Collection agencies have been known to "sit on" client funds for anywhere from 30 to 120 days before remitting them. An agency might be using the funds for working capital purposes or simply earning interest on the funds after investing them — as opposed to remitting them to the client on a timely and ethical basis.

Unless a credit person keeps in close contact with the agency, it will be difficult to track how long an agency is holding on to the company's collected funds. The only other way a company might get wind of an agency's poor performance in this area is if a referred customer advises the company that a payment has been made. This might happen if the referred customer wants to buy from the company on a cash-in-advance basis, or if the referred account wants the company to surrender a lien that has been perfected.

Don't be naive about the remittance practices of certain collection agencies. Create safeguards to protect recovered cash flow. For instance, to keep close tabs on the agency's performance, always ask it for a copy of the referred account's check along with the envelope that was remitted by the referred customer to the agency.

Another yardstick of performance is the average turnaround time for initial recoveries made by the agency on new referrals. Thus, on an annual basis, the credit department should review all the newly referred accounts. How long did it take the agency before it made its initial recovery? Thirty days? Forty-five? More than 90?

With respect to pricing and fees, the credit person needs to measure the total fees paid the agency as a percentage of the total dollars collected or recovered by the agency. Fees could include non-contingency fees paid upfront at the time of referral, attorneys' fees, or other legal fees, as well as the collection fee on the actual recovery. Most often the agency may apply a non-contingency fee against collection fees; this means that recovery fees are not collected by the agency until the recovery fees to be paid exceed the non-contingency fee paid.

In addition, a company might want to compare the non-contingency fee and collection fee pricing of one agency to those of another agency to gauge if the firm is getting a competitive deal.

Other informal performance measurements include an overall rating of the agency's collection style, the total number of disputes between the company and the agency regarding referred accounts, the number of complaints registered by referred accounts against the agency due to illegal collection practices, and the number of accounts the company took away from the agency due to inefficiency or legal violations.

The formal and informal yardsticks outlined here should be reviewed at least on an annual basis. This will ensure that unethical agency conduct, declines in collection performance, and out-of-line fee structures do not go unnoticed. Formalize annual reviews of collection agency activity as part of written credit department policies and procedures.

ABSTRACT SUMMARY

- Monitoring a collection agency's performance is necessary to ensure that it is charging competitive fees and meeting expected performance standards.
- A simple measure of collection performance is to track the percentage of dollars collected as a function of total dollars referred.
- A credit practitioner might also want to measure collection agency performance on a per-customer basis, focusing particularly on major accounts.

- Other performance measures might include the average turnaround time for initial recoveries on new referrals, the total fees paid as a percentage of total dollars collected, and the total number of disputes between the company and the agency.

- The credit department should also keep track of how long it takes for various agencies to remit funds collected from referred accounts.

MONITORING BAD-DEBT WRITE-OFF ACCOUNTS

There are basically four reasons why a company might write off bad debt:

1. A customer may file for bankruptcy via a Chapter 11 or Chapter 13 filing.
2. A customer cannot or refuses to pay its account, and the customer is placed for collection through an attorney or collection agency.
3. A customer goes out of business, sells the business, closes its doors, skips town, or files for Chapter 7 of the Bankruptcy Code (business liquidation).
4. A dispute arises over price, quantity received, or whether the customer received product or services, and the supplier is unable to prove that the price or quantity was correct, or that the product or services were received. In this case, the supplier may still be selling to the customer but writes off certain invoices or deductions to its bad-debt account.

Under the first three scenarios, the supplier may be able to recover the bad-debt write-off amount. Under the fourth scenario there will be no recovery unless the supplier decides to litigate the dispute or amount in question.

In each case, the supplier's credit department needs to establish a mechanism for tracking bad-debt write-offs. And, for the first three scenarios, the credit department needs to track any recoveries made for reporting and monitoring purposes.

For reporting purposes, the credit practitioner wants to be able to identify the exact amount of dollars written off, as well as the exact amount of dollars that have been recovered and credited to the income statement. At the same time, the credit person needs a formal, computerized means of tracking the status of customers from which there is the potential for recovery. Manual tracking of bad-debt write-offs and recoveries is subject to human error and can be very time-consuming.

As an alternative, the credit practitioner could record all the detailed information either on mainframe computer or via a personal computer. Using a PC, details of a master suspense account and sub-accounts would be maintained on the PC while making monthly journal entries to the general ledger to record the month's total write-off and recovery activity.

Under the mainframe scenario, within the general ledger, the credit practitioner should establish a master suspense account that keeps track of total bad-debt write-offs by customer and dollar amount, and provides detail for each of the individual write-offs sustained. For each bad-debt write-off sustained, there should be a sub-account for potential recoveries. The individual sub-accounts for each bad-debt write-off should list the following information:

Write-Off Name/ Date	Reason Code	Original Write-Off Amount	Recovery Date	Recovery Amount	Check Number	Moving Net Loss	Comments (payments)
ABC	CH. 11	$35,750	2/12/86	$2,500	125	$33,250	1st of 4
12/15/84			6/17/86	$3,000	920	$30,250	2nd of 4

The main suspense account should have a dollar total for total recoveries, whereas the sub-accounts should provide individual customer detail of the recoveries that have been made, thus serving as an audit trail for total company recoveries.

The Reason Code section enables one to classify bad debts based on the reason for the write-off, e.g., collection agency referral, attorney referral, bankruptcy, or unresolvable customer dispute. This way, the credit department can advise management of the type and quality of bad debts that have been sustained by the firm. A complete analysis of bad debts by customer reason code may reveal that write-offs can be primarily attributed to unresolvable customer disputes as opposed to presumed poor credit analysis and extension (see Exhibit 8.4).

Each time a payment is received, a credit practitioner can enter the detailed information into the sub-account and obtain a total moving net loss figure for the respective bad-debt write-off account. The comments section allows the user to elaborate on the nature of the payment received.

The sub-accounts are helpful not only for monitoring and reporting purposes, but they will also provide a red flag if an old bad-debt account resurfaces and wants to buy from the firm again on open-account credit terms. The red flag provided by the sub-accounts might lead to the company denying credit to the old customer, or it could lead to a more guarded granting of credit. In either case, it's good to know about the customer's payment history.

Exhibit 8.4
ABC Co. 1988 Write-Off Summary

Write-Off Reason Code	Write-Offs	Percent of Total Write-Offs	Recoveries	Percent of Total Recoveries
Collection Agency	15718	15.25%	6216	27.98%
Attorney Referral	2789	2.71%	1000	4.50%
Chapter 7	0	.00%	0	.00%
Chapter 11	14295	13.87%	2500	11.25%
Chapter 13	3169	3.07%	0	.00%
Unresolvable Dispute	67114	65.11%	12500	56.27%
Total 1988 Write-Offs	103085	100.00%	22216	100.00%

With the suspense account and sub-accounts in place, a credit person can provide timely and accurate reports to senior management—either on a quarterly or annual basis. The reports can provide classification of bad debts, total write-offs to date, total recoveries to date, as well as individual customer detail of total write-offs and recoveries.

This process enhances the reportability of bad-debt write-off data and uses the tracking process as a management tool to enhance potential recoveries.

ABSTRACT SUMMARY

- Companies write off bad debt for four reasons (customer files Chapter 11 or 13; customer refuses to pay; customer goes out of business; or there is a customer dispute that can't be reconciled).
- In each case, the supplier's credit department needs to establish a mechanism for tracking the write-offs.
- The credit person needs a formal, computerized means of tracking the status of customers from which there is the potential for recovery.
- Using a PC, the credit person can make monthly journal entries to the general ledger to record the month's activity.
- Under the mainframe scenario, within the general ledger, the credit practitioner should establish a suspense account that keeps track of total bad-debt write-offs by customer and dollar amount; and for each bad-debt write-off sustained, there should be a sub-account for potential recoveries.

CLASSES OF BANKRUPTCY

There are three classes of bankruptcy that generally impact standard trade accounts receivable creditors: Chapter 7, Chapter 11, or Chapter 13.

Chapter 7 of the Bankruptcy Code is referred to as a straight bankruptcy. The debtor's nonexempt property is liquidated by the bankruptcy trustee and the net proceeds are distributed to the creditors accordingly. In a Chapter 7 bankruptcy, no provision is made for a reorganization plan.

In Chapter 7, the Bankruptcy Court appoints an interim trustee or the creditors can elect an acceptable trustee. Creditors can make the selection only if they hold 20 percent in dollar value of allowable and undisputed claims.

Under Chapter 7, the Bankruptcy Court can dismiss the debtor's petition for liquidation if it finds that the granting of such relief would be an abuse of the federal Bankruptcy Code. For example, it would be considered an abuse of the code if the debtor committed fraud prior to filing the petition.

The most common form of bankruptcy impacting trade creditors is the Chapter 11 bankruptcy. A debtor files for Chapter 11 seeking court protection or relief while it files a reorganization plan with the court. The debtor filing for bankruptcy under Chapter 11 of the Bankruptcy Code is referred to as a "debtor in possession."

A debtor in possession is allowed to continue to operate the business during the reorganization period. However, under Chapter 11, creditors can request a court-appointed trustee if they believe the debtor is mismanaging the reorganization.

Under this form of bankruptcy, the court appoints a creditors committee holding unsecured claims. The committee is usually comprised of the seven largest unsecured creditors. The creditors committee has the right to employ a secretary, attorney and accountants at the debtor's expense.

Whenever it is economically feasible, a creditor should seek representation on the committee; it's the best way to protect the company's claim. Committee representation offers a creditor a first-hand look at the debtor's plan for reorganization, and for participating credit staffers it can be quite an educational experience.

Any debtor's plan for reorganization must be accepted by more than half the creditors. The plan must also be accepted by creditors representing two-thirds of the dollar value of outstanding debts. However, if a designated group of creditors does not vote in favor of the proposed plan, it can still be confirmed if the Bankruptcy Court finds that the class of creditors will be unimpaired by the proposed plan for reorganization. Under Chapter 11, the plan for reorganization must be submitted within 120 days of filing bankruptcy.

A Chapter 13 bankruptcy proceeding is designed for individuals who operate as small unincorporated businesses. In order to file for Chapter 13, the individual's unsecured debts must be less than $100,000 and secured debts must be less than $350,000. Chapter 13 allows the debtor to reorganize through a court-approved plan. Like Chapter 11, Chapter 13 is not a self-terminating or liquidation proceeding. (Other bankruptcy proceedings less common to standard trade creditors include Chapters 9 and 12 of the Bankruptcy Code, which relate to municipalities and the family farmer.)

Bankruptcies can be classified in another important fashion. There are voluntary petitions, in which the debtor seeks to reorganize (Chapters 11 and 13) or liquidate (Chapter 7). And there are involuntary petitions, in which the bankruptcy proceeding is initiated by creditors.

A group of three or more creditors holding uncontingent and unsecured claims totaling at least $5,000 can file for involuntary proceedings against their common customer and debtor. If there are fewer than 12 creditors, however, it only takes one or more creditors with total claims of $5,000 to file an involuntary petition. An involuntary petition can be filed seeking either a liquidation or reorganization of the debtor's business.

Filing an involuntary petition against a debtor can be risky. If the court ultimately dismisses the petition, it can require the petitioners to file a bond to indemnify the debtor for costs, damages, and attorney fees.

With Chapters 7 and 13, once a creditor receives notice of a debtor's petition for a bankruptcy proceeding, the creditor must file a proof-of-claim form (see Filing a Bankruptcy Proof-of-Claim Form, in this chapter) with the Bankruptcy Court within 90 days of the first creditors meeting. On the other hand, with a Chapter 11 proceeding, unless the debtor has omitted its claim from the schedule of claims or has listed an incorrect amount, the creditor is not required to file a proof-of-claim form.

To be on the safe side, file a timely proof-of-claim form for all classes of bankruptcy.

ABSTRACT SUMMARY

- There are three classes of bankruptcy that generally impact standard trade accounts receivable creditors; they correspond to Chapters 7, 11 and 13 of the Bankruptcy Code.

- In a Chapter 11 filing, the most common form of bankruptcy impacting trade creditors, a debtor files for court protection while it forms a reorganization plan for the court's approval.

- A debtor filing for bankruptcy under Chapter 11 is referred to as a "debtor in possession."

- Chapter 7 and 13 proceedings require a proof-of-claim to be filed within 90 days of the first creditor's meeting. Under Chapter 11, a proof-of-claim is not required unless the debtor has omitted your claim from the schedule of claims.

■ Bankruptcy filings can be voluntary or involuntary; a group of three or more creditors holding uncontingent and unsecured claims totaling at least $5,000 can file for involuntary proceedings against their common debtor.

FILING A BANKRUPTCY PROOF-OF-CLAIM FORM

A company receiving written notice from the Bankruptcy Court that one of its debtors has filed a bankruptcy petition must generally file a proof-of-claim form with the court. With respect to Chapters 7 and 13 of the Bankruptcy Code, the law requires that the form be filed within 90 days of the first creditors' meeting.

In a Chapter 11 filing, a creditor is not required to file a proof of claim unless the claim has been omitted from the debtor's schedule of claims or unless the amount of the claim is listed incorrectly. However, filing a proof-of-claim form for all classes of bankruptcy is still advisable.

The bankruptcy proof-of-claim form is a standard form that can be obtained from any legal stationery store at a reasonable cost (see Exhibit 8.5).

Any needless delay in filing the proof-of-claim form is foolish. Failing to file this form in a timely fashion could jeopardize the status of a creditor's claim, or possibly spoil the company's chance of gaining representation on the creditors' committee.

The form is fairly clear-cut and easy to fill out. The first task is to fill out the cover sheet. At the top of that sheet, enter the case number and jurisdiction district of the court. In the middle of the cover sheet indicate the name of the debtor, and at the bottom of the sheet enter the total dollar amount of the claim and the creditor's legal address.

Here are some basic instructions to follow when filling out the rest of the form:

Section 1.   Enter the name of the company's agent (who is preparing the form), the agent's address, and the creditor's address. Note that the form provides three different places for the creditor's address information, depending on whether the creditor is a proprietorship, a partnership, or a corporation.

Section 2.   Enter the total dollar amount of the claim.

Section 3.   Indicate the grounds for the claim, such as "for services or raw materials rendered."

Section 4.   Applies only if the claim is founded in writing.

Section 5.   If appropriate, this section indicates the creditor does not possess a note or collateral supporting the claim.

Section 6.   Complete only if the creditor possesses a valid judgment against the debtor.

Exhibit 8.5
The Bankruptcy Proof-of-Claim Form

POWER OF ATTORNEY

To

of *

The undersigned claimant hereby authorizes you. or any one of you, as attorney in fact for the undersigned and with full power of substitution, to vote on any question that may be lawfully submitted to creditors of the debtor in the above-entitled case; [if appropriate] to vote for a trustee of the estate of the debtor and for a committee of creditors; to receive dividends; and in general to perform any act not constituting the practice of law for the undersigned in all matters arising in this case.

Dated: Signed:...

            [If appropriate] By..As..

            Address:...

ACKNOWLEDGMENT

STATE OF   COUNTY OF   ss.:

INDIVIDUAL-PARTNERSHIP-CORPORATION: Acknowledged before me on

PARTNERSHIP: by   who says that he is a member of the partnership named above and is authorized to execute this power of attorney in its behalf.

CORPORATION: by   who says that he is the   of the corporation named above and is authorized to execute this power of attorney in its behalf.

            ....

            ....

* State post-office address.   *official character*

No.............................

United States Bankruptcy Court

.....................DISTRICT OF

In Bankruptcy

IN THE MATTER OF

Debtor

**Proof of Claim
and
Power of Attorney**

AMOUNT OF CLAIM $...................

(NAME)

(ADDRESS)

JULIUS BLUMBERG, INC. NEW YORK CITY 10013

Exhibit 8.5 (continued)
The Bankruptcy Proof-of-Claim Form

T 1031— Proof of Claim : Bankruptcy : Official Form 15 : Power of Attorney :
Individual, Partnership or Corporation, letter size. 9-80

© 1973 BY JULIUS BLUMBERG, INC.,
PUBLISHER, NYC 10013

TYPE OR PRINT ALL NECESSARY PARTS. INCOMPLETE OR ILLEGIBLE CLAIMS MAY RESULT IN DISALLOWANCE.

UNITED STATES BANKRUPTCY COURT FOR THE _____ DISTRICT OF

In re

CASE NO.

PROOF OF CLAIM

Include here all names used by debtor within last 6 years.   Debtor

1. **If claimant is an individual claiming for himself** The undersigned, who is the claimant herein, resides at *

   If claimant is a partnership claiming through a member The undersigned who resides at *

   is a member of _____ a partnership, composed of the undersigned and †

   and doing business at *
   and is authorized to make this proof of claim on behalf of the partnership.
   If claimant is a corporation claiming through an authorized officer The undersigned, who resides at *

   is the _____ of _____ , a corporation organized under the laws of
   and doing business at *
   and is authorized to make this proof of claim on behalf of the corporation.
   If claim is made by agent The undersigned, who resides at *
   is the agent of
   of * _____ and is authorized to make this proof of claim on behalf of the claimant.

2. The debtor was, at the time of the filing of the petition initiating this case, and still is indebted [*or* liable] to the claimant, in the sum of $

3. The consideration for this debt [*or* ground of liability] is as follows:

4. [*If the claim is founded on writing*] The writing on which this claim is founded (or a duplicate thereof) is attached hereto [*or* cannot be attached for the reason set forth in the statement attached hereto].

5. [*If appropriate*] This claim is founded on an open account, which became [*or* will become] due on
as shown by the itemized statement attached hereto. Unless it is attached hereto or its absence is explained in an attached statement, no note or other negotiable instrument has been received for the account or any part of it.

6. No judgment has been rendered on the claim except

7. The amount of all payments on this claim has been credited and deducted for the purpose of making this proof of claim.

8. This claim is not subject to any setoff or counter-claim except

9. No security interest is held for this claim except

[*If security interest in property of the debtor is claimed*] The undersigned claims the security interest under the writing referred to in paragraph 4 hereof [*or* under a separate writing which (or a duplicate of which) is attached hereto, *or* under a separate writing which cannot be attached hereto for the reason set forth in the statement attached hereto]. Evidence of perfection of such security interest is also attached hereto.

10. This claim is a general unsecured claim, except to the extent that the security interest, if any, described in paragraph 9 is sufficient to satisfy the claim. [*If priority is claimed, state the amount and basis thereof.*]

11. This claim is filed as ☐ an Unsecured ☐ a Priority ☐ a Secured claim.

Dated: Signed:

$ ....
Total amount claimed

Claim Number
(For Office Use Only)

....
* State post-office address.
† Name and post-office address of each partner.

Type or Print Name Signed

(left margin, vertical text): PENALTY FOR PRESENTING FRAUDULENT CLAIMS.—Fine of not more than $5,000 or imprisonment for not more than five years or both—Title 18, U.S.C., Sec. 152.

Section 7.   Make the following notation: "See attached statement of account."

Section 8.   Complete if there is to be a valid setoff or counterclaim.

Section 9.   Indicates there is no security interest perfected with the claim.

Section 10.   Simply reiterates that there is no security interest as part of the claim.

Section 11.   Indicate in the appropriate box whether the claim is unsecured, priority, or secured. On the same line again indicate in writing the dollar amount of the claim.

Below Section 11 sign and date the claim form, again noting the creditor's legal address.

Within the standard proof-of-claim form, there is a power-of-attorney section in which the creditor can designate its collection agency or legal counsel as having power of attorney in the jurisdiction on the creditor's behalf. Utilizing this section lets the creditor give the collection agency or legal counsel power to make decisions relating to the proceedings on its behalf.

The creditor's attorney or legal department should proofread the executed proof-of-claim form to ensure that the filing of the claim is properly executed and accepted by the Bankruptcy Court.

The proof-of-claim form should be prepared by senior credit management and signed by an authorized officer. The form should be prepared and submitted to the court in duplicate, along with an itemized statement of account. Attach a self-addressed, stamped envelope and request in a cover letter to the Bankruptcy Court that the court acknowledge receipt of the claim using an attached duplicate form. If after a period of six weeks the court has failed to acknowledge the claim in writing, contact the court by telephone to verify that the claim has been filed. If it has been filed, once again request a written acknowledgment.

ABSTRACT SUMMARY

- A vendor must file a proof-of-claim form with the Bankruptcy Court within 90 days of the first creditors meeting in Chapter 7 and 13 bankruptcies.
- Chapter 11 filings do not require the creditor to file a proof-of-claim form unless the creditor has been omitted from the debtor's schedule of claims or the amount of the claim is listed incorrectly. Nevertheless, it remains sound credit policy to file a proof-of-claim form for all classes of bankruptcy.

- A standard proof-of-claim form can be obtained from any legal stationery store.

- A creditor can use the proof-of-claim form to give its collection agency or legal counsel the power to act on its behalf in the bankruptcy proceeding (power of attorney).

- In order to ensure that the claim is properly executed, the creditor should have its attorney or legal department proofread the proof-of-claim form.

PERSONAL GUARANTEES

A personal guarantee represents a guarantee of payment by an individual on behalf of a business entity. Under most circumstances it is probably the weakest form of guarantee, security, or collateral that a credit practitioner can obtain from a customer in return for extending open account credit. Letters of credit, UCC1s (Uniform Commercial Code liens), subordination agreements, and corporate guarantees are all more readily enforceable and offer greater protection.

Personal guarantees can be collateralized or uncollateralized. Most trade creditors utilize uncollateralized personal guarantees in which there are no specific assets pledged in the form of a lien that stand behind the guarantee. Banks, on the other hand, generally require personal guarantees to be collateralized.

Although uncollateralized personal guarantees aren't the best protection for a creditor, they can be strengthened by taking certain steps. For instance, before executing a personal guarantee, the creditor should thoroughly review the personal guarantor's finances. This will entail asking for a personal financial statement or a copy of the individual's tax return.

A company can also benefit by using a standard form for executing the uncollateralized personal guarantee (see Exhibit 8.6). The form should state that the guarantee shall be interpreted according to the laws of the creditor's state of domicile. This allows a company to initiate court proceedings in its own state.

The creditor should include in the form a clause that provides a window of protection in the event that the guarantee is canceled by the personal guarantor. It should state that the personal guarantor is personally liable for a period of 30 days or more after written notice of cancellation. The form should also include a clause stating that the personal guarantor is prohibited from taking a security interest in his company that could supercede the creditor's unsecured claim.

The creditor should acknowledge receipt of the personal guarantee via a letter to the guarantor(s) stating that the creditor is relying on the personal guarantee as the sole means of extending credit to the company.

Unfortunately, no matter how many steps one takes to strengthen the uncollateralized personal guarantee, it may still turn out to be almost impossible to execute. In most cases, a bank will be holding a collateralized position, making it that much harder to successfully attach personal assets.

The major downside to an uncollateralized personal guarantee is that when the guarantor's company files for bankruptcy, the guarantor can also file for personal bankruptcy, which negates the enforceability of the uncollateralized personal guarantee.

Another downside of the personal guarantee is that most are negotiated without obtaining the guarantee of the individual's spouse. Without the spouse's guarantee, when the credit practitioner goes to enforce the guarantee, he often finds no personal assets remaining in the individual's name. They, of course, have been transferred to the spouse.

Exhibit 8.6

APM Co.
30389 Lincoln Blvd.
Emerson, NJ 07630

Gentlemen:

To induce you to extend credit to _____ a
_____ corporation having an office and place of business at
_____ (hereinafter
referred to as the "customer") and in consideration of your supplying to the customer goods upon credit
and in accepting the customer as a credit risk and for other good and valuable consideration, the undersigned, jointly and severally, guarantee to you, the partners named above, and your and their respective
successors and assigns, performance by the customer of all its contracts with you and prompt payment
by the customer for any goods purchased by it from you prior to this date and in the future, and the
prompt payment at maturity of any notes and other documents given by the customer in payment for
such goods and for performance of said contracts. This guarantee shall be effective immediately and
shall apply to all purchases and contracts made by the customer prior to your receipt of written notice of
cancellation from the undersigned, in which event this guarantee shall also be effective as to all purchases made by the customer within a period of thirty (30) days after the date of receipt by you of such
written notice of cancellation.

Each of the undersigned hereby agrees and consents that, without the further consent of or notice to any
of the undersigned, you may, from time to time, make any agreements or arrangements whatsoever with
the customer, including, but not limited to, agreements and arrangements for payment, extension of time
therefor, subordination, composition, compromise, discharge, or release of the whole or any part of such
obligations of performance and prompt payment, whether by way of acceptance of part payment or of
dividends or any settlement or otherwise, or for the change or surrender of any or all collateral security,
and the making of such arrangements or agreements shall in no way impair, release, or discharge the
liability of any of the undersigned hereunder.

Each of the undersigned hereby waives notice of acceptance of this guarantee and all other notices of
any kind to which the customer and/or any of the undersigned may be entitled by law, including, without
limitation, notice of the sale of any goods made under this guarantee, all demands of payment on, and
notice of nonpayment, protest, and dishonor to, the customer and any of the undersigned.

Your books and records showing the account between you and the customer shall be admissible in
evidence in any action or proceeding hereon, for the purpose of establishing the facts set forth therein,
and shall constitute prima facie proof thereof.

(Exhibit 8.6 continues on following page)

Exhibit 8.6 (continued)

This guarantee shall not be affected by the taking by you of any notes or other obligations for the payment of the price of any goods sold by you to the customer or by the taking of any security or security interest for such payment and/or for the payment of any charges in connection with said sales, or the termination of this guarantee for any reason whatsoever, and nothing shall discharge or satisfy the liability of the undersigned hereon except the full payment of the said indebtedness with interest.

No discharge of or compromise with any of the undersigned shall discharge or affect any obligation or indebtedness hereunder of any other of the undersigned.

This guarantee shall be deemed to have been made in the State of _____ and shall be construed and interpreted in accordance with the laws of said state.

This agreement shall be binding upon the undersigned, their heirs, and assigns. The names, home addresses and relationships of the undersigned to the customer are as follows:

Dated this _____ day of _____ , 19 ___ .

Very truly yours,

Attest:

_____   _____
Signature   Signature

_____   _____
Print Name   Print Name

_____   _____
Home No. & Street   Home No. & Street

_____   _____
City & State   City & State

_____   _____
Relationship to Customer   Relationship to Customer

WITNESS:

_____
Signature

_____
Print Name

_____
Home No. & Street

Even if none of these specific conditions exist — personal bankruptcy, attachment by bank or other creditors, or assets shifted to the spouse — the individual's assets are still often otherwise hidden or difficult to locate and attach.

A collateralized personal guarantee provides a greater degree of protection, as long as lien rights are properly perfected. Thus, the credit person should try to get the individual to pledge his home, stocks, bonds, government securities, or real property as collateral for the guarantee.

A note of caution: Be careful about collateralizing a personal guarantor's real property. The laws vary from state to state regarding enforceability.

One of the less tangible benefits of the personal guarantee is psychological. A company that has a personal guarantee might find that it gets paid better than other vendors in the period just prior to the customer's bankruptcy filing. The possibility of losing a home or other personal goods certainly will ensure that the personal guarantor will take the potential for insolvency quite seriously. He isn't likely to be found on the golf course while his company goes down for the count.

In the case of an insolvency, however, be aware that a bankruptcy judge will be on the lookout for preferential payments and may ask that they be returned to the debtor.

A personal guarantee is a tool of limited value. The credit person should attempt to procure a better form of guarantee or collateral. But when all else fails, it is wise to seek the personal guarantee so that the company will have some sort of protection against a customer's potential future inability to pay.

ABSTRACT SUMMARY

- A personal guarantee — probably the weakest form of guarantee a trade creditor can extract from a customer — represents a guarantee of payment by an individual on behalf of a business entity.

- Although they are quite difficult to enforce, personal guarantees accepted by trade creditors are most often uncollateralized.

- Before executing a personal guarantee, the creditor should thoroughly review the guarantor's finances.

- The biggest problem with an uncollateralized personal guarantee is that when the guarator's company files for bankruptcy, the guarantor can also file for bankruptcy, which negates the guarantee.

- A creditor is better off with a collateralized personal guarantee, one in which the guarantor pledges his home, stocks, bonds, or other assets as collateral for the guarantee.

CORPORATE GUARANTEES

A corporate guarantee represents a guarantee of payment made by a business entity on behalf of another business entity. In return for the guarantee, the vendor agrees to extend open account credit.

Quite often, parent companies provide guarantees on behalf of their subsidiaries. Or, a corporation could guarantee the obligations of an affiliate company. In still other cases, a company could provide corporate guarantees for a sister company instead of their parent providing the guarantee.

Another common scenario is a corporation providing a guarantee on behalf of a key supplier.

The vendor should have a standard corporate guarantee form that can be executed by business entities (see Exhibit 8.7). A creditor should take some of the same precautions as with the personal guarantee. For instance, the creditor should make sure the guarantee form:

- States that the guarantee will be interpreted according to the laws of the vendor's state of domicile.

- Provides an open window with respect to cancellation. It should indicate that the guarantor is responsible for all purchases made by the customer for a period of 30 days after the cancellation has been received.

- Includes a clause prohibiting the guarantor from taking a security interest in the customer that could supersede the creditor's potential claims.

The form should also state that the execution of the guarantee was duly authorized by the officers and directors of the guarantor. The guarantee form should be attested to by the corporate secretary by affixing the corporate seal in the lower left-hand corner of the document. The form is officially executed and signed by an officer in the lower right-hand corner of the form.

The creditor should further obtain a resolution of the guarantor's board of directors that attests to the guarantee's validity (see Exhibit 8.8). The resolution of the board of directors should state that the guarantee was taken into consideration on a particular date and was approved for execution by an authorized officer of the company.

Before accepting a guarantee, efforts should also be made by the creditor to confirm the corporate guarantor's financial wherewithal. In theory, by accepting the corporate guarantee, a creditor extends credit based on the financial wherewithal of the guarantor rather than that of the customer. Thus, a creditor should request an audited year-end financial statement from the guarantor, as well as bank and trade references. In essence, the creditor should perform a complete credit investiga-

Exhibit 8.7

APM Co.
30389 Lincoln Blvd.
Emerson, NJ 07630

Gentlemen:

To induce you to extend credit to _____ a
_____ corporation having an office and place of business at
_____ (hereinafter
referred to as the "customer") and in consideration of your supplying to the customer goods upon credit
and in accepting the customer as a credit risk and for other good and valuable consideration, the undersigned guarantees to you, the partners named above, and your and their respective successors and assigns, performance by the customer of all its contracts with you and prompt payment by the customer for
any goods purchased by it from you prior to this date and in the future, and the prompt payment at
maturity of any notes and other documents given by the customer in payment for such goods and for
performance of said contracts. This guarantee shall be effective immediately and shall apply to all purchases and contracts made by the customer until canceled by the undersigned, in which event this guarantee shall also be effective as to all purchases made by the customer within a period of thirty (30) days
after the date of receipt by you of notice of termination by the undersigned of said guarantee.

The undersigned hereby agrees and consents that, without the further consent of or notice to the undersigned, you may, from time to time, make any agreements or arrangements whatsoever with the customer, including, but not limited to, agreements and arrangements for payment, extension of time
therefor, subordination, composition, compromise, discharge or release of the whole or any part of such
obligations of performance and prompt payment, whether by way of acceptance of part payment or of
dividends or any settlement or otherwise, or for the change or surrender of any or all collateral security,
and the making of such arrangements or agreements shall in no way impair, release, or discharge the
liability of the undersigned hereunder.

The undersigned hereby waives notice of acceptance of this guarantee and all other notices of any kind
to which the customer and/or any of the undersigned may be entitled by law, including, without limitation, notice of the sale of any goods made under this guarantee, all demands of payment on, and notice
of nonpayment, protest and dishonor to, the customer and the undersigned.

Your books and records showing the account between you and the customer shall be admissible in
evidence in any action or proceeding hereon, for the purpose of establishing the facts set forth therein,
and shall constitute prima facie proof thereof.

(Exhibit 8.7 continues on following page)

Exhibit 8.7 (Continued)

This guarantee shall not be affected by the taking by you of any notes or other obligations for the payment of the price of any goods sold by you to the customer or by the taking of any security or security interest for such payment and/or for the payment of any charges in connection with said sales, or the termination of this guarantee for any reason whatsoever, and nothing shall discharge or satisfy the liability of the undersigned hereon except the full payment of the said indebtedness with interest.

All references to you in this guarantee shall include your subsidiaries.

This guarantee shall be deemed to have been made in the State of _____ and shall be construed and interpreted in accordance with the laws of said state.

This agreement has been duly authorized by the officers and directors of the undersigned, as indicated in the certified copy of its corporate resolution, attached hereto, and shall be binding upon the undersigned, its successors, and assigns.

Dated this _____ day of _____ , 19 ___ .

Very truly yours,

Attest:

_____   _____
       Secretary   Corporate Guarantor

By: _____

Title: _____

   Affix Corporate
Seal in space above

tion—just as if credit were actually being extended to the guarantor. As such, a credit professional might want to make a field visit to the guarantor.

It makes no sense to extend credit to a company based on a corporate guarantee that has no financial substance.

A creditor should acknowledge receipt of the guarantee in writing. The acknowledgment letter should be addressed to the officer of the company who signed the guarantee. The letter should state that the creditor is relying on the guarantee as the sole means of extending credit to the company.

Remember, by obtaining a corporate guarantee, a creditor obtains only partial protection of its investment in accounts receivable. Credit risk has been minimized by the guarantee, but not totally eliminated. In the event of nonpayment by the customer, the creditor will still have to successfully invoke its guarantee and collect from the corporate guarantor.

Exhibit 8.8
Certified Copy of Corporate Resolutions

The undersigned _____ , Secretary of a corporation, (hereinafter called the "Corporation") does hereby certify:

1. That he is the duly elected, qualified, and acting Secretary of the Corporation and has the custody of the corporate records, minutes, and corporate seal.

2. That at a meeting of the Board of Directors of the Corporation, duly called, convened and held on _____ 19__ , at which meeting a quorom was present and voted throughout, the following resolutions were duly adopted by said Board and said resolutions have not been amended, altered, or repealed and remain in full force and effect on the date hereof:

RESOLVED, that this Corporation guarantees the payment of the obligation of _____ to APM Co., and it was further

RESOLVED, that the officers of this Corporation hereby are authorized and directed to perform all things necessary to carry the foregoing resolution into effect including executing a guarantee to APM Co. in the form attached to and made a part of these minutes.

In witness whereof the undersigned has caused this certificate to be executed and the seal of the Corporation to be hereunto this _____ day of _____ , 19 ___ .

_____
Secretary

Affix Corporate
Seal in space above

ABSTRACT SUMMARY

- A corporate guarantee is one business entity's guarantee that another business entity will make a trade payment.

- The creditor should use a standard corporate guarantee form that should state that the execution of the guarantee was duly authorized by the officers and directors of the guarantor.

- The creditor should also obtain a separate resolution of the guarantor's board of directors that attests to the guarantee's validity.

- The creditor should investigate the guarantor's financial wherewithal just as if it were the company being extended credit.

- In effect, a corporate guarantee does not guarantee payment; if the customer fails to pay off its debts, the creditor may still face an uphill battle to successfully invoke the guarantee and extract payment from the guarantor.

LETTERS OF CREDIT

A letter of credit (LC) is a written promise by a bank or other issuer made at the request of a customer. The letter of credit promises that the issuer will honor and pay drafts or other demands for payment if the entity drawing the drafts or making demands complies with the terms and conditions outlined in the LC. The issuer's promise is a primary obligation, independent of any promise made by the customer. Therefore, the bank does not guarantee payment in the conventional sense, but substitutes its own credit for that of the customer.

Thus, before accepting a letter of credit from a customer, a company should scrutinize the bank issuing the LC. The party accepting an LC needs to take a keen interest in the issuing bank's creditworthiness. This is more important than ever today, in light of the financial problems experienced by many savings and loan institutions and commercial banks suffering as a result of bad real estate and oil loans.

To find out more about a particular bank, a credit professional should use a valuable reference source — Polk's World Bank Directory. This publication will provide a bank's statement of condition, and list its officers, directors, correspondent banks, and other banking data.

A credit person should probably get suspicious if the issuing bank is not listed in the Polk's directory. If such is the case, contact the bank and request a recent financial statement. The credit decision will be based on the creditworthiness of the bank issuing the LC, so it's wise to get all the information one can about that bank's financial condition.

There are two basic kinds of letters of credit, and the credit person in most cases should only accept one of these from a customer — the irrevocable letter of credit. A revocable letter of credit can be canceled or revoked by either the customer or the issuing bank.

A letter of credit must be executed according to the terms and conditions outlined in the document — exactly according to them. If it is not, the customer will face possible payment delays due to "discrepancies" in the document. A simple example of a discrepancy would be shipping product whose weight exceeds the weight indicated in the LC. Discrepancies often delay payment, because they can only be waived by the customer.

Unfortunately, customers are often slow to waive discrepancies. If the customer likes to play cat and mouse, it can delay payment for days or even weeks based on a discrepancy. The lesson here: Before drafting on a letter of credit, take great pains to ensure that all the outlined terms and conditions of the LC have been met. Draft and presentation documents should be reviewed by another party to minimize discrepancies.

To prevent hassles with letters of credit, a company needs to give an LC close scrutiny upon initial receipt of the document. The credit person should review the LC to ensure that the company can comply with its terms and conditions. If the review turns up any problems with documentation requirements, the company will probably need to ask the customer to amend the letter of credit.

A better alternative to going through the amendment process would be to use a preferred letter-of-credit format. When negotiating with a customer, a vendor can provide the customer with a copy of the preferred irrevocable standby letter of credit format and ask the customer to have its bank issue the LC in that format (see Exhibit 8.9).

The preferred letter-of-credit format should avoid references to bills of lading or other shipping documents—especially when dealing with domestic transactions. Under the preferred scenario you will have a clean LC that simply requires a draft and a signed statement in order to be paid, as opposed to a documentary LC, which requires timely presentation of various documents. The vendor should also press for sight payment terms, and should refuse any stipulation that invoices must be past due a certain number of days before presentation for payment can be made. In essence, the vendor should strive to get the customer's bank to issue what is referred to as a "clean" LC—one that will not be difficult to draft against. The term standby letter of credit generally refers to a domestic letter of credit which is provided to cover shipments overtime. The idea is that if the customer does not pay their bills you have the recourse to draft on the letter of credit.

With export LCs, the vendor needs to be especially cautious in regard to discrepancies. Export LCs are documentary, in that the LC will probably require the vendor to provide a bill of lading and other documents. However, the vendor should try to avoid certain other requirements, such as provisos calling for the appointment of outside inspectors or the establishment of shipping deadlines. Unless stated otherwise, there is a 21-day time frame from the day after the shipment for presentation of documents. Otherwise, you have a discrepancy in the form of stale documents. If faced with time constraints, request your customer to authorize the bank to issue an amendment extending the presentation time frame.

The export LC will also state a dollar amount. Another way to avoid a discrepancy is to hedge the language here a bit. For instance, the LC should not state "$50,000." Rather, it should include the wording "approximately $50,000." By adding the word "approximately," a vendor gives the letter of credit a value of plus or minus 5 percent of the issued amount.

Make sure that your export LC is a confirmed letter of credit, which means that you will present your documents and receive payment from a confirming U.S. bank as opposed to the buyer's issuing bank, which most likely is a non-U.S. bank.

Compliance with LC documentation should not be taken lightly. Whenever there are questions related to compliance, it is always wise to contact the issuing bank before presenting documents for payment.

A final caveat: If an LC states that the vendor's invoices must be past due before it can draft on the LC—and terms are net 30 days—don't ship product in the last month before expiry. The vendor must ensure that the LC does not expire before it can legally draft against the document.

Exhibit 8.9
Sample Preferred Irrevocable Standby Letter of Credit Format

DPM Inc.
617 Avenue of the Americas
New York, NY 10171

Attention: Credit Department

We hereby open our Irrevocable Letter of Credit No. ____#1____ in your favor for the account of ____#2____ for up to $ ____#3____ available by your drafts at sight drawn on ____#4____ accompanied by statement that the drawing is to cover amount due from ____#5____, which amount has not been paid in accordance with the agreed-upon terms. Multiple drawings for partial amounts permitted. Drawings for partial invoice values permitted.

All drafts must bear the clause "Drawn under the ____#6____ Letter of Credit No. __ #7____ dated ____#8____," and must be drawn and presented for payment no later than ____#9____ .

We hereby engage with drawers, endorsers, and bonafide holders that all drafts drawn in compliance with the terms of this credit shall be duly honored upon presentation and delivery of documents.

Except as expressly stated herein, this credit is subject to the "Uniform Customs and Practice for Commercial Documentary Credits" of the International Chamber of Commerce (International Chamber of Commerce Publication Number 400, 1983 Revision).

Very truly yours,

Instructions Legend

1. To be assigned by bank
2. Your customer's name
3. Amount
4. To be decided by bank
5. Customer's name
6. Name of bank
7. Same as # 1
8. LC date
9. One year from today

The vendor needs to leave an open window for collection. So the credit person might want to follow up with the customer and request renewal of the LC 90 days prior to expiration.

All letters of credit should be recorded in a collateral register in order to avoid having good collateral expire due to human oversight.

As of Oct. 1, 1975, letters of credit issued by banks worldwide became subject to the Uniform Customs and Practice for Documentary Credits, Publication 290, of the International Chamber of Commerce. The Uniform Customs and Practice for Documentary Credits was revised in 1983 through Publication 400. As a result, all LCs should contain the following language: "The abovementioned documentary credit is subject to the Uniform Customs and Practice for Documentary Credits (1983 revision, International Chamber of Commerce, Paris, France, publication number 400). This way, in the event of a dispute, the ground rules for resolving the dispute are uniformly recognized.

ABSTRACT SUMMARY

- A letter of credit is a written promise by a bank or other issuer made at the request of a customer.
- The LC promises that the issuer will honor and pay drafts or other demands for payment if the entity drawing the drafts or making demands complies with the terms and conditions outlined in the document.
- Before accepting a bank's letter of credit, a vendor should conduct a financial investigation of the bank.
- The creditor must avoid "discrepancies" when following the terms and conditions of the document; failure to follow these terms and conditions could lead to payment delays.
- In most cases, the only kind of letter of credit worth accepting is an irrevocable letter of credit.

SUBORDINATION AGREEMENTS

A subordination agreement involves three parties—a vendor, a customer, and a third party. The third party is often the principal owner of the customer or the customer's corporate parent. In most cases, the principal or corporate parent has made a loan to the customer. In the straight subordination agreement, the third party agrees to subordinate this debt to the debt the customer owes to the vendor. In another situation, the vendor could serve as a third party subordinating its secured debt to the secured debt of a new bank being brought on by the customer. In this case, an intercreditor subordination agreement would be drawn up.

According to the subordination agreement, the third party should not get paid by the customer until the customer first pays off the vendor. Any exceptions have to be approved in writing by the vendor. In the case of the bank intercreditor subordination agreement, the vendor is not paid in a liquidation until the secured debt of the new bank is paid.

A subordination agreement should state that all collateral held by the third party is subordinated to the vendor's claim with the customer. The agreement should also state that the customer's books and records and any evidence of indebtedness held by the third party shall be marked and endorsed to indicate the subordination of debt to the vendor (see Exhibit 8.10).

Furthermore, the subordination agreement should make a provision for the possible liquidation or dissolution of the customer. The agreement should state that any distribution of funds or assets resulting from the liquidation will benefit the vendor before the third party. To be more specific, the agreement should state that any amount the third party is entitled to shall be received in trust by the third party and paid to the vendor.

The trust proviso only applies up to the dollar amount of indebtedness due the vendor. This is necessary because individual proprietors and corporate parents often secure their loans to the company by filing a UCC1 security interest.

The subordination agreement should be executed by an authorized officer of the third party. If the third party is an individual, the vendor should make sure he or she signs the agreement as an individual with no corporate references. Otherwise, the vendor may have problems enforcing the agreement.

Upon receipt of the executed subordination agreement, the vendor should send an acknowledgment letter to the third party, either to the individual principal or to the company officer that executed the agreement. The letter should state that the vendor is relying on the subordination agreement as the sole means of extending credit to the customer.

Exhibit 8.10

PLM Industries, Inc.
100 Medallion Road
Kastoria, NJ 08885

SUBORDINATION AGREEMENT

In consideration of PLM Industries, Inc., a corporation, granting credit to
_____ ("Debtor"), the undersigned
_____ ("Creditor"), hereby subordinates all indebtedness now or hereafter incurred by the Debtor to the Creditor in favor of any indebtedness, present or future, of the Debtor to PLM Industries, Inc. and any extension or renewals thereof.

In furtherance of such subordination, it is hereby agreed that until such indebtedness of the Debtor to PLM Industries, Inc. has been paid, no payments shall be made by the Debtor or received by the Creditor on account of the principal or interest on such indebtedness to the Creditor, without the written consent of PLM Industries, Inc.; that the books and records of the Debtor and any evidence of the indebtedness held by the Creditor shall be appropriately marked and endorsed to indicate this subordination; and that, upon any liquidation or dissolution involving any distribution to creditors of the Debtor, any amount which the Creditor would be entitled to receive, to the extent necessary to meet any deficiency in the payment in full of the indebtedness to PLM Industries, Inc., shall be received by the Creditor in trust for PLM Industries, Inc. and shall forthwith be paid over to it.

IN WITNESS WHEEROF, this instrument has been executed this _____ day of _____ , 19 ___ .

(CREDITOR)   (CREDITOR)

Name: Name:
Title: Title:

the undersigned, being the Debtor referred to in the foregoing Subordination Agreement, hereby acknowledges receipt of a copy thereof and agrees to be bound by the terms thereof.

NAME OF COMPANY

AUTHORIZED SIGNATURE
Title:

ABSTRACT SUMMARY

- A subordination agreement involves three parties—a vendor, a customer, and a third party.
- Generally, the third party has made a loan to the customer; in the subordination agreement, the third party agrees to subordinate this debt to the debt the customer owes the vendor.
- The subordination agreement should make a provision for the possible liquidation of the customer; it should state that any proceeds from the liquidation will go to the vendor before it goes to the third party.
- The subordination agreement should be executed by an authorized officer of the third party.
- Upon receipt of the executed subordination agreement, the vendor should send an acknowledgment letter to the third party.

UCC1 SECURITY INTERESTS

The best kind of creditor to be is a secured creditor. When a company files for bankruptcy and is dissolved, its secured assets are liquidated by the court and paid to secured creditors in order of priority. Once all the secured parties are paid in full, which rarely happens, the remaining proceeds from the bankruptcy are distributed as dividends to unsecured creditors. So it's easy to see that obtaining a security interest in a customer's assets makes good sense as a condition of extending credit to marginal or high-risk customers.

All transactions creating a collateralized security interest on stipulated assets are governed by Article 9 of the Uniform Commercial Code (UCC). In order to perfect a security interest, a creditor and its debtor need to jointly execute a UCC1 financing statement form, which is filed with the appropriate state and/or local governmental bodies. The security interest establishes lien rights for the creditor.

A UCC1 financing statement (see Exhibit 8.11) identifies the debtor, the secured party (creditor), and the exact nature of the collateral. The financing statement must be signed by officers from both parties.

In most states, the secured party files the UCC1 form with the secretary of state and, if necessary, an appropriate local office. The Credit Manual of Commercial Laws, published by the National Association of Credit Management (NACM) in Columbia, MD, defines all aspects of Article 9 of the Uniform Commercial Code with respect to the filing requirements for each of the 50 states.

Following proper filing procedures is important; an improper filing could jeopardize a creditor's security interest and lien rights. For instance, creditors need to know how many separate filings they need to make. If a debtor operates in another state, the creditor will have to execute and file a separate UCC1 financing statement in that state in order to create a security interest in specified assets.

Let's say the customer is a retailer who operates in five states. The creditor will want to make five separate UCC1 filings. On the other hand, if the creditor has five stores but they are all in one state, the creditor would need to file the statement only once.

Before making a credit decision based on creating a security interest, a vendor should request from the secretary of state a lien search on the debtor. The lien search, which usually costs about $5, will turn up a list of all other companies that are secured creditors of the customer in question, explain what priority each one has, and specify which assets are secured.

Pay close attention to the information provided by the lien search, especially noting who has what priority. It will do a creditor no good to have a third lien on accounts receivable and inventory. In case of a bankruptcy and liquidation, the holder of a third lien may find he is holding a security interest in nothing.

The point is: Don't accept a collateralized position that can never be enforced. Instead, review the subject's balance sheet and the dollar amounts of other secured

Exhibit 8.11
The UCC1 Financing Statement

Uniform Commercial Code — FINANCING STATEMENT — Form UCC-1

JULIUS BLUMBERG, INC. N. Y. C. 10013

IMPORTANT — Read instructions on back before filling out form

This FINANCING STATEMENT is presented to a Filing Officer for filing pursuant to the Uniform Commercial Code.

No. of Additional Sheets Presented:	3. ☐ The Debtor is a transmitting utility

1. Debtor(s) (Last Name First) and Address(es): | 2. Secured Party(ies) Name(s) and Address(es)

4. For Filing Officer: Date, Time, No. Filing Office

6. Assignee(s) of Secured Party and Address(es)

5. This Financing Statement covers the following types (or items) of property:

7. ☐ The described crops are growing or to be grown on:*
   ☐ The described goods are or are to be affixed to:*
   ☐ The lumber to be cut or minerals or the like
     (including oil and gas) is on:*
     *(Describe Real Estate Below)

☐ Products of the Collateral are also covered.

8. Describe Real Estate Here: | ☐ This statement is to be indexed in the Real Estate Records:

9. Name of a Record Owner

No. & Street	Town or City	County	Section	Block	Lot

10. This statement is filed without the debtor's signature to perfect a security interest in collateral (check appropriate box)
   ☐ under a security agreement signed by debtor authorizing secured party to file this statement, or
   ☐ which is proceeds of the original collateral described above in which a security interest was perfected, or
   ☐ acquired after a change of name, identity or corporate structure of the debtor, or ☐ as to which the filing has lapsed, or
   already subject to a security interest in another jurisdiction:
   ☐ when the collateral was brought into the state, or ☐ when the debtor's location was changed to this state.

By _____ | By _____
Signature(s) of Debtor(s) | Signature(s) of Secured Party(ies)

(1) Filing Officer Copy-Numerical
STANDARD FORM - FORM UCC-1 — Approved by Secretary of State of New York
(5/82)

creditors' claims, and make sure that once creditors with higher-priority lien rights are paid in full, there are still excess assets to cover the company's exposure.

When analyzing asset coverage for UCC1s covering accounts receivable and inventory filings, discount balance sheet inventory by at least 50 percent, because a liquidation of the inventory will probably yield 50 cents on the dollar for inventory. On the other hand, receivables should be discounted by 15-20 percent to allow for valid disputes and claims.

All security interests should be accompanied by a security agreement, a longer document that spells out the general terms and conditions of the security filing. The security agreement will define collateral in detail, clearly spell out events of default, and protect the creditor when it comes time to enforce a security interest.

Unlike the UCC1 financing statement, the security agreement does not have to be filed with any secretaries of state.

ABSTRACT SUMMARY

- In a bankruptcy situation, a secured creditor has a much better chance to collect from the debtor than an unsecured creditor.

- A creditor can establish a security interest by filing a UCC1 financing statement with the appropriate state and/or local governmental bodies.

- To perfect a nationwide lien, a creditor must file a UCC1 financing statement with each state that the debtor operates in.

- For a nominal fee, state governments can conduct lien searches that will tell the creditor what other parties have secured interests involving the debtor, and what priorities these other secured parties have.

- All security interests need to be accompanied by a security agreement, a document that spells out the general terms and conditions of the security filing; it does not have to be filed with any governmental body.

BULK TRANSFERS

The Uniform Commercial Code defines a bulk transfer as the sale or transfer of goods, wares, merchandise, and fixtures in bulk. The code contains statutes for each state that govern these transfers. The statutes are designed to ensure that a bulk transfer proceeds without causing harm to creditors of the company selling or transferring the assets.

A bulk transfer is generally transacted when a company is going out of business. In some cases, a company will try to use a bulk transfer to shift assets to another legal entity so as to avoid paying off debts. Existing statutes are meant to protect creditors from this fraud and the possible loss of accounts receivable.

Bulk sale transfers are covered under Section 6 of the Uniform Commercial Code. The rules governing these transfers vary considerably from state to state. Thus, in order to gain the full protection of the Code, a credit professional needs to be familiar with the proper state statute in each bulk transfer situation. One should also note that not all asset transfers are considered bulk transfers. For instance, transfers resulting from a general assignment for the benefit of creditors, sales by bankruptcy trustees, public auctions to enforce liens, or settlements of liens or security interests are not considered bulk transfers and are not subject to the code.

Statutes generally require that the transferor (the company selling or transferring the goods) draw up a list of creditors — including disputed creditors — that contains names, addresses, and amounts due. The transferee (the recipient in the transaction) is then required to maintain the creditor list on file for six months. This is because, ultimately, it is the transferee that is responsible for payment of the transferor's credit obligations.

Some important points to remember: First, a creditor remains protected by the code if it is omitted from the creditor's list. In such a case, the creditor merely has to show proof of the debt. Second, the transfer can be declared void unless, within 10 days of executing the transfer, the transferee provides creditors with written notice of the transaction.

Generally, the transferee will discharge its responsibility for paying creditors by establishing an escrow account in the county where the transferor's principal place of business is domiciled. With such an account in place, a creditor must seek its accounts receivable from the courts by filing a claim. Expect payment from the courts — out of the escrow account — to take anywhere from 30 to 45 days.

A creditor has six months from the official transfer date to begin a proceeding against the transferee to enforce a claim. The exception occurs when a transfer is concealed. In such a case, creditors have until six months after discovery of the transfer to initiate a proceeding.

Valid creditors need not fear bulk transfers. They are protected by the Uniform Commercial Code. On the other hand, one can never be too careful. Thus it makes sense for a credit professional to stay right on top of the details of any such transfer.

An additional consideration: A credit person should probably investigate the finances of the transferee, which could soon become a new customer.

ABSTRACT SUMMARY

- A bulk transfer—the sale or transfer of goods, wares, merchandise, and fixtures in bulk—usually is transacted when the transferor is going out of business.

- Section 6 of the Uniform Commercial Code provides guidelines for transacting bulk transfers—guidelines designed to protect the transferor's creditors.

- A transfer can be declared void unless, within 10 days of executing the transfer, the transferee provides creditors with written notice of the transaction.

- The transferor is generally required to draw up a list of creditors that must be maintained by the party receiving the bulk transfer; the "transferee," as it is called, becomes ultimately responsible for the transferor's credit obligations.

- Transferees often discharge their responsibility by establishing an escrow account from which the courts pay off the transferor's creditors.

COLLECTING FUNDS ON BAD CHECKS

The scenario is all too common. On a one-time-only sale, the customer's check is returned for non-sufficient funds, or else the customer stops payment on the check. The customer is contacted for a replacement check but then the runaround begins. Arrangements are made, but ultimately the customer fails to replace the bad check with good funds.

The need for serious and swift action soon becomes apparent. But what is the best action to take?

A credit professional has a number of options. He can refer the account to a collection agency or an attorney. However, probably the action that will get the best results is to refer the customer's check to the creditor's bank for collection.

The bank collection process is the swiftest and most practical method of recovering these funds. The creditor's bank will present the check as a collection item to the collection department of the customer's bank, which holds the referred check and collects on it as soon as there are sufficient funds in the customer's account. Oftentimes, collection will be possible when, for instance, the debtor makes a deposit to cover his weekly or monthly payroll.

Successfully collecting on such an item generally takes anywhere from three to 21 or more days. Be prepared to pay a fee, however. The customer's bank may charge up to 10 percent of the check's face amount.

If this avenue is unsuccessful, a credit professional should probably make an attempt to gain some psychological leverage using local bad-check laws. Information on these laws by state is available through the Uniform Commercial Code.

For example, in the state of Florida, it's a felony offense to write bad checks in the amount of $50 or more. The penalty is up to five years in prison or a $1,000 fine. For a misdemeanor in Florida, the penalty can be up to six months imprisonment or a $300 fine. Explaining these penalties to a customer can often speed the process of getting the customer to replace a bad check with good funds. In fact, in many cases it's a good idea to highlight the bad-check laws for an NSF customer during the very first call or meeting regarding the returned item.

Timing will be critical in successfully recovering cash flow on a returned item. In many cases, waiting as long as 30 days for a customer to replace a returned check is simply too long. It might only be days after notification of the returned item before the debtor becomes insolvent or skips town. So move quickly. Don't wait until the debtor's phone has been disconnected before taking firm action.

ABSTRACT SUMMARY

■ One of the best options when faced with a customer that refuses to replace a bad check is to place the returned item for collection with the creditor's bank.

■ Once an item is placed with a bank for collection, it generally takes the bank from three to 21 or more days to collect on the item, at a cost of up to 10 percent of the check's amount.

■ Information on local bad-check laws is available in the Uniform Commercial Code.

■ A creditor can use the penalties associated with bad-check laws to encourage a debtor to replace a bad check in order to avoid prosecution.

■ Timing is critical when trying to recover cash flow on a returned item, so act quickly. Don't wait until the debtor has skipped town or become insolvent before taking firm action.

POSTDATED CHECKS

When a company accepts a postdated check from a customer, it forfeits all its rights related to bad-check laws. Nevertheless, there are situations when accepting a postdated check might make sense.

A check can be defined as a draft drawn on a bank or financial institution that is payable on demand. A postdated check, however, is an altogether different kind of instrument; it merely represents a promise to pay in the future, and suggests that sufficient funds currently are not available.

If a payee accepts a postdated check with the understanding that the maker presently has insufficient funds to cover presentation, then the maker is not in violation of any bad-check laws. The reasoning: The maker has not tendered a check with true intent and representation.

So why accept a postdated check? To put it simply, a postdated check might be better than no check at all, but generally only if the credit professional conducts proper follow-up procedures.

Accepting a postdated check should be considered as an alternative if the debtor continually fails to mail or commit to making payments. In this situation, one might take the chance of accepting a postdated check—given that the alternative usually is to refer the customer to a collection agency or attorney.

Some credit practitioners also accept postdated checks from long-term customers who have a sound track record of having such checks clear without any problems. This appears to be an acceptable practice, as long as the credit professional remembers that bad-check law rights are forfeited in the process.

If circumstances warrant accepting postdated checks, the key is to proceed with caution. On the date that the check is postdated for, contact the customer's bank and ask if there are sufficient funds on hand in the customer's account to cover the check. If there are, deposit the check immediately. If there are not, contact the customer and confront him about the lack of sufficient funds.

If the item is presented and returned for non-sufficient funds, it can still be placed as a collection item through the creditor's bank.

The issue of whether to accept postdated checks is ticklish. The credit person wants to protect his company's rights. Yet it is also clear that the postdated check may not turn out to be a cashable check instrument.

When accepting a postdated check, a credit person must at a minimum understand the major risk—namely, the fact that he is surrendering his right to recourse via bad-check laws.

ABSTRACT SUMMARY

- A postdated check simply represents a promise to pay in the future; it implies that sufficient funds are not presently available to pay off the debt.

- A company that accepts a postdated check from a customer forfeits its bad-check law rights.

- In some credit scenarios, having a postdated check is better than having no check at all; in others, it represents the continuation of a routine business practice between long-term trade partners.

- If circumstances warrant accepting postdated checks, the key is to proceed with caution. On the date that the check is postdated for, contact the maker's bank and ask if there are sufficient funds on hand to honor the check.

- The holder of a postdated check presented and returned for non-sufficient funds can place the returned item as a collection item through its bank.

9

CREDIT AND
CASH FLOW STRATEGY

CREDIT FUNCTION STRUCTURE

The three elements of credit department structure are physical operational structure (centralization vs. decentralization), internal reporting structure (chain of command), and level of approval-authority structure. The latter covers credit-limit approvals for new and existing accounts, order approvals, and bad-debt write-off approvals.

Physical operational structure relates to the geographic structure of the credit function. The centralization vs. decentralization debate has gone on for years. There are pros and cons to both sides. However, it is clear that a centralized credit function is more effective in providing uniformity when executing policy, procedure, and credit strategy. Under a centralized credit function, credit investigations, existing file reviews, order approvals, and collateral negotiations are performed under one roof and not open to interpretation.

A centralized credit function makes it easier for the credit manager to be aware of day-to-day credit operations. It also provides more control by offering greater access to credit information and data.

Supporters of decentralization stress the benefit of geographic proximity to the customer base. However, it isn't really all that big of a problem to hop on an airplane to visit a customer, nor is it a big problem to pick up a check from a distant customer when necessary; the local salesperson can usually handle that task.

Whichever geographic approach the company chooses, credit personnel must make sure that the approach does not conflict with the company's credit and cash management strategy.

Turning to the second element of structure—internal reporting—it's clear that every credit department should have an organizational chart detailing reporting lines and responsibilities. All credit personnel, including clerical and secretarial personnel, should be listed on the organizational chart.

The corporate credit manager should report to the treasurer or controller. This enables the credit manager to keep the chief financial officer abreast of cash flow and risk, while staying aware of the CFO's cash flow and liquidity needs. Written job descriptions for all credit personnel will enforce this organizational structure.

A key point when putting together an organizational structure is to make sure there are no major conflicts of interest. For instance, when manpower permits, personnel that apply cash to customer ledgers and generate credit memos should not report directly to the credit manager. If possible, these employees should report to the accounting department.

If the company operates overseas, it should also have an overseas organizational chart that reflects reporting lines to headquarters. The overseas company will probably need to have foreign nationals staffing the overseas credit function. The native credit manager should report directly to the overseas chief financial officer and on a dotted-line basis to the corporate credit manager for control purposes.

Corporate credit managers should have access to overseas credit information and reports, and they should at least have indirect input into the overseas policy and procedure. If corporate credit managers have no input, they cannot successfully protect the company's assets of accounts receivable and cash.

The final element of credit function structure relates to credit authority. Written policy should detail who can approve new and existing credit limits, customer orders and bad-debt write-offs. In addition to the "who," this written policy should also designate dollar limits for each person with approval authority. The policy should cover all levels of credit personnel, as well as the treasurer or controller and the company president. It should also provide procedures for handling exceptions to approval-authority limits.

Formalized authority levels create a uniform and clearly defined approach to approvals while maintaining accountability.

ABSTRACT SUMMARY

■ The three elements of credit department structure are physical operational structure, internal reporting structure, and level of approval-authority structure.

■ The debate in the area of physical operational structure has been between a centralized credit department and a decentralized department.

■ With respect to internal reporting structure, every credit department should have an organizational chart that details reporting lines and responsibilities for all credit employees.

■ If the company operates overseas, it should have an overseas organizational chart that reflects reporting lines to headquarters.

■ A written policy should identify credit department personnel with authority to approve new and existing credit limits, customer orders, and bad-debt write-offs. This policy should also designate dollar levels of authority for these personnel, as well as for the treasurer or controller and the company president.

CREDIT POLICIES AND PROCEDURES

Regardless of their size, all companies should have written credit policies and procedures. Policies should clearly state the objectives of the credit department, as well as the specific procedures required to execute these objectives.

Having policies and procedures in place promotes greater control over the accounts receivable function. Sound and clearly elaborated credit policies and procedures provide credit employees with direction. Without these written guidelines, the department might be operated using an intuitive process that would provide no direction or continuity. Ultimately, written credit policies and procedures protect and maximize cash flow.

Furthermore, with guidelines in place, credit tasks are performed with objectivity, which is especially critical when the department is decentralized. And, with formal policies and procedures, there will be minimal problems when employees retire or leave the company.

Credit policies should promote several basic objectives that clearly define credit's role. Examples include:

1. Acceptance and retention of desirable business
2. Proper protection of accounts receivable
3. Maximum receivable turnover and the ensuing conversion to cash
4. Maximum sales volume
5. Minimal bad-debt write-offs

These objectives reveal the dynamic and constructive role of the credit department. Notice that the credit policy objectives above are marketing and cash-flow oriented. Credit must walk a fine line in generating the required cash flow and protecting the company's investment in accounts receivable, while meeting company objectives with respect to sales and new customer development.

In addition to a general policy statement, the credit department should have specific policy statements covering job descriptions, employee evaluations or appraisals, collections, granting extended credit terms, and levels of authority. The policy statements for levels of authority should cover specified dollar levels for credit authority, bad debt and charge-off authority, and order approval authority. The dollar levels of authority should be assigned to each job classification within the credit department. Positions with no authority should be assigned a $0 level of authority to eliminate confusion.

Typical credit tasks requiring written procedures are as follows:

1. Operating the credit and accounts receivable software system
2. Operating the order entry system to release or approve orders on credit hold
3. Reviewing extended credit term requests

4. Updating and approving existing customer credit files and limits
5. Investigating and approving new customer accounts
6. Investigating and approving accounts with foreign ownership
7. Writing off bad debts and charge-offs
8. Selecting a collection agency
9. Referring an account for collection to an agency or attorney
10. Evaluating collection agency performance
11. Handling collateral taken as security
12. Monitoring and updating the collateral register data base
13. Preparing for a customer visit and plant tour
14. Writing up a customer-visit trip report
15. Calculating days sales outstanding (DSO) and Best DSO
16. Classifying customers by risk code
17. Preparing weekly, monthly, and quarterly reports
18. Performing employee performance evaluations
19. Sharing credit information on credit references
20. Obtaining bank and trade information—both written and verbal

Procedures should be "how to" oriented; they should explain in a step-by-step fashion how the particular credit task or function should be carried out. Sample forms and exhibits should accompany credit procedures, translating the narrative into documented action elements.

Where applicable, the credit department should have the legal department review and approve the proposed policies and procedures manual. Once policies and procedures are place, credit managers should review the manual on an annual basis to update, add, or delete sections as the scope of the credit department changes.

ABSTRACT SUMMARY

- All companies, regardless of size, should have written credit policies and procedures.

- Written policies and procedures should clearly state the objectives of the credit department, as well as the specific procedures required to execute these objectives.

- Credit policy objectives are both marketing and cash-flow oriented, requiring department personnel to walk a fine line in both protecting the company's accounts receivable investment and helping to achieve corporate sales objectives.

- In addition to a general policy statement, the credit department should have specific statements regarding job descriptions, employee evaluations, collections, granting extended credit terms, and levels of authority.
- Procedures should be explained in a step-by-step fashion to clearly outline how each credit task should be carried out. They should be accompanied by sample forms and exhibits.

LEVELS OF CREDIT APPROVAL AUTHORITY

A corporation should have written policies that contain dollar levels of approval authority for specific credit and noncredit employees. These dollar levels should apply to authority in the following areas:

1. New and existing customer credit-limit approvals
2. Bad-debt write-off approvals
3. Customer order approvals

Designated levels of credit authority are essential for placing accountability with the proper personnel. Including these designations as part of written policies—both corporate policy and credit department policy—also ensures that senior management participates in the process when dollar levels exceed the specified limits.

All credit department personnel should be assigned dollar levels of approval authority for all three types of approval, even if the approval amount is zero. Setting a specific dollar level for each employee—even if that level is zero—enables the firm to clearly define levels of authority. To stress these designations, all job descriptions should reflect the specified levels.

Certain individuals outside of the credit department should also be given either a specific level of authority or a zero level of authority. For example, the manager of customer service, the order processing manager, and marketing managers should all be given such designations. From a credit control standpoint, it's probably best that these individuals are given zero-dollar authority limits.

Written policy should indicate that approval beyond an employee's designated level can only be granted through the chain of corporate command.

Senior management personnel outside of the credit area—such as the controller, treasurer, director of marketing, and even the company president—should also be given levels of authority. A company might give the company president an unlimited level of authority, or the president might receive a specific limit. Exception cases, where the president seeks approval authority beyond specified limits, could be subject to the approval of the board of directors or the finance committee.

Under the approval authority process, bad-debt write-offs and major customer workouts will be minimized due to senior management involvement in the decision-making process. For example, a credit representative might be given a $25,000 credit-limit approval level; customer credit limits in excess of that amount would have to be approved or countersigned by the assistant credit manager and/or the credit manager. In this way, senior management will be required to review exposures of any consequence.

Clearly defining levels of authority promote an objective approach to critical credit responsibilities, rather than a subjective or haphazard approach.

ABSTRACT SUMMARY

- Dollar levels of authority should be designated in writing for credit-limit approvals, bad-debt write-offs, and customer order approvals.
- Approval levels should be incorporated into the credit department's written policies and procedures.
- Levels of authority place accountability, promote objectivity, and ensure control of the credit function.
- All credit department personnel should be designated dollar levels of approval authority for all three types of approval—even if the approval amount is zero.
- Certain individuals outside of the credit department should be given either a specific level of authority or a zero level of authority.

CLASSIFICATION OF TRADE ACCOUNTS RECEIVABLE

As part of its credit strategy, a company should evaluate and classify each of its customers annually based on risk. This risk classification should be determined using four factors:

1. The probability that the customer's cash flow (payments) will be according to standard terms
2. The customer's ability to live within its credit line and exposure
3. The customer's overall financial condition
4. The likelihood of an insolvency over the next one to three years

By assessing the four risk factors, credit personnel can thoroughly evaluate risk for both new and existing customers.

Generally, customers are classified as either minimum credit risks, standard credit risks, or high credit risks.

A customer classified as a minimum credit risk pays the trade in discount to prompt, displays a strong financial condition, and reflects no signs or characteristics of potential insolvency. The standard-risk customer's payments range from generally prompt to slow 15 days; it displays a sound to fair financial condition, as well as some risk of insolvency. The high-risk customer generally pays slow 16 to 30 or more days, displays an unbalanced, leveraged, and undercapitalized financial condition, and projects the potential for an insolvency over the near term. Effectively monitoring and controlling high-risk exposures is where credit personnel really earn their pay.

Each customer should have its classification reviewed and designated at the time of its annual credit-limit review. This review should be performed about three to four months after the customer's annual year-end statement date. New customers should be assigned a classification when the initial credit investigation is performed.

Classifications should be documented in the customer credit file and input in the accounts receivable software system. This enables credit personnel unfamiliar with the account to learn quickly about the quality of the customer. Credit personnel will also have a better perspective on when to change classifications if the classifcations are readily accessible.

When the credit limits of customers classified as minimum risks or standard risks exceed the credit manager's credit approval authority, a joint authorization form (see Joint Authorization, in this chapter, p. 312) should be prepared for joint action by the corporate credit manager and the treasurer or controller. The high-risk customer evaluation form (see High-Risk Evaluation, in this chapter, p. 315) should be prepared annually and should coincide with the credit-limit review. This form provides the credit department with a formalized channel for asking the marketing department to justify its desire to sell to the customer on credit despite the perceived risk.

Classifying trade accounts receivable according to risk enables the credit department to develop specific strategies, policies, and procedures for customers falling within each risk category. Corrective strategies can be associated directly with specific customers. The joint authorization and high-risk evaluation forms provide formal mechanisms to justify credit extension to these exception cases.

Only by classifying trade accounts receivable are credit practitioners able to derive individual and overall accounts receivable portfolio risk standards. Classifying trade receivables should also help credit personnel understand the nuances of DSO and Best DSO. Total DSO can be broken down into minimum, standard, and high-risk DSO components to determine the overall quality of accounts receivable. Based on the accounts receivable dollar breakdowns of risk classifications, they can determine whether projected DSO performance is attainable.

Classifying customers according to risk will promote a more consistent approach to credit analysis by all credit personnel.

ABSTRACT SUMMARY

- Credit departments should annually evaluate each of their customers and place them in one of three risk classifications: minimum, standard, or high risk.

- Risk classifications should be based on a combination of the customer's ability to pay on time, to live within its credit line, to display a sound financial condition, and to remain solvent.

- A high-risk customer is one that generally pays slow 16 to 30 or more days, displays an unbalanced financial condition, and projects the potential for an insolvency over the near term.

- Risk classifications should be documented within the customer credit file and input into the accounts receivable system.

- When the credit limits of customers classified as minimum risks or standard risks exceed the credit manager's credit approval authority, a joint authorization form should be prepared for joint action by the credit manager and the treasurer or controller.

JOINT AUTHORIZATION EVALUATIONS

The joint authorization evaluation form (see Exhibit 9.1) is designed for use with accounts classified as either minimum or standard risks whose credit limits exceed the credit manager's credit-limit approval authority. The credit manager and the treasurer or controller must jointly approve or deny the annual required credit limit being reviewed.

The credit manager prepares the form and submits it to the treasurer or controller. The essence of the evaluation is in the customer and credit information and justification sections of the form. Specific marketing information such as product purchased, purchase point, year-to-date sales, and prior year sales is provided. Credit and financial data are fairly comprehensive, including credit line required, terms of sale, Dun & Bradstreet credit rating, security on hand, credit scoring model score, if applicable, current payments, high credit, prior year payments, and prior year high credit. The credit and financial data presented should clearly document evidence of creditworthiness.

In addition to the marketing and credit header data, the credit manager must include a brief explanation of why the subject's required credit limit should be approved. The credit manager will usually want to comment on the customer's financial condition, bank facilities, and scope of operations. The text can also refer to the marketing and credit header information. The goal here is to state in a succinct manner the financial and marketing justification for approving the required credit limit.

Credit managers will want to make every effort in these situations to obtain financial disclosure from the customer. Remember, the customer probably requires a fairly large credit limit if it exceeds the credit manager's approval authority. In such a situation, making a joint authorization recommendation for a standard risk account without financial disclosure may be hard to justify.

It might be wise to visit the customer at his location before preparing the joint authorization. The visit will give the credit manager the opportunity to make the customer's numbers come to life. The credit manager can assess the strength of the customer's management and also ask any additional questions regarding the customer's financial condition.

The joint authorization form brings the treasurer or controller into the process when required credit limits exceed the credit manager's approval authority. And, of course, that makes good sense. The treasurer or controller, like the credit manager, is extremely concerned about the potential for lost or delayed cash flow.

The credit and treasury/controller interface is a natural fit. Both parties have the same goals in mind of providing financial support and protecting the company's assets.

If the customer is denied credit approval, the treasurer or controller should indicate the action required. One option would be to perform a high-risk evaluation for commercial underwriting by marketing. Such a "commercial underwriting" im-

Exhibit 9.1
Joint Credit Authorization For Accounts in Excess of $200,000

Account Name	Credit Line Required	Terms	Current High Credit	YTD Sales	Prior Year High Credit	Prior Year Payments	Products Purchased	Purchase Point	D + B Rating	Security	Credit Warning Score
ABC Co.	$1.6M	Net 30	$1.3M	3.6M	$1.1M	Prompt	Rod & Bar	Dukey Works	5A1	None	19 - Good

ABC Corporation has been a customer since 1977 with payments consistently prompt. They are rated 5A1 by Dun & Bradstreet with trades in the moderate six figure range and payments prompt. Working Capital as of the fiscal year-end, December, 19XX, was $205M with a current ratio of 1.73, which is an increase over 19XX of 1.45. Sales for 19XX were $1,758M with a net profit of $158M. Their debt to worth is .22 with their net worth being $892M. Based on six-month figures ending June, 19XX, sales were $930M with a net income of $83M, a 7% increase in sales and 14% increase in net income from the comparable period in 19XX. Sales at that time were $867M with a net income of $73M. They have available through their domestic banks, a line of credit for $300M, which is presently all available. We sell to two locations, Chicago, IL and Green Bay, WI.

Prepared By: _____

Approved By:

_____   _____
Credit Manager   Date

_____   _____
Controller   Date

_____   _____
President   Date

plies that the credit department has deemed a customer uncreditworthy, but the marketing department is willing to accept financial responsibility for the account by underwriting the high-risk evaluation submitted.

The joint authorization evaluation form should be included in the credit department's written policy and procedure.

ABSTRACT SUMMARY

- When a minimum-risk or standard-risk customer requires a credit limit beyond the credit manager's approval authority, the credit manager can seek approval through a joint authorization with the treasurer or controller.
- To pursue joint authorization, the credit manager must fill out a joint authorization form and submit it to the treasurer or controller.
- The credit manager should attempt to include credit and financial data that will present a clear indication of the customer's creditworthiness.
- Joint authorizations may be difficult to justify unless the credit manager can get the customer to provide updated financial disclosure.
- Credit personnel might consider making a visit to the customer's location during the process of preparing the joint authorization form. This will give them an opportunity to assess the strength of the customer's management, as well as ask any further questions about the customer's financial condition.

HIGH-RISK EVALUATIONS

The high-risk evaluation might be described as the alter ego of the joint authorization (see Joint Authorization Evaluation, in this chapter, p. 312). While the joint authorization process deals with minimum- and standard-risk customers, the high-risk evaluation considers the more marginal, or high-risk customers. These are the customers who always pay slow by 15 to 30 or more days, display an unbalanced financial condition, and have the potential to become insolvent within a one- to three-year period.

Each high-risk customer should be evaluated on an annual basis using the high-risk evaluation form. The form (see Exhibit 9.2) is prepared by the credit department and submitted to marketing for endorsement and underwriting. Copies go to the treasurer, credit manager, and director of marketing.

The high-risk customer is one to whom credit personnel feel they cannot extend credit. The high-risk form enables marketing to accept partial or full accountability and responsibility for continuing to sell to the customer in light of the highlighted risk.

The high-risk form is similar to the joint authorization form. Both contain marketing and credit header information and require a narrative. Where they differ is that the high-risk form requires the marketing department to justify why the company should continue selling to the customer despite the highlighted risk. The form also gives credit personnel an opportunity to document in writing why the customer is classified as "high risk."

The marketing department might want to endorse the business despite the high-risk classification. On the high-risk evaluation form, marketing personnel might offer a number of potential justifications:

- The gross profitability on sales to the customer is high.
- The high-risk customer is a growth company whose business will increase over time.
- The business would be difficult to replace.
- The high-risk customer is a major customer for a specific company plant or marketing region.
- The customer buys a lot of a new product that is being developed and that requires market penetration.

If marketing is unable to underwrite the business, then a strategy must be devised to "unwind" the customer's accounts receivable balance. Failure to get approval on a high-risk evaluation means the decision has been made that the firm can no longer extend open credit terms to the customer.

Exhibit 9.2
Credit Department High-Risk Evaluation Form

Referral Requesting Marketing Endorsement:

Customer and Credit Information

Prepared by: Peter Jason
Submitted to: Mary Karavida
Date: 12/06/XX
Date Response Requested: 12/20/XX

Customer Name and Address: Jones Industries, Inc., Irving, Texas
Product Line: Tube
Main Purchase Point: Dallas
Credit Line Required: $350,000

Nature of Security Held	Credit Alert Score	Current Terms	19XX YTD Sales	198XX Pmts.	19XX H/C	19XX Sales	19XX Pmts.	19XX H/C	Sold Since	Date Inc.	Current D&B Rating
None	46	Get Out 1%3 on 60	$880k	PPTSL5	$326k	$979k	PPT	$301k	6/76	1975	1A3

Credit Department justification for high-risk designation:

Despite satisfactory prompt payment performance the subject displays an unbalanced and highly leveraged financial condition. Current and quick ratios of .97 and .44 are extremely tight. Bank debt of $1.393M is extremely heavy representing 76% of total liabilities. It appears expansion into the aerospace industry has contributed to the decline of Jones's financial condition. Overall, a $399,000 net worth is based on $2.236M total assets and $1.837M total liabilities, reflecting a 4.6 debt to worth ratio. Note, in the event payments decline orders will be restricted and credit will press for security. Despite the decline in financial condition, there appears no imminent danger of insolvency.

Marketing Department justification for underwriting required credit line:

Jones represents $1M account using all material to manufacture a proprietary product which is sold through distributors. Jones's volume would be very hard to replace if their financial position should worsen. The record of payment has been good & we have built this volume over 3-4 years. I would recommend we continue to sell as long as they are prompt paying.

(A) Marketing Manager Approval _____ Date: 12/13/XX   Expiration Date: 07/31/XX
(B) Joint action required if Marketing unable to endorse required credit line:

Conversely, if the high-risk evaluation receives approval, the review and analysis process doesn't stop. The credit department will need to generate a high-risk report on such customers on a monthly basis. This report will go to the marketing department and to financial management. The report keeps all parties informed regarding the customer's most recent month-end accounts receivable exposure, along with other financial details and comments.

The high-risk evaluation form should not be used by the credit department as a "cop out." A marketing department endorsement doesn't mean that the credit department shouldn't hold a high-risk customer's order if its account is past due.

The evaluation form is part of the credit strategy of classifying trade accounts receivable by risk. The credit department must use good judgment in determining which customers are designated with the high-risk classification. Some customers, in fact, do not even merit this classification. No form should be prepared for these customers; they simply should not be extended open account trade credit.

If a high-risk customer's financial condition or payments decline dramatically, its classification should be terminated and an action plan to eventually terminate the business should be devised.

ABSTRACT SUMMARY

- The high-risk evaluation form is prepared by the credit department and submitted to marketing for endorsement and underwriting; copies go to the treasurer, credit manager, and director of marketing.

- The high-risk customer is one to whom credit personnel feel they cannot extend credit.

- Each month a high-risk report should be prepared on high-risk customer exposures and generated to marketing and financial management.

- The high-risk evaluation form should not be used by credit as a cop out; if a high-risk customer later fails to keep its account current, the credit department should still consider holding the customer's current order.

- The evaluation form is part of the credit strategy of classifying trade accounts receivable by risk.

PROTECTING ACCOUNTS RECEIVABLE ASSETS WITH A COLLATERAL REGISTER

With certain high-risk customers, the credit department will need to negotiate guarantees and/or collateral. These arrangements may involve an irrevocable letter of credit, a corporate or personal guarantee, a UCC1 filing, an accounts receivable note, a subordination agreement, or some other instrument of legal recourse. Most of these instruments have an expiration date. Or, in some cases they automatically expire at the end of a predetermined time period—as with a UCC1, which in most states automatically expires in five years unless there is a renewal.

Credit personnel need ready access to detailed customer information about each negotiated instrument that is still in force and valid. They can accomplish this by keeping a collateral register data base. Elements in the data base should include customer name, product purchased, date that the collateral became effective, a description of collateral (e.g., guarantee or letter of credit), expiry date, dollar limit (if applicable), and credit limit. The information might be detailed in a format like the one shown in Exhibit 9.3, and reported to management.

The expiry date entry might be the most critical element of the data base. The credit limit is also an important entry. A credit practitioner will want to note whether a high-risk account's credit limit exceeds the coverage provided by a legal recourse instrument. For instance, it's probably not wise to allow a high-risk customer to have a $250,000 credit limit but only a $25,000 letter of credit covering that exposure.

The description of the collateral will indicate its overall enforceability. Holding a first position UCC1 filing on a customer's accounts receivable and inventory is much more desirable than having a third position where there may not be sufficient secured assets to satisfy the secured claim in a bankruptcy filing.

As the credit department negotiates new forms of collateral, it updates the data base. If the format is on a computer disk, the updated information can be automatically alpha-sorted into the data base. The department can then run reports requesting collateral by customer and ascending order of expiry. It's also possible to break out product line collateral by type and in total.

A credit manager can report to management on the total number and types of collateral that the credit department has successfully negotiated. By keeping a collateral register, the credit department is virtually assured that collateral will not expire without management's prior knowledge and approval.

Allowing collateral to expire and thus failing to collect a receivable is one of the worst sins that a credit practitioner can commit. The way to limit such human error is to create a formalized mechanism to monitor collateral in force. Keeping a collateral register is one credit strategy that is simple to implement and pays big dividends by protecting corporate assets and collateral rights. It would be advisable

Exhibit 9.3

Co. Name	Product	Effective Date	Description	Expiry Date	Coverage or Dollar Limit	Credit Limit
BPM Co.	Liner	7/19/86	Irr. LC	7/19/87	$1,000,000	$1,000,000
BJM Co.	Board	12/06/86	UCC1/Cal.	12/06/91	2nd A.R. & Inv.	50,000
PJM Co.	Board	9/20/82	PG/D. Jones	Open	Open	25,000
LPM Co.	Fiber	11/26/85	CG/Lee Co.	Open	$100,000 MAX	100,000
ARM Co.	Fiber	6/20/87	UCC1/N. J.	6/20/92	1st A.R. & Inv.	250,000

Legend: Irr. LC – Irrevocable Letter of Credit
UCC1 – Uniform Commerical Code Lien
PG – Personal Guarantee

to include use of a collateral register in the department's written policies and procedures.

ABSTRACT SUMMARY

- Credit departments have a clear need to have ready access to detailed customer information about each negotiated instrument that is still in force and valid.
- A collateral register data base should contain customer name, product purchased, date collateral effective, description of collateral (e.g., corporate guarantee or letter of credit), expiry date, coverage or dollar limit, and credit limit.
- The expiry date may be the most important element of the data base; allowing collateral to expire without collecting a receivable is one of the worst sins a credit practitioner can commit.
- The description of the collateral — e.g., "first position UCCI filing" — will indicate its overall enforceability.
- As new forms of collateral are negotiated, the credit department will update the collateral register data base.

NEGOTIATING GUARANTEES AND COLLATERAL: PLANT THE SEED FIRST

Customers don't get a lot of pleasure out of providing guarantees or collateral in exchange for trade credit. Yet they are more likely to find these conditions acceptable if their supplier's credit department eases into them. In other words, from the credit practitioner's perspective, it's wise to "plant the seed" before harvesting a guarantee or collateral. Obviously, if there is a near-term threat of visibility the collateral should be negotiated immediately.

Customers don't appreciate a "shotgun" approach to guarantees or collateral. If, as they begin a relationship with a new vendor, the first thing they hear is a demand for a guarantee or collateral, the relationship will more than likely get off on the wrong foot. An alternative approach is to throw down a challenge to the customer — let the customer know it has an opportunity to avoid these credit requirements.

For example, if it's July, the credit manager might want to challenge the customer to bring its exposure under, say $100,000, by the end of October. By doing so, the customer can avoid providing a guarantee or collateral; however, at the time of the challenge, credit practitioners should make it clear that they want a promise that if the customer fails to bring the exposure below the required level, it will provide a guarantee or specified collateral.

This is referred to as "planting the seed." Whenever credit practitioners plant such a seed with a customer, they should write a memo to the file documenting the date and tenor of the agreement. It's also advisable to confirm in writing to the customer the challenge that has been thrown down, as well as the customer's promise to provide a guarantee or collateral if the challenge is not met.

In most cases this approach is preferable to the "shotgun" approach to negotiations. If the credit practitioner immediately demands a guarantee, the new customer often feels it is receiving an ultimatum. And, of course, this is not likely to be conducive to cultivating the vendor/customer relationship.

An immediate demand for collateral or guarantee puts the customer on the defensive before it has time to understand the supplier's perspective on the relationship. The shotgun approach is sometimes necessary, but in most cases it builds a wall in the relationship that need not exist.

Another point to keep in mind during these negotiations: They can be used as a selling tool when credit personnel feel comfortable with the company's exposure from risk and bad-debt standpoints. A credit practitioner can offer to increase the customer's credit limit or tolerate existing delinquency in exchange for the guarantee or collateral being sought.

It's much easier to obtain a guarantee or collateral after showing some flexibility in granting the customer a reasonable amount of time to meet a challenge. When using the "plant the seed" method of negotiation, credit practitioners usually end up winners. If the customer meets the challenge, they win; and if the customer fails to meet the challenge, they get the collateral or guarantee they sought while appearing to be reasonable with regard to requirements and timing.

ABSTRACT SUMMARY

- When negotiating guarantees or collateral from customers, don't make point-blank demands; negotiate the credit requirements over time.

- A good strategy is to throw down a challenge to a customer, qualifying the challenge with the company's need for guarantees or collateral if the customer is unable to meet the challenge.

- Taking the "shotgun" approach can make the customer feel that it is receiving a hostile ultimatum, which will not be conducive to cultivating the vendor/customer relationship.

- Consider using negotiations for collateral as a selling tool; a credit practitioner might attempt to exchange a higher credit limit for collateral or a guarantee.

- Credit practitioners will find it is much easier to obtain a guarantee or collateral after granting the customer a reasonable amount of time to meet a challenge related to payment performance.

REVOKING CREDIT TERMS

Unfortunately, on occasion the credit department must revoke a customer's open account trade-credit status. There are several reasons why this action might be necessary.

Sometimes, the credit department will encounter customers who are chronic promise breakers with respect to meeting their payment commitments. These are the customers who usually don't call the credit department if they can't meet their commitment, and often make payment commitments only because they have orders pending. Credit managers can only give these types of customers so many chances before they must revoke their open account trade credit.

About 99 percent of the time, promise breakers are extremely slow-paying customers. However, in the rare instance that credit personnel are dealing with a promise breaker who generally pays within terms, they should think twice before revoking their credit.

The second type of customer whose trade credit a company might want to revoke is the customer whose financial condition over time has evolved into an unbalanced and marginal condition. The customer's financial condition may have been borderline in the past, but now it has deteriorated — in some cases to a deficit net worth; the customer's current and quick ratios are well under 1.0, or it has consistently sustained loss operations for a period of three to five years. Their financial condition is beyond being classified as high-risk for marketing endorsement.

Timing is crucial when a company revokes credit from a marginal or unbalanced customer. The goal is to "pull the plug" on the customer's credit before it becomes insolvent. To be on the safe side and remain unscathed by the customer's financial difficulties, the company might have to revoke credit six to 18 months before the customer's unbalanced financial condition peaks. This decision requires the credit practitioner to almost have a sixth sense with respect to the customer's ongoing viability. The challenge is to interpret the red flags that arise before the customer finds itself in a deficit net worth situation.

A third type of customer whose trade credit might need to be revoked is the new customer who appears to be a marginal credit risk but is given a trial period with open account terms. At any time during the beginning of the relationship, the credit manager might determine that the customer is not creditworthy. Again, the reasons may be due to derogatory credit information or extremely slow payment performance. Revoking credit in a new relationship may be slightly easier than the other two cases noted above.

With either of the three scenarios outlined here, it will be extremely difficult if not impossible to "zero out" the customer overnight. The first step is sometimes a two-for-one paydown program each time an order is placed, which in essence is a veiled form of applying COD credit terms. Under a two-for-one scenario, each time the customer places an order, it must pay for the full amount of the order at the

322

time of shipment along with a like amount to offset the outstanding and past due balance.

The credit department needs to be careful once it has determined it wants to revoke credit. If the company simply cuts the customer off from its product, the customer will seek alternative suppliers and cash flow from the customer will simply cease. This approach will leave the company with only one option for pursuing payment and extending the cash flow benefits of the customer relationship: a lawsuit. Thus, it is better to revoke credit in several phases.

ABSTRACT SUMMARY

- Generally, there are three classes of customers that might need to have their credit revoked: 1) Chronic promise breakers, who are generally slow payers; 2) Customers whose financial condition has become unbalanced and marginal; and 3) New, marginal customers who exhibit poor payment performance during a trial period with open account credit.

- In rare instances, promise breakers will be customers who normally pay on time; think twice before revoking their credit.

- When revoking credit for a marginal or unbalanced customer, the key is timing.

- Knowing when to revoke credit demands a sixth sense of sorts. Even so, to be on the safe side, a supplier sometimes has to revoke credit from six to 18 months prior to the time that the customer's financial situation hits rock bottom.

- When revoking a customer's credit, don't immediately cut off the customer from product; cut the customer's credit off in phases as a way to maintain some cash flow benefits from the relationship.

SELLING TO LBOs: A WHOLE NEW BALL GAME

Leveraged buyouts have proliferated during the 1980s, changing the face and makeup of corporate America. The ultimate impact of LBOs on creditors and corporate liquidity is still unclear. However, one thing is clear: When selling to a firm that has just been purchased in an LBO, the credit department needs to be aware that it is selling to a totally new entity. Everything credit personnel had established about that company in terms of financial wherewithal and payment performance is now history.

Following an LBO, companies that previously had AAA or AA debt ratings are likely to be considered speculative grade investments. The reason is that there will often be concern about the LBO's ability to meet obligations to the holders of debt instruments that have been issued.

An LBO's funding costs always will rise. While before the LBO those costs may have been 90-125 basis points over the 90-day Treasury bill rate, funding costs could rise to 600-800 basis points or more over the T-bill rate. Furthermore, the "new" company's debt-to-worth ratio will often skyrocket. If it was 1:1 or smaller before, that ratio could rise to 10:1 or greater.

The makeup of the company can also be expected to change drastically following an LBO. Fixed assets, product lines, divisions, and subsidiaries that were previously an integral part of the company may be sold off to reduce debt and the intense burden of interest expense. Productivity may suffer as a result of significant cutbacks and layoffs. In the future, restrictions will be placed on the total annual amounts of capital expenditures that can be made by the LBO, possibly blunting the LBO's competitive posture.

From a vendor's standpoint, the company's payment performance might take a major turn. Previously a prompt payer, the new LBO firm might be a slow payer or request extended terms.

The vendor needs to realize that selling to the LBO firm is an entirely new ball game. For that reason, the supplier needs to start early to set the tone for an entirely new trade relationship. When the LBO is announced, and it appears that it will be successfully executed, credit personnel at the vendor need to start planning to deal with the "new regime." The first step will be to contact the management of the LBO to discuss what the company will need once the LBO is finalized in order to establish a line of credit for the "new" firm. Depending on the magnitude of the credit limit the firm will extend, the credit department should request the following considerations to qualify the LBO for credit:

- A visit and tour of the headquarters or primary operating/manufacturing location that includes a meeting with the treasurer or CFO.
- Pro forma balance sheet and income statement financial information. This, in essence, represents the LBO's estimated or forecasted opening

balance sheet and income statement projections. Credit personnel should ask that this information be supplemented with ongoing financial disclosure once the LBO is in place.

- A review of the LBO's business plan, which should project financial information three to five years beyond the initial pro forma statements.
- A review of forecasts for the first year's monthly cash flows based on estimated monthly receipts and disbursements.
- A listing of the amounts, interest rates, and sources of debt that will be utilized to fund the LBO.
- An updated listing of banks that will be extending credit lines to the LBO, in addition to banks and financial institutions that will be providing the buyout funding.

Once again, the important thing is to act quickly so there will be plenty of time to satisfy information needs regarding the LBO firm. A supplier and its credit department do not want to enter into the new relationship unprepared.

Credit personnel need time to carefully scrutinize all financial data on the LBO firm and compare that data to what the company already knows about the predecessor firm. The results could be enlightening. For example, the LBO firm may be projecting a 33-day turnover for accounts receivable in its monthly receipts and disbursement projections, whereas the predecessor company's turnover may have been 45 days. Credit staff will want to consider whether the LBO can realistically reduce its AR levels by 12 days without losing sales and customers.

Other cross-comparisons can be made. Credit practitioners can calculate interest expense as a percent of sales, for instance, and then compare this ratio to the gross margin percent or to the operating profit percent to see how tight margins are. There may be very little room for profitability and amortization of debt, even under favorable operating circumstances.

When reviewing the LBO firm's financial information, credit personnel need to pay close attention to the liquidity, leverage, and profitability/operating ratios. If the firm is selling five or more LBO accounts, they need to develop financial ratio standards for this group of accounts. The credit department can establish high, mean, and low averages for the liquidity, leverage, and profitability/operating ratios analyzed.

Furthermore, if the information is not provided, credit personnel should reconstruct and perform an annual source and application of funds analysis with data that is provided. The analysis will help determine whether operations will provide sufficient cash flow to reduce debt while meeting the internal funding needs and requirements of the business. The source and application of funds analysis may reveal that additional borrowings will be required to fund operations, which would put a further strain on profitability and leverage.

Questions that credit personnel need to ask when they interview the LBO firm's treasurer or CFO include:

- Has bridge financing been replaced by permanent financing yet?

- What are the ratings, maturities, and rates for junk bonds to be issued? Have any private placements been arranged and what are the specific arrangements?

- Are there any future plans down the road to go public in order to boost equity and/or retire debt via a stock issue?

- What asset sales are being contemplated to reduce the initial debt levels?

- What cost reduction programs are going into effect to reduce expenses?

- What are the "new" firm's goals and objectives over the next three to five years, and how will the LBO strategically achieve these goals?

- Who are the firm's main competitors and on what basis? Price? Quality? Service?

- Does the LBO face any foreign competition?

- How will the LBO successfully and profitably compete against the competition in light of the significant acquisition expense?

- Do the competitors now have a competitive advantage from an operating standpoint?

- What is the LBO's game plan to cope with a price war, industry downturn, or nationwide recession?

- Are any suppliers balking at extending credit to the new LBO entity? (Avoid asking if any suppliers are providing extended credit terms.)

- What selling price and purchase price assumptions are incorporated into sales and expense projections?

- What is the impact to the bottom line if selling prices are increased or reduced (Ask same question for purchases.)

- What are the capital spending plans for the next three to five years for facilities and existing technology?

- Are capital spending levels limited by the bondholders or bank covenants?

- Have any sectors of management left the company since the leveraged buyout?

Once the initial credit limit is established for the LBO firm, the credit department should continue to monitor the account closely from payment and financial disclosure standpoints. At a minimum, credit personnel should be prepared to visit the customer on an annual basis.

By establishing lead time, performing a thorough analysis, and making a face-to-face visit with financial management of the new firm, credit personnel should get a clear picture of the liquidity and viability risks of doing business with an LBO customer.

ABSTRACT SUMMARY

- When selling to a firm that has just completed an LBO, credit personnel must realize they are selling to an entirley new and different entity. Previous information about financial wherewithal and payment performance is valuable only for comparison purposes.

- After being purchased in an LBO, a company with AAA or AA debt ratings may find that it is rated as a speculative grade investment. With an LBO, there are often significant doubts about the company's ability to meet its obligations, and funding costs and leverage increase dramatically.

- The new LBO firm may exhibit entirely different payment performance. Whereas the old firm may have payed promptly, the new LBO firm might pay beyond terms or request extended credit terms.

- If the company sells to five or more LBO firms, it should develop financial ratio standards for these firms — e.g., standards for current, quick, and debt-to-worth ratios.

- Credit personnel should try to set up a personal visit to the customer to see its operations and meet with its treasurer or chief financial officer.

SELLING NON-CREDITWORTHY NEW ACCOUNTS

Often times, a credit investigation for a new account will be performed and the customer will not qualify for open account credit terms. The investigation could reveal an unbalanced financial condition, excessively poor trade payments, or the firm could be a start-up company with no payment or financial track record.

When the credit investigation produces these results, the credit department should not immediately reject the customer's request for credit and invoke COD (cash on delivery) or CIA (cash in advance) terms. Instead, credit personnel should make every effort to sell to the customer on open account. After all, their objectives should include maximizing sales as well as protecting assets and minimizing bad debt. The credit department must serve marketing needs from commercial and profitability standpoints while meeting treasury needs with respect to liquidity and cash flow. And, yes, it's a fine line to walk!

Alternatives to rejecting the sale but at the same time protecting the investment in accounts receivable include the following:

- Irrevocable standby letter of credit
- UCC1 lien on accounts receivable and inventory
- Corporate guarantee, if applicable
- Personal guarantee of principal, preferably collateralized
- Subordination agreement

If administered properly, the irrevocable standby letter of credit (see Letters of Credit, in Chapter 8, p. 285) will probably afford the most protection. With an LC, the credit department relies not on the customer's creditworthiness, but rather on the creditworthiness of the customer's bank.

When utilizing an irrevocable standby LC, credit personnel can advise the customer that they don't intend to use the LC as a means for payment unless payments are well beyond terms—and these boundaries should be specified—or unless at the time of expiry the account is not within terms. The irrevocable standby letter of credit gives the customer a time frame for establishing a strong payment track record. Under no circumstances should the credit department accept a revocable letter of credit, which can be cancelled unilaterally by the bank or customer at any time.

Another alternative with an LC would be to procure an LC for only half of the subject's credit line. This strategy gives the subject open credit on the back end of the exposure for half of its credit needs. For example, the customer may require a $100,000 line that cannot be justified. In that case, credit could extend a $100,000 line protected by a $50,000 irrevocable letter of credit. As an inducement for the customer to provide the LC, the credit department could offer to pay for the cost of opening the LC.

A UCC1 filing lien on the debtor's accounts receivable and inventory will protect the dollar exposure if there are sufficient accounts receivable and inventory assets that can be liquidated to pay the balance (see UCC1 Security Interests, in Chapter 8, p. 292). The UCC1 filing establishes the firm as a secured creditor. In bankruptcies, secured creditors must be paid in full before unsecured creditors can be paid at all.

A note of caution: If the company's lien is a second or third lien on accounts receivable and inventory, credit personnel must make sure there are sufficient assets to pay the secured creditors and those with a second or third lien. Otherwise, the second or third lien is worthless.

Most often, the corporate guarantee (see Corporate Guarantee, in Chapter 8, p. 280) is less desirable than the LC and UCC1 options, yet it is still a viable alternative for asset protection. In essence, the guarantee substitutes the guarantee of a third-party corporation for the creditworthiness of the new customer. From an insolvency standpoint, the credit department would look to collect the debtor's (customer's) balance from the corporate guarantor. A guarantee does not establish lien rights, however.

The personal guarantee (see Personal Guarantee, in Chapter 8, p. 276) is probably the least desirable form of protection—especially if it is an uncollateralized guarantee. With an uncollateralized guarantee, there are no specific assets of the guarantor pledged to back the guarantee.

If credit personnel seek a personal guarantee, they should always obtain a personal financial statement from the individual guarantor. They should also seek a corresponding guarantee with the individual's spouse; this will hinder the primary guarantor from transferring assets to the spouse to avoid having those assets attached if the creditor attempts to enforce the primary guarantee.

A subordination agreement (see Subordination Agreement, in Chapter 8, p. 289) is another vehicle that might allow a company to offer credit to a customer who is not creditworthy. A subordination agreement can be constructed if the customer owes another party, in many instances its parent company, a significant debt. In the subordination agreement, the third party agrees to subordinate that debt to the debt owed to the customer's supplier. In other words, in the normal course of business or in the event of an insolvency, the customer must pay its supplier before it pays the debt it owes to the third party.

Under any of these alternatives, the credit department should convey to the customer that the formalized asset protection is not a blank check for slow trade payments. The customer must know that it is expected to meet its obligations reasonably within terms, and failure to do so could lead to enforcement of the asset protection or the revoking of open account credit terms.

A customer should be advised that a termination of asset protection will be based on the combination of payment performance and financial condition, not just payment performance.

A final alternative that will not protect a supplier's investment, but which will minimize its initial exposure, is providing the customer with a reduced credit line for a trial period of three to six months. Before offering this alternative to the customer, credit personnel must be convinced that the customer's financial condition is such that it will remain viable through the trial period.

Remember, before refusing credit to a potential customer, it is the credit person's duty to determine if there are any viable asset protection alternatives that will enable the company to sell to the customer on an open account basis.

ABSTRACT SUMMARY

- Although new customers don't always meet the criteria for open account credit terms, credit personnel can consider various strategies that offer such credit while protecting the firm's accounts receivable investment.

- Options for protecting the AR investment include: irrevocable letter of credit, UCC1 lien on accounts receivable and inventory, corporate guarantee, personal guarantee, or a subordination agreement.

- Irrevocable letters of credit generally provide the best form of asset protection if administered properly.

- Personal guarantees are generally the least desired form of asset protection; uncollateralized personal guarantees are particularly weak.

- If none of these methods of asset protection apply, the company might consider selling the account on a limited credit line basis for a specified time period, e.g., three to six months. This strategy only makes sense if the customer presents no near-term viability problems.

SELLING ACCOUNTS WITH FOREIGN OWNERSHIP

Extending credit to companies with foreign ownership is somewhat different from routine credit extension. For these companies, most funding and key company decisions come from the overseas headquarters. The subsidiary cannot make any significant commitments without first conferring with the parent.

The U.S.-based subsidiary will never make the "ultimate decision" to cease operations and file for bankruptcy in the United States. The decision to cease operations will always be made by the foreign parent. If the U.S. subsidiary ever does file for bankruptcy, the supplier's credit department generally has no legal recourse with the foreign parent — even though the parent may be financially strong. There is a legal recourse only for companies holding guarantees from the parent, or possibly a strongly worded comfort letter.

Rule No. 1: When dealing with a foreign-owned U.S. subsidiary: Always obtain financial disclosure on the U.S. sub and the foreign parent. If both exhibit strong financial conditions, then there really is no problem. However, if the U.S. sub reflects an undercapitalized and/or a leveraged financial condition, credit personnel may have to take additional action to protect the company's investment in accounts receivable.

One action might be to propose that the U.S. sub open an irrevocable standby letter of credit in the supplier's favor for a period of one year. As a marketing concession, the company could offer to pay the cost to open the irrevocable standby LC. Additional bank charges related to the letter of credit would have to be paid by the U.S. sub, however. At the end of one year, credit personnel could reconsider extending open credit based on payment performance.

Rule No. 2: With exposures possessing significant risk, credit personnel should attempt to negotiate a corporate guarantee from the foreign parent when an LC cannot be negotiated. The guarantee of payment will nullify the negative effects of the U.S. sub filing for bankruptcy.

The supplier should seek to get the guarantee on its own corporate guarantee form to ensure that U.S. authorities have jurisdiction to rule on matters related to the guarantee. A letter from the foreign parent guaranteeing the U.S. sub's indebtedness may later pose a jurisdiction problem.

The credit department should acknowledge receipt of a foreign parents' corporate guarantee. The acknowledgement letter to the sub and the foreign guarantor should be sent within 30 days of receiving the guarantee. It should note that the company is relying on the guarantee as the sole means of extending credit to the U.S.-based sub.

Rule No. 3: Always attempt to secure a "comfort letter" if the foreign parent declines to provide a guarantee or irrevocable stand by letter of credit. A comfort letter is generally not enforceable in a court of law unless the wording resembles that of a guarantee of payment. The comfort letter usually states that the parent generally stands behind the U.S. sub's operations (without issuing a formal guarantee), the sub is adequately capitalized to honor trade obligations, there is no intent to cease operations in the U.S., and that the parent will notify the supplier if there is a change in the sub's financial condition. The letter provides "comfort" insofar as the foreign parent declares it is aware and approves of the business relationship between the supplier and its subsidiary.

If the supplier is unable to obtain either a guarantee or a comfort letter, then it must decide whether it still wants to sell the account. If the supplier goes forward, it must proceed in the relationship with due diligence.

It is sound credit strategy to develop written policy and procedure for extending credit to foreign-owned U.S. subsidiaries. Credit practitioners may want to establish an approval authority structure that differs from the firm's structure related to pure U.S. customers. Approval levels could be lowered in order to get senior credit and finacial management more involved in the decision-making process.

As part of the policy, credit personnel should clearly define the criteria for high-risk customer classification of foreign-owned customers.

ABSTRACT SUMMARY

- Selling to companies that are foreign-owned demands different credit strategies — and sometimes more involvement by senior financial management.
- If a foreign-owned company files for bankruptcy, a U.S. supplier's credit department generally has no legal recourse with the foreign parent — even though the parent may be financially strong.
- *Rule No. 1*: When dealing with a foreign-owned U.S. subsidiary always obtain financial disclosure on the U.S. sub and its foreign parent.
- *Rule No. 2*: With exposures possessing significant risk, the credit department should try to negotiate a corporate guarantee from the foreign parent or obtain an irrevocable standby letter of credit.
- *Rule No. 3*: Always try to secure a "comfort letter" if the foreign parent declines to provide a guarantee. This type of letter generally is not enforceable in a court, but it does indicate that the foreign parent stands behind its U.S. subsidiary and is aware of its new trade relationship.

SELLING WORKOUT ACCOUNTS

Selling to workout accounts is where credit professionals earn their pay.

A workout account can be defined as an account with a past-due balance that will not be current or significantly reduced within the next three to nine months, or in some cases may never become current. Some workout accounts face the imminent possibility of bankruptcy, while others are in a somewhat more viable position.

So, in essence, there are two types of workout accounts. With the first, there is a true question of viability. With this type of account, credit personnel need to be concerned about how payments against the account are applied in order to avoid a bankruptcy trustee's declaration that "preferential" payments were received by the firm. Preferential payments can be defined as payments for an antecedent debt received by a supplier within 90 days or greater of the insolvent customer's filing of a bankruptcy petition.

The supplier can continue to service the "potentially insolvent" customer on a COD (cash on delivery) or CIA (cash in advance) basis for all new shipments. In this way, the company can generate cash from the customer relationshp that will not be lost in the case of a bankruptcy filing, when the customer's assets will be frozen. Remember: For customers that fall into this category, don't apply payments against the unpaid past-due items if there appears to be a strong likelihood of a bankruptcy filing within the next 90 days. If the customer goes bankrupt, a supplier may not be able to recoup the past-due balance.

Current payments should be applied against antecedent debt only if it appears the customer is in no danger of bankruptcy within the next three to five months. And, even then, credit personnel would be wise to confer first with senior management and the legal department regarding the firm's payment application strategy.

The second type of workout customer poses much less of a risk of bankruptcy and creates less concern regarding preferential payments. With these customers, the goal is simpler: reduce the past-due and overall balance.

Here is where credit personnel can get creative. They might establish a weekly payment program to reduce the past due while making sure that all new invoices coming due are kept current. Short of placing the customer on a true COD or CIA basis, they should make every effort to reduce the outstanding balance.

With these customers, it's important not to let the exposure get any higher without securing some form of collateral or a guarantee. For example, let's say a customer has a balance of $168,000, of which $105,000 is past due. A credit practitioner can put the customer on a payment program requiring $5,000 weekly payments against the past due and payment of all future invoices coming due on a current basis. Unless the customer violates the agreement, its account should be completely current in 21 weeks. Of course, the weekly paydown of existing past due must be a realistic and feasible dollar amount for the customer.

Another strategy would be to require that for every shipment the customer must provide a commitment or a payment of twice the dollar amount of the shipment. The payment would not have to be made the same day as the delivery; a commitment could be accepted whereby the payment would be sent at the time of shipment or within a specified number of days after the shipment. With the "two-for-one" strategy, the ratio of payments to new orders does not necessarily have to be 2:1, but the ratio should exceed 1:1 to ensure that the balance does not rise.

Under the "solvent workout" scenario, current payments can be applied against the antecedent balance. However, if the customer breaks its promise, then the supplier may have to shift to a true COD or CIA shipping arrangement.

When working with either type of workout account, the supplier's credit personnel need to keep accurate manual records of the customer's commitments, incoming payments, and outgoing shipments. This is necessary to ensure that the company's exposure does not increase (see The Total Exposure Concept, in Chapter 6, p. 183).

In either case, the negotiating skills of the credit practitioner will be tested.

ABSTRACT SUMMARY

- A workout account is one whose past-due balance will not be current or significantly reduced within the next three to nine months, or in some cases may never become current, and may possibly file for bankruptcy over the near term.

- There are two basic types of workout accounts—the "potentially insolvent" accounts and those that are expected to remain solvent through the near term.

- With "potentially insolvent" workouts, credit personnel must be concerned about how payments against the account are applied in order to avoid a bankruptcy trustee's declaration that preferential payments were received by the supplier.

- Don't apply current payments against antecedent debt unless it appears the customer will remain solvent beyond the next three to five months.

- When dealing with workout accounts of either variety, credit personnel need to maintain accurate manual records of the customers' commitments, incoming payments, and outgoing shipments. The goal is to ensure that the company's total exposure does not increase.

BAD-DEBT WRITE-OFF CONTROLS

Bad-debt write-offs cannot be eliminated, but they can be controlled and minimized by the credit department. And, in fact, they must be. With the Tax Reform Act of 1986—which requires the direct write-off method for bad debts instead of the accrual method—a large dollar bad-debt write-off could push the company's monthly, quarterly, or year-end profit and loss statement into the red.

Effective bad-debt write-off controls begin with a written credit department policies and procedures manual. The manual should contain a policy statement regarding bad-debt write-off approval authority for all credit positions. It should also have a policy statement regarding credit-limit approval authority for all credit positions. Without credit-limit approval authority, the company takes the chance that a junior credit staffer will incur a major bad-debt write-off that could otherwise have been avoided if senior managers were aware of the situation.

The tone and enforcement of credit policy will have an impact on bad-debt write-offs. Credit managers should ask themselves: How closely does their credit policy coincide with overall company goals? How do they justify the extension or rejection of trade credit?

Collection efforts need to be reviewed for their impact on controlling bad debts. For instance, if certain high-risk customers are significantly past due in their payments, credit holds may have to be placed on their current orders in order to control further exposure and minimize bad-debt potential. Is the credit department confronting slow-paying customers that need to be confronted?

One way to monitor high-risk customers is through a high-risk report generated for both internal and management reporting purposes. High-risk customer balances should be monitored closely and collateral should be negotiated where possible to cover the company's downside. In this way mangement can avoid surprises.

Written job descriptions for credit department positions will also help control bad debts. These job descriptions should elaborate on cash flow responsibility and accountability. Clearly written job descriptions ensure that all credit employees are aware of their roles with respect to generating cash flow and minimizing bad-debt write-offs.

An additional control mechanism is a form that should be used whenever bad debts are written off (see Exhibit 9.4). The form needs to be prepared by the credit individual directly handling the account. It should be approved by credit personnel according to the department's bad-debt write-off approval authority designations.

The form for writing off bad debts should contain the date of the write-off, the dollar amount of the write-off, the oldest invoice date, the credit limit at the time of write-off, the date the credit limit was last approved, and the reason for the write-off.

The credit department should have a written procedure for filling out and executing the bad-debt write-off form. The form will promote a uniform approach to

Exhibit 9.4
Referred Account

Date _____

To: _____   Amount_____

Location: _____   Oldest invoice date (after
adjusting credits to
oldest items) _____
Last Payment Received _____
A/C No. _____

Customer: _____
Address: _____
Person Contacted: _____   Phone No: _____
Title: _____

Agency Rating: _____
Latest Credit Limit $ _____   Date: _____   Assigned by: _____
Previous Credit Limit $ _____   Date: _____   Assigned by: _____
Comments: _____

_____

Enclose: Verified Statement—5 copies
Correspondence
Credit Information
Notices
From:
(Location) _____
By: _____

_____

Credit Manager's Recommendations: _____

_____

_____

_____

By _____

Countersigned By _____

documenting bad-debt write-offs and prevent the nonreporting of write-offs. Once approved, the form should serve as a backup for the journal entry to the general ledger that must be made against accounts receivable. Credit personnel should keep a log and copies of the forms for all bad-debt write-offs to remain aware of, and be able to report on, the moving write-off dollar level in detail by customer.

The form serves three purposes. It acts as a control mechanism, as a monitoring or tracking tool, and as a reporting tool.

Although a certain number of bad-debt write-offs are unavoidable, a conscious effort to control them is certainly better than having no action plan. Designated bad-debt approval levels and the bad-debt write-off form will be central to this effort, allowing the credit department to place responsibility and accountability at the appropriate levels. An audit of these controls and procedures for reducing bad debts should be performed on an annual basis.

Credit personnel shouldn't be passive when it comes to bad-debt write-offs. They need to take steps to minimize these setbacks to the cash flow effort.

ABSTRACT SUMMARY

- Every company will experience bad-debt write-offs, but a credit department needs to have controls in place to minimize these write-offs and prevent possible bad-debt write-off catastrophies.
- The Tax Reform Act of 1986 requires the direct write-off method for bad debts as opposed to the accrual method, which is reserved for future bad debts.
- Effective bad-debt write-off controls begin with a written credit department policies and procedures manual.
- When writing off bad debts, the credit department needs to use a standard form. The form should be prepared by the credit individual directly handling the account.
- Having designated bad-debt approval levels in writing and using a bad-debt write-off form are two ways to control bad debts. These mechanisms place responsibility and accountability at the appropriate levels.

CUSTOMER REFUNDS

Make sure that your company's policies and procedures manual incorporates a section on how to handle, process, and refund customer credit balances. Written policies and procedures with tight controls should eliminate customer fraud and employee misconduct.

You want to establish controls of the credit department to oversee the customer refund process. Your policy should state in writing that, before a refund can be processed, you must have a letter from the customer requesting a refund of the specific credits on the customer account. Beyond the letter, you also should require a refund voucher request highlighting the nature of the credit and why the customer is requesting a refund.

In lieu of a refund check you might ask the customer to deduct the open credit from their next payment. This method of clearing the credit eliminates the opportunity for fraud while minimizing the accounting gymnastics you must perform to remove the credit from the customer's account and from the accounts receivable records.

The refund voucher should require two separate approvals when dollar amounts exceed your designated limit. The voucher also should be accompanied by a photocopy of the open credit items.

Despite having controls in place, there is still the danger of employee fraud, especially when tempted by personal hardship or other circumstances. Therefore, for refunds in excess of a certain dollar threshold, you should send a letter under separate cover confirming the refund. Such a refund letter is designed to prevent cases where a firm's credit employee fraudulently submits a refund request on behalf of a customer and subsequently personally cashes the check.

As a further precaution against fraud, for large dollar refunds you may want to follow up the refund letter with a phone call to the customer confirming that the check was received. Yet an additional precaution for large dollar refunds is to pull a copy of a cleared refund check and review it to make sure it has a valid customer endorsement stamp on the back of the check.

Controls on requests, refund processing, and encashment will ensure that customer refund requests will be properly processed and administered. The controls are simple and not elaborate. Most important of all, the controls and procedures to be followed must be in writing. Without written control procedures there will be widespread interpretation of policies. In contrast, with written controls there is a sound mechanism to monitor and control the flow of customer refunds.

ABSTRACT SUMMARY

- Incorporate in your policies and procedures a section for the handling, processing, and refunding of customer credit balances.

- Written policy and procedure with tight controls should eliminate potential employee or customer fraud and misconduct.

- Require a refund voucher request highlighting how the credit balance occurred and why the customer is requesting a refund check.

- For refunds exceeding a certain threshold, send a letter under separate cover confirming that a refund will be made and that the customer, indeed, requested the refund.

- Controls over both refund requests, processing, and encashment ensure that customer refund requests will be properly processed and administered.

PERFORMING POST AUDITS
OF CREDIT OBJECTIVES

Once departmental budgets and objectives have been set for DSO, Best DSO, Past-Due DSO, percent past due, aging of past due, monthly collections, and bad-debt write-offs, credit personnel should evaluate actual performance to budget on a monthly, quarterly, and annual basis.

The idea of a budget is to set performance standards that coincide with the company's overall goals and objectives for sales, profitability, and cash flow. Thus, on a monthly, quarterly, and annual basis, credit personnel should review actual performance against budget to determine whether changes to credit policy and or manpower are required to meet the established budgets.

Most of the targeted objectives will be budgeted on a monthly basis. Bad-debt write-offs are the exception; they are often reviewed less frequently. That's OK, but credit personnel should not audit bad-debt write-offs only on an annual basis. It's not wise to wait until year-end to assess actual bad-debt write-off performance; at that point, it might be too late to make adjustments in credit policy, philosophy, or departmental headcount.

When conducting a post audit, a credit professional might discover that credit department performance budgets are set too high; the department could be having an easy time in achieving DSO targets, for instance. Or, quite the opposite could be the case. The post audit might reveal that budgeted targets for such measures as DSO are too low and too difficult to achieve. In either case, these discoveries may lead credit personnel to alter their budgets and their action plans.

One conclusion of a post audit might be that employee headcount is insufficient to meet the budgeted targets for DSO, Best DSO, Past-Due DSO, and monthly collections. If the department does not have sufficient staff to meet budgeted objectives, existing staffers may soon realize it and give up on attaining the goals. Credit department goals must remain realistic.

After credit managers compare actual performance against budget, they can advise the department of the results during monthly staff meetings. At these meetings, the credit manager may get either positive or negative feedback relating to the attainability of the budgets. Remember, successful credit department communications involve a two-way flow of information. The credit manager needs to be willing to listen and hear what is being said by staffers about the budgets. Credit employees will get the most satisfaction when they are able to meet aggressive but realistic budgets.

On a quarterly and annual basis, the credit or treasury manager might want to issue to senior management a highlight letter that details actual performance against budget. The letter should list each month's specific budget, actual performance, and variance, along with a short narrative explaining how or why the budget was attained (or not attained) for each particular time period. If the results are favorable, this gives the credit or treasury managers a great opportunity to blow their horns with senior management. If the results are unfavorable, they have an opportunity to express to senior management what they want or need in terms of resources to attain the targeted budgets.

This same type of post audit of budgeted objectives should be applied to the objectives and actual performance of individual credit employees, and this analysis should be performed at least quarterly. By doing so, the credit manager will be able to give more timely and accurate performance appraisals.

ABSTRACT SUMMARY

- Credit managers should evaluate actual performance to budget on a monthly, quarterly, and annual basis using a post audit of goals and objectives.
- Most of the targeted objectives will be budgeted for on a monthly basis with the primary exception being bad-debt write-offs.
- The idea of a budget is to set performance standards that coincide with the company's overall goals and objectives for sales and profitability.
- The post audit may reveal that credit department performance budgets are set too high or too low, providing the credit manager with the information needed to make adjustments in the budgets or to seek additional resources.
- In some cases, this analysis may indicate that the credit department lacks the necessary staffing to meet the budgeted targets for DSO, Best DSO, Past-Due DSO, and monthly collections.

AUDITING THE CREDIT FUNCTION

Credit management should audit the credit department on an annual basis. The audit should include a review of the following 10 areas of the credit function:

1. Policy and philosophy
2. Procedures
3. Controls
4. The annual review process for ongoing customers
5. New customer credit investigations
6. Collections
7. Credit reporting and forecasting scope
8. Collection agency activity
9. Credit department performance measurement
10. Departmental credit budget

The audit should be conducted to ensure that the credit department is functioning at its full capabilities in these areas. Credit managers should address the 10 functions and take action if necessary to meet credit and cash flow needs (see Exhibit 9.5).

Credit managers should probe each and every area and challenge the effectiveness of credit operations as currently executed. Questions about the nature of operations for each of these areas must be resolved.

In simple terms, the audit will allow the credit department to maximize its corporate role of protecting the company's investment in accounts receivable while generating the required levels of cash flow on a consistent basis.

In the first part of the audit, credit managers should review credit policy, philosophy, procedures, and controls. Without these four elements of credit administration, a credit department has no direction or safeguards. Some questions to ask include:

- Does the firm have written policies and procedures? If not, the first post-audit step will be to write a credit policies and procedures manual covering all areas of the credit function.

- Are there written procedures on how to operate the accounts receivable system and on how to refer an account for collection?

- Does the firm have a policy statement relating to unearned discounts?

- What types of internal and external controls are in place for bad-debt write-offs, customer offsets, customer refunds of credit balances, and accounts receivable system access and input?

Exhibit 9.5
Variables Impacting Credit and Cash Flow Needs & Objectives

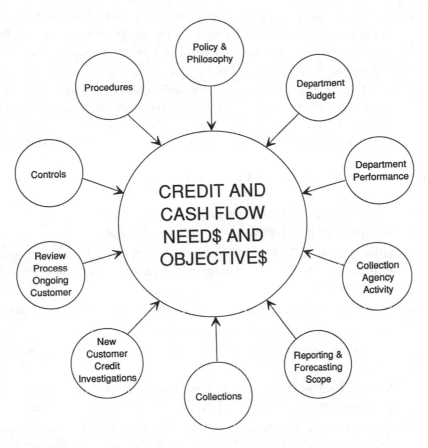

Credit managers will also want to audit the review and annual approval process for ongoing customers' credit limits. Questions to ask include:

- Are there specific criteria established for approving designated dollar levels for credit limits?

- If so, are the criteria based on job classifications, or are they determined by individual merit?

- What type of file documentation is required for the annual renewal of customer credit limits?

- To what degree is the credit department obtaining financial disclosure to justify and approve ongoing credit extension with high-risk customers?

And, regarding new customers:

- Is the company using a formal credit application for new customers? (A credit application will speed up the review process while enabling credit personnel to perform a more complete and standard credit investigation.)

- Does the company have an automatic credit approval model for new customers whose orders fall within the prescribed automatic approval limits? (Automatic credit approval for small dollar limits enables credit personnel to allocate their time to other credit priorities.)

With respect to the collections function, questions to ask are:

- How are the collection assignments broken down? Are they by product lines, by geographic location, or by the alphabet?

- How are the collection assignments for individual credit personnel determined? Are the assignments based on experience or are they made randomly?

- Does the credit department employ any rotation of assignments?

- What types of collection output measurements are in place? Are staffers assigned a formalized objective for average daily collection calls made?

- Is the credit staff making quality collection calls, and how is the department measuring the level of quality collection calls made?

- Has the credit department performed a ship date/invoice date audit to determine if the billing function is assigning free payment days to customers due to the lag between the shipment date and actual invoice date?

- Has the credit department performed a lockbox audit to measure and accelerate cash flow?

Regarding credit reporting and forecasting, ask:

- What credit reports are being generated by the credit department? What is the frequency and distribution of these reports, and how effective are they?

- Can the department effectively manage the receivables function with the current flow of information?

- What reports are being derived manually and how time-consuming is the exercise? Are there any other viable alternatives to the manual environment?

- What type of reports is the credit department generating via the PC? How does PC utilization fit in with the skills and capabilities of existing credit personnel?

- Is there any forecasting being performed? If so, how effective is it?

- What forecasting methodologies are being used and what ones might be used?

- Does forecasting require additional data processing support?

Collection agency activity needs to be probed. The credit manager might ask:

- Are the fee schedules of those agencies being used competitive?

- Does the company use only one agency? If so, why?

- How effective is each agency's collection performance for referred accounts?

- What type of record keeping does the company maintain for referred accounts? Are the records kept on a manual basis or on a mainframe?

- Are the firm's collection agencies remitting recoveries on a timely basis?

With regard to credit department performance, there are a number of issues to explore:

- What performance measurements are being used to judge overall credit performance? Does the company have formal budgets for DSO, Best DSO, Past-Due DSO? If so, is there a post audit performed to compare actual performance to the established budgets? How does the level of bad-debt write-offs correspond to the DSO performance?

- How is the department evaluating individual performance? What criteria are being used?

- Is the credit department procuring the required level of financial statements, guarantees, and collateral?

- Can the credit manager quantify that the credit department as a whole is meeting the company's cash flow needs and objectives?

With respect to the department budget:

- Are funds being spent in the right places?
- Is staff size sufficient to meet the company's cash flow objectives?
- Is money being spent on conferences, seminars, and continuing education to challenge and develop credit personnel?
- Does the department have a travel budget for customer visits?
- Is the software in use meeting department needs or will the department require a new system in the near future?

The end result of a complete audit should be clearer policy and procedure, enhanced controls, stronger credit analysis and credit extension, accelerated collections, enhanced credit reporting and communications, enhanced collection agency performance, and a higher level of overall credit performance compared to the credit standards established.

After the audit, the credit manager will be able to formulate an action plan to correct and revise the areas that must be addressed.

ABSTRACT SUMMARY

- Credit management should audit the credit department on an annual basis.
- The audit should cover: 1) Policy and philosophy, 2) Procedures, 3) Controls, 4) The annual credit review process, 5) New customer credit investigations, 6) Collections, 7) Credit reporting and forecasting scope, 8) Collection agency activity, 9) Credit department performance measurement, and 10) The department credit budget.
- The objective of the audit is to review all areas of the credit function to ensure that the department is operating as effectively as possible.
- Once the audit has been performed, credit management can create an action plan to eliminate problem areas.
- The audit enables the credit department to maximize its corporate role of protecting the company's investment in accounts receivable while generating the required levels of cash flow on a consistent basis.

10

PERSPECTIVES

COD TERMS DO CARRY CREDIT RISK

Credit department personnel often mistakenly believe that they are taking on absolutely no credit risk when they sell to a customer on a cash-on-delivery (COD) basis. But this isn't the case at all.

With both certified checks and regular demand deposit checks, customers can execute "stop payment" instructions through their payor banks. A certified check implies that good funds from the customer's demand deposit account have been allocated to the check that has been written. It does not imply that the customer cannot stop payment on the check. And, of course, with a regular demand deposit check, the customer can execute a stop payment order at any time with no constraints, provided that the check has not already cleared the payor's account.

Additionally, there is usually a lag of one to three days and sometimes more before the COD check is deposited to the vendor's account, and then another one to two days before the item is processed for check presentment through the check-clearing system. By the time the regular demand deposit check is presented to a payor bank for payment, the customer may no longer have sufficient funds in its account.

Sometimes, the common carrier picking up the check at the delivery won't immediately remit the check to the vendor, adding to the lag time. If this is often the case, the vendor may want to make arrangements up front with the carrier to remit the check directly to its lockbox on the same working day that the item was received from the customer. However, many carriers will insist on depositing the customer's check in their account first, and only when it clears will they remit funds to the vendor. This type of scenario only increases the probability that there won't be good funds to clear the item or there will be an additional delay in getting funds credited to the vendor's account. Cash flow in this case is not only at risk, but also delayed at an implicit opportunity cost.

At a minimum, when arranging for a COD customer delivery, credit personnel should contact the customer's bank and inquire if there are sufficient funds in the customer's account to honor the check amount for the COD order in question. If the bank advises that there are insufficient funds on hand to cover the check, credit personnel should advise the customer, and at that time the vendor may want to arrange for a certified check to be given to the common carrier.

One way to eliminate any credit risk when making COD deliveries is to make the terms of sale cash in advance (CIA), either by wire transfer or by a regular check that must pass for presentment before the actual shipment can be made. Obviously, this payment mode may require a bit of lead time prior to shipment.

So remember: COD terms carry with them implicit credit risk. Credit practitioners that fail to recognize this fact are likely to get burned.

ABSTRACT SUMMARY

- Credit department personnel sometimes mistakenly believe that they are taking on absolutely no credit risk when they sell to a customer on a cash-on-delivery (COD) basis.

- Customers can stop payments on both certified checks and regular demand deposit checks through their payor banks.

- When arranging for a COD delivery, the credit department should contact the customer's bank and inquire if there are sufficient funds in the customer's account to honor the check amount for the COD order in question.

- Processing a check takes time. By the time that the regular demand deposit check is deposited with the vendor's bank, the customer making the COD payment may no longer have sufficient funds in its account.

- One way to eliminate any credit risk when making COD deliveries is to make the terms of sale cash in advance (CIA), either by wire transfer or by regular check.

BEWARE OF HOMEMADE FINANCIAL STATEMENTS

With small and midsize businesses beginning to use personal computers in the late 1970s and the 1980s, more and more customer financial statements began to be generated on PCs. Most PC-generated statements are for interim reporting periods, primarily for internal review and evaluation purposes. And most of the time these internally driven statements are accurate representations of the firm's financial position as of the statement date.

However, when credit personnel receive financial statements generated on a PC, they should not treat them as they would audited statements prepared by an accounting firm in accordance with generally accepted accounting principles (GAAP).

When credit personnel are provided with PC-generated customer statements — statements that are not on the letterhead of an accounting firm — they should proceed with caution. They should be cautious when the customer claims that the PC-generated statement is a year-end statement. Without the scrutiny of an accounting firm, it would be easy for a company to generate such a year-end statement — making sure that the sum of total assets equal total liabilities and equity — and pass it off as a "balanced statement" and proof of the company's creditworthiness.

Under these circumstances, additional due diligence regarding the customer's financial condition is required. If credit personnel are provided with a questionable year-end PC-generated statement, they could ask for a copy of the customer's tax return, which by law must contain a year-end balance sheet. If credit personnel have statements from prior years on hand, they should attempt to reconcile them to the current statement. In this comparison, they should look for continuity with respect to the currently reported levels of cash, accounts receivable, inventory, accounts payable, and net worth.

In essence, credit personnel will need to perform a full reconciliation of the newly reported levels for the asset and liability accounts. Does the reported level of stockholders' equity tie in with the prior year's statement when one rolls forward the retained earnings from the current PC-generated statement?

Another test of the PC-generated statement would be a source and application of funds analysis of the current statement to see if the reported level of cash agrees with the changes in the balance sheet accounts.

If credit personnel still feel uncomfortable with extending credit based on the PC-generated statement, they should ask for an on-site review and audit of the customer's accounts receivable and accounts payable ledgers. They should ask management to explain why the statements don't reconcile. Unless they take this step, credit practitioners will end up basing their credit decision on a financial statement that may or may not be valid.

ABSTRACT SUMMARY

- Customer financial statements generated on personal computers are un-audited and primarily used for internal purposes.
- PC-generated statements should not be confused with audited statements prepared by an accounting firm.
- When credit personnel are provided with PC-generated statements that are not on an accounting firm's letterhead, they should proceed with caution.
- When credit personnel are provided with questionable year-end PC-generated statements, they could ask for a copy of the customer's tax return, which must contain a year-end balance sheet.
- If necessary, credit personnel may want to ask for an on-site review and audit of the customer's accounts receivable and accounts payable ledgers.

BEWARE OF CUSTOMERS THAT MOVE

When small to midsize companies move into larger facilities, either renting them or buying them, their vendors become unofficial silent partners in either amortizing the moving expenses or the new mortgages.

Customers experiencing growth are often encouraged to purchase their own facilities. They believe by owning a facility they will be getting a better "deal." What they don't realize is that their new facility will not add anything to their current productivity.

In fact, quite to the contrary, a move from a rental facility to a company-owned facility is a cash drain that usually trickles down to primary suppliers. Not only is there the cost to physically move the contents of the prior facility, but there will also be significantly higher monthly payments to be made, both to pay off the mortgage and to maintain the property.

When a Fortune 500 company buys a facility, there may not be as severe a cash drain, but the company is still dedicating cash to an asset that bears no productive benefits.

The customer will also have to pay higher property taxes, which are an expenditure with no return relating to productivity. And it is likely that the customer will also be faced with the need to do a certain amount of remodeling in its new corporate home. Additionally, there are many hidden costs related to a move that are never factored into the purchase/move economics.

Usually once a customer moves into a company-owned facility, it will experience a drain on cash flow for the next 12-18 months. The drain can run even longer if the company doesn't meet growth projections.

In this situation, a major supplier literally becomes an unofficial silent partner in the venture, as partial cash flow that should be earmarked to pay off the supplier is redirected to funding the move. This cash-flow drain scenario is even more evident when a marginal customer moves into a new facility. Here again, it will appear as if the customer's cash flow is solely dedicated to the support of the move.

Thus, when credit personnel are advised that a customer is moving into a new facility, it may be wise to perform a complete credit review of the account, including updates of both bank and trade information. Other steps to take include:

- If there is a financial statement on hand, factor the cost of the facility purchase into the customer's existing statement to gauge the impact of the debt on cash flow.
- If there is no financial statement on hand, renew efforts to secure one from the customer.
- If credit personnel were contemplating a move to negotiate for a guarantee or a collateralized position, plant the seeds for the negotiations.

Credit personnel should also try to find out from the customer if the company is purchasing the building or if one of the principals will be purchasing the building and leasing it back to the company. Either way, there will be an impact on trade payments. The only difference is that the added leverage won't be reflected on the company's balance sheet if the principals are purchasing the building.

Even when customers move and rent a larger facility, there will be an impact on trade payments. The added rental cost, combined with moving expenses and changes to the newly rented facility, will surely drain the customer's cash flow. In the rental scenario, the cash flow drain usually runs from six to 12 months, depending upon the magnitude of the move.

ABSTRACT SUMMARY

- When any small to midsize company moves into a larger facility, either by renting it or buying it, the company's suppliers become unofficial silent partners in funding the move.

- A newly owned facility will not add to or enhance a firm's productivity, but it will increase monthly operating expenses.

- Once a customer moves into a company-owned facility, the customer can be expected to suffer a drain on cash flow for the next 12-18 months, or longer.

- When credit personnel are advised by a customer that it is moving into a new facility, they would be wise to perform a complete credit review of the account.

- A supplier should beware when a customer's owners buy a facility personally. The leverage won't be reflected in their financial statement, but it will surface in their trade payments.

ALWAYS LET CUSTOMERS KNOW
WHEN THEY'RE ON CREDIT HOLD

One of the cardinal rules of credit is "Always tell customers when they are on credit hold." A credit practitioner who fails to do so will jeopardize his or her individual credibility with a customer, as well as possibly the entire vendor/customer relationship.

Here's how the scenario might play out. Let's say a company manufactures bicycle tires and its customer—Smith Co.—assembles bicycles and sells them to bicycle shops. Believing that its order for more tires is on the way, the Smith Co. advises one of its customers that it will deliver X number of bicycles by tomorrow. When the bicycles are not delivered, the bicycle shop calls the Smith Co. and wants to know the status of its order. Someone at the Smith Co. learns that the reason is a holdup on a delivery of bicycle tires and gives the tire manufacturer a call. "Where is that order of bicycle tires?" he wants to know.

If the answer is, "Sorry, but your order is on credit hold," and the customer hasn't been previously informed, the tire manufacturer is likely to have one angry customer on its hands.

The customer, of course, will want to know why it was not informed of the credit hold. By failing to inform the customer of the credit hold, a supplier leaves himself open to criticism and excuses. The most common is: "I had all the funds you required three to four days ago, if only you had told me that the order was being held up due to past-due items."

Telling customers they are on credit hold is sometimes difficult. Nevertheless, the credit person in most cases needs to call up past-due customers before shipment of their next order can be approved. One strategy for making this call can be to begin by inquiring about the status of invoices, asking about them by invoice number and indicating the dollar amount they total. "Can you tell me if or when the items will be paid?" the credit person should ask.

At this point, the customer has no idea that his order is being held.

If the customer is trustworthy and says the check has already been mailed or will be mailed shortly, the credit practitioner can record the information and politely terminate the conversation—without referring to the pending order that requires credit approval for shipment. The order can simply be approved without any mention to the customer about a credit hold. What customers don't know won't hurt them.

In some cases, the customer will not immediately offer any sort of commitment. In these cases, the credit person needs to press for one. It may take some discussion, but if the commitment is forthcoming and it is satisfactory, then once again the credit person will be able to terminate the conversation and say nothing about a credit hold. And again the order can be approved.

However, sometimes, after lengthy discussion, there are situations where the credit person will not obtain a satisfactory payment commitment from the past-due customer. If all collection efforts appear to be exhausted, then, and only then, is it time to advise the customer that the order is on hold due to the past-due items that are unresolved.

Once credit practitioners let on about the credit hold situation, they can expect one of two responses. The customer might become more responsive to the supplier's payment needs, or the customer might simply say, "OK, hold my order, I can't do any better."

The strength of this strategy is that the credit person makes every possible effort to learn the status of the items before "lowering the boom" on customers and advising them they are on credit hold. The theory is simple: Why ruffle customers' feathers and insult their egos if they have already paid, or are planning to pay, the past-due items?

Customers should not be told they are on credit hold unless it is clear that they have no plans to pay off their past-due items. But once this is clear, they have to be told. Failing to advise customers of a credit hold altogether will, in the end, give the customer leverage. And that will make it more likely that the supplier will lose the account and the business relationship.

ABSTRACT SUMMARY

- One of the cardinal rules of credit is to always let customers know when they are on credit hold.
- By not advising customers when they are on hold, the credit person jeopardizes his or her credibility with the customer, and possibly the entire relationship.
- By not advising the customer of the credit hold, the credit person is potentially conceding payment leverage to the customer.
- When calling a customer on credit hold, try to secure a payment commitment before breaking the news that the customer is on hold.
- Only advise customers they are on credit hold after all attempts to obtain a satisfactory payment commitment have been exhausted.

ALWAYS SECURE AN UP-FRONT PAYMENT COMMITMENT FROM POTENTIAL SLOW-PAYING NEW CUSTOMERS

What should a credit practitioner do when a new customer's trade references report slow payment performance?

As long as there is no question about the customer's viability, the company may still want to pursue the business. If so, credit personnel should start by contacting the customer's accounts payable manager or treasurer to discuss concerns about potential slow payments and to affirm the terms of sale.

If the company is a small, privately owned concern, the credit practitioner may want to contact the new customer's president or owner. The goal will be to secure a satisfactory up-front payment commitment that meets the terms of sale. In doing so, the credit person needs to make sure that whoever is contacted on behalf of the customer has the responsibility and authority to make a payment commitment.

Credit personnel should diplomatically advise the customer that, when questioned about the customer's payment habits, trade references revealed that the customer tends to pay slow in excess of terms. Credit personnel should restate the terms and ask the customer in a direct manner if there will be problems paying within those terms. If the customer says it can meet the terms, document the commitment in writing, with both a letter to the customer and a memo to the new customer's credit and collection files.

If the customer admits that it can't meet the terms of sale, then credit personnel will be faced with a business decision. Should the company sell to this customer? In some cases the answer will be "no." But in others, rather than turning their backs on the business, credit personnel may be willing to tolerate a negotiated level of delinquency representing a middle ground that both parties can accept.

When late payments are assessed an interest charge, credit personnel need to make sure that the customer is aware of the fact. The two parties then need to establish an acceptable and legal payment range where interest will not be assessed for late payments. A letter should also be sent to the new customer highlighting the commitments that have been made during the telephone conversation. Part of the text of the letter could read as follows:

"As a follow-up to our July 19 telephone conversation, we mutually agreed to the following:

- The ABC Company's terms of sale are net 30 days.
- Your firm, the XYZ Company, is aware of the net 30-day terms and will make every effort to adhere to our standard terms of sale.

357

- Credit may be restricted and orders put on hold if payments are in excess of our terms.

- A late charge of 1.5 percent monthly or .0005 percent daily is assessed on past-due payments.

- Payments received at our lockbox in under 35 days from date of invoice will not be assessed a late payment service charge.

We will rely on your verbal commitment as the means of extending credit to the XYZ Company. In closing, we at the ABC Company look forward to establishing a mutually profitable relationship with the XYZ Company."

Credit personnel should contact the customer the first time its payments do not reasonably adhere to the payment commitment. The customer should be reminded of the initial telephone conversation, as well as the letter the supplier sent that detailed the verbal commitments. By documenting the commitments in writing to the customer and the credit file, credit personnel are armed with specifics as opposed to vague details about the discussion and the commitment.

If they are properly documented, the customer really has no opportunity to question the commitments. They have been outlined in a letter and the customer has been given a chance to respond to this letter. Questioning the commitments only after they are broken would not be credible on the customer's part.

Securing an up-front commitment from the new customer's management "short-circuits" any ideas they might have about pleading ignorance regarding terms of sale when the first payment is required. By contacting a management individual, credit personnel can appeal to the customer on a personal basis to keep his or her word relating to commitments made.

ABSTRACT SUMMARY

- Credit personnel should secure a satisfactory up-front payment commitment from new customers whose credit investigations reveal the strong likelihood of slow payments.

- The commitment should be secured from a management employee who has the responsibility and authority to make a payment commitment.

- A letter should be sent to the new customer highlighting the payment commitment that was made during the initial telephone conversation.

- Credit personnel should contact the customer the first time its payments do not reasonably adhere to terms of sale. The customer should again be reminded of the initial telephone conversation and the commitments it made.

- Securing an up-front commitment from the new customer's management will "short-circuit" any attempts to plead ignorance about terms of sale.

CREDIT ADMINISTRATION: THE NEGOTIATING GAME

The job of the credit practitioner is one of almost constant negotiation. Credit personnel spend most of their time negotiating with customers in order to protect their companies' investments in accounts receivable.

These negotiating sessions can range from making a simple collection call with the purpose of securing a payment commitment to soliciting and obtaining financial disclosure from a customer.

Credit personnel might find themselves negotiating with a customer to obtain a guarantee or a form of secured collateral via a UCC1 filing in order to support the credit exposure. Or, they may make a visit to the customer's facility to negotiate a payout on a customer's account.

Negotiations with a customer can involve resolving old items and deductions that are still outstanding and represent lost cash flow. Or, a credit person might negotiate with a customer regarding its required credit limit.

The bottom line is that credit practitioners are literally negotiating with customers on an ongoing and daily basis. The credit person needs to be prepared to negotiate with customers on a variety of fronts at almost every turn.

The key to success, of course, is to be prepared. Credit personnel should plan in advance of negotiations. They should establish exactly what it is they want to derive from the negotiating process.

Advance planning is crucial for even simple tasks—like making a collection call. Before making collection calls, credit personnel should review the customer's account in detail and identify specific invoices that they want to be paid. Credit personnel should strive to be so prepared that the collection call will require them to do little thinking on their feet. They should have specific targets and objectives for the negotiations before they begin.

Credit personnel need to be prepared with alternative negotiating tactics in the event they are initially unsuccessful in achieving their primary goals. Through careful planning and by anticipating negotiating scenarios, they can maximize each negotiating session and thereby protect the firm's best interests.

Another strategy for improving negotiating techniques is to enroll in a negotiating class or seminar.

ABSTRACT SUMMARY

- Credit practitioners are almost constantly negotiating with customers in order to protect their companies' investments in accounts receivable.

- Credit personnel need to be prepared when negotiating, whether the subject of the negotiations is securing a personal guarantee or simply trying to get the customer to pay more promptly.

- In advance of any negotiations, credit personnel should outline their goals. They must establish what they want to accomplish in specific terms.

- Credit personnel should be prepared with alternative negotiating tactics in the event they are initially unsuccessful in negotiating their primary objectives.

- Another strategy for improving negotiating techniques is to enroll in a negotiating class or seminar.

CENTRALIZATION vs. DECENTRALIZATION

Should all credit personnel be under one roof? Or, should credit professionals be dispersed throughout the nation, where they can be nearer to the customers? Should distinct product lines or product groups be serviced on a centralized basis or by separate credit groups located close by the product group? For years, both credit pros and senior corporate management have debated the pros and cons of a centralized versus a decentralized credit department.

Should credit policy and procedure be administered on a centralized or decentralized basis? Should basic credit policy and procedure be uniform throughout all of a firm's credit offices?

Who determines which credit services to use, such as lockboxes and collection agencies?

When considering centralization versus decentralization, you must consider not only how it relates to credit personnel, but also how it will impact distinct product lines, policy, procedure, and use of outside credit services. For example, credit personnel might be physically decentralized while headquarters still decide personnel policy and which credit services to use and when. If and when should any of these decisions, as well as authority to change customer credit terms, be decentralized?

An obvious advantage of centralization is having all credit employees under one roof. This affords both tighter day-to-day control over operations and control over execution of policies and procedures. Centralization also gives senior management ready access to customer credit data.

In contrast, with a decentralized credit operation, senior credit management has less direct control over the day-to-day operations as well as over how remote credit personnel carry out these policies and procedures. Staffers at various locations may differ in interpreting how credit policy ought to be carried out. This can be an even greater problem if your firm does not have formalized written credit policies and procedures.

Decentralization does enable credit practitioners to get closer to the customers. However, does this single benefit justify having a decentralized credit function? If there are problems, cannot a credit representative from your centralized staff travel to the customer's location to review and resolve matters? If it is a matter of picking up a customer check, cannot your firm's local sales representative do the job?

Before making any changes, you must fully explore the tradeoffs of both the centralized and decentralized approaches to credit management.

ABSTRACT SUMMARY

- Centralization implies that all credit personnel are under one roof.
- Decentralization implies that credit personnel are geographically dispersed to be nearer to customers.
- In choosing a decentralized versus a centralized approach, you must consider where physically to locate your credit staff. You also need to decide who will select outside credit services and how much latitude you want to allow remote credit staff in interpreting corporatewide policies and procedures.
- Centralization enables senior management to have far more ready access to credit information.
- Decentralization diminishes senior management's direct control over day-to-day credit operations and over how local credit pros interpret policies and procedures.

OBJECTIVES ENHANCE PERFORMANCE

All credit department employees should be striving to meet both formal and informal objectives. Meeting such goals will create an atmosphere of achievement and instill a greater sense of pride in these employees.

Setting objectives provides employees with direction and helps clarify their mission. One of the major benefits of objectives-setting is that credit personnel become more cash-flow oriented.

Formal objectives should be readily quantifiable, whereas informal objectives should be more educational or developmental.

Formal objectives can be set for DSO (days sales outstanding), Best DSO, Past-Due DSO, past due percentage, bad-debt write-offs, daily collection calls, and the number of customer visits. Monthly targets should be set for DSO, Best DSO, Past-Due DSO, and past due percentage, while annual objectives can be set for bad-debt write-offs and visits. Weekly objectives could be set for the number of collection calls made per representative, and daily objectives might be set for the number of customer orders on credit hold.

Informal objectives are usually not dollar-oriented. Instead, they are geared toward the development of the employee. Plant tours, seminars, MBA programs, and association memberships are just a few of the many informal objectives that might be set.

Although not readily quantifiable in terms of dollars, informal objectives do pay "invisible" dividends to the company. By attending seminars or participating in associations, employees remain in the mainstream of their profession. Greater knowledge and a growing number of industry contacts are likely to be gained from attending these functions.

Both forms of objectives-setting offer a motivational factor that goes far beyond the immediate benefits of meeting any particular objective.

Reasonable objectives also give the credit manager yardsticks for measuring the performance of employees. These objectives can even be incorporated into the employee's performance evaluation. After all, most formal and informal objectives fall within the realm of either responsibilities or expectations in a written job description.

Objectives should be reviewed quarterly with each credit department employee. Progress or deficiency in achieving objectives should be noted during these reviews. Even objectives that involve annual targets, such as bad-debt write-offs, should be reviewed quarterly.

ABSTRACT SUMMARY

- Formal and informal objectives for credit department personnel pose challenges that enhance credit performance.

- Formalized objectives provide employees with direction and they also help to clarify their mission within the credit department.

- Formal objectives are readily quantifiable, whereas informal objectives are more educational or developmental.

- Although not readily quantifiable, informal objectives do pay off in "invisible" dividends to the company.

- Reasonable objectives provide credit managers with yardsticks for measuring the performance of employees, and can be incorporated into the employee's performance evaluation.

MONTHLY CREDIT STAFF MEETINGS

Regular staff meetings can enhance communications both up and down the organizational structure of the credit department. Staff meetings should be held on a monthly basis with credit management and credit nonmanagement personnel in attendance.

The meetings can be used as forums to review and discuss current results relating to DSO, month-end accounts receivable, collections, past due, and bad-debt write-offs. The credit manager can also use the meetings to reinforce for all credit personnel the department's formalized objectives regarding individual and overall credit department performance.

Enlisting the help of credit staffers in achieving goals is a vital effort. If credit staffers aren't aware of the monthly results or formalized credit objectives, how can they help the credit manager meet the predetermined targets related to DSO, month-end accounts receivable, collections, past due, and bad-debt write-offs?

Credit management is often guilty of promoting a one-way line of communication—managers talk, staffers listen. The proactive credit manager, however, will use the staff as a valuable source of information to help determine whether the department can attain the outlined goals.

Staff meetings should be run based on predetermined agendas that allow credit managers and credit reps to report on their areas of responsibility. Corporate credit managers might want to use their time to update the month's performance and discuss how the results compare to the budgeted objectives. They might also present any changes in credit policy and procedure, review the status of long-range credit projects, and seek comments from the staff. In this way, the entire credit department can be used as a sounding board.

Credit managers can discuss marketing issues and problems, potential problem accounts, the status of existing problem accounts, upcoming visits to customers, and guarantees or collateral recently negotiated. They might also want to provide an update on any ongoing projects they are working on.

Credit representatives can discuss their outlook from the "trenches." In many cases, credit reps will be more aware than the credit manager of exactly what is going on with a high-risk customer.

The staff meeting might also be a good time to review marginal customers and even develop action plans related to particular customers. Action items discussed at the meeting should be put into writing to ensure follow-up and implementation.

Staff meetings can be a great benefit, if only as a way to clearly communicate the goals and objectives of the credit department. These meetings provide credit managers and credit reps with an opportunity to "blow their horns" with respect to recent accomplishments and achievements. They also offer a forum for communicating and discussing accountability in a positive manner.

After a staff meeting, everyone in attendance—from top to bottom—should really feel that they have a finger on the pulse of the credit department.

ABSTRACT SUMMARY

- Monthly credit department staff meetings can enhance communications both and up and down the department's organizational structure.
- Staff meetings can be used to review and discuss current results relating to DSO, month-end accounts receivable, collections, past due, and bad-debt write-offs.
- Credit managers are often guilty of promoting a one-way line of communication—managers talk, staffers listen.
- Staff meetings should have predetermined agendas that allow credit managers and credit reps to report on their areas of responsibility.
- Action items discussed at the staff meeting should be put into writing and distributed accordingly, in order to ensure follow-up and implementation.

CLAIMING NEW AREAS OF
CASH FLOW RESPONSIBILITY

Credit and accounts receivable management traditionally has been viewed as a "backroom" operation consisting of collections, credit analysis, and extending credit to new and existing customers. Most have overlooked how an ambitious credit manager can significantly accelerate a company's cash flow.

Customer visits are also a part of the job of the traditional credit professional. Credit pros use their visits to negotiate payouts and collateral, to establish a customer's credit limit, and to legally settle accounts with customers in liquidation. These and several other credit management duties can significantly impact how much cash a company will receive and when.

Today, credit professionals have the opportunity to involve themselves in new areas of financial responsibility — areas that treasurers and controllers have traditionally managed.

In many middle-market companies, the controller or treasurer may be preoccupied with other responsibilities. This leaves an opportunity for the ambitious credit pro to take on additional responsibilities such as lockbox and accounts payable management.

Taking over responsibility for lockbox management is a good place to start. If credit is going to collect the funds, why not also manage the funds and payment detail flowing through your lockbox? And, who better than the credit manager knows whether your lockbox geographic configuration matches the dispersion of your customers? Also, the credit manager is much more aware of your firm's order entry and billing system than is your treasurer or controller. Therefore, he or she is better positioned to accelerate cash flow by speeding up customer billings.

Depending on the size of your firm, the credit manager may also have an opportunity to manage the accounts payable function. If you're going to be collecting the company's receipts, why not also be involved with the outflow of funds? The opportunity to manage accounts payable will more likely arise when a treasurer or cash manager leaves, and his or her duties would default to the firm's controller. An ambitious credit pro could volunteer to take on accounts payable responsibility, citing its natural fit with the receivables function, which he or she already manages.

Credit practitioners can involve themselves in discussions about whether to negotiate extended credit terms from a vendor. The credit pro is usually the first person in your firm a customer asks for trade support. He or she, therefore, is familiar with all the arguments for extended terms and is well positioned to make your firm's case with a vendor.

Credit pros can forecast trade receipts. Such a forecast might augment other forecasts developed by your treasury department or may, in fact, be the only forecast provided.

In smaller companies, the credit professional can work with the controller to help arrange corporate investments and borrowings. Because the credit manager already understands the nuances of incoming receipt patterns, he or she is well positioned to manage liquidity while maximizing investments and minimizing borrowings.

ABSTRACT SUMMARY

- Credit analysis, credit extension, collections, and order approvals are key elements that influence cash flow.
- Credit's activities play a significant role in generating corporate cash flow.
- The investment, borrowing, lockbox, and accounts payable functions are areas the credit pro can logically assume responsibility.
- Because of experience in granting credit to customers, the credit manager may be the person in your firm best equipped to negotiate terms with your vendors.
- Monthly credit department receipt forecasts can be used to augment the treasury department forecast.

CREDIT'S CODE OF ETHICS

Credit practitioners should always follow certain unwritten guidelines when they carry out their job responsibilities. Like other professionals, credit practitioners should adhere to certain standards of conduct in their work. Some of these standards include:

- *Never use abusive or foul language with a customer, even when provoked.* The credit practitioner should not stoop to that level, regardless of the circumstances. Engaging in such discussion is unprofessional, and furthermore, it isn't likely to accomplish anything.

If during the course of a conversation a customer gets abusive or uses foul language, credit practitioners should advise the customer that they can't continue the conversation. Prior to ending the conversation, they can tell the customer that a member of the firm's management will be in touch. After the call, the credit person should document the experience in writing and immediately advise management of the situation.

A credit practitioner should always be polite, cheerful, and courteous when engaging a customer in conversation. There is no possible benefit to being derogatory. By acting in a derogatory manner, the credit practitioner could actually turn a winning hand into a losing hand. Furthermore, a credit person who initiates a derogatory conversation could end up losing his or her job.

- *Never reveal credit file financial information to non-company contacts.* A credit person must be especially careful to heed this standard during the course of trade references, verbal discussions with trade competitors, or discussions with other customers.

Whenever financial information is shared by a customer, it is always with the implicit understanding that the information will be treated with confidentiality. A credit representative is expected to treat the information in a professional and confidential manner. The information was provided for the sole purpose of assisting the supplier in making a credit decision; it was not intended to be shared with outside parties.

Sharing financial information with outside parties could be considered collusion in administering credit, and it could have legal ramifications and consequences. Who needs that kind of aggravation and grief?

If an outsider or a trade contact requests that a credit person share his customers' financial information, he should politely advise them that it's against personal and company policy. Management should be advised of any such requests, and co-workers should be made aware of these incidents.

Discussing confidential financial information with the firm's sales department or order processing personnel should also be taboo. These employees don't need this information to do their jobs. For instance, if the credit department decides that a customer's deteriorating financial condition warrants putting a hold on the customer's order, someone in the company will have to be told not to ship product to the customer. However, they don't have to be given a detailed financial justification for the decision.

- *Never bad-mouth a customer with employees or outside parties.* A credit practitioner's job is not to criticize or condemn customers. His or her job is to perform the credit function in a professional manner. Derogatory opinions about customers should not be shared with company employees, as they simply serve no beneficial purpose.

- *Never base a credit decision on personal feelings.* The credit person's function is to protect the company's investment in accounts receivable and to generate cash flow. Basing credit decisions on personality — on whether the customer is or is not a likable sort — is not sound credit philosophy. Credit decisions need to be made on a uniform and fair basis.

- *Never accept a gift or tangible benefit from a customer.* Clearly, to accept a gift or benefit would create a conflict of interest. Credit practitioners should never place themselves in a position to fall prey to temptation. Remember, credit practitioners must always act in the best interests of their firms.

These are but a few of the many ethical guidelines credit professionals should adhere to in their work. There are others, of course. The important thing to note is that adhering to such guidelines as these will increase professionalism without compromising success.

ABSTRACT SUMMARY

- Never use abusive or foul language with a customer, even if provoked by the customer.
- Never reveal credit file financial information to non-company contacts — especially during the course of trade references, discussions with trade competitors, or any discussions with other customers.
- Never bad-mouth a customer with employees or outside parties.
- Never make a negative credit decision on the basis of personal feelings about a customer.
- Never accept a gift or benefit from a customer.

THE 60 COMMANDMENTS OF CREDIT

Successful credit practitioners generally have a set of commandments or guidelines that they abide by in performing day-to-day credit tasks. Awareness of and adherence to these commandments should promote sound and consistent credit administration while minimizing the likelihood of a credit disaster.

These informal rules may vary slightly from credit department to credit department based on company policies and philosophies. However, the majority of commandments detailed below should have application to most credit practitioners and credit departments. Like most rules, there will be exceptions to these. But it's important to know the rules before one breaks them.

The ideas expressed in many of these 60 commandments are already contained within this handbook. The commandments are as follows:

- Never knowingly break the law, and never test the law without prior legal approval.
- Always perform at least a cursory review of a financial statement within two days of receiving it.
- When guarantees or collateral are put into effect, always acknowledge it in writing to the customer.
- Never hold a customer order without letting the customer know it is on hold.
- Never accept postdated checks except as a last resort in collection efforts.
- Always deposit or mail customer checks to the bank or lockbox on the same day they are received.
- Never give an opinion of a customer's operations during a trade or bank reference.
- Never accept a revocable letter of credit in lieu of an irrevocable letter of credit.
- Never unknowingly allow a letter of credit to expire where a drawing may be required on the LC.
- Never unknowingly allow any collateral or guarantees to expire.
- Always secure the personal guarantee of the guarantor's spouse.
- Never make a critical credit decision without the benefit of reviewing all the facts first.
- Never bad-mouth the competition, another customer, or your company during a customer visit.
- Always keep your unattended briefcase locked during a customer visit.

- Never play "god" with the company's funds concerning write-offs, settlements, or when extending credit. It's not funny money.

- Never trust the marketing department on matters related to the customer's financial condition without first-hand verification.

- Never extend credit to an unknown new customer without at least performing a minimal credit investigation.

- Never revoke a customer's credit terms without first advising the marketing department.

- Always notify the marketing department when customers are being referred for collection.

- Always advise the marketing department or customer service when holding a customer order.

- Always review credit files and limits on an annual basis or when the account has exceeded its credit limit.

- Never raise credit limits without a minimal credit review.

- Never provide extended credit terms without legal documentation.

- Never refer an account for collection when it is clear that the balance eventually will be collected.

- Never make a collection call without at least securing a follow-up date for contacting the customer.

- Never understate or overstate data on credit reports due to perceived management pressure.

- Never hold out or delay on advising senior management of bad-debt write-offs or bad news due to perceived management pressure.

- Always document customer visits in writing.

- Never start a lockbox or collection agency relationship without contacting references.

- Never purchase an accounts receivable system without receiving a live demonstration and contacting user references.

- Always draw up a systems needs and wants list when purchasing accounts receivable software.

- Never extend credit to a company with a negative net worth without having sound overriding reasons.

- Never extend credit to a company involved in bankruptcy proceedings without having sound overriding reasons.

- Never succumb to marketing pressure if there is an immediate customer viability problem.
- Always avoid telling customers what their credit limit is, unless they specifically ask.
- Never make a critical credit decision without an understanding of all the data.
- Never lie on behalf of the company or a customer.
- Always review the customer's internally generated interim, and especially year-end, financial statements with caution.
- Never believe a trade rumor about a customer unless it can be substantiated.
- Always ask for the notes and accompanying schedules to financial statements if they are not included.
- Always ask for a profit and loss statement if it is not included with the balance sheet.
- Always remember that a balance sheet only represents the financial condition of a firm as of a particular date.
- Never stop attempting to get financial disclosure from excessively slow-paying customers.
- Always be wary and watchful of a customer that is sustaining loss operations.
- Always remember that COD terms carry credit risk.
- Never make a commitment to a customer that exceeds your level of credit authority.
- Never argue with a salesperson or other company employee during a customer visit.
- When in doubt, always clarify legal "sold to" name styles in writing.
- Never visit a customer without first reviewing the credit file in detail.
- Never make a promise or commitment to a customer, knowing that the promise will have to be broken.
- Never treat one customer preferentially over another customer.
- When in doubt concerning the law, always confer with an attorney.
- Never make the same critical credit mistake twice.
- Always conduct conversations concerning legal matters or revoking credit terms with the customer's senior management only.

- When the ownership of a customer changes, always perform a complete credit investigation, especially when the customer has undergone a leveraged buyout.

- Never accept a gift or benefit from a customer nor socialize with one where it might be possible to develop a conflict of interest.

- Always save the envelope in which customer financial statements or other critical correspondence was mailed. It's a felony to commit fraud through the federal postal system!

- Avoid comparing financial ratios across industries.

- Always perform a complete customer credit investigation upon learning of individual suits, judgments, and IRS tax liens.

- Always remember that credit is a privilege, not a right.

ABSTRACT SUMMARY

- Successful credit practitioners generally live by a set of commandments or rules in their work.
- Awareness of and adherence to the commandments or rules should promote sound and consistent credit administration.
- Following these commandments should minimize credit disasters.
- The rules may vary slightly from credit department to credit department because of differences in company policy and philosophy.
- Exceptions to the rules should be made only under justifiable circumstances.

CREDIT MYTH:
"DON'T WORRY, WE'RE FULLY RESERVED"

Credit personnel sometimes have misconceptions about the true mechanics of a bad-debt reserve or allowance for doubtful accounts. How many times have credit managers heard one of their staffers say, "Don't worry. We are fully reserved for that bad-debt loss"?

Sure, from a GAAP (generally accepted accounting principles) standpoint the company might be reserved; the bad-debt write-off will not impact the current month's profit and loss statement. However, when a company writes off a doubtful account against its allowance for bad debts, there *is* an impact on cash flow. The company will not collect any cash from the customer until bankruptcy dividends are paid out. That, of course, assumes that there is any recovery or dividend paid. If a payment does come, it must be recorded as a bad-debt recovery and credited to income.

A bad-debt reserve should be looked upon as an accounting device that is used to allocate potential losses evenly over the years. Accruals to the bad-debt reserve are made either monthly, quarterly, or at year end, in order to reserve for potential losses. However, there is no real pool of cash that has been set aside for a rainy day when bad-debt losses are sustained. That is where the company loses cash flow!

With the Tax Reform Act of 1986, the Internal Revenue Service, from a tax accounting standpoint, no longer recognizes accruing for bad debts. They must now be charged directly against current income. The company must charge current income based on the direct write-off method as opposed to the accrual method.

Companies must maintain an allowance reserve for GAAP reporting purposes to stockholders, while at the same time they must utilize the direct write-off method for tax purposes. It's like keeping two sets of books.

Just remember, a bad-debt loss is a bad-debt loss is a bad-debt loss. It always negatively impacts cash flow. A company may be fully reserved from a GAAP standpoint, but it will receive no true replenishment from a cash flow standpoint.

ABSTRACT SUMMARY

- Credit personnel are often too willing to accept bad-debt losses based on the fact that the company is "fully reserved for the loss."
- While from an accounting perspective the company might be reserved for a bad-debt loss, any such loss is bound to have a negative impact on cash flow.
- A bad-debt reserve should be looked upon as an accounting device that is used to allocate potential losses evenly over the years.

- With the Tax Reform Act of 1986, the Internal Revenue Service no longer recognizes accruing for bad debts. They must now be charged directly against current income.
- The rules are somewhat paradoxical: Companies must maintain an allowance reserve for GAAP reporting purposes, but at the same time they must use the direct write-off method for tax purposes.

CREDIT MYTH: THERE'S NO PROBLEM WITH DEFICIT RETAINED EARNINGS

Credit professionals sometimes lose perspective when performing credit analysis on customer financial statements. Credit pros need to look carefully at net worth to make sure the customer is adequately capitalized.

You need to look beyond the reported net worth to the elements that comprise that number. For example, a customer may report a net worth of $1 million and not be as creditworthy as you might think. That net worth may be comprised of $100,000 capital stock, $1.5 million paid-in capital, and −$600,000 in retained earnings. A closer look would tell you that the deficit retained earnings will have a significant negative impact on the customer's long-term financial health.

When analyzing financial statements look at each component of the customer's equity or tangible net worth. Look at capital stock, paid-in capital, preferred stock, and, most important of all, retained earnings. Retained earnings are the most critical component of net worth, since they reveal the firm's ability to turn a profit over the long haul. If you are dealing with a start-up company just beginning to generate revenues, deficit retained earnings are to be expected for a few years. However, deficit retained earnings for a long-established company should cause you to question a company's long-term viability.

Make sure that you especially understand the net worth component of an LBO customer. Remember, with LBOs you must also factor out of net worth intangibles, such as cost in excess of assets required.

Companies with deficit retained earnings most likely already have dissipated their capital stock and paid-in capital. And their ability to issue new stock or to raise other types of equity may be severely limited because of deficit retained earnings in recent reporting periods.

ABSTRACT SUMMARY

- Not looking into the fine detail of a customer's net worth can lead you to erroneously conclude that a customer is adequately capitalized.
- Don't look at a firm's net worth just as a whole. Instead, examine all the components that make up the customer's equity or tangible net worth.
- Examine the levels of capital stock, paid-in capital, preferred stock, and, most important of all, retained earnings.
- Retained earnings are the most critical component of net worth, because they reveal the historical capabilities of the firm's earnings power.
- A firm with deficit retained earnings may not be financially viable in the long-term.

CREDIT MYTH: THE CHECK IS IN THE MAIL

How often has a marginal or high-risk customer told you that the check is going in the mail? An all too familiar scenario arises, a high-risk customer who has exceeded its credit limit and/or is past due beyond your standard terms of sale places an order. Credit phones the customer and you are advised that the check "is in the mail." You monitor your lockbox for the next five days but there is still no check.

When you make a follow-up phone call the customer says that accounts payable "forgot to mail the check." Or, that your check is being held until the customer receives payment from one of its customers. A third common delay tactic is that the customer was unable to obtain the required two signatures for your check until two days ago and that they mailed the check "yesterday."

Credit managers hear these "white lies" from marginal customers all too often. Unfortunately, however, you can't be as trusting or naive with such "promise breaker" customers. You must develop a "Doubting Thomas" attitude and press the customer to make sure that the check really will go into the mail. You may have to diplomatically remind the customer of their previously broken promises.

In your initial collection call always request that the customer contact you if, for any reason, they are unable to mail the check. You may want to call the next day advising a customer that you did, indeed, ship its order. While on the phone, you can get the customer to confirm that the check was mailed as promised. While these approaches may sound pushy or aggressive you must confront customers who chronically break promises and remind them of their payment commitments. Fortunately, however, these types of customers usually represent a very small percentage of your total customer base.

In the above scenarios we're not talking about a customer who is late one time because of an honest oversight. We're talking about customers who repeatedly break their promise and then always have ready excuses why the check was not mailed when they said it would be. Clearly, you must remind these customers that credit is a privilege and not a right and that it can be revoked. If promises are broken too frequently, you may have to change the customer's terms to cash on delivery (COD) or cash in advance (CIA) via check, certified check, or wire transfer payment.

ABSTRACT SUMMARY

- Marginal customers sometimes tell white lies.
- Do not be as trusting with customers characterized as "promise breaker" customers.
- Take a "Doubting Thomas" attitude with "promise breakers," pressing the customer to make sure that the check really will go into the mail.

■ Remind slow payers that credit is a privilege and not a right and that can be revoked.

■ If a customer fails repeatedly to make promised payments, you may have to revoke that customer's open account credit terms.

CREDIT MYTH: YOU CAN COUNT ON MARKETING PERSONNEL'S FINANCIAL JUDGMENT

The marketing manager's job is to market, promote, and sell a company's product. Nowhere does the job description state that a marketing executive must exercise sound financial judgment.

Companies evaluate and promote marketing personnel on how much product they sell. Marketing professionals rarely consider the economic impact their pricing and other marketing actions have on the company. However, this is not to imply that marketing or sales personnel are dishonest or without integrity.

At the same time, most companies do not charge back bad debts to the individual when computing the salesperson's compensation. So there is little incentive for a salesperson to scrutinize the risk the way credit personnel do.

So credit professionals need to beware when marketing personnel tell you that they know a new customer is "good" for the pending order. In most cases their judgment may be correct. The only problem is that the marketing person doesn't base his or her judgment on sound financial analysis. Marketing people generally don't think about the potential economic consequences that might arise from the sale.

Therefore, despite assurances from the marketing staff, credit professionals must take the time to investigate new customer accounts when the initial information is either incomplete or not provided.

ABSTRACT SUMMARY

- Marketing personnel's job is to promote and sell product. Nowhere does their job description require them to exercise sound economic judgment.
- Marketing personnel don't have an incentive to minimize bad debts if there are not chargebacks to sales.
- Beware of marketing personnel who assure you that the new customer is "good" for the pending order.
- Take the time to investigate new customer accounts when the initial information is either incomplete or not provided.
- Always beware of a marketing person's economic philosophy on credit and risk management.

CREDIT MYTH: I'M GOING TO BUY ELSEWHERE

When pushed for financial disclosure, a marginal customer may threaten to take his business elsewhere.

You may be negotiating for financial disclosure, improved payments, guarantees, or another form of security. You feel a need for the customer to comply with your request in order to strengthen the credit relationship.

When the customer threatens to "buy elsewhere," many credit practitioners back off for fear of losing the business and being personally blamed for losing the account. By backing off, however, you are simply ignoring the problem that led you to press for better disclosure or revised terms in the first place.

Many times the customer is bluffing. The customer generally needs your firm as a supplier as much as you need them. And, unless you are being very unfair and narrow-minded in your negotiations, your customer isn't likely to walk away from a long-standing and profitable relationship. The customer has invested years in developing a pricing, service, and quality rapport with your marketing department that can't be reproduced overnight—especially if the customer is a slow-paying and/or a high-risk account.

Before negotiating with the customer, confer with your marketing managers and advise them what you need from the customer and why. Informing marketing is a good strategy because, if your requests are fair, marketing will not only support you but also will participate in the negotiations to try to preserve the relationship.

Also, drawing on its marketplace intelligence, marketing can help you determine whether the customer has a reasonable chance of taking its business elsewhere. If marketing disagrees with your tact, it should cite specific reasons not to press your case with the customer. Whenever I've pressed for increased disclosure or changed terms with marginal customers, the marketing department has supported my efforts 90% of the time once I outlined the big picture and the risk to our company without the changes.

Over the years don't recall losing a single customer because of disputes regarding disclosure or change in terms. The secret to successful negotiations are twofold. First, make sure the customer understands why you are persuing your course. Second, try to look at the situation from the customer's perspective and see why they might object to the changes you request. In some cases you may have to modify what you require from the customer. But you need to be firm about making the kind of change necessary to resolve the problem while continuing to negotiate with the customer.

While you cannot be inflexible, you must be both persistent and professional in your negotiations.

ABSTRACT SUMMARY

- Marginal customers are often bluffing when they threaten to buy elsewhere.
- It's very difficult for the customer to walk away from a long-standing vendor relationship and quickly develop a rapport with a new vendor.
- Before negotiating, consult with your marketing department and advise them what changes you need from the customer and why.
- Marketing can tell you whether a customer is in a position to establish a new vendor relationship.
- When negotiating, don't be inflexible. It's also necessary to be both persistent and professional in negotiations.

11

"YOU MAKE THE CREDIT CALL"

"YOU MAKE THE CREDIT CALL": AN INTRODUCTION

The "You Make the Credit Call" case study approach lets you test your credit and cash flow expertise. Read and respond in writing to each of the hypothetical cases described below, detailing your objectives, action items, and options. When you are done, compare your responses to the follow-up guidelines in Chapter 12 for each case.

Each of the 12 case studies challenges you to make a credit decision based on descriptions and information from actual credit scenarios. The cases aren't geared toward any one particular audience; anyone from a junior credit representative to a senior financial manager can take a shot at "making the credit call."

The cases are designed to be thought provoking. Each one requires you to make an executive decision regarding individual customer risk and cash flow. In most cases, there will be no right or wrong answers. Your responses will probably be a function of your credit department's credit policy and philosophy.

The cases are structured to allow you to use the facts provided to formulate specific recommendations to management. You may want to have several credit employees respond to the cases to measure the variety of responses that can be expected. You are called on to detail in writing objectives, action items, and options for each case presented, and to elaborate on the rationale for these.

Four of the case studies presented include full balance sheets offering vital information relating to the customer's financial condition. With the remaining eight cases, financial information is discussed but not presented in financial statement form.

Most of the cases include information relating to bank and trade information. Your firm's hypothetical exposure is noted, and based on the facts, you are to recommend a credit decision, as well as alternative options. Your objectives, action items, and specific options should clearly support your final credit decision.

During the course of reviewing a case, you may determine that additional information would be needed from the customer; in some cases, the author has omitted such information intentionally. If you feel the need for additional information, note this in your response. For instance, you might see the need for more complete bank information. These additional requirements should be a part of your "action items." In most of the cases, however, there will be sufficient information upon which to base your credit decisions.

Before rendering these decisions, you might find it helpful to refer back in the handbook to key abstracts, such as those that discuss customer visits or bad-debt warning signals.

Immediately following the 12 cases are follow-up guidelines in Chapter 12, where the author provides some objectives, action items, and options for each one. These are listed in bullet form for review and for comparison to your responses.

The "You Make the Credit Call" section is an important, interactive part of this handbook. It offers you an opportunity to express your credit and cash flow perceptions and insights as you react to "real life" credit situations.

CASE ONE: QUICK DECISION ON MARGINAL NEW CUSTOMER

The credit department receives a completed credit application from the marketing department. You are advised by the salesperson that the prospective new customer will be purchasing a product that has a very high profit on sales return as compared to your firm's other products. The required credit limit is $50,000, and you are advised that the credit requirements will probably double within the year. The required credit limit assumes that there will be no delinquency as items come due and new orders are placed. Your firm's terms of sale are net 30 days.

It's Tuesday and you have a $25,000 order pending that marketing advises must be shipped to the customer no later than early Wednesday morning. The alternative is that the competition will ship the order and the new business will be jeopardized. Thus, you may not be able to review a hard copy of the customer's most recent year-end financial statement before making a credit decision relating to the order.

The two trade references contacted during the new customer's credit investigation revealed trade payments were slow 29 and slow 36 days with high credits of $21,000 and $34,000 respectively on terms of net 30 days. One of the trade references indicated that it had received NSF (non-sufficient funds) checks on two occasions in the past. Bank information reveals average balances of low five-figure proportions on hand with no lending relationship at the present time.

You order a D&B on the new customer and it indicates that the company filed for bankruptcy years earlier. Details are sketchy on the reorganization plan. The customer has been out of Chapter 11 for 21 months.

Your marketing department calls within hours of the first contact inquiring about the status of the new customer's order. YOU MAKE THE CALL!

[Detail in writing your objectives, action items, and options with respect to the pending order and the customer's required $50,000 credit limit. Formalize your credit and cash flow strategy in writing. Then compare your findings with the author's follow-up guidelines on p. 403.]

CASE TWO: LETTER OF CREDIT SET TO EXPIRE

Your credit department has been selling to an active account for the past two years. Since the customer has only been in business for three years, you have required a $50,000 irrevocable standby letter of credit.

Payments for the first year of your business relationship were 100 percent slow 31 days. During the past year, your customer's payments were 100 percent slow 22 days beyond your net 30-day standard terms of sale. Despite the delinquency, you have never had to draft and drawdown on the letter of credit to be paid.

The customer has never broken any promises with respect to making payments.

Twice during the past year the customer's balances exceeded the $50,000 irrevocable letter of credit. The two high credits were $71,500 and $69,000.

In its first two years of existence, the customer operated in the red. Losses of $54,000 during that period were attributed to one-time start-up costs. Operations for the third year were profitable, however, with a net income of $28,000 on sales of $581,000.

The credit department has never been out to the customer's plant for a tour of operations. This is partly due to the fact that the customer is located 750 miles away; the other reason is that the exposure was covered by the standby irrevocable letter of credit.

But now the LC is set to expire in five weeks and your customer calls and requests that the credit department not ask for a renewed letter of credit upon expiry. YOU MAKE THE CALL!

[Detail in writing your objectives, action items, and options with respect to the customer's request to not renew the letter of credit. Formalize your credit and cash flow strategy in writing. Then compare your findings with the follow-up guidelines offered by the author on p. 405.]

CASE THREE: EXTENDED TERMS TO MEET COMPETITIVE SITUATION

At the top of the completed credit application is a handwritten note from your company's salesperson indicating that the proposed new business will require net 60-day terms. Upon contacting marketing to discuss the extended credit terms request, you are advised by the salesperson that the terms are required to meet a competitive situation. Marketing further advises that a refusal of the terms request will probably result in a loss of the business.

The four trade references contacted advise of slow payments ranging from slow 29 days to slow 49 days. None of the references contacted indicate they are providing formalized extended credit terms to the subject. One of the references is a competitive supplier who indicates that the customer is carrying a current and high credit balance of $114,000, and the entire account balance due is past due 15-39 days beyond terms. The reference also notes that the customer is on credit hold.

Your bank reference reveals average balances of medium five figures with secured loans granted up to a low six-figure amount. Security on the loan is comprised of UCC1 liens on accounts receivable, inventory, and fixed assets. The bank refuses to disclose if the loan is guaranteed by the principals of the firm.

The year-end balance sheet received from the customer is as follows:

ASSETS:		LIABILITIES & EQUITY:	
Cash	$ 14,000	Accounts payable	$ 259,000
Accounts receivable	127,500	Accrued liabilities	81,000
Inventory	354,000	Short-term loans	125,000
Total current assets	$ 495,500	Income tax payable	20,000
		Total current liabilities	$ 485,000
Fixed assets	$ 54,500	Deferred income tax	$ 6,500
		Stockholders Equity:	
		Common stock	$ 75,000
		Retained earnings	(11,000)
		Total equity	64,000
Total assets	$ 550,500	Total liab. & equity	$ 550,500

Your salesperson calls and inquires about the status. YOU MAKE THE CALL!

[Detail in writing your objectives, action items, and options with respect to the new customer's request for extended credit terms. Formalize your credit and cash flow strategy in writing. Then compare your findings with the follow-up guidelines provided by the author on p. 407.]

CASE FOUR: RUMORS OF BANKRUPTCY

Your credit department has been dealing with a customer for more than seven years, during which time the relationship has been rocky. The customer has been a chronic slow payer with good intent but apparently insufficient wherewithal. Currently the customer is carrying a $122,000 balance, of which $88,000 is anywhere from one to 60 days past due.

The customer has had loss operations the past three years. The company really hit rock bottom at the most recent year-end; a $350,000 loss created deficit retained earnings of $55,000. Losses during the past three years aggregate to $675,000.

The customer appears to be in violation of loan covenants with its bank—covering earnings, debt to cash flow, and working capital requirements. The bank has not called in its loan but in the past three months has begun to bounce checks when the customer hasn't had sufficient funds in its account. Previously, the bank would always honor checks presented in an overdraft situation. It appears that the bank will not advance beyond their current dollar exposure.

You are the customer's major supplier for the product purchased. Other small vendors have begun to cut off the customer. You cannot completely cut off the customer because that will probably put them out of business; there is no competitor willing to jump in and take on your risk dollars.

There are rumors in the trade that the customer is about to file for bankruptcy. These rumors are bolstered by additional rumors, reported by your sales personnel, that key personnel are contemplating leaving the company.

The customer's annual credit limit approval must now be approved or revoked, and there may be some conditions attached to either decision. YOU MAKE THE CALL!

[Detail in writing your objectives, action items, and options with respect to approving or revoking the subject's required credit limit. Formalize your credit and cash flow strategy in writing. Then compare your findings with the follow-up guidelines provided by the author on p. 409.]

CASE FIVE: COMMON LAW WRITE-OFF

You have been selling to a marginal customer for the past five years. Payments have historically been 100 percent slow 30 or more days beyond your standard terms of net 30 days. During the course of the relationship you have held orders on the customer to control the exposure. You have no guarantees or collateral protecting that exposure.

The subject's financial condition has deteriorated to the point that it is carrying a deficit net worth of $325,000. The most recent year-end results showed operating losses of $145,000, up from $105,000 the previous year. Clearly the customer is very close to insolvency and rumors in the trade indicate it may be filing for bankruptcy by year end.

Most suppliers have already cut off the customer from trading past due dollars for new orders. Your company has taken the same action over the past six months, putting the customer on a two-for-one program of payments when new orders are placed. Through the two-for-one paydown program, your firm has reduced the exposure from $135,000 to the current balance due of $89,000, reflecting a $46,000 reduction in your exposure.

The customer's bank has stopped advancing funds to the customer because it is in violation of its loan covenants. Bank debt is said to be in excess of $1 million and secured by a first lien on virtually all of the firm's assets.

One day you get a letter from your customer's attorney advising that his client is undergoing financial problems and requesting that you attend a meeting of the major creditors. At the informal creditors meeting, you are informed that there is a potential buyer for the firm who is willing to make a capital infusion into the company subject to one condition. The condition is that the prospective buyer will assume 100 percent of the bank debt, but 90 percent of the trade creditors (based on dollar volume) must accept a 20 percent settlement for their accounts receivable balances due.

The customer's attorney notes that if the 20 percent settlement is not approved by 90 percent of the creditors (based on dollar volume), the customer will file for bankruptcy by month end. As of the date of the informal creditors' meeting, accounts payable due creditors totalled $2.15 million, making your $89,000 exposure 4.1 percent of the total payables.

The creditors have been advised by the customer's attorney that they can form an informal creditors' committee, which can seek counsel.

Do you join the informal creditors' committee or begin litigation? YOU MAKE THE CALL!

[Detail in writing your objectives, action items, and options with respect to the proposed common law write-off. Formalize your credit and cash flow strategy in writing. Then compare your findings with the follow-up guidelines provided by the author on p. 411.]

CASE SIX: POSTPONED ORDER
FOR CUSTOMIZED GOODS

The customer is an active account that has grown dramatically during the last four years, during which time it has paid generally prompt to slow 15 days on terms of net 30 days. All of its orders are customized.

The business itself has only been operating for five and a half years. During its first four years, the company was a subchapter S company whose earnings had to be distributed annually to the individual principals, as opposed to traditionally retaining net earnings after taxes. Thus, the customer is somewhat leveraged and undercapitalized based on its annual sales volume and credit limit requirements.

The customer's most recent year-end financial information is as follows:

ASSETS:		LIABILITIES & EQUITY:	
Cash	$ 12,750	Accounts payable	$ 185,000
Accounts receivable	221,000	Accrued liabilities	16,000
Inventory	179,000	Short-term debt	140,000
Other current	2,250	Other current liab.	7,500
Total current assets	$ 415,000	Total current liabilities	$ 348,500
Fixed assets net	$ 109,000	Long-term debt	$ 45,000
		EQUITY	
		Capital stock	$ 75,000
		Retained earnings	55,500
		Total equity	$ 130,500
Total assets	$ 524,000	Total liab. & equity	$ 524,000

Operations for the Dec. 31 year end recorded a net income after taxes of $83,000 based on sales of $1.05 million. Earnings for the prior year were $12,750 based on sales of $675,000, although bank debt was $95,000 lower than at the current year-end.

About two months ago in March you produced and shipped to the customer $50,000 of custom goods; however, the customer's customer postponed an order for finished goods by six months. The customer's balance is now at $95,000, $50,000 of which is past due representing the postponed order's balance due.

Your customer contacts the credit department advising that it has a new major order for $85,000 from another customer, but advises that it will not be able to retire the $50,000 past due. The customer further requests that you convert the $50,000 past due into a nine-month unsecured promissory note.

Customer service calls you today and advises it wants to place the order for production. YOU MAKE THE CREDIT CALL!

[Detail in writing your objectives, action items, and options with respect to the pending order and the request for a nine-month promissory note. Formalize your credit and cash flow strategy in writing. Then compare your findings with the follow-up guidelines provided by the author on p. 413.]

CASE SEVEN: THE IMPORTANT NEW BUYER

You receive a completed credit application from marketing sales personnel for a potential new customer that has been in business less than two years. The marketing department says it's trying to build up sales for the particular product line in question and notes that the account has the potential to be a key customer within the next three to five years. Marketing implicitly asks for the credit department's assistance in opening the new account.

The potential new customer's purchasing needs require a credit limit of $25,000. The customer advises you up front that on occasion it pays beyond the company's standard net-30-day terms of sale.

On the credit application, the customer provides three trade references to contact, not all of which reflect the high credit levels you are being asked to extend. The trade references reveal that payments have been generally prompt, there is no history of NSF (non-sufficient funds) checks, and the customer hasn't broken any promises. None of the three trade references provided on the credit application are from your industry, however.

Bank information reveals a routine non-borrowing account with no NSF check history and average balances in the low five figures. The account has been opened for less than two years. The bank indicates that although the subject is now a non-borrowing account, it would consider extending credit upon a detailed review of the new customer's finances.

The customer does not have an audited financial statement to provide. It does, however, offer to provide an internally generated statement covering the first year of operations.

Your marketing department wants to arrange for the credit department to visit the customer's facility to review and discuss the situation. YOU MAKE THE CALL!

[Detail in writing your objectives, action items, and options with respect to the new customer request for a $25,000 credit limit. Formalize your credit and cash flow strategy in writing. When you are finished, compare your findings with the author's follow-up guidelines provided on p. 415.]

CASE EIGHT: AFTER PLANT EXPANSION, RELIABLE CUSTOMER SLOW PAYS

For the past five years, your firm has been selling to a customer that has always retired trade obligations within the net-30-day terms of sale. The customer annually buys more than $850,000 in product, with monthly purchases of about $75,000. The customer currently has a $100,000 credit limit and is looked upon as a valued account by the marketing department.

Recently, the customer underwent plant expansion, and its payments have begun to run slow anywhere from six to 15 days beyond standard terms of sale. Until now you have tolerated the delinquency, looking upon the recent slow payment trend as a temporary aberration that would correct itself.

Your customer now formally requests additional trade support from the marketing department, asking that terms of sale be extended to net 75 days for an indefinite period of time to accommodate the customer's cash flow problems.

Your credit file is somewhat incomplete; the customer has never been required to provide a financial statement in the past based on its previously strong payment record. Trade references on hand are at least two years old — also reflecting prompt payment experience. Bank information is recent and reveals high five-figure average balances with credit extended on a secured basis to a low six-figure amount with low six figures outstanding; there is no borrowing availability at the present time. The Dun & Bradstreet report on file contains no derogatory information and is dated within the past 18 months.

If you decide to extend 75-day credit terms to the customer, your credit exposure will probably double to $200,000. YOU MAKE THE CREDIT CALL!

[Detail in writing your objectives, action items, and options with respect to justifying *or* refusing to support the customer's extended terms request and increased credit requirements. Formalize your credit and cash flow strategy in writing. You can compare your findings with the author's follow-up responses on p. 417.]

CASE NINE: CUSTOMER GETS A FORTUNE 500 CONTRACT

For the past three years, your firm has been selling to a customer that has now received a contract from a Fortune 500 company. As a result of procuring the new contract, the customer asks you to triple its $50,000 credit limit. Your current exposure with the customer is somewhat leveraged; the current credit limit represents 79 percent of the subject's stated net worth. But the new exposure will represent 236 percent of net worth. The contract is expected to run for a minimum of one year and could be renewed and possibly increased at the end of year one.

Your standard terms of sale are net 30 days and the customer has historically paid its account slow 21-30+ days beyond terms. On occasion, the credit department has had to hold orders on the customer's account to control the exposure.

Credit representatives have visited the customer's operations twice during the past three years. The customer has only been in business for five full years.

In a highly competitive marketplace driven by price, terms, and quality, your firm is currently the customer's No. 1 supplier.

Within your credit file you have an unaudited balance sheet for the customer's most recent year end. The financial information contained in the credit file is as follows:

ASSETS:		LIABILITIES & EQUITY:	
Cash	$ 12,500	Accounts payable	$ 99,500
Accounts receivable	59,000	Short-term loans	10,000
Inventory	112,000	Accrued liabilities	24,000
Total current assets	$ 183,500	Total current liabilities	$ 133,500
Fixed assets net	$ 37,000	Long-term bank loans	$ 24,000
		Stockholders' equity:	
		Common stock	$ 20,000
		Retained earnings	43,500
		Stockholders' equity	63,500
Total assets	$ 220,500	Total liab. & equity	$ 220,500

The marketing department advises you that the customer's orders cannot be held if they are designated for contract work. Your firm in the past has obtained an uncollateralized personal guarantee from the chairman, which is not cosigned by his wife. YOU MAKE THE CREDIT CALL!

[Detail in writing your objectives, action items, and options with respect to increasing the customer's credit limit and servicing the contract business. Formalize your credit and cash flow strategy in writing. Then compare your findings with the follow-up guidelines provided by the author on p. 418.]

CASE TEN: FORTUNE 200 CUSTOMER ALTERS TERMS UNILATERALLY

Your firm has been selling to a Fortune 200 company for the past three years. From a marketing standpoint, the customer is a key account that generates annual sales in excess of $1 million. The product being purchased is extremely profitable.

The customer has historically paid promptly within your standard net-30-day terms of sale. But recently the customer's payments have been slow by six to 15 days or more beyond those terms.

A routine collection call to the customer reveals that the customer has decentralized its payables function and is now going to pay net 30 days from the date the material is used. You confront the customer's accounts payable department regarding the new payment mode but get no satisfaction. The customer will provide no reasonable explanation as to why payment terms are being changed unilaterally. The customer's accounts payable department advises you to confer with the firm's purchasing agent.

A call to the customer's purchasing agent reveals that the customer intends to pay invoices 30 days from the date that the material is used. You diplomatically remind the purchasing agent that the agreed to and standard terms of sale are net 30 days. The purchasing agent doesn't disagree with your contention, but he notes there is now a competitive situation with a competitive supplier. The new supplier has agreed to quasi consignment terms—its 30-day terms' "clock" does not start until the material has been unloaded and used for processing.

Compounding your competitive problem is the fact that the customer has now decentralized its accounts payable function. The purchasing agent advises credit that unless the new terms are revoked, his firm will continue to pay in the new manner.

The purchasing agent also makes it known in a low-key manner that if the new terms are revoked, the business will be transferred to your competitor.

By now you are in contact with your marketing department, which is 100 percent in favor of extending the terms. YOU MAKE THE CALL!

[Detail below your objectives, questions, recommendations, alternative options, and primary action plan with respect to the customer's request that your firm meet the competitive credit terms. Formalize your credit and cash flow strategy in writing. Then compare your findings with the follow-up guidelines provided by the author on p. 420.]

CASE ELEVEN: ENFORCE THE FINANCE CHARGES?

As a rule, your firm collects finance charges only from chronic slow-paying customers. Thus, you do not assess a charge to generally prompt customers who occasionally pay an invoice beyond terms.

Your industry is highly competitive; both price and terms are competitive factors. On occasion the credit department uses the finance charge assessment as a negotiating tool to resolve other credit issues with customers. Reduced payments are sometimes accepted from even chronically slow-paying customers. After all, you don't want to lose the business if you're satisfied with your credit risk.

You have been selling to a customer for 22 months. The customer has been in business for three and a half years, is currently undercapitalized, and is using slow payments as a form of working capital. The product you sell the customer is a low-margin commodity product.

In the first year of the relationship, payments were slow 26 to 30 days. The customer was a slow payer from the onset of the relationship. From the beginning the credit department advised the customer that finance charges were accruing. During that time the customer refused to resolve the finance charge issue. Credit did not press the issue, instead trying to give the customer additional time to review the matter and improve payments.

Finally, at the end of year one, the credit department, in an effort to be accommodating from a marketing standpoint, agreed to negotiate a significantly reduced payment percentage on the outstanding finance charges. The amount paid by the customer could be characterized as a token amount; but the credit department pressed the issue as a matter of principle, as a way of establishing a firm posture with respect to slow customer payments.

At present, your customer's earnings are down significantly and the firm is in a borrowing mode. It's almost the end of year two with the customer, and its payments have deteriorated to slow 44 days. During the entire second year, the customer has dodged and skirted the finance charge issue. Specifically, on two separate occasions, statements of the finance charges outstanding were sent to the customer with no action taken by the customer. Within the past 10 days, the credit department has mailed the customer a third statement of finance charges.

The customer calls back and is adamant: It won't pay the finance charges. The customer claims that the competition is willing to tolerate excessive delinquency without enforcing a finance charge.

At the time of the call the customer was carrying a relatively small open balance. The customer closes the discussion by advising you that if your firm makes the finance charges an issue, it will buy elsewhere. YOU MAKE THE CALL!

[Detail in writing your objectives, action items, and options with respect to the issue of enforcing the finance charges. Formalize your credit and cash flow strategy in writing. Then compare your findings with the follow-up guidelines provided by the author on p. 422.]

CASE TWELVE: CUSTOMER SELLING OUT, BUYER HAS DEMANDS

You are selling to a high-risk customer whose $355,000 credit exposure is secured by a UCC1 lien on accounts receivable and inventory. Your lien rights are second to that of the subject's lending bank, which is owed $1.1 million.

Payments have historically been 100 percent slow 15 to 30 days.

The historic high credit during the past six years of the relationship is $415,000 attained late last year. The customer's current credit limit is $375,000.

The account is now past due $305,000 by one to 90 or more days, with the entire account balance coming past due shortly. This year, payments have been slow 60+ days well beyond the historical norm. Until now there have been no NSF (non-sufficient funds) checks deposited.

Last year there were loss operations sustaining a loss of $250,000. In the prior year, the company recorded break-even results, although bank debt increased by $300,000. During the past four years the subject's bank debt has increased by $800,000. Detailed below is the subject's most recent year-end balance sheet:

ASSETS:		LIABILITIES & EQUITY:	
Cash	$ 21,000	Accounts payable	$ 745,000
Accounts receivable	450,000	Accrued liabilities	200,000
Inventory	925,000	Short-term loans	450,000
Total curr. assets	$ 1,396,000	Total current liab.	$ 1,395,000
Fixed assets net	$ 1,050,000	Long-term loans	$ 700,000
		Stockholders' equity:	
		Common stock	$ 25,000
		Retained earnings	324,000
		Total equity	$ 349,000
Total assets	$ 2,444,000	Total liab. & equity	$ 2,444,000

Your customer has lined up a potential buyer for the business. However there are some preconditions to the sale that directly relate to your company. First, the prospective buyer wants your company to drop all lien rights by terminating the UCC1. Second, the new customer wants to convert the $355,000 balance into a note receivable that will be uncollateralized, non-interest-bearing, and payable bi-monthly over the next eight months.

The prospective buyer has sent the credit department a letter outlining its requirements to make the sale. YOU MAKE THE CALL!

[Detail in writing your objectives, action items, and options with respect to the prospective buyer's letter and/or the customer's status. Formalize your credit and cash flow strategy in writing. Then compare your findings with the follow-up guidelines provided by the author on p. 424.]

12

FOLLOW–UP GUIDELINES TO "YOU MAKE THE CREDIT CALL"

CASE ONE FOLLOW-UP

OBJECTIVES:

- Determine the likelihood of an insolvency over the short and long term.
- Determine customer profitability based on prompt payments and slow payments.
- Perform a complete credit investigation to assess liquidity and viability.
- Negotiate prompt payments in light of the prior bankruptcy.

ACTION ITEMS:

- Identify the competitor willing to supply the product if you cannot meet the shipping deadline.
- Obtain product profitability from marketing or accounting.
- Request verbal summary figures if the customer does not have a telecopier to send you its statement.
- Request that the customer send the statement to you today via courier. (Get statement before noon; you could halt delivery in transit if necessary.)
- Determine why the customer does not have a borrowing relationship with its bank.
- Ask the customer why it generates NSF checks.
- Find out details of the reorganization plan.

OPTIONS:

- Require wire transfer to ship order based on NSF and bankruptcy history.
- Ship first order COD with carrier picking up check in light of time constraints. Contact bank to determine if sufficient funds are on hand.
- Ship first order with terms of 50 percent on delivery and 50 percent in 30 days.
- Ship first order on standard terms with no credit restrictions.
- Request $50,000 letter of credit—with or without tolerating slowness.
- Consider collateralized personal guarantee of principal and spouse before providing $50,000 credit limit. Must be collateralized in light of prior bankruptcy. Payments must be prompt.

- Consider UCC1 filing on accounts receivable and inventory in light of no bank security interests. Payments must be prompt.

- Approve credit limit but require prompt payments or credit will be revoked.

- Approve $50,000 credit limit while tolerating delinquency.

- Refuse to extend credit without LC. Offer COD terms.

- Refuse credit; offer CIA terms.

CASE TWO FOLLOW-UP

OBJECTIVES:

- Continue to do business with the customer on mutually agreeable terms.
- Assess viability risk if LC weren't renewed.
- Perform complete credit investigation to determine if LC can be dropped.
- Visit the customer to view operations and assess character firsthand.
- Negotiate improved payment performance.

ACTION ITEMS:

- Obtain updated year-end or interim financial information, if available.
- Ask customer for permission to call accountant to discuss customer's financial condition.
- Obtain from the customer a business plan, if available, or projections relating to the coming year.
- Review with the customer the details relating to the $28,000 net income for its third year of operations.
- Ask the customer if it plans to negotiate a bank credit line.
- Obtain updated bank information.
- Update trade references.
- Reorder D&B report.
- Request personal financial statement or tax return.
- Identify competition and end-users.
- Determine why customer has paid slowly.
- Through marketing and customer, identify likely purchases for the year. Factor in delinquency to assess peak credit needs.

OPTIONS:

- Require that $50,000 LC be renewed for another year until payments and/or financial conditions significantly improve. Either agree to exceed LC amount or refuse to exceed LC amount. Either impose prompt payment requirements or do not.

- Require $25,000 LC, agreeing to absorb half the risk. Either agree to exceed LC amount or refuse to exceed LC amount. Either impose prompt payment requirements or don't.

- Allow LC to expire, but request UCC1 filing for accounts receivable and inventory in light of the customer being a new business entity and historically a slow payer.

- Drop LC but require personal guarantee of principal and spouse along with prompt payments under the threat of holding orders.

- Drop LC and agree to tolerate delinquency.

CASE THREE FOLLOW-UP

OBJECTIVES:

- Confirm competitive offer.
- Perform complete credit investigation to justify possible credit extension.
- Determine viability in light of deficit retained earnings.
- Determine the opportunity cost to extend credit terms.
- Determine net customer profitability.
- Negotiate mutually acceptable payment terms to clarify cash flow status.

ACTION ITEMS:

- Obtain hard copy documentation of the competitive situation from marketing or the customer. Documentation could include a copy of the competitor's invoice, a letter from the competitive vendor outlining terms, or a letter from the customer explaining the competitive situation.
- Obtain product profitability information from marketing or accounting.
- Derive opportunity cost of extended terms in scenarios with and without delinquency.
- Determine the history of the deficit retained earnings position.
- Question the potential customer as to why it is on credit hold with another vendor. Determine why trade reference payments are slow.
- Obtain financial statements for the previous two years.
- Request a personal financial statement.
- Consider making a customer visit to better assess the request and potential exposure.

OPTIONS:

- Agree to extended terms, but require irrevocable letter of credit for full exposure without exceeding LC amount.
- Agree to extended terms, but require irrevocable letter of credit for half the exposure. Require prompt payments before allowing the exposure to exceed the LC amount.

- Agree to terms, but request a second position UCC1 filing on accounts receivable and inventory. Base the strategy on satisfactory asset coverage beyond the bank's first position.

- Consider requesting a collateralized personal guarantee to support credit exposure in light of extended terms and overall financial condition.

- Refuse terms and offer standard terms on a trial basis subject to continuance based on payment performance.

- Refuse terms and refuse to extend any credit. Terms offered could be COD or CIA. The customer may buy on restricted terms.

CASE FOUR FOLLOW-UP

OBJECTIVES:

- Determine the likelihood of a bankruptcy over the immediate near term.
- Determine the customer's ability to operate as an "ongoing" business.
- Render a fair credit decision following the customer's credit limit review.
- Protect your investment with the customer.
- Perform a complete credit investigation to confirm the status of the first four objectives.

ACTION ITEMS:

- Set up a customer visit to discuss issues face to face.
- Determine why losses have been sustained.
- Determine if the customer has a formalized game plan to return to profitability.
- Verify whether key personnel are leaving the company.
- Determine the bank's position and intent relating to the covenant violations.
- Ask the customer how it will rectify the covenant violations.
- Find out what the bank's posture is toward returning checks.
- Ask the customer if a capital infusion is planned.
- Question the customer directly as to whether it is considering filing for bankruptcy.
- Update trade references on file and determine the posture of other vendors toward continued credit extension.
- Identify alternative suppliers.
- Reorder D&B and look for derogatory information such as IRS tax liens, customer suits, or judgments.

OPTIONS:

- Do not approve credit and advise the customer that you want to terminate relationship over the next 90 days. (Remember, this could force the customer into bankruptcy.) Offer COD terms during paydown.

- Do not approve credit limit and set a goal to gradually reduce the exposure to under $100,000 over the next 90 days. Then seek another gradual reduction over the next 90 days. Propose three for two payments or better and hope to avoid a preference.

- Write note receivable for $122,000 balance secured by lien on AR and inventory and collateralized personal guarantee. This could be interpreted by the bank as a sign of good faith by your firm as a vendor. Sell account on small credit exposure that must be paid within terms provided the note is paid as agreed.

- Approve the credit limit supported by a collateralized personal guarantee that covers your full exposure.

- Approve credit limit with no guarantees, collateral, or payment provisos.

CASE FIVE FOLLOW-UP

OBJECTIVES:

- Minimize bad debts and protect your $89,000 credit exposure.
- Assess the economics of the buyer's offer.
- Assess the overall merits of the buyer's offer in light of your customer's financial condition.
- Determine existing customer viability.
- Determine economic payout from a potential bankruptcy.

ACTION PLAN:

- Obtain a copy of the buyer's common law write-off offer.
- Retain counsel to review legal paperwork from the prospective buyer.
- Obtain a list of other creditors in descending dollar value of claims.
- Contact other large creditors to discuss their feelings regarding the offer.
- Attend the meeting but don't join the creditors' committee if formed. This way you avoid a potential conflict of interest and could vote no and reject the plan.
- Perform a complete credit investigation of the buyer.
- Confront the customer and find out if it plans to file bankrupcty if the sale falls through. Find out if the principal has personally guaranteed the bank indebtedness.
- Contact the bank and determine its posture if the sale is not executed.
- Conduct a review of the customer's records to determine if any fraud has been committed.

OPTIONS:

- Reject the plan, hoping that in doing so you will be part of a minority under 10 percent of total claims. Under this scenario, the buyer may pay all of these claims in full. No counteroffer is made.
- Reject the plan and in a counteroffer propose a more favorable payoff for creditors. To be effective you must gather the support of the majority of creditors.
- Reject the plan and immediately file suit against your customer. This is probably not a good idea as the suit may trigger a bankruptcy filing. However, this option could cause the creditors to panic and agree to

pay your claim in full, fearing a bankruptcy will pay less and delay the proceedings unnecessarily.

- Accept the plan contingent upon minor modifications. This option will require the support of the majority of creditors.

- Accept the plan with no modifications to the proposed common law write-off.

CASE SIX FOLLOW-UP

OBJECTIVES:

- Determine if a potential $180,000+ credit exposure can be justified in light of the risk at hand.
- Determine profitability on the new order.
- Perform a complete credit investigation in light of the new potential credit exposure.
- Review the economics of converting the $50,000 balance to a note or propose an alternative solution that is mutually agreeable.
- Protect your investment in accounts receivable.

ACTION ITEMS:

- Consider a customer visit to enhance and support your ultimate credit decision.
- If available, request interim financial information from the customer.
- Contact trade references to compare credit exposures and payment performance.
- Update bank information to assess availability.
- Perform a lien search in the state of venue.
- Reorder D&B for public filings and derogatory information.
- Obtain product profitability information from marketing or accounting regarding the new order.
- Find out when your customer will be paid by its customer.
- Determine your potential high exposure by reviewing the customer's unfilled order backlog with your firm.

OPTIONS:

- Agree to write the note and support increased credit requirements, but require that the note be secured by a UCC1 filing with or without interest.
- Agree to write the note and support increased credit requirements, but require the note to be backed by collateralized personal guarantees with or without interest.
- Agree to the note and credit requirements on an unsecured and unguaranteed basis.

- On any agreeable option you could negotiate down the term of the note to six months from nine months to accelerate delayed cash flow.

- On any agreeable option consider requesting that you be named as a joint payee on payments to your customer for the new $85,000 order.

- Offer to take back the $50,000 of goods either for resale purposes or for your firm to hold until the customer needs the goods once again.

- Refuse to write a note, but agree to process the new order while not pressing the issue of the $50,000 past due.

- Refuse to write a note under any conditions and require immediate payment of the $50,000 past due in order for your firm to approve the pending $85,000 order.

CASE SEVEN FOLLOW-UP

OBJECTIVES:

- Justify credit extension through a customer visit.
- Protect the company against potential new customer exposure.
- Assess the possibility of customer insolvency in light of its recent entry into business (two years).
- Negotiate satisfactory payment parameters.
- Reach an accord with the customer in order to accommodate product line emphasis.

ACTION ITEMS:

- Ask for a copy of the company's most recent year-end tax return.
- Ask to see a copy of the individual's most recent tax return.
- Obtain the company and the individual's tax returns for the first year of operation.
- Request additional trade references with similar exposures that are industry related.
- Ask the customer if it can secure bank financing.
- Ask the customer if it is considering bank financing.
- Ask the owner how much additional capital he or she intends to invest in the business.
- Ask the customer what means will allow it to pay invoices within terms.
- Ask for a tour of the operating facilities.
- Determine end uses for the customer's products.
- Identify the customer's competition and the level of that competition.

OPTIONS:

- Request a $25,000 irrevocable letter of credit. (You could offer to pay the fee the customer will incur for opening the LC.)
- Request a $12,500 LC where half the exposure is secured.
- Request a collateralized or uncollateralized personal guarantee executed by the principal and his or her spouse.
- Consider UCC1 filing on accounts receivable, inventory, and possibly other specified assets.

- Extend open credit with no legal guarantees and restrictively enforce terms of sale when necessary.
- Extend credit and tolerate delinquency.

CASE EIGHT FOLLOW-UP

OBJECTIVES:

- Determine if there are any other reasons, aside from plant expansion, why the customer has been paying slow.
- Assess risk in light of the incomplete file information on hand.
- Perform a complete customer credit investigation.
- Quantify the cost of extended terms to net customer profitability.

ACTION ITEMS:

- Make the issue of providing a financial statement a MUST.
- Request the last two year-ending financial statements and the most recent interim statement available.
- Update trade references and determine if other vendors are providing trade support.
- Acquire an up-to-date credit report from Dun & Bradstreet.
- Consider making a customer visit.
- Ask the customer about any plans to increase its bank credit line.
- Consider having your bank perform a new update to confirm current availability without identifying you as the customer requesting the inquiry.
- Obtain customer profitability information from marketing or accounting and derive the opportunity cost of the extended terms request.

OPTIONS:

- Agree to terms for a set time frame subject to renewal, but support the extension of credit terms with a guarantee, UCC1 filing or letter of credit.
- Agree to terms for a set time frame subject to renewal, but restrict the credit limit to under $200,000, with or without legal guarantees.
- Agree to terms for a set time frame subject to renewal, without any legal guarantees supporting credit extension.
- Refuse the terms request but continue to extend a $100,000 credit limit and enforce the current standard terms of sale, with or without legal guarantees.
- Refuse terms and consider reducing the $100,000 credit limit.

CASE NINE FOLLOW-UP

OBJECTIVES:

- Protect your exposure by possibly negotiating a legal guarantee.
- Determine customer viability.
- Negotiate acceptable cash flow from customer.
- Maintain a reasonable and manageable customer exposure.
- Perform a complete customer credit investigation.
- Justify the increased credit requirements to meet marketing's needs.

ACTION ITEMS:

- Identify the contract customer and the risk at hand for your customer in servicing the contract.
- Determine the payment terms for the contract.
- Analyze an unaudited year-end financial statement.
- Request an interim statement and corporate tax return to verify unaudited year-end financial information on hand.
- Update trade references and determine other vendors' posture toward slowness.
- Update bank information to determine current outstandings and availability.
- Update Dun & Bradstreet information.
- Consider making a customer visit to discuss contract, payments, and overall exposure.
- Obtain profit information from marketing on the margins relating to the contract sales. Determine overall profitability of the subject customer.

OPTIONS:

- Request to be named joint payee on checks issued by the contracting party to your customer.
- Request a $150,000 irrevocable letter of credit. You could offer to pay the cost to open the LC.
- Request a $75,000 irrevocable letter of credit, thereby agreeing to bear half the risk.

422

- Request a UCC1 security interest in accounts receivable and inventory in light of minimal bank debt.
- Request that the guarantee now be collateralized by personal assets of the chairman.
- Request that the uncollateralized guarantee now be countersigned by the chairman's spouse.
- Provide increased credit requirements with no legal guarantees and the stipulation that the customer will utilize bank borrowings if neccessary in order to meet your standard terms of sale.
- Provide increased credit requirements with no legal guarantees without requiring prompt payment.
- Reject the marketing request for the increased credit requirements.

CASE TEN FOLLOW-UP

OBJECTIVES:

- Confirm the competitive offer.
- Determine the opportunity cost associated with the "free consignment" days.
- Determine net customer profitability.
- Maintain business while improving the current payment scenario.

ACTION ITEMS:

- Ask marketing or the customer for written documentation to support the request for the expansion of terms. The best form of documentation would be a competitor's letter to the customer (the terms net 30 days from date of usage will probably not appear on a customer invoice).
- Find out the proposed time frame for the competitive arrangement.
- Find out why there is a need for significant lag time in days between shipments and usage.
- Determine the average lag time between the date a shipment is received and the date the product is used. (Use to quantify opportunity cost calculation.)
- Obtain profitability information from marketing or accounting.
- Derive opportunity cost and net profitability.
- Identify and confirm decentralized payables locations to ensure timely cash flow.

OPTIONS:

- Approve terms request, but attempt to have customer consciously reduce lag time. Establish mechanism to confirm usage and strictly enforce payment terms.
- Approve terms request with no overtures made to reduce lag time. Say nothing about enforcing terms.
- Consider requesting a maximum payment date such as net 40 days from invoice date. With such a proviso, even if the material goes unused, it will have to be paid for.
- Consider drafting a consignment agreement to legally formalize the request.

• Refuse the competitive request and seek to enforce standard terms of sale. (This is the worst possible option, unless there is a perceived viability problem with the Fortune 200 customer or net customer profitability is unacceptable. Taking this step will probably cost you the business.)

CASE ELEVEN FOLLOW-UP

OBJECTIVES:

- Resolve outstanding service charge issue.
- Perform complete credit investigation to determine if credit should continue selling to the subject in light of payments, service, and current low balance.
- Determine customer profitability on purchases.
- Determine whether competitors are enforcing service charges.
- Maintain business and negotiate improved payment performance if objective No. 2 is satisfied.

ACTION ITEMS:

- Confirm that a competitor is not enforcing late payment service charges.
- Obtain product profitability data from marketing or accounting.
- Derive net customer profitability, factoring into the calculation the customer's slow payment performance.
- Obtain year-end and interim financial information from the customer.
- Update trade references and find out if any vendors are restricting credit. Obtain reference from a competitor; no harm can be done if handled professionally.
- Update bank information.
- Find out from marketing if the customer's volume can be replaced by other business.
- Consider making a customer visit to resolve the issue face to face.

OPTIONS:

- Enforce 100 percent collection of service charges. Advise the customer that you may pursue litigation if the customer is not willing to resolve the matter.
- Enforce 100 percent collection of service charges. Advise the customer that if service charges are not paid, credit will be revoked. Make it clear to the customer that all future late charges must also be paid in full. Don't discuss the issue of litigation.
- Enforce 100 percent collection of service charges without threatening to revoke credit. But make it clear the issue must be amicably re-

solved. Attempt to have the customer understand your perspective on the issue. You may or may not want to press the issue of future service charges generated or discuss possible litigation.

- Enforce the collection of service charges but agree to accept a fair settlement offer. Seek no less than 50 percent payment.

- Agree to write off outstanding service charges. But insist that future service charges be paid in full or terms may possibly be restricted.

- Agree to write off outstanding service charges without discussing your posture on future finance charges generated.

CASE TWELVE FOLLOW-UP

OBJECTIVES:

- Perform due diligence with respect to prospective buyer's offer.
- Determine financial wherewithal and viability of prospective buyer.
- Determine if there are any other potential buyers.
- Develop alternative plans of action in the event the sale falls through.
- Assess customer viability in the event the sale falls through.
- Protect your current $355,000 exposure.

ACTION ITEMS:

- Request a copy of the proposed sale agreement.
- Retain legal counsel to review the proposed sale agreement.
- Request from the proposed buyer audited year-end financial information covering the past three years.
- Obtain bank and trade information from the prospective buyer.
- Contact bank reference. Determine credit arrangements and attempt to speak with the loan officer about the nature of the buyer's operations.
- Contact prospective buyer's trade references and find out if there is slowness.
- Order D&B on prospective buyer and customer to review for derogatory information.
- Discuss with the customer the reasons for the poor operating results in the past two years.
- Find out if your customer has any other prospective buyers in the wings.
- Ask the customer if it has a game plan to turn around the business in the event the sale falls through.
- Request interim financial information from the customer in order to make an up-to-date assessment of viability.
- Contact the customer's references in the event the sale is not consummated. Find out which vendors have the customer in a restricted credit scenario.
- Find out if the customer is in violation of bank covenants. If so, explore further.

428

- Determine the bank's commitment to your customer.

OPTIONS:

- Agree to a non-interest-bearing note under the condition that the note be supported by a collateralized security interest in accounts receivable and inventory. The note would be subject to defined events of default and acceleration. Note payments received at your lockbox three days beyond the due date would be subject to a finance charge.

- Agree to an interest-bearing note without collateral. However, the note would be subject to defined events of default and acceleration.

- Agree to a non-interest-bearing note with no collateral or guarantees.

- Under either of the three options above, you could stipulate that payments be made monthly and/or the length of the note be six months instead of eight.

- Refuse to write the note due—either because of the non-interest-bearing or uncollateralized stipulations. Insist on maintaining second position and seek to reduce exposure over time. This option could force the buyer to make a sweetened counteroffer.

- Refuse to write the note due to the same reasons as above but seek to enforce the lien if necessary over the next 30 to 90 days. This option could force the prospective buyer into being more agreeable about some of your requirements.

- Refuse to write the note due to the same reasons as above. Seek to work out the exposure with your existing customer in an amicable and non-threatening manner. Maintain collateral in a passive manner.

GLOSSARY

Glossary of Terms

Acceleration clause: A clause in a bank note, bond, or mortgage that says in the event of a default, all obligations outstanding are immediately due and payable regardless of their original maturity dates. Generally, when an acceleration clause is formally executed, the next step for the customer is bankruptcy.

Accrual for bad debts: An accounting method for reserving against future bad-debt losses. The practice was employed prior to the Tax Reform Act of 1986, which requires the direct write-off method when accounting for bad debts.

Asset-based lending: A form of collateralized lending where the lender makes loans to the borrower based on having a collateralized interest in specified assets. Borrowings are generally advanced in accordance with a formula relating to the assets pledged.

Attachment: The legal act of taking a subject's property into the custody of the court to ultimately satisfy a judgment rendered against a defendant.

Audit opinion - adverse: One of four possible opinions rendered by auditors as part of the audit report for financial statements. The adverse opinion is rendered when statements are considered misleading or do not reflect generally accepted accounting principles (GAAP).

Audit opinion - disclaimer: One of four possible opinions rendered by auditors as part of the audit report for financial statements. The disclaimer means that the auditors issue no opinion on the statements, generally due to the uncertainty of the statements or the scope of the audit being severely restricted.

Audit opinion - qualified: One of four possible opinions rendered by auditors as part of the audit report for financial statements. The qualified opinion means the statements taken as a whole were presented fairly but have material deficiency. The terms "subject to" and "except for" are generally reference points for determining why the opinion was qualified.

Audit opinion - unqualified: One of four possible opinions rendered by auditors as part of the audit report for financial statements. The term unqualified means

433

the auditor has no reservations concerning the financial statements presented. The auditor found no deficiencies in the financial statements or the audit of accounting standards employed.

Automatic cash application: An accounts receivable software system feature, usually utilizing algorithms, that automatically applies customer cash payments against open invoices without human assistance.

Automatic credit approval model: A credit decision-making tool that can be designed to automatically review new customer requests for credit based on predetermined financial criteria. The model alleviates the need for a formal credit investigation.

Bad check laws: Defined by the Uniform Commercial Code and in effect in every state, these laws are designed to prosecute check makers who write bad checks. The laws can be very severe in certain states, like Florida and New Mexico, or lenient and less favorable toward creditors, as in Vermont and Maine.

Bad-debt write-off: Represents an accounts receivable balance deemed uncollectable that has been charged to the income statement and removed from the accounts receivable ledger. Write-offs can result from disputed invoices, customers referred for collection or lawsuit, and bankruptcies. The Tax Reform Act of 1986 requires use of the direct write-off method for bad debts.

Bank collection: A process that can be used to collect returned customer checks when customers do not voluntarily comply with providing replacement funds. The customer's check is presented for collection to the supplier's bank, which presents the check to the customer's bank collection department as a collection item. The customer's collection department holds the check and collects on the check when there are sufficient funds in the customer's account to honor the check.

Bank compensation: Compensation paid to a bank by its customers in the form of fees and/or balances in return for cash management and credit services.

Bank credit line: A term used to describe a type of borrowing arrangement. The credit line usually runs for a period of one year, at which time it is reviewed. The bank credit line can be canceled at any time by the bank, even if the bank customer is not in violation of the credit line. On the other hand, the bank cannot call in its customer's outstanding debt until maturity, unless the customer is in violation of the line. Credit lines can be on a secured or unsecured basis. The bank credit line is usually not supported by a detailed document such as with a revolving credit agreement, although there usually is legal wording relating to conditions of default.

Bank loan availability: Represents the remaining amount of dollars that a borrower has available to draw down on its credit facility. For example, if a borrower had a $1 million credit facility and $250,000 was outstanding in borrowings, the bank availability would be $750,000.

Bankruptcy proceeding - involuntary: Initiated through a bankruptcy petition filed by three or more creditors who hold non-contingent and unsecured claims totaling at least $5,000. If total creditors number less than 12, any one creditor can file the petition.

Bankruptcy proceeding - voluntary: A bankruptcy proceeding filed for by the debtor to either reorganize or liquidate its business. The most common voluntary proceedings are Chapter 7 and Chapter 11 proceedings.

Bankruptcy proof of claim: The process of filing a formal dollar claim against a debtor in a bankruptcy proceeding. The form is filed with the Bankruptcy Court to ensure the validity of the claim. The form should be filed within 90 days of the first creditors' meeting.

Bill of lading: A shipping document issued by a carrier. The bill of lading acknowledges receipt of the goods by the customer. Bills of lading are commonly used by rail, common, air, and ocean carriers. They can be used for proof of delivery to clear outstanding invoices.

Borrowing instruments: The specific borrowing options that are extended to the borrower by the bank. Options could include prime or CD-based borrowings, banker's acceptances, and possibly Eurodollar-based borrowings. Borrowings are usually fixed for 30, 60, 90, 120, or 180 days, and there is usually a provision for overnight borrowings. The bank will usually put a margin on all borrowing instruments with the possible exception of prime-based borrowings. For instance, the bank might require the banker's acceptance rate plus 50 basis points.

Borrowing margin: The premium a bank attaches to its base rate for a specified type of borrowing instrument for a specified customer. A customer's margin could be 75 basis points on banker's acceptance borrowings and 65 basis points for CD-based borrowings. To calculate the "all in" cost, one would add the margin to the bank's base rate for the specific instrument.

Build-up method accounts receivable forecast: Forecasting technique to project month-, quarter-, or year-ending dollar levels for accounts receivable.

The forecast utilizes assumptions about projected sales and DSO to "build-up" the dollar level of projected accounts receivable.

Bulk transfer: The Uniform Commercial Code (UCC) defines a bulk transfer as the sale or transfer of goods, wares, merchandise, and fixtures in bulk. Every state has enacted statutes within the UCC governing bulk transfers. The statutes are designed to ensure that the bulk transfer proceeds without causing harm to creditors of the transferor.

Cash flow: Term used to describe the cash inflows (cash receipts) for the operations of a business. The term can also be used to refer to a source and application of funds analysis, whereby the term net cash flow represents the difference between sources and applications.

Cash flow timeline: Cash management term used to describe the cycle for customer cash flow. The cycle begins at the time an order is received from a customer and is completed when the customer's check has cleared and available funds are granted relating to the order that has been received. Intermediate steps are invoicing the customer, making a collection call, and the customer vouchering and initiating payment.

Centralized credit department: All credit employees are housed under one roof. The alternative is a decentralized credit function where credit employees are geographically disbursed.

Chapter 7 Bankruptcy: Bankruptcy proceeding commonly referred to as a "straight bankruptcy." The debtor's nonexempt property is liquidated by a bankruptcy trustee and distributed to creditors in order of claim rights. There is no intention of continuing the business by reorganizing.

Chapter 11 Bankruptcy: Bankruptcy proceeding in which the debtor seeks court protection or relief in order to file a plan of reorganization. The debtor is allowed to remain in possession of the business as the debtor in possession, unless mismanagement claims can be substantiated by creditors.

Chapter 13 Bankruptcy: Bankruptcy proceeding designed for individuals who operate small, unincorporated businesses and seek reorganization relief.

CIA (cash in advance) terms: Nonstandard, restrictive terms of sale utilized for credit risks that are not deemed to be creditworthy. With CIA terms, the payment must be received before delivery is made to the customer. CIA payments can be executed by electronic transfer or paper check.

Classification of trade accounts receivable: The credit strategy of assigning customer classifications based on risk. Policy and strategy can then be customized for each level of classification.

Cleanup period: Relates to bank credit lines rather than revolving credit agreements. As a liquidity test, a borrower may be required to be debt-free of the bank for a period of generally 30 to 60 days—the cleanup period. The requirement is invoked because the bank doesn't want to get into an evergreen loan situation where a borrower's credit line is being renewed annually by the customer without any evidence of loan reduction wherewithal.

COD (cash on delivery) terms: Nonstandard, restrictive terms of sale used for credit risks that are not extended credit. Payment is made to the carrier at the time the goods are delivered. Some credit risk is attached to COD sales, however, as the customer can subsequently stop payment on its check.

Collateral register: Credit management tool and safeguard for tracking the status of collateral. The register tracks by collateral type, expiration date, and dollar amount among the collateral elements. The register prevents the unintentional expiry of collateral.

Comfort letter: A letter of financial assurance obtained by the credit department from a domestic or foreign parent of a customer that is being extended credit. The comfort letter will generally not be enforceable in court as a guarantee of payment.

Commitment fee: The fee a borrower is charged by a bank for a credit facility. The fee can be based on the total dollar amount of the credit facility or on the unused portion of borrowings.

Competitive marketing situation: A marketing scenario in which an existing or potential customer requests that a supplier match a competitive supplier's selling price and/or terms.

Computeritis: The unfounded fear of using personal computers for business applications.

Concentration bank: Banking and cash management term used to describe a company's principal or main bank of account. It is the account where cash is directed to for funding purposes. Funds are concentrated from lockboxes and decentralized subsidiary accounts to avoid having idle balances and to maximize investment yield.

Controlled disbursement account: A cash management disbursement service offered by banks. Generally a demand deposit account that provides same-day check presentment information, thereby creating certainty in funding. Such an account can be funded by balances or serve as a zero-balance disbursement account.

Cost of goods sold: Represents an accounting term and entry that is a component of the income statement. The calculation for cost of goods sold would be: Opening Inventory + Inventory Purchases − Ending Inventory = Cost of Goods Sold. Also known as "cost of sales."

Credit approval authority: The policy whereby all credit employees are assigned dollar levels of authority for customer credit limit approval, customer order approvals, and for bad-debt write-off approvals.

Credit function audit: A credit strategy calling for a thorough review of the credit function to ensure that all potential sources and tools of cash flow are being maximized and that policies and procedures are being followed. The audit covers policy and philosophy, procedures, controls, annual review process, new customer investigations, collections, reporting scope, collection agency activity, credit department performance, and the credit department budget.

Credit hold: The credit terminology used to define when a customer's order is not being shipped due to a credit problem, such as a past-due or overexposed condition.

Credit limit/tangible net worth ratio: A credit analysis ratio used to determine customer leverage. The ratio is calculated by dividing the customer's credit limit by its tangible net worth. The higher the ratio, the more dependent the customer is on its supplier as a creditor.

Credit limit review: The process in which credit personnel review a customer's credit limit or perceived credit needs. The review can be performed on an annual or on an exception basis. Financial, bank, trade, credit agency, and customer payment information are generally analyzed in the decision-making process.

Credit save: Credit term used to describe the process of reducing or "zeroing out" a high-risk customer's balance successfully before the customer files for bankruptcy. The amount of the exposure reduced from the supplier's high credit for that time period represents the credit save. The save is the dollar amount collected that would have been written off as bad debt.

Credit scoring model: A model that evaluates individual customer payment and financial criteria in order to make a risk assessment. Scores are assigned to each review criteria and the total score is compared to a legend indicating risk.

Credit strategy: A formalized decision-making process for generating an action plan, which includes alternative options for managing accounts receivable in general or for individual customers.

Creditor - secured: Refers to a creditor's status in a bankruptcy. The claims of a secured creditor must be paid before those of an unsecured creditor. Secured claims are paid in the order that they were filed. The term can also be used to refer to a trade creditor who has perfected a security interest via a UCC1 filing on specified assets.

Creditor - unsecured: A term denoting a creditor's secondary status in a bankruptcy. Unsecured creditors are compensated for outstanding accounts receivable only after secured creditors are paid in full. "Unsecured creditor" can also be used to define a trade creditor who possesses no collateral interests.

Current ratio: A liquidity measure derived by dividing total current assets by total current liabilities—figures that are extracted from a balance sheet. A 1.5 current ratio reveals that there are $1.50 of current assets for every $1 of current liabilities.

Customer bank information: The process of obtaining the latest information available from a bank regarding a customer's banking relationship. Checking and credit accommodations are usually covered in the update, which can be performed via telephone or in writing.

Customer contact card: The credit form used for individual customers that details collection call information and notes directions for follow-up. The card provides an audit trail of individual customer collection activity. For each call made to a customer, the card should note the date, balance, past due, and any comments.

Customer counseling: Credit task of providing guidance to a customer relating to its credit policy, procedures, and collections. The counseling should be requested by the customer rather than volunteered by the credit practitioner.

Customer DSO: Cash management tool that measures days sales outstanding (DSO) based on an individual customer's accounts receivable and sales. A useful barometer for monitoring high-risk customers. Customer DSO trend lines can be plotted.

Customer remittance audit: A cash management study performed to determine the geographic dispersion of a company's customers, to redirect cash flow due to coding errors and changes in the company's customer base, and to verify the geographic configuration of the company's lockbox network. Only major customers are included in the study in order to obtain a broad picture of cash flow dispersion.

Cycle value forecasting: A method of forecasting whereby forecast values are given to each day of the month based on historical data. For example, by reviewing the past 12 months' receipts data, a credit practitioner might determine that 14 percent of total monthly cash receipts are derived on the first Monday of the month, whereas the second Monday of the month only represents 9.8 percent of total monthly receipts. Historical data cycle values can be used to forecast receipts or specified disbursement categories.

Daily collection call budget: Formalized budgets for daily collection call output for either the department as a whole or for individual personnel. For example, an individual may be assigned a budget of making 10 calls per day. Collection call budgets can be formalized into job descriptions and employee objectives.

Decentralized credit department: The concept that calls for credit employees to be located in different geographic locations. The alternative is a centralized credit function where all employees are under one roof.

Deficit net worth: An unbalanced financial condition in which the sum of a company's total liabilities exceeds the total assets of the firm. In essence, the equity of the company is negative or in a deficit. There must be deficit retained earnings for there to be a deficit net worth.

Deficit retained earnings: An unbalanced financial condition characterized by retained earnings that are negative and that reduce net worth commensurately. The retained earnings in effect represent losses sustained and not income retained. Deficit retained earnings are a clear indicator of a potential insolvency.

Delinquent: Term used to describe a customer who has not retired an invoice that is due for payment according to terms. The customer could be delinquent on standard or extended credit terms. There is an implicit cost attached to customer delinquency.

Demand deposit account (regular): A checking account, funded by balances, that does not provide timely same-day check information.

Depreciation expense: Accounting method for allocating the cost of a tangible asset over the useful life of the asset. Depreciable assets could include buildings, tools, or equipment. The equipment could be a personal computer or an extruder. The total cost of the asset (purchase price) would be amortized over the useful life as opposed to directly expensing the purchase in year one.

Direct write-off method: Method for accounting for bad-debt write-offs that is required by the Tax Reform Act of 1986. Companies can no longer accrue or reserve for future bad debts, but must directly write bad debts off against their income statements when they are incurred.

DSO: DSO (days sales outstanding) is a calculation of total accounts receivable that measures month-end accounts receivable dollars to sales for the current and prior months, if necessary, and then allocates sales days to the outstanding receivables.

DSO - Best: Best DSO is the DSO measurement that only takes into account current (non-past-due) month-end accounts receivable dollars when performing the calculation. It is the "best" the DSO could have performed if there were no past-due dollars. [Note: Total DSO = Best DSO + Past-Due DSO]

DSO - Past-Due: Past-Due DSO is the DSO measurement of month-end past-due accounts receivable dollars. Past-Due DSO can be calculated or derived by subtracting Best DSO from the Total DSO.

DSO calibration: The concept of aging out Past-Due DSO days for past-due accounts receivable dollars. For example, if there were 12 total Past-Due DSO days, a credit practitioner would assign DSO days to 1-30 days past due, 31-60 days past due, 61-90 days past due, 91-120 days past due, and 120+ days past due, based on the past-due accounts receivable balances.

EDI (electronic data interchange): The electronic transaction of business information using standardized formats that are machine-readable. EDI applications include receiving electronic payments via the ACH payment network, invoicing electronically, and electronically receiving and confirming purchase orders.

Events of default for bank loans: Conditions or events that might arise during the course of a borrowing arrangement that allow the lender to immediately demand full payment of outstanding borrowings prior to the maturity date for the loan. In essence, the event of default allows the lender to unilaterally accelerate the maturity of all outstanding loans. Violating covenants or filing for bankruptcy are typical conditions leading to an event of default.

Evergreen account: The term used to describe a customer whose accounts receivable balance has not been reduced over time and shows no signs of reducing the exposure in the future. Such a customer might be making payments against the account, but it never achieves any appreciable reduction of exposure.

Expiration date: The date that a legal document or contract legally expires and is no longer legally effective. An expiration date could apply to a letter of credit, guarantee, or UCC1 security agreement.

Extended credit terms: Legally extended terms that represent a temporary expansion of a company's standard terms of sale with a specified customer. Terms are part of price and thus extending credit terms must comply with the Robinson-Patman Act (see definition).

Extended credit terms documentation: The cash management process of legally documenting in writing the temporary expansion of standard credit terms for specific individual customers. The reason for approving the extended terms must be in order to meet a competitive situation or due to financial hardship.

Extended credit terms opportunity cost calculation: The calculation used to determine the cost of providing extended credit terms to a customer over a specified time period. The calculation is based on the firm's cost of funds, total sales dollars being underwritten within a specified time period, and the number of additional days beyond standard terms for extended terms. The opportunity cost of the terms can be compared to profitability to determine the net economics of the proposed extension of terms.

Factoring: Factoring, or asset-based lending, generally describes a nonbank source of funding that is available to borrowers. There is no unsecured relationship. The factor will generally possess a lien on accounts receivable, inventory, and possibly all other assets. Factoring does not necessarily imply that the borrower is a poor credit risk—although for certain firms factoring may be the only funding alternative due to their inability to negotiate conventional bank financing.

Free final demand: Service offered by a collection agency. The agency will send a final demand letter to an account that has been referred for collection. Generally, if the debtor pays within 7-10 days, the agency does not charge its client a fee.

Funds availability: The assignment and crediting of good funds to checks deposited at a bank or lockbox. For example, two-day availability on a check means that the beneficiary of the check will not be entitled to spend the funds for two days from the date that the item was deposited.

General ledger: A company's complete chart of accounts that on a monthly basis classifies, records, and summarizes all financial transactions. The general ledger provides audit trails for the balance sheet and P&L statement.

Goodwill: An intangible asset that is carried on a balance sheet. Goodwill is a result of the purchase price exceeding the book value.

Gross profitability: A profitability measure based on the excess of net sales over the cost of goods sold. Also known as "gross margin." It represents a good measure of a firm's manufacturing and materials handling processes. Gross profitability does not include general, administrative, selling, or interest expense.

Guarantee - collateralized personal: A personal guarantee made by an individual or individuals where the creditor is pledged specific personal assets in support of the guarantee. With an uncollateralized personal guarantee, no specific assets are pledged.

Guarantee - corporate: Guarantee of payment made by a corporation on behalf of another business entity. The guarantee is provided in consideration of the vendor providing credit to the business on whose behalf the guarantee is made.

Guarantee - cross-corporate: A scenario in which a single company holds separate guarantees from two specific corporations that are on behalf of each other. For example, a supplier might hold a corporate guarantee in which company A guarantees the obligations of company B, and another guarantee in which company B guarantees the obligations of company A. Both A and B are customers and usually have a parent-subsidiary relationship with each other.

Guarantee - personal: A guarantee of payment made by an individual or individuals, usually on behalf of a business entity, in consideration of the vendor extending credit to the business entity. Personal guarantees can be either collateralized or uncollateralized, and can also be made on behalf of individuals.

High credit: The highest amount of outstanding accounts receivable dollars for a customer over a specified time period. For example, a credit practitioner could monitor high credit for the year, past 12 months, or historical high credit. High credit is used to gauge exposure as well as to adjust individual customer credit limits. High credit information is also used externally when providing trade references.

Insolvent: Describes an unbalanced financial condition in which the debtor is no longer able to pay its obligations due to poor cash flow.

Intangible asset: An asset that is carrying value on a balance sheet but has no real quantifiable dollar value. Examples are trademarks, patents, and goodwill. Intangible assets should be subtracted from total assets with the offset entry to net worth.

Interchange of credit experience: The credit term used to describe the sharing of trade payment information between two vendors concerning a common customer or potential customer. Trade reference information usually includes sold since date, high credit, current outstandings, and payment performance.

Job description: A written document that defines the responsibility and accountability for a specified position, as well as the purpose of the position, regular and occasional duties, and knowledge, skills, and experience required.

Legal cycle: Term used to describe a successful legal proceeding from filing suit to collection. The full cycle would include: 1) filing suit against another party for nonpayment; 2) winning a judgment; 3) attaching assets; and 4) satisfying the judgment monetarily.

Letter of credit - irrevocable: An instrument issued by a bank or other issuer on behalf of a customer to an individual or business entity by which the bank substitutes its own credit for that of its customer. The letter of credit cannot be canceled.

Letter of credit - revocable: A letter of credit that can be canceled at any time without the beneficiary's permission. A revocable letter of credit is not recommended as a means of protecting risk at hand if there is any probability of the issuer or customer revoking the LC.

Letter of credit discrepancy: Refers to any deviation from the outlined terms of a letter of credit. A company that drafts on a letter of credit but has not complied with the outlined terms and conditions of the letter is subject to the bank subsequently rejecting the presentation. A simple example of a discrepancy would be shipping product whose weight exceeds the weight outlined under the conditions. Payment can be delayed until the customer waives the discrepancy.

Leveraged: A financial condition characterized by heavy bank debt or total debt in relation to the firm's net worth.

Liquidity ratios: A series of financial ratios, derived from the balance sheet, that measure customer liquidity. The ratios are helpful in assessing customer payment wherewithal. A generally illiquid financial condition is a leading sign of insolvency.

Loan covenants: Written actions or conditions that the borrower agrees to adhere to during the course of a lending agreement. Violation of covenants will cause the borrower to be in default. Covenants could include performance covenants such as maintaining minimum working capital levels, current ratio requirements, and debt-to-cash flow requirements.

Lockbox: A cash management service generally provided by a bank. The bank receives customer remittances, processes the remittances for check presentation, and grants availability of funds for the incoming customer checks.

Lockbox availability: The assignment and crediting of good funds to checks deposited at a bank or lockbox. For example, two-day availability on a check means that the beneficiary of the check will not be entitled to utilize the funds for two days from the date that the item was deposited.

Lockbox location: The city or town where a company has its lockbox or where it has decided to open a lockbox. Lockbox selection is usually based on the geographic dispersion of a company's customer base and achieving reduced mail float and maximum availability of funds.

Lockbox mail pick-up: The daily task of picking up customer remittances that have been mailed to a lockbox at a post office. Mail in the form of customer checks and other backup materials is then brought to the lockbox center for sorting, distribution, processing, and check presentment.

Lockbox receipts: Customer remittances generally in check form that are directed to a designated lockbox address. The daily lockbox receipts can be left on account with the lockbox bank or transferred to another bank. Lockbox receipts generally comprise 80 percent or more of a firm's incoming cash flow.

Magnetic Ink Character Recognition (MICR) number: A series of numbers on a check that reveals the paying or drawee bank, customer's account number, and a check number in serial form. The MICR numbers are located at the bottom left-hand side of the check. MICR numbers are recaptured by lockboxes to facilitate the automatic input of cash and eliminate the need for manually inputting cash. MICR usage speeds up the communication and processing of incoming cash flow.

Mail float: The number of days between the mailing of a remittance and its arrival at a customer location or lockbox.

Major customer listing: A form of credit analysis that isolates major customers based on sales. The rule of thumb is that a company's major customers, while they make up only 10 percent to 15 percent of total customers, still represent

80% or more of all incoming cash flow. The analysis should yield insight into DSO capabilities and the overall quality of the firm's accounts receivable portfolio.

National Association of Credit Management (NACM): The national professional trade organization for credit practitioners. The NACM has a national office in Columbia, MD, and state and regional NACM groups throughout the nation. The NACM publishes credit publications and conducts seminars nationally for the benefit of its members. The NACM is also the principal lobbyist for the credit profession.

Net working capital: An accounting and balance sheet definition of the difference between total current assets and total current liabilities. Positive working capital implies that current assets are in excess of current liabilities. Working capital is a good measure of liquidity.

Non-contingency fee basis: Refers to the terms under which a collection agency or attorney requires an upfront fee. If they accept a case on a contingency basis, they are not paid unless they are successful in collecting from the debtor.

NSF check: A customer check that has been returned by the customer's bank to the supplier's bank due to non-sufficient funds in the customer's account. An NSF check is subject to bad-check laws unless it is postdated.

Open account credit: Term used to describe the extension of credit based on standard terms of sale. Open account credit implies there are no restrictions on securing trade credit up to a designated credit limit.

Order entry interface with accounts receivable: A company's order entry system can interface with its accounts receivable system to perform an automatic credit check based on predetermined criteria. An interface generally accelerates the processing and approval of pending orders.

Overnight floating-rate debt: Banking and borrowing term used to describe borrowings where the rate is not fixed. The rate is set or pegged on a daily basis. Thus, there is no set maturity date for the borrowings; they can be paid down at any time.

Quality collection call: Based on dollar volume, a collection call that can have a cumulative impact on reducing DSO, current, and past-due accounts receivable. Credit personnel should be urged to pursue a customer with $25,000 past due (a quality collection call) before pursuing a customer with only $1,000 past due.

Payment performance: The degree to which a customer adheres to a supplier's terms of sale. Payment performance is either prompt, slow, or a weighted combination of the two.

PC spreadsheet software: Software that provides the PC user with columns and rows. The term for where a row meets a column is a "cell." Text, data, or formulas can be entered into the cell. For example, the location column C row 5 is referred to as cell C5. Common spreadsheet software packages include Lotus 1-2-3 and Framework II.

Plant tour: A tour of a customer's facility taken by a credit practitioner. The objective is to make financial information come to life and provide the credit person with additional insight into the customer's ability to pay.

Postdated check: A check that is dated on a date subsequent to the current date because sufficient funds are not presently on hand. When a postdated check is returned to the supplier's bank because of non-sufficient funds, the customer is not subject to bad-check laws. The presenting of a postdated check by the maker is not considered an implied representation that the maker has sufficient funds on deposit to meet the check's presentation for payment.

Prime rate: Once known as the benchmark rate for the bank's best customers. That definition has changed over the past 10+ years with the surge in Eurodollar borrowings and commercial paper issuance.

Private placement: A borrowing arrangement where the lender is not a bank. Nonbank private placement lenders usually include insurance companies, trusts, pension funds, or foundations. The borrower may be introduced to the lender by a bank or investment banking firm.

Promise breaker: A customer who chronically breaks promises, including payment commitments.

Quick ratio: Also referred to as the acid ratio, the quick ratio is another liquidity measure. The ratio is calculated by dividing cash and equivalents by total current liabilities. A .95 quick ratio indicates that there are 95 cents of cash and equivalents for every $1 of current liabilities.

Ratios - leverage: A series of financial ratios, derived from balance sheet and P&L sources, that measures customer debt. The ratios are helpful in assessing wherewithal and viability. A high degree of leverage generally reveals an undercapitalized firm that is dependent upon bank and trade credit.

Ratios - profitability: A series of financial ratios, derived from balance sheet and P&L sources, that measures customer profitability. The ratios are helpful in assessing management and overall viability. The ratios reveal how efficiently share-holder capital has been deployed.

Remote disbursement account: A cash management disbursement service offered by banks. Such demand deposit accounts are used by companies that want to take advantage of extended mail and presentation float. Banks do not market these accounts as remote disbursement accounts; however, they act as such because of geographic and presentation considerations. The account provides same-day check presentment information, thereby creating certainty in funding. Such an account can be funded by balances or serve as a zero-balance disbursement account.

Retained earnings: A balance sheet entry that is a key component of net worth. Retained earnings represent the net income that has been "retained" by the business rather than distributed to shareholders in the form of dividends. The retained earnings are in essence reinvested in the business.

Revolving credit agreement: Committed credit facilities; involves a detailed loan agreement that spells out terms and conditions. Unless the borrower is in violation of the agreement or in default, the bank cannot refuse to lend to the borrower. The text of the agreement will cover definitions, loans, conditions to borrowing, representations and warranties, covenants, defaults and remedies, changes in circumstances, opinion of counsel, and a promissory note. Revolvers can be on a secured or unsecured basis.

Revolving credit commitment reductions: Financial requirements sometimes incorporated into straight revolvers and revolvers with term periods. The commitment reduction implies that the borrower must reduce its outstanding borrowings over time to coincide with predetermined reductions of the total lending commitment.

Robinson-Patman Act: Federal law governing price discrimination. It states that terms must be treated as part of price. Thus, in order for extended credit terms to be in compliance with the federal law, the request for extended credit terms must be an unsolicited price change based on financial hardship or a request to meet a competitive situation.

Roll-forward cash receipts forecast: Forecasting procedure utilizing opening accounts receivable, forecasted DSO, and sales to forecast monthly cash receipts. The theory is that opening AR plus projected sales minus projected ending AR (use DSO projection to quantify) will equal projected monthly cash receipts.

Ship date/invoice date audit: A study that reviews the date of shipment against the invoice date for individual customer invoices to determine if there is a lag in billings that could negatively impact cash flow and DSO. If a lag is identified, it means that the customer is being assigned free payment days due to billing inefficiency.

Software needs and wants: The process of prioritizing system software characteristics and specifications when purchasing or internally programming system software. The credit practitioner can classify desired characteristics as either needs or wants. Once this hierarchy is developed, the needs should take priority over the wants (system luxuries).

Sold since: A credit term referring to the starting date of a vendor-customer relationship. The term is helpful in assessing the value of trade payment information.

Source and application of funds: A form of cash flow analysis in which the sources and uses of cash are reviewed. Sources of cash are net income, depreciation, deferred income taxes, stock and bond proceeds, and borrowings. Typical applications include capital spending, working capital changes, and dividends. The difference between sources and applications should agree with the change in the cash position reflected on the balance sheet.

Subordination agreement: A legal agreement involving three parties—often a supplier, its customer, and the customer's corporate parent. The corporate parent agrees to subordinate the debt it is owed by the customer to the debt that the customer owes the supplier. Thus, until the supplier's debt is paid off or the supplier provides written consent, the customer cannot pay off the debt it owes to the parent company (or other third party).

Summary figures: Financial information conveyed in summary form either verbally or in writing. Summary figures represent limited financial disclosure as opposed to full financial disclosure. For example, summary figures could include total current assets, total assets, current liabilities, total liabilities, and net worth, without breaking down the components. Summary figures can serve as an alternative when the customer declines to provide full financial disclosure.

Tangible net worth: The balance sheet item that represents the equity of the company once intangible assets such as goodwill or trademarks have been netted out of net worth. Net worth represents the difference between total assets and total liabilities. Net worth can be comprised of common and preferred stock, additional paid-in capital, retained earnings, and treasury stock.

Total debt to tangible net worth ratio: A leverage ratio derived by dividing tangible net worth by total liabilities. If a subject's debt-to-worth ratio was 2.2 to 1, that would mean it has $2.20 of total debt for every $1 of net worth.

Total exposure: A cash management concept for credit extension and analysis that looks at risk beyond the accounts receivable balance due. Total exposure is comprised of the months opening accounts receivable balance + new orders shipped (invoiced and uninvoiced) + orders ready to ship + order backlog − cash received to date and credits issued. The idea is that potential credit loss is greater than just open accounts receivable.

Total funded debt/tangible net worth ratio: A leverage ratio of total funded debt to tangible net worth. Funded debt is comprised of bank debt, bonds, debentures, private placements, and other similar debt instruments. It is a very common covenant used by banks for credit agreements. The ratio can be used as a source of comparison to other leverage ratios to measure overall leverage.

Trading assets: Accounts receivable and inventory − the two primary assets that generate cash on an ongoing basis.

Trade support: The degree to which accounts receivable creditors (credit department) either tolerate delinquency or grant extended credit terms with specific customers.

UCC1 financing statement form: A form executed between a debtor and a secured party that, if filed and perfected properly with the appropriate state and local entities, creates a collateralized security interest in the assets stipulated on the form for the secured party.

Vendor: A business entity or individual who sells or agrees to sell another business entity or individual goods and/or services. Vendors are commonly referred to as suppliers.

Weeding: The term used for housekeeping with respect to the information contained in a customer credit file.

Wire transfer: The means of making payment to another party electronically. Same-day availability of funds is granted on incoming wire transfers. They can be used with customers as a means of executing cash in advance (CIA) terms.

Workout account: A customer that is unable to retire all or part of its accounts receivable balance. As a result, a payment plan is usually derived to provide for a gradual but orderly reduction of the account balance.

Zero-balance accounts (ZBAs): A formal interrelationship among demand deposit accounts in one institution; the company has a master or consolidation account and potentially an unlimited number of subsidiary accounts that are writing demand deposit checks. All debit and credit transactions flow through the subsidiary accounts to the master account. This cash management process allows subsidiary obligations to be funded by the master account, and thus no balances are maintained at the subsidiary accounts.

Index

About the Author

Mr. Mavrovitis is Vice President and Treasurer for Bertelsmann, Inc., a $2+ billion media and entertainment company. At Bertelsmann he is responsible for the treasury/cash management function. Mr. Mavrovitis holds professional designations as a Certified Credit Executive (CCE) and Certified Cash Manager (CCM).

He has authored credit and treasury related articles for *Business Credit* magazine, the *Journal of Cash Management, CashFlow* magazine, *Practical Cash Management* and the bi-monthly newsletter *CREDIT INSIGHTS*, where he currently serves as the editor. Mr. Mavrovitis also serves on the *Journal of Cash Management*'s editorial advisory board.

Currently, Mr. Mavrovitis is an adjunct professor teaching the course, "Working Capital Management," at the Rutgers Undergraduate School of Business located in New Brunswick, New Jersey. A graduate of Rutgers College, he earned his MBA in finance from the Rutgers Graduate School of Business. Before joining Bertelsmann, Inc., he was employed by Cyro Industries, United States Steel Corporation (now USX Corp.), and the Amerada Hess Corporation.